Film Policy is the first comprehensive overview of the workings of the international film industry. The authors examine film cultures and film policy across
the world, explaining why Hollywood cinema dominates the global film market,
and the effec
a series of ca
and Australi
product and
national film
censorship.

Albert Mor
University.
including *Pr*
(1993).

CULTURE: POLICIES AND POLITICS

Series editors: Tony Bennett, Jennifer Craik, Ian Hunter,
Colin Mercer and Dugald Williamson

What are the relations between cultural policies and cultural politics? Too often, none at all. In the history of cultural studies so far, there has been no shortage of discussion of cultural politics. Only rarely, however, have such discussions taken account of the policy instruments through which cultural activities and institutions are funded and regulated in the mundane politics of bureaucratic and corporate life. *Cultural Policies and Politics* will address this imbalance. The books in this series will interrogate the role of culture in the organization of social relations of power, inlcuding those of class, nation, ethnicity and gender. They will also explore the ways in which political agendas in these areas are related to, and shaped by, policy processes and outcomes. In its commitment to the need for a fuller and clearer policy calculus in the cultural sphere, *Culture: Policies and Politics* will help to promote a significant transformation in the political ambit and orientation of cultural studies and related fields.

Also in this series:

Rock and Popular Music: politics, policies, institutions
Edited by Tony Bennett, Simon Frith, Lawrence Crossberg,
John Shepherd, Graeme Turner

The Birth of the Museum: history, theory, politics
Tony Bennett

Gambling Cultures: studies in history and interpretation
Edited by Jan McMillen

FILM POLICY

International, National and Regional Perspectives

Edited by Albert Moran

London and New York

First published 1996
by Routledge
11 New Fetter Lane, London EC4P 4EE

Simultaneously published in the USA and Canada
by Routledge
29 West 35th Street, New York, NY 10001

Routledge is an International Thomson Publishing company

© 1996 selection and editorial matter: Albert Moran;
individual chapters: the contributors

Typeset in Times by
Ponting–Green Publishing Services, Chesham, Bucks
Printed and bound in Great Britain by
Clays Ltd, St. Ives PLC

British Library Cataloging in Publication Data
A catalogue record for this book is available from the
British Library

Library of Congress Cataloguing in Publication Data
Film policy: international, national, and regional perspectives /
edited by Albert Moran
p.   cm. – (Culture, policy, and politics)
Includes bibliographical references and index.
ISBN 0–415–09790–8 (hardcover). – ISBN 0–415–09791–6 (pbk.)
1. Motion picture history–Economic aspects.   2. Motion picture
industry–Government aspects.   I. Moran, Albert.   II. Series.
PN1993.5.A1F513   1996
384'.83–dc20   95–48260
                                    CIP

ISBN 0–415–09790–8 (hbk)
ISBN 0–415–09791–6 (pbk)

To Peter Morris
Film policy scholar and Canadian nationalist

CONTENTS

CONTENTS

viii

TABLES

CONTRIBUTORS

Manuel Alvarado is currently Senior Research Fellow at the University of Luton, UK, and editorial director of John Libby Media Publications. He has been Head of Education at the British Film Institute; Director of the UNESCO Global Video Project; Research Fellow at the Broadcasting Research Unit, London; Lecturer in Television and Film at the University of London Institute of Education; National Organiser to the Society of Education in Film and Television and editor of the academic quarterly *Screen Education*. He has co-authored and edited numerous books and has published widely in the fields of cinema, television mass media and broadcasting.

Tino Balio is Professor of Communication Arts and Chair of the Arts Consortium at the University of Wisconsin-Madison, USA. His most recent books are *Grand Design: Hollywood as a Modern Business Enterprise 1930–1939* (1993), *Hollywood in the Age of Television* (editor, 1990), and *United Artists: The Company that Changed the Film industry* (1987).

David Birch is Professor of Communication and Media Studies at the Central Queensland University, Australia. He is Co-Director of the Asia and Pacific Research Centre, Australia at CQU and a fellow of the Asia Research Centre, Murdoch University. Recent publications include the book *Singapore Media: Communication Strategies and Practices* (1993). He edited 'Cultural studies in the Asia Pacific', a special double issue of the *Southeast Asian Journal of Social Science* (1994), and contributed a chapter 'Staging crises: media and citizenship' to the book *Singapore Changes Guard: Social, Political and Economic Developments in the 1990s* (1993). He has edited two issues of *The Southern Review* – 'Teaching the postmodern' (1994) and 'Framing (post-colonial) cultures' (1995). He is also completing a major project on the management of information in Singapore.

Ron Burnett is Director of the Graduate Program in Communications and Professor in Cultural Studies at McGill University, Canada. He is also a member on the editorial boards for *Arena Journal*, *International Journal of Communications*, and *Communications*, Laval. He is presently completing research into the history and practice of lowcast media with an emphasis on video. His book, *These Images which Rain Down into the Imaginary*, appeared in 1995.

Michael Dorland is Assistant Professor, School of Journalism and Communication at Carleton University, Ottawa, Canada. Recent publications include: 'Telefilm Canada et la production audiovisuelle independante: la longue errance d'une politique gouvernementale' (*Communication* 1993); 'A thoroughly hidden country: *ressentiment*, Canadian nationalism, Canadian culture', in Jessica Bradley and Lesley Johnstone (eds) *Sightlines: Reading Contemporary Canadian Art* (1994); co-editor with Blaine Allan and Zuzana M. Pick of *Responses: In Honour of Peter Harcourt* (1993). He is currently editing an anthology on Canadian cultural industries policies, *Canada's Cultural Industries: Into the 21st Century*. He is also researching a history of the development of rhetoric in the Canadian context.

John Hill is Senior Lecturer in Media Studies at the University of Ulster, Northern Ireland. He has written widely on film, television and the theatre and his publications include *Sex, Class and Realism: British Cinema 1956–63* (1986), *Cinema and Ireland* (1987) and *Border Crossing: Film in Ireland, Britain and Europe* (1994). He is the author of the forthcoming *Oxford Guide to Film Studies*. He is also chairman of the Northern Ireland Film Council and a governor of the British Film Institute.

Anne Jäckel is Senior Lecturer in the Faculty of Languages and European Studies at the University of the West of England, where she teaches French and Film Studies. She has been visiting lecturer and guest speaker at various European Film Societies and universities lecturing on European film policy and French cinema. She has contributed articles to such journals as *Cinema Papers*, *Journal of Communications* and *Media Policy Review*. Her current research interests include: European cinemas, culture and economic implications of film policy, and cinematographic co-productions.

Randal Johnson is Professor of Brazilian Literature and Culture at the University of California, Los Angeles, USA, where he also serves as Director of the Latin American Centers Program in Brazil. He is the author of *Cinema Novox 5: Masters of Contemporary Brazilian Film, The Film Industry in Brazil: Culture and the State* and *Literatura e Cinema*, as well as many articles on Brazilian cinema, literature and culture. He is also co-editor (with Robert Stam) of *Brazilian Cinema* and editor of *Tropical Paths: Essays on Modern Brazilian Literature* and Pierre Bourdieu and Randal Johnson *The Field of Cultural Production: Essays on Art and Literature*. His current research focuses on relations between culture and the state in Brazil.

Jonathan D. Levy is Senior Staff Economist in the Office of Plans and Policy at the US Federal Communications Commission, having taught economics at the University of Wisconsin-Milwaukee, USA. In 1993 he was a Fulbright Senior

Scholar at the University of Technology, Sydney, researching US–Australian trade in television programming and film. At the FCC his primary activities include analysis of competition in mass media markets and a review of proposed changes in government regulation of the mass media, in particular in broadcasting, cable television and satellite television. He is co-author of *Broadcast, Television in a Multichannel Marketplace* and the author of *Implications of Content Regulation for Trade and Television Programs: A US Perspective* (1994).

Steve McIntyre is Chief Executive at the London Film and Video Development Agency. He is currently working with a number of local authorities in London and across the UK assisting and advising on local cultural industries policies. Recent publications include: 'Vanishing point: feature film production in a small country' in John Hill, Martin McLoone and Paul Hainsworth (eds) *Border Crossing: Film in Ireland, Britain and Europe* (1994); 'Inventing the future: in praise of small films' (*Scottish Film and Visual Arts* 1993). He is currently researching three linked areas: cultural industries as a tool of economic re-generation; regional film and video policy in the UK; and film policy in the regions of the UK, in particular in Scotland.

Michael Meadows lectured in the School of Media and Journalism at the Queensland University of Technology in Brisbane, Australia, until his recent appointment as Lecturer in the Humanities Faculty at Griffith University, Australia His main research interests include media representation and indigenous media production and policy. Recent publications include a 1992 monograph, *A Watering Can in the Desert*, and two book chapters in 1994. 'Voice blo mipla all ilan man' concerns community perceptions of the recent arrival of satellite television in the Torres Strait region in northern Australia, and 'The cultural frontier' examines indigenous media production in Australia and Canada. Dr Meadows' interest in the development of indigenous media in Australia and Canada continues as does his research focus on racism in the media.

Toby Miller is Assistant Professor and Director of Graduate Studies and Cinema Studies at New York University, USA. He has worked as an information officer in the Australian Senate, an announcer and commentator for the Australian Broadcasting Corporation and has taught at Murdoch and Griffith Universities in Australia. He is the author of the *The Well-Tempered Self: Citizenship, Culture and the Postmodern Subject* (1993) and *Contemporary Australian Television* (1994). He is currently researching media globalization, sport, popular culture and everyday life.

Albert Moran is Senior Research Fellow at Griffith University, Australia. He has published widely on Australian film and television and his books include *Image and Industry, Australian Television Drama Production* and *Projecting Australia: Government Films Since 1945*. He was the director of the 1991 Film Policy Conference held at Griffith University. His current areas of research include the international traffic in television programme formats and a social history of Australian broadcasting.

Manjunath Pendakur is Professor of the Political Economy of Communications and Chair of the Department of Radio-TV-Film at Northwestern University, USA. He was trained as a cinematographer in India and worked on feature films and documentaries before migrating to North America. He is author of *Canadian Dreams and American Control: The Political Economy of Canadian Film Industry* (1990) and co-editor of *Illuminating the Blindspots*: *Essays Honoring Dallas Smythe* (1993). He is in the process of completing a book on India's popular cinema. His current research interests include global expansion of television and its impact on rural culture and film/television in the India diaspora communities. Pendakur is President of the Political Economy Section of the International Association for Mass Communication Research and the National Coordinator of India Alert, a human rights activist group based in Chicago.

Krishna Sen is Senior Lecturer in Communications and Fellow of the Asia Research Centre on Social, Political and Economic Change at Murdoch University, Australia. She has published many journal articles and book chapters and lectured in various public fora on the Indonesian electronic media and on Indian cinema. She is also involved in teaching, research and publishing in the area of Women's Studies. Her book *Indonesian Cinema: Framing the New Order* appeared in 1994, and she co-edited *Sex and Power in Affluent Asia* (1996). She is founding editor of the magazine *Inside Indonesia*.

Carole Sklan was Project Coordinator in the Film Development Branch of the Australian Film Commission, working in the Melbourne office. She wrote and directed *Guns and Roses*, which won the AFI Award for Best Television Documentary in 1991, and co-wrote *Fifty Years of Silence*, which won the AFI Award, 1994, and the Logie Award for Best Television Documentary in 1995. She has also worked on the research and development of three major television dramas, *Scales of Justice, Leaving of Liverpool*, and *Brides of Christ*, and a documentary drama, *The Last Dream*.

SERIES EDITORS' PREFACE

Culture is a political matter. So too, and inevitably, is its analysis. This is not simply because of the personal biases and investments which inescapably inform any particular individual's approach to a given topic. Rather, the issue is that of the political relation that is implied and produced by the manner in which intellectuals think of their work and the manner and circumstances in which they envisage it having practical effects. In the sphere of culture no less than any other, the ways in which intellectual work is conducted and circulated – that is, the contexts in which it is undertaken, the forms in which it is expressed, the constituencies to which it is addressed – have a crucial bearing on the ways in which such work might connect with and contribute to contemporary political issues and concerns.

In these respects, the *Culture: Policies and Politics* series is intended to help bring about a significant transformation in the political ambit and orientation of cultural studies. The direction of the change is indicated by the conjunction of the key terms 'policy' and 'politics'. Closely linked in many areas of social and political life and analysis, these terms have often been strangers in the discipline of cultural studies. If practitioners of cultural studies have talked about politics – as they have, for example, when discussing resistance and empowerment – they have rarely shown any interest in the policy instruments through which cultural activities and institutions are funded and regulated in the mundane politics of bureaucratic and corporate life.

There are a number of reasons for this striking silence. The most obvious is the political leaning that was given to cultural studies in the Anglophone world by its formative passage through the work of Raymond Williams and the New Left. In defining culture as a 'whole way of life' – and in promising to reclaim the cultural totality by restoring the popular and the political to the realm of the aesthetic – this tradition provided cultural studies with a prophetic and oppositional political voice which aspired to rise above the mundane calculations and procedures of the world of policy. In this way, through entertaining the possibility that it might bypass them, cultural studies has failed to link its discussions of culture and politics to the instruments and ethos of policy. That is to say, it has lacked a policy calculus.

If it is to prove more than a passing intellectual fad and develop a capacity to make a sustained and long-term contribution to the governmental and industrial processes through which our cultural futures will most actively be shaped, cultural studies urgently needs to develop such a calculus. And this, in turn, can only be accomplished through more detailed and scrupulous attention to the various policy structures and processes – from government inquiries through the activities of the statutory bodies which regulate the legal environment of the cultural industries to specific industry practices and procedures – which influence the ways in which the relations between culture and politics are practically mediated.

It is work of this kind, therefore, that we shall publish in this series – work which, in recognizing the role which many forms of contemporary culture play in the relay of forms of power across relations of class, nation, race, ethnicity and gender, also takes account, both theoretically and practically, of the need to accord policy considerations their due in the formulation of political objectives and ways of pursuing them that are likely to be both practicable and effective. This is, to speak plainly, an advocacy for pragmatism which, given the more idealistic aspirations on which cultural studies has customarily been nurtured, will no doubt, in some quarters, be rejected as unprincipled by those who remain committed to the project of a wholly oppositional politics.

To view this as a cause for alarm, however, can now only count as backward-looking. Once we have ceased to think of cultural studies as the intellectual delegate of the subaltern fragments of human totality, then there is no reason to assume that it will speak with a single ethnical or political voice. The private and civic environments in which cultural activities are funded and regulated are far too various – their ethical, legal, and economic orientations far too mundanely complex – to permit a single exemplary oppositional relation to them. It is the purpose of this series to trace some of the multifarious paths cut through the field of cultural activities by the instruments of policy – instruments that shape the often unpredictable, gritty and compromised ways in which such activities are pursued, thought about and argued over.

Tony Bennett
Jennifer Craik
Ian Hunter
Colin Mercer
Dugald Williamson

ACKNOWLEDGEMENTS

This collection has developed out of some of the papers delivered at the Film Policy Conference held at Griffith University by the Institute for Cultural Policy Studies. I would like to thank all the participants, especially Colin Mercer and Robyn Pratten, the then Director and Administrative Officer of the Centre. Since the Conference, the project has received the continued support and encouragement of Tony Bennett, the Director of the Key Centre for Cultural and Media Policy, successor to the former Centre, and Rebecca Barden, Commissioning Editor at Routledge. I am enormously grateful to them both. In gathering this collection, I am very much indebted to the contributors for the various drafts they supplied and the many deadlines they met. I should also, especially, like to thank Karen Yarrow and Margaret Pullar for hleping to physically pull the manuscript together. My thanks to Dugald Williamson who read the manuscript and made many useful suggestions. In seeing the manuscript into print, I have much to be grateful to Diane Stafford for, who copy edited the text. Staff at Routledge did a wonderful job in the production of the book and I would especially like to mention Leigh Wilson and Alastair Jenkinson.

TERMS FOR A READER
Film, Hollywood, national cinema, cultural identity and film policy
Albert Moran

Film is an economic commodity as well as a cultural good. As a commodity, film, like other manufactured objects, has been brought about by the labour of many workers with no personal relationship or connection existing between them and those who will end up using or ingesting the commodity. Manufactured goods exist in successive moments of production, distribution and consumption. 'Consumption' applied to material goods refers to that kind of appropriation whereby the object is digested or used so that it is subject to physical decay and disintegration. Cultural goods such as films are not subject to the same laws of entropy. While the material bearer or carrier of the cultural good, in this case a reel of celluloid or a length of videotape, will suffer the same fate as other material goods, the cultural object will not be affected for new copies can be struck from the original. Rather, the consumption of cultural objects refers to the dimension of their ideological meanings and focuses on the moment of decoding. While this dualism of materiality and meaning, commerce and culture, is repeatedly insisted upon in the chapters that follow, nevertheless it is worth remembering that the material existence of a film is a prior, necessary condition to its capacity to engender any ideological effects. In other words, before film can be considered as a cultural object, it must first be conceived as an industry.

FILM AS INDUSTRY

First instituted as a novelty and a working-class entertainment in competition with the penny arcade, the travelling tent show and, later, vaudeville and the popular stage, the cinema is now beginning its second century of existence. And while many of the technologies of the cinema, considered not only in the mechanical or physical sense such as film cameras, recording equipment, editing facilities and so on, as well as in the conceptual sense of organizational mechanisms such as film stars and patterns of narration, nevertheless films have to be produced, promoted, and made available to an audience before any meaning or ideological effect can be derived from the film. As an industrial enterprise, film is divided into three interdependent yet separate sectors. Of the three – production, distribution and exhibition – the middle activitiy is the most crucial, not least because it

1

connects the other sectors. Distribution is that part of the physical cycle of the film industry whereby the finished film (in the form of celluloid stored in cans) is warehoused and shipped to various destinations. The general activity of distribution also includes systems for booking particular films for showing in various exhibition outlets, preview arrangements, and publicity and advertising. The sector is staffed by accountants, sales personnel, warehouse managers and others and is low not only on glamour but also on contact with the public. Distribution is seen as a distinctly mundane and prosaic activity, perhaps the most commercial part of the film industry; it is not surprising that it receives the least amount of public attention. Yet as has recently been emphasized (Aksoy and Robins 1992), echoing investigation from nearly fifty years ago (Huettig 1944), distribution is the key to the film industry. Production exists to meet the demand created by the mechanism of distribution rather than distribution existing to serve production.

Exhibition on the other hand is that sector where the society, in the form of an audience, is able to watch films. Since the 1950s, beginning with broadcast television, there has been a growing number of secondary viewing outlets other than motion picture theatres, nevertheless the hard-top theatre continues to be the primary vehicle of film exhibition. This 'first-run' circuit usually generates a substantial proportion of the film's overall profit. It is also the point where most of the publicity and promotion for the film is produced. Given these industrial circumstances, it is not surprising that this sector receives its fair share of popular and serious attention.

Production is, in a nutshell, the business of making pictures. Thanks to publicity in the popular media, society sees film making principally in terms of film stars, but the actor is only one of a large number of personnel, ranging from writer to editor, who are engaged in the manufacture of this particular industrial object. Nor is human labour the only resource tied up in the making of films. Film production also involves the use of, among other things, film making equipment, sound stages, processing laboratories and editing suites, and the large amounts of financial investment that these facilities require.

Historically the cinema has been organized in three very different institutional sets of arrangements. Cinema emerged in France, Britain and the United States in the 1890s at a time of small-scale industry. Thanks to recent historical scholarship on early cinema (Fell 1974; Bordwell, Staiger and Thompson 1985; Thompson 1985; Elsaesser 1987), the general situation of the industry in its first years is better understood. The artisanal phase of production lasted from 1894 to around 1907. It was the French company, Pathé Frères, that was the major international film producer and distributor during this period. The company was, however, exceptional in its organization. Most film making and film screening was local in its territorial operation, with small amounts of capital underpinning the activities.

The second period in the history of the film industry began after 1907 and was characterized by massive financial investment, the creation of national and international markets for American film, and the reorganization of production such that it became large scale and systematized. In the US, Hollywood, California, became the major centre of production and the 'dream factory' itself became a symbol of the industrialization of cinema. Often (and inappropriately) characterized as the Hollywood studio period, lasting until around 1960, the era is better understood as one of market oligopoly, with eight American motion picture companies dominating the film business, not just in the United States but internationally. Of course this did not happen immediately or without resistance. The major American motion picture companies formed in the 1910s and 1920s, vertically integrated production, distribution and exhibition and thus came to dominate the vast American film market (Gomery 1986). In turn, this became a most advantageous stepping stone to international market domination, which this group achieved by around 1934. However, the 1950s saw a major upheaval in the American film industry that was to force significant changes in the three sectors of activity. Anti-trust action by the federal government caused the majors to divest themselves of their exhibition interests while television's erosion of the domestic theatrical market made the international exhibition market more important than it had been in the past (Balio 1990). In addition, the majors also began to find it profitable to distribute films produced outside of Hollywood. Post-war moves by European governments to protect their national film industries, for instance, inadvertently advantaged American film makers working on the continent. This repositioning of the American film companies continued until well into the next decade when the much-trumpeted 'death of Hollywood' was an indication not of a demise but of continued transition (Mayersburg 1967). The anti-trust action had forced the break up of vertical integration. The companies recognized distribution as the key to continued control of the market and they sold off their investments and interests in production and exhibition. The Hollywood studio era came to an end and film production now came about under the package or agency system. Exhibition also changed from being the province solely of theatres to a succession of outlets prefaced by theatrical screening. In the recent era, receipts from the cinema release of a film are part of a gross that includes the sale of rights for network and cable television screenings, subsidiary rights to novelization, books about the making of the film, television spin-offs, sound track recordings and cassettes, commercially retailed videotapes, and merchandising tie-ins such as T-shirts, toys, games, comics, and so on (Armes 1987). Nor are the major motion picture companies like their counterparts in the studio era. Instead, as Tino Balio discusses in Chapter 1 in this collection, they are often huge entertainment and leisure service conglomerates with interests not only in film but in other areas such as publishing, television, music, hotels and theme parks.

The key to an understanding of Hollywood's domination of global film business lies not only in historical events such as the First World War, which was crucial in allowing American film producers to begin to wrest control of international film markets from hitherto dominant interests such as that of the French, but also in the international communicability of silent film, the creation in the United States of the most profitable domestic market in the world and especially in the particular

3

nature of the film commodity (Armes 1987). Most of the production costs of a film go into making the master negative and the first print. Prints from this original can be struck at a small fraction of the overall cost of production so that, once that negative has been made, an ever-wider market can be serviced at little additional cost. Historically, Hollywood has been able to amortise its development and production costs in a particular market or markets so that revenue derived from other markets, being almost pure profit, would mean film rental and admission prices could be set at what those other markets could bear.

FILM AS CULTURE

Film occupies an uneasy, ambiguous position as one of the mass media of communication. Cinema came into existence in the late nineteenth century, being inscribed in existing social arrangements (public mass consumption of content, the consumer purchasing, not the content, but attendance, and so on) that mark film as institutionally different from an earlier media form such as the newspaper as well as later forms such as television. Perhaps because early cinema was in the hands of private companies and individuals and because much of the content fell into the category of entertainment (and, to a much lesser extent, art), the state historically has not felt the same need to bring the cinema under its control as it did in the 1920s and 1930s with broadcasting. (Of course, there have been exceptions: Soviet Russia, for example, had state controlled film production studios, while in France, the state has put complementary exhibition regulations in place for television and cinema.) And yet, as so many of the present chapters demonstrate, the state is everywhere concerned with the cinema.

As the production of propaganda films during the First World War and early moves to switch censorship from the place of exhibition to the content of films recognized, cinema is a powerful instrument for generating and spreading ideas (Jowett 1976). Such ideas are important not just at the immediate level in the promotion of particular forms of behaviour, emotions and sentiment, but also at the more general level where cumulatively they produce a mental landscape, a world view, a particular way of thinking about reality. Thomas Guback, for example, quotes official American sources that see the export of American films as doubly ideological. On the one hand, American films act as promotional vehicles for American manufacturing and secondary industries publicizing everything from cars to clothes and cosmetics and, on the other, even beyond the promotion of any particular good or item, the films promote consumption as an American value, part of the American world outlook (Guback 1969). Thomas Elsaesser has further elaborated on the ideological dimensions of the Hollywood action film:

> There is a central energy at the heart of any good Hollywood film which seeks to live itself out as completely as possible. The prevailing plot-mechanisms invariably conform to the same basic pattern. There is always

4

a central dynamic drive, always the same graph of maximum energetic investment. . . . [What remains consistent is] a fundamentally affirmative attitude a kind of *a priori* optimism located in the very structure of the narrative about the usefulness of positive action.

(Elsaesser 1975: 14)

THE NEW HOLLYWOOD

Although the phrase was first used as early as the 1970s, 'new Hollywood' is an especially apt designation of the most recent incarnation of the motion picture industry which has been headquartered for so long on the west coast of the United States. In its present form, the industry is no longer simply a film industry nor is it solely American. New Hollywood defines a field of commercial interests that include film, broadcast television, cable televison, satellite broadcasting, music and recording interests, newspaper, magazine and book publishing, theme parks, merchandising, professional sport, and a range of other activities in the areas of entertainment and leisure. Nor are the major companies in this new Hollywood content to restrict themselves only to this very broad arena of business activity but are instead constantly seeking to expand their activities even further. Disney, for example, is currently building a complete housing village in Florida which combines physical security, the most up to date technology and enviromental sensitivity (BBC 1995). Such a venture is, for the moment, marginal to the company's main business orientation although in the future it may come to have a commercial importance for the company. The point is that the Hollywood majors can pursue such commercial research and development because their central activities, most especially the motion picture industry, are so financially secure. As Balio shows in detail in Chapter 1, this core activity has in the 1980s and early 1990s been further strengthened by horizontal and vertical integration. The Hollywood majors have conglomaratized themselves by establishing links with other areas of the communications industries including publishing, television, video and music so that the theatrical release of a feature film will cause a succession of commercial ripples in a series of adjacent ponds, all to the financial benefit of the initial distributor of the film. Most significantly starting in 1985 with Rupert Murdoch's News International takeover of Twentieth-Century Fox, all four of the US commercial broadcast networks are now in the hands of new owners, mega media conglomerates, thus ensuring these companies a guaranteed outlet for their feature films and television programmes.

Ownership of the networks gives these companies access to two other significant markets – the US domestic cable industry and overseas television markets. In addition the majors have also recently moved to vertically re-integrating their theatrical distribution activities. Historically the companies had owned key theatres in the United States during the studio era but had been forced by anti-trust action to off load these. A recent change in the rules by the federal government has allowed the companies to purchase cinema chains so that they

5

are again a significant force in the domestic theatrical exhibition industry. They are also involved in the building of new theatrical complexes in Europe and elsewhere.

If Hollywood is now enormously more profitable, capitalized and powerful than it was in the studio era, it has also drawn many other elements into its sphere of influence so that the line of demarcation between what is Hollywood and what is not has become sometimes hard to draw. Hollywood has changed considerably in the past half century. One of these changes has to do with the ownership of the major Hollywood companies. The 1980s and the early 1990s witnessed a series of take-overs and buy-outs that saw some of the majors no longer in the hands of American multinationals. And indeed further foreign takeover is expected. A long term forecast for the Hollywood industry is that by early in the next century the majors will include one or two European giants, several Japanese conglomerates as well as some American companies. These changes in ownership appear likely to have few cultural effects on Hollywood films (Aksoy and Robins 1992; McAnany and Wilkinson 1992). Nevertheless the shift is indicative of a more profound transformation.

Distribution remains the key sector of the motion picture industry and distribution has long paid little respect to national cinemas. A brief consideration of two particular film genres helps make this point. The action spectacle has long been a component of Hollywood's output, with particular cycles and sub-generic inflexions such as the biblical and historical epics of the 1950s. However, the genre is by no means unique to Hollywood. Not only are there individual action films made outside of the United States that yet gain international distribution by Hollywood, there is also the example of foreign film production cycles such as the Italian spaghetti western or the Hong Kong kung fu films that also gained global distribution through Hollywood. The other genre of particular significance to new Hollywood is art cinema. While Hollywood, even before the consolidation of the studio era, had found it financially and culturally useful to occasionally produce 'quality' films, nevertheless art cinema was essentially engendered elsewhere, most especially in Europe after the Second World War. However, the model was recuperated by Hollywood in the 1960s as part of a massive process of re-organization after the end of the studio era. By the 1990s art cinema is very much a Euro-American genre, as Toby Miller notes in his chapter, so that Hollywood is once again ready to distribute films made outside the United States.

This dialectic between Hollywood and the rest of the world also operates at other levels. Since as early as the 1930s, when German emigrant film makers gained a foothold in the American film production industry after fleeing from Nazi Germany, Hollywood has been receptive to overseas film makers coming to work there. However, a qualitative change has occurred over the past twenty years with the development of a global Hollywood. With the increasing transnationalization of film production, of motion picture financing, the articulation of a long chain of distribution outlets and their domination by the majors, and the growth of independent producers who themselves frequently act as brokers between film

6

makers and the principal distributors, the system now exists whereby national film making is, through a series of commercial linkages, also a part of Hollywood. Recent analyses of national cinemas in nation-states as diverse as Ireland and Canada have come to the same conclusion that Hollywood is no longer out there, beyond their national borders, but is instead very much a component of their own national cinema (Rockett 1994; Magder 1993).

HOLLYWOOD AND NATIONAL CINEMAS

As the historical sketch developed above suggests, the Hollywood film industry has been and continues to be the dominant film industry in world terms. No cinema has escaped its force field and historically Hollywood has to a large extent defined the range of options for other cinemas in both economic and cultural terms. Thus, whether national cinemas or not, these other cinemas have variously imitated Hollywood, attempted to transform and vary the Hollywood model or else resisted and rejected its example in favour of alternative aesthetics, funding arrangements, systems of production and distribution, and ways of constituting and relating to an audience. So far as national cinemas are concerned, the early pattern, evident from the time of the First World War onwards, was for American dominance of local distribution and exhibition leading to a situation where the local production industry languished, facing the possibility of complete extinction. Nation-states everywhere confronted this crisis and were slowly drawn into regulatory and legislative actions to support their local production industries. The measures were sometimes protective against film imports and sometimes supportive of local production and were undertaken for economic reasons such as the safeguarding of local employment, and, less frequently, cultural motives such as lessening the 'American' influence on the culture. Some governments in Europe and in parts of Latin America had measures in place by the 1930s, whereas in other parts of the world, particular nation-states, often with smaller populations, such as Australia and New Zealand, did not undertake support and protection until the 1960s and the 1970s. However, the general pattern is evident: national governments across the world in recent times have in varying degrees been involved in promoting and supporting their national production industries. In other words the invariable rule is that in nation-states outside of the USA, it is the case that the term 'film industry' is one that refers to a bipartite or dual system. Such a system is marked by a distribution/exhibition sector that is under the control of private commercial entrepreneurial interests, and which whether locally owned or else operating under joint venture arrangements is tied very much to the Hollywood majors for much of the programmes that they screen. The second sector of national film industries is concerned with film production within the national territory and is characterized by the active support of government and other elements of the state. Mostly governments have set up agencies, commissions, boards, corporations and so on as instruments through which a wide range of supportive and protective measures are put in place. Randal Johnson in his chapter mentions some of these measures

7

and, although he is writing about Latin American film industries, the use of these measures is not confined to that area. These policy tools include: financing credits; low-interest loans; state backed co-productions; various kinds of subsidies and subventions; distribution advances; co-productions between the state and private producers or between the state, private producers and foreign concerns; box-office taxes; taxes on profits, remittances by foreign distributors; and taxes on the production sector.

While a more detailed delineation of the two sectors would certainly have to note the many occasions on which, in particular national settings, the distribution/exhibition sector is frequently involved in production, and the state is involved in exhibition, nevertheless for the sake of this sketch this second sector can be thought of as the public service face of national film industries. When television is included as another component of national film industries, then this duality is further emphasized. The state has historically been intimately involved in television broadcasting and although the 1980s and 1990s have seen the emergence of private, commercial television in many parts of the world where hitherto there was only either direct state control or public-service broadcasting, nevertheless the state continues to play an important role in the audio-visual industries. In other words the public/private structure of national film industries seems well nigh universal. This dual structure is present across the globe – from Ireland to India and from Britain to Brazil – and it constitutes the backbone of the different national cinemas discussed in Part II.

NATIONAL CINEMA AND CULTURAL IDENTITY

Up to this point, the phrase 'national cinema' has been used in an unproblematic way to designate the range of film activities and institutions within a nation-state. There are, however, conceptual difficulties surrounding the phrase. Some inflexions of the term 'cinema' have already been suggested. 'Cinema' can be used in both a restricted and a more general sense: on the one hand, the term can refer to the venue of theatrical exhibition while, on the other, it can apply in an inclusive sense to the three sectors of film production, distribution and exhibition. The designation here is economic. Applied in this way, the phrase 'national cinema' corresponds to 'domestic film industry' and invites such questions as: What are the principal government agencies that are involved in protecting and supporting film inside the national territory? What form does this encouragement take? Who are the main production houses in the domestic situation? Who owns the principal film exhibition circuits? (Higson 1989)

However, the phrase is often used to refer to several other conceptual objects. 'National cinema' can, for example, refer to a particular *oeuvre* of films, unified in style and theme, that directly interrogate national issues, including the question of national identity. It can also apply to the perceived cultural implications of inbalances between the proportion of imported and locally produced films that are shown to national audiences. It sometimes designates a particular range of

8

'quality' domestically-produced films that are principally of value and importance to a high culture audience. And finally there is the possibility of further considering the term from a *consumptive* rather than a *productive* perspective by using it to refer to the historical appropriation of cinema by the different subcultures of the national film audience (Higson 1989).

'National cinema' then is a slippery phrase whose meaning, in practice, will shift between various referents. And, acting as a semantic base, anchoring these various meanings of the phrase is the the apparent reality of a domestic film industry. However, when 'national cinema' is used in an inclusive sense to refer not just to the domestic film industry but to the production sector as the cinematic expression and imaginative projection of a national community then caution is necessary. The cultural imperialist research of the 1960s and 1970s used the term 'national' in this way, whether referring to cinema, broadcasting or mass communications in general in discussing the cultural and economic impact of US film and television programmes on national audio-visual systems. Underlying much of this work is the assumption that the presence of a production sector in local culture industries is a necessary and sufficient condition for the cultural expression of a population. Imported material cannot have this kind of authentic relationship with national audiences and this leads to cultural debilitation. Thus, for example, Guback's ground-breaking study of the post-war impact of the American film industry on Europe contrasts imported films with those of a particular European national cinema in the following terms:

> international financing, international settings, international stars and pro-
> duction teams, and dependence on world markets, breed international films
> appealing to most people in most places. True, many films not made under
> these conditions have become universal favourites. As examples, consider
> the Chaplin films or those in the Italian neo-realist tradition. They were
> international, but in a much different sense. They were able to convey a
> *human* message in terms understandable to people everywhere. While the
> neo-realist films were grounded in conditions and times of a particular
> country, they spoke to diverse cultures because they struck a chord of human
> sensitivity. But so many of the new international films border on de-
> humanization by brutalizing sensitivy, often deflecting attention from
> reality. They count on developing audience response with synthetic,
> machine-made images. Their shallowness and cardboard characters are
> camouflaged with dazzling colours, wide-screens, and directorial slickness.
> Films of this genre are not a form of cultural exchange. In reality, they are
> anti-culture, the antithesis of human culture.
>
> (Guback 1969)

However, this kind of argument as a reason for supporting national cinema is difficult to maintain. For one thing, realist aesthetics in the cinema have come under increased scrutiny, particularly with the advent of Russian formalism, structuralism and semiotics. More importantly, the terms in which Guback

9

chooses to celebrate Italian neo-realism as an example of national cinema and to condemn the films of Hollywood are very much the terms of the mass culture debate. In other words, by arguing for national cinemas in this way, Guback inadvertently makes it clear that the cultural imperialist argument is in part a rerun of the mass culture/high culture debate. What Guback does is to indicate his own aesthetic taste, preferring the film products of Euro-American art cinema (Chaplin and Italian neo-realism) to those of popular or mass culture (Hollywood films of the 1950s and 1960s). That this kind of rhetoric, defending national culture, turns out, on closer inspection, to be a version of the high culture/mass culture debate has been noted by others (Collins 1990; Routt 1991). Certainly the cultural imperialist argument is an area that warrants further investigation of the kind recently initiated by Tomlinson (1991). It is not surprising that this thesis has found it hard going in the European context in the 1980s, where various European mass communications scholars have insisted on the liberatory potential of Hollywood films and television (De la Garde *et al.*, 1993; Skovmand, and Schroder 1992; Buscombe 1990).

A second conceptual problem with the term 'national cinema' concerns the socially constructed nature of the nation. As, for example, recent historical investigation of the social history of British broadcasting has demonstrated, the 'nation' is an imagined community that attempts to supersede loyalties to other communities such as those based on class, region or gender and thereby marginalizes and displaces identities based on those other sources (Scannell and Cardiff 1991). In other words, championing national cinemas in the face of the power of Hollywood may seem politically progressive. However, considered from a sub-national or multicultural perspective such a defence is more problematic. Thus Meadows in his chapter on the struggle of first peoples in Australia, New Zealand and Canada for the resources to create their own film and video culture speaks not of national cinema under cultural threat from outside but rather of a 'mainstream' (which includes national cinema and television) which has mostly marginalized these peoples. Where champions of national cinemas see cultural struggle in the arena of film occurring between a heroic, David-like, national cinema and an overwhelming, Goliath-like, Hollywood, an emphasis on the mini-national or the regional such as that adopted, for example, by Sklan and Meadows in Part III of this book, leads to a perception of national cinema not only as Goliath-like in its denial of material resources and opportunities to marginal communities but, even more importantly, as blocking the very legitimacy of communities to control their own images and sounds.

The argument then can be briefly recapped. There is no such thing as a 'national cinema' if the phrase is used to designate a single, unitary object. National populations are marked by a multiplicity of cultural communities to which individuals belong in varying degrees: there is no such thing as a single national cultural identity. As two scholars in the field of mass communications research pointed out over twenty years ago, the nation-state is characterized by a heterogeneity of subjects within its national boundaries. There are differences of

10

class, gender, ethnicity, language and accent, region, history and religion, to name some of the principal points of difference across populations (Nordenstreng and Varis 1973). Such differences are partly historical, brought about by military and political annexation (Snyder 1982). In the past thirty-five years, because of social upheavals due to war, famine, natural disasters, shifting patterns in the international labour market and changes in transportation and mass communications, national populations have become even more diverse and variegated (Anderson 1992).

If then it is necessary to problematize the notion of 'national cinema' as a monolithic cultural apparatus acting on behalf of a unified, homogeneous population within a national boundary, one should be careful not to surrender the opportunities for the film construction of cultural differences provided by a national cinema. The authors in this collection are aware of the conceptual difficulties that surround the notion but they are similarly aware of the potential for the representation of national multiculturalism offered by a national cinema. As John Hill has suggested elsewhere, 'national cinema' is worth defending precisely because it is capable of registering the 'lived complexities' of 'national' life (Hill 1992).

FILM POLICY RESEARCH

Although research on the particular national economic impact of American film began as early as 1937 (Legg and Klingender 1937), it was not until the end of the Second World War that research began on the international film industry (Bàchlin 1945). However, Bàchlin's pioneering study was available only in French and German. Another quarter century passed before there was any English-language study of the international context of national film policies. Thomas Guback's 1969 analysis of the American film industry in Western Europe has already been referred to. It was the first study of the post-war, overseas activities of the Hollywood film industry and had begun life as a thesis under the supervision of Dallas Smythe, the 'father' of political economy research on mass communications (Wasko *et al.* 1993). The study was not a lone one. Instead it was soon joined by a series of others, operating within a 'cultural dependency' paradigm, and examining such areas as the overseas reach of American television and the cultural import of Disney comics (Schiller 1969; Wells 1972; Mattelart and Dorfman 1975). This 'cultural dependency' research has been critically reviewed elsewhere and there is no need to rehearse that discussion here (Schlesinger 1987; Tomlinson 1991; McAnany and Wilkinson 1992). In any case, some of the conceptual problems of the approach have been raised above. Despite these difficulties, Guback's study of the relationship between Hollywood and the largest Western European film industries is a major work of film policy research. The continuing value of that study lies in the detail and clarity of Guback's diagnosis of the prevailing situation in national film industries in Britain, Italy, Germany and France in the 1960s. His account of the film policies not only of the

Hollywood majors and the particular national governments but also of the US government itself is a model piece of research into the political economy of a cultural industry at a particular moment in time.

The other major study that forms a backdrop to the present collection was published in France in 1983 and appeared in English in 1984 (Mattelart, Delcourt and Mattelart 1984). *International Image Markets* grew out of the report of a French government mission to explore the feasibility of a 'Latin audio-visual space' that would include several European and South American countries. Again, the study is of most interest and continuing value in the details it produces about the international film and television industries in the 1980s. Equally, the book is at its weakest in its assumptions about the homogeneity of an 'audio-visual space', the latter being a modern label for 'national cinema' or 'national television'. (Schlesinger 1993).

REVISIONIST RESEARCH

Since the appearance of these two studies, a new world order (or disorder) has emerged. New international configurations have appeared not only in the areas of economics and trade but also in areas such as culture and politics. In particular with the collapse of the Soviet Communist bloc, the Cold War has come to an end and this has triggered a renewed wave of nationalism (anderson 1992; Schlesinger 1993). While the authors in this collection do not deal directly with this new wave of nationalism, nevertheless its effects are registered in many of the chapters. Modernization and the spread of popular culture has made it impossible to use terms such as nation and national identity without a good deal of conceptual qualification. The volume thus represents a revision of the political economy tradition of film policy research, inspired by its scholarship and attention to economic and political detail but with more awareness of national cultural differences.

The particular occasion for the book lay in the conference on film policy organized by the Institute for Cultural Policy Studies at Griffith University and held in Brisbane in December 1991. The Institute (now known as the Key Centre for Media and Cultural Policy) has published two volumes of papers delivered at the conference (Moran 1992, 1994). A number of the original papers, five in all, were identified as being of international interest and it was decided to organize a collection that built on this foundation. As this reader was initially conceived, it was thought that a subtitle for the volume might be 'Film Policy: International, National and Regional Perspectives'. However, when it came to commissioning new chapters and having the original papers revised and rewritten, it was found that it was not so easy to delineate between these three levels. In the world of the very late twentieth century, film policy inevitably has ramifications at many levels. However, the broad scheme was of some use in organizing the chapters that follow.

A short introduction to both the parts and the individual chapters follows.

A GLOBAL INDUSTRY

Part I of the collection is concerned with the international film industry. Despite the changes in ownership of some of the major companies, noted above, as well as the emergence of local feature film production in many parts of the world, the industry continues to be headquartered in Hollywood. Tino Balio in his chapter examines the international entertainment industry over the course of the past fifteen years from an American point of view. He concentrates not only on the output of particular films but also on their significance from an industry perspective. More importantly, he also analyses the changing parameters of the conduit, the distribution system collectively controlled by the Hollywood majors, through which these films pass. In the 1980s and the 1990s even the majors have been confronted by some degree of uncertainty in protecting and expanding their profitability. From the late 1970s into the early 1980s, the majors had followed a course of horizontal disaggregation, offloading some of their operations in order to concentrate on core industries related to the business of film. However, Murdoch's 1985 move to acquire Twentieth Century Fox as a means of ensuring a ready supply of feature films and television for his television outlets in the United States, Europe and Asia caused an abandonment of the strategy of disaggregation in favour of a new round of integration along vertical as well as horizontal lines. Although some of the new partnerships are somewhat shaky both in market and organizational terms, nevertheless the net effect of the new alliances has been to guarantee Hollywood's continued domination of global film markets well into the next century.

Broadcast television is a crucial means of distributing feature films and television programmes. Recent alliances between the major film companies and the American television broadcast networks has put Hollywood in a pivotal position not only in the home market but also in the international market. Recent relaxation of broadcast regulations in the US, enabling the American television networks to engage in foreign syndication, means that the networks are now important players in overseas television markets. The US domestic and the international television markets are the respective subjects of the next two chapters. In Chapter 2, Jonathan Levy outlines the likely expansion of exhibition windows in film and video, being brought about through new technologies such as satellite delivery, increased cable penetration and digital signal compression. The significant issue is that of content and who will provide it for the new delivery systems. While there will be an increasing series of interactive services available Hollywood is likely to be the principal source of programming for the multi-channel systems of the not too distant future. Thus, like the development of cable TV and video cassettes as exhibition outlets in the 1980s, developments which the film majors did nothing to foster and yet was a major beneficiary from their operation, Hollywood is likely to again derive significant market advantage from the new systems.

As suggested above, America is not the only country to play an important role

13

in the global film and television industry. Several of the advanced capitalist nations, especially in Europe, are also important players. The next chapter, written by European researcher Manuel Alvarado, examines the principal global television marketplace. Several national television systems are significant exporters of television programmes. The most important factor underlying such market power is not, as might be thought, the size of the national population but rather the size of the domestic viewing audience. Significant national systems in the world market then include America, Britain, France, Germany, China, Japan and Brazil. Thus Alvarado's analysis supports the contention, quoted earlier, that the world marketplace in film and television of the near future is likely to contain several major players whose roots lie outside the United States.

The last two chapters in Part I concern the recent European response to Hollywood. Toby Miller analyses the 'moment' of the Uruguay Round of the General Agreement on Tariffs and Trade (GATT), especially the move of delegates from outside the US to exempt audio-visual products from trading terms agreed upon for other goods. However, the perception that this was a 'victory' for France and other countries who insisted that audio-visual goods needed protection considerably simplifies and blurs the actual situation in the international audio-visual industry. France's protective stance on 'cultural heritage' is likely to be of most benefit to large capitalist interests in Western Europe and of little assistance to film producers in countries such as those in Africa. Indeed, as Miller shows, there is good reason to suggest that, just as once upon a time in the studio era what were ostensibly rival firms were in fact working together in oligopoly, something similar is in place as far as film industries in the US and other advanced capitalist nations is concerned. Anne Jäckel in her chapter on feature film co-production, especially the case of the Anglo-French Agreement, offers more material for this kind of reflection. As one of the Western nations, France is caught between economic ambition (to be a dominant force in the world film industry) and cultural ambition (to support domestic production, emphasizing cultural plurality and artistic merit). Certain film makers pay the price for this kind of policy, not least those domestic writers and directors whose subject matter is more local in scope or are prepared to deal with subject matter that stresses the multicultural reality of Europe.

CINEMA AND NATION-STATES

Part II of the collection takes the form of a series of case studies of one or more nation-states and the particular film policies that they have recently pursued. The six chapter topics were chosen both to highlight different components of film policy and to achieve a cultural and geographic spread. With the exception of Hill's chapter on Britain, the chapters here deal with the policies of nation-states that were offshoots of European colonialism and which have come into existence only in the past two centuries. Nationhood has often been achieved through the imposition of political unity on disparate ethnicities, regions, religions and languages. Particular national film policies are then frequently selective in terms of the particular cultural and economic interests inside the nation that they promote.

John Hill's chapter on British film policy in the 1980s and early 1990s has already been referred to. It is particularly interesting to read his discussion in the light of Miller's and Jäckel's passing remarks on film policy in France. What is clear from comparing the two is that British film producers did not fare well under an economically rationalist goverment. French film makers fared a lot better under a socialist government.

Although inspired by Britain's long-standing support for its film production industry, Canada has had a more recent history of government support for feature film production. In turn, Canada's 1967 decision to develop a government-supported feature production infrastructure led several other countries, including Australia, to follow a similar policy. Michael Dorland's chapter is concerned with the historic moment of that intervention in both Canada and Australia and especially with the discursive formations it provoked. These rhetorics are characterized by a verbal slippage between two key terms, industry and culture. Dorland sees this as a weakness in arguments for a film production infrastructure.

However, there is the equally strong possibility that it is precisely this slippage that is the *strength* of government-supported film production industries: financial shortcomings can be excused by a cultural mandate and artistic successes, while cultural shortcomings can be excused on the basis that some films at least have to be commercially profitable.

Randal Johnson in his chapter on film policies in Latin America pays particular attention to Brazil, a nation with a long history of state support for its film industry. This support has recently included an exhibition quota, designed to ensure that locally produced films were screened in Brazilian theatres, and a state-run film agency which co-produced films with local private producers. Neither of these measures have been very effective. Theatre-owners have not observed the quota and the state agency system has turned out to be a form of patronage for particular local producers which has not resulted in good distribution of their films. Johnson therefore sees the need for the Brazilian state to achieve new legitimacy as far as the film industry is concerned both by ensuring that the exhibition quota is met and also by having an arms length relationship with private film producers.

The last three chapters concern three Asian nations. With significant differences in religion, language and culture, the three countries – India, Indonesia and Singapore – all gained political independence soon after the end of the Second World War. Yet all three have found themselves still affected by their former colonial rulers in terms of their response to perceived threats to the new political order. To protect the 'social order', the state in India, Indonesia and Singapore has exercised strict film censorship. Manjunath Pendakur in his chapter on Indian film policy marries an account of film censorship, particularly as it is applied to Indian films, with a broader discussion of the Indian film industry, most especially the private and the state-supported sectors. The relationship between the state and the Indian film industry is a patron–client one although this may be changing with recent significant rises in the number of US films being imported. Krishna Sen's chapter centres on one of the 'Asian (economic) tigers', an economy that has grown remarkably in the past fifteen years. The Indonesian state has pursued a ruthless policy of military control, economic nationalism and cultural laissez faire. In a striking argument that challenges the orthodoxies of cultural dependency theory, Sen concludes that opening the floodgates to the import of foreign media products represents no threat to the Indonesian state. Cultural liberalization does not lead to a loosening of control. Instead, filling the audio-visual space with an endless flood of films and television programmes from the US, Europe, Australia and elsewhere helps remove the threat to the state that could be posed by the cultural work, including films and videos, of its own citizens. The last chapter in Part II is in striking contrast to Sen's. David Birch is concerned with Singapore, another of the booming economies of South East Asia, which has also pursued a policy of economic nationalism coupled with strict social and political control. With the imminent return of Hong Kong to China in 1997, the Singaporean government has undertaken a sustained attempt to build this island state as a production centre for information and communication services, including cinema. Unlike Indonesia, Singapore does not operate a liberal regime so far as the circulation of foreign cultural material, especially Western films and books, is concerned. There is repressive censorship of film and Birch explores the rhetoric, contradictions and tensions that surround this particular aspect of Singaporean film policy.

POLICY AND NEW FILMIC SPACES

Part III focuses on cultural policy, especially film, at a level below that of the nation and doubly below that of the supra-national. If such a metaphor implies a set of spatial relations arranged along a vertical axis then we can equally invoke a horizontal axis in referring to peripheries, with the latter being peripheries to larger metropolitan centres. Film policy at the regional levels is the subject of the first two chapters in this part. Steve McIntyre is concerned with the relatively recent initiatives in the United Kingdom for local government bodies to adopt cultural industry initiatives, including various forms of support and funding for local film and video production. Part of the seeds of this initiative lie in the cultural industries strategy of the Greater London Council between 1981 and 1984. The GLC's policy was conceived as a series of interventions in existing culture industries located in London so as to give culturally marginal groups a voice that they had hitherto lacked. Although it failed to meet this ambition, the policy initiative has served as a crucial example for regional cultural policy strategies. However, there has been a significant change of emphasis, away from cultural empowerment of minorities and towards notions of regional development and job creating initiatives.

Carole Sklan's chapter is concerned with film policy in regional Australia.

16

Various Australian state governments have undertaken film policy initiatives and these have harboured not only economic but also cultural ambitions. However, the nationalist claim of the Australian regions is a 'weak' one with no foundation in such arenas of difference as language, religion, or ethnicity.

In this respect the case of French-speaking province of Quebec in predominantly English-speaking Canada is far more interesting. Ron Burnett in Chapter 14 analyses some of the contradictions surrounding state nationalism in Quebec especially as it operates in cultural arenas such as that of film policy. Quebec nationalism is very much the cultural nationalism of a particular state apparatus. It operates with a monoculturalist sense of what it is to be a Quebecois. At the same time, Quebec turns a blind eye to the integration of its national economy into the economy of the North American transnationals such that Quebec film makers are easily and readily absorbed by Hollywood. The last chapter deals with a series of nations that lack control both of a state apparatus and their own territory. Meadows examines the cultural plight of indigenous peoples in three white settler societies and ties this to their political and economic plight. The chapter is concerned with Australia, New Zealand and Canada but it might equally have focused on several other terrritories such as the US, South America and northern Europe where indigenous peoples have a marginal existence. As cultural resources, film and video are especially important for these people in the task of building positive images of themselves for self-identity and as a means of communication in their political struggles. By adopting a cross-national and cross-cultural perspective, Meadows underlines the non-homogeneity of the nation-state. Groups inside national boundaries often have more in common with groups within other national boundaries than they do with other groups within the same boundary.

This emphasis on the multicultural nature of the nation-state contained in the last chapter is a fitting note on which not only to end the collection but also this Introduction. The concern here has been to register some of the conceptual complexities that surround a series of key terms for this film policy reader. These include notions of film as culture, film as industry, the meaning of 'Hollywood' in the past and in the present, Hollywood and national cinemas, national cinema and film policy, and national identity and cultural identity. Historical process is invariably at work so that new connections, arrangements, practices and ideas are inevitably being forged. The past thirty years have seen large-scale transformations in the film industry, film technologies, and government philosophy and policy, not to mention the conceptual terrain within which film policy is researched. This collection then offers new bearings in this changed environment.

REFERENCES

Aksoy, A. and Robins, K. (1992) 'Hollywood for the 21st century: global competition for the critical mass in image markets'. *Cambridge Journal of Economics*. 16(1): 1–22.
Anderson, B. (1992) *24 Hours* (Supplement) February: 40–6.

Armes, R. (1987) *Third World Film Making and the West*. Berkeley: University of California Press.

Balio, T. (1990) *Hollywood in the Age of Television*. North Sydney: Allen & Unwin.

Bächlin, P. (1945) *Der Film als Ware*. Basel: Burg.

BBC World Service (1995) *Aint No Mickey Business*.

Borwell, D., Staiger, J. and Thompson, C. (1985) *The Classic Hollywood Cinema: Film Style and Mode of Production to 1960*. New York: Columbia University Press.

Buscombe, E. (1990) 'Coca-Cola satellites? Hollywood and the de-regulation of European television' in Balio, T. (ed.) *Hollywood in the Age of Television*. Boston: Unwin Hyman.

Collins, R. (1990) *Culture, Communication and National Identity: The Case of Canadian Television*. Toronto: University of Toronto Press.

Elsaesser, T. (1975), 'The pathos of failure: American films in the 1970s.' *Monogram*, No. 6.

Elsaesser, T. and Barker, A. (eds) (1990) *Early Cinema: Space, Frame, Narrative*. London: BFI Publishing.

Fell, J. (1974) *Film and Narrative Tradition*. Oklahoma: Oklahoma Press.

De la Garde, R., Gilsdorf, W. and Wechselmann, I. (1993) *Small Nations, Big Neighbour: Denmark and Quebec/Canada Compare Notes on American Popular Culture*. London: John Libby.

Gomery, D. (1986) *The Hollywood Studio System*. London: Macmillan.

Guback, T. (1969) *The International Film Industry: Western Europe and America Since 1945*. Bloomington: Indiana University Press.

Guback, T. (1974) 'Film as International Business', *Journal of Communications*, 24, Winter: 297–314.

Higson, A. (1989) 'The Concept of National Cinema', *Screen*, 30 (4): 36–46.

Hill, J. (1992) 'The issue of national cinema and British film production', in Petrie, D. (ed) *New Questions of British Cinema*. London: BFI.

Huettig, M. (1944) *Economic Control of the Motion Picture Industry*. Philadelphia: University of Pennsylvania Press.

Jowett, G. (1976) *Film: The Democratic Art*. Boston: Little, Brown.

Legg, S. and Klingender, F.D. (1937) *Money Behind the Screen: A Report*. London: Lawrence and Wishart.

McAnany, E. G. and Wilkinson, K. T. (1992) 'From cultural imperialists to takeover victims: questions on Hollywood's buyouts from the critical tradition', *Communications Research*. 19(6): 742–7.

Magder, T. (1993) *Canada's Hollywood: The Canadian State and Feature Films*. Toronto: University of Toronto Press.

Mattelart, A. and Dorfman, A. (1975) *How to Read Donald Duck*. New York: International General.

Mattelart, A., Delcourt, C. X. and Mattelart, M. (1984) *International Image Markets: In Search of An Alternative Perspective*. London: Canadian Publishing Group.

Mayersburg, P. (1967) *Hollywood: The Haunted House*. London: Penguin.

Moran, A. (ed.) (1992) *Film Education and Training: Policy and Performance*. Griffith University, Brisbane: Institute of Cultural Policy Studies.

Moran, A. (ed.) (1994) *Film Policy: An Australian Reader*. Griffith University, Brisbane: Institute of Cultural Policy Studies.

Nordenstreng, K. and Varis, T. (1973) 'The non-homogeneity of the nation-state', in Gerbner, G., Gross, L. and Melody, W. (eds) *Communications Technology and Social Policy: Understanding the New 'Cultural Revolution'*. New York: Wiley.

Rockett, K. (1994) 'Culture, industry and Irish cinema', in Hill, J., McLoone, M. and Hainsworth, P. (eds) *Border Crossing: Film in Ireland, Britain and Europe*. Belfast/London: Institute of Irish Studies and BFI.

Routt, W. D. (1991) 'New Zealand', *Continuum*, 4(2): 218–26.

Scannell, P. and Cardiff, D. (1991) *A Social History of British Broadcasting*. Oxford: Blackwells.

Schiller, H. (1969) *Mass Communications and American Empire*. New York: A. M. Kelly.

Schlesinger, P. (1987) 'On national identity: some conceptions and misconceptions criticized', *Social Science Information*, 26(2): 219–64.

Schlesinger, P. (1993) 'Wishful thinking: cultural politics, media and collective identities in Europe', *Journal of Communications*, 43(2) Spring: 6–17.

Skovmand, M. and Schroder, K. (1992) *Media Cultures: Reappraising Transnational Media*. London: Routledge.

Snyder, L. (1982) *Global Mini-nationalism: Autonomy or Independence*. Westport, Connecticut: Greenswood.

Thompson, C. (1985) *Exporting Entertainment: America in the World Film Market 1907–1934*. London: BFI.

Tomlinson, J. (1991) *Cultural Imperialism: A Critical Introduction*. London: Pinter.

Wasko, J., Mosco, V. and Pendakur, M. (eds) (1993) *Illuminating the Blindspots: Essays Honouring Dallas W. Smythe*. Norwood, New Jersey: Ablex.

Wells, A. (1972) *Picture-tube Imperialism? The Impact of U.S. Television on Latin America*. New York: Orbis Books.

Part I

POLICY IN
A GLOBAL INDUSTRY

1

ADJUSTING TO THE NEW GLOBAL ECONOMY

Hollywood in the 1990s

Tino Balio

The 1980s were good to Hollywood. Without having nurtured the new television distribution technologies, Hollywood became the beneficiary of two lucrative ancillary markets, pay-TV and home video (Balio 1990: 262–70). Contrary to predictions, the new technologies did not kill the motion picture theatre; rather, they stimulated demand for more motion pictures, spread the risk of production financing, and enhanced the value of film libraries. Changes in the global political and economic environment, particularly the commercialization of broadcasting systems worldwide, created additional sources of profit. And on the horizon, still newer technologies offered even more intriguing opportunities for growth.

Conditions such as these led to the 'globalization' of the film industry. Describing its rationale for merging, Time Warner explained,

> In the Eighties we witnessed the most profound political and economic changes since the end of the Second World War. As these changes unfolded globalization was rapidly evolving from a prophecy to a fact of life. No serious competitor could hope for any long-term success unless, building on a secure home base, it achieved a major presence in all of the world's important markets.
>
> (Time Warner 1989)

Upgrading international operations to a privileged position, the Hollywood majors expanded 'horizontally' to tap emerging markets worldwide, formed 'downstream' alliances with independent producers to enlarge their rosters, and 'partnered' with foreign investors to acquire new sources of financing. Achieving these goals led to a merger movement that has yet to run its course.

THE DOMESTIC MARKET

Home video and pay-TV invigorated motion picture exhibition during the 1980s by enhancing the status of the theatre in the distribution chain. To consumers, the performance of a feature film at the box office established its value at the video store and on cable television. The vitality of the theatrical market, coupled with the laissez-faire approach to anti-trust by the Reagan administration, convinced the majors 'to take another fling with vertical integration' (Gold 1990). The logic seemed to be this. Since only a few movies at any one time succeed at the box office, why not go into exhibition and profit from the hit films on the market? Columbia started the trend in 1986 by purchasing a small chain of theatres in New York City. Within a year, MCA, Paramount Communications and Warner Communications bought or acquired stakes in important theatre chains around the country (Noglows 1992).

Home video and pay-TV also stimulated demand for product. Domestic feature film production jumped from around 350 pictures a year in 1983 to nearly 600 in 1988. Oddly, the majors contributed little to the increase; in fact, the number of in-house productions of the majors held steady during this period, between seventy and eighty films a year (Cohn 1990). The additional films came from the so-called 'mini-majors' – Orion Pictures, Cannon Films, and Dino de Laurentiis Entertainment – and from independents like Atlantic Release, Carolco, New World, Hemdale, Troma, Island Alive, Vestron and New Line who were eager to fill the void. These companies took the plunge thinking that even a modest picture could earn money from the sale of distribution rights to pay-cable and home video. Although the proceeds from such sales were insignificant by Hollywood standards, the 'pre-selling' of rights to these markets could offset the entire production cost for an inexpensive picture and might make the difference between profit and loss for a more ambitious project.

Rather than producing more pictures, the majors exploited a new feature film format, the 'ultra-high budget' film (Logsdon 1990: 11). The format was popularized by Carolco Pictures, an independent production company headed by Mario F. Kassar and Peter Hoffman that got its start with the *Rambo* movies starring Sylvester Stallone in the 1980s. Carving a niche for itself in the fast-growing foreign market, Carolco specialized in action-filled blockbusters and paid top stars like Sylvester Stallone and Arnold Schwarzenegger enormous fees to carry them. Following this tack, the majors upped the ante and production costs rose from around $9 million in 1980 to close to $24 million in 1989, on the average. The most expensive pictures in 1989, such as *Batman* (Warner), *The Abyss* (20th-Fox), and *Tango & Cash* (Warner) cost twice the average (Fabrikant 1990a).

'Ultra-high' budgets and saturation booking went hand in hand. To recoup their investments as quickly as possible, film companies regularly booked new releases into 2,000 and more screens. Print and advertising costs tripled as a result to over $12 million per film on the average by 1989. For 'event' films, companies spent $10 million and more on pre-opening weekend advertising alone (Natale 1992a). The strategy resulted in 'ultra-high' grosses; for example in 1989, six pictures grossed over $100 million in the US, among them *Batman* (Warner, $250 million), *Indiana Jones and The Last Crusade* (Paramount, $195 million), *Lethal Weapon 2* (Warner, $147 million) and *Honey, I Shrunk the Kids* (Disney, $130 million) (*Velvet Light Trap*, 1991).

With pictures like these in distribution, it was no surprise that the 1980s concluded with record-breaking box office results. In 1989, admissions reached a five-year high of 1.13 billion, and the box office a high of over $5 billion (*Velvet Light Trap* 1991). (Much of this increase at the box office resulted from ticket price inflation, which saw the average price of a ticket increase from $2.69 to $4.44 over the decade.) Capitalizing on the appeal of such pictures, the majors were able to extract better terms, longer play dates, and higher up front guarantees from exhibitors.

The blockbuster had the desired effect from the majors' perspective of raising the expectations of movie goers for high production values, special effects and big-name stars. But in the process, the 'ultra-high budget' picture seriously undermined the ability of smaller firms to play the game. A shake out occurred in the independent market in 1989 as many independent producers went bankrupt. For one thing, the lure of pre-sales had created a product glut. From 1984 to 1987, annual output of the mini-majors and independents nearly doubled, causing a logjam at the exhibition level. Marginal films – those judged unlikely to recoup print and advertising costs – were shelved; others were lucky if they secured any playing time. Without national exposure or a theatrical run, few films found takers in the ancillary markets. To get national exposure, a picture had to open in New York and receive favourable reviews. Because this meant going up against the majors, independents were forced to spend more on advertising for a longer period of time. Few firms had the money to pull this off (Goldman 1989).

THE FOREIGN MARKET

The growth of the overseas market during the 1980s was a result of the upgrading of motion picture theatres, the emancipation of state-controlled broadcasting, the spread of cable and satellite services, and the pent-up demand for entertainment of all types. At one time, theatrical rentals constituted nearly all of the foreign revenues of American film companies, but by 1989 they accounted for little more than a quarter. The largest revenue components for Hollywood product overseas had become video, theatrical and TV, in that order. From 1985 to 1989, video cassette sales increased from $1.5 billion to $3.25 billion; theatrical film rentals rose from $800 million to $1.25 billion; and TV sales grew from $300 million to $800 million (Logsdon 1990: 49).

The largest influx came from Western European television. When governments liberated the broadcast spectrum, the number of privately-owned commercial television stations and cable and satellite services grew enormously. In Great Britain, where consumers had long been restricted to two BBC and two quasi-independent stations, British Satellite Broadcasting and Sky Television introduced nine new satellite channels of pay-TV services (*Variety* 1990). In France, Canal Plus, the country's first pay-TV service, attracted three million subscribers within five years (Fabrikant 1990d). By 1989, Western European television reached 320 million people and 125 million households (vs 250 million people and 90 million households in the United States) and showed the potential of becoming the largest single market for Hollywood entertainment (Logsdon 1990: 50).

Although Hollywood had become the principal supplier of programming to these new services, the value of this trade was considerably less than theatrical distribution. This disparity existed because in most major European markets, governments had erected import quotas on television programmes similar to those imposed on motion pictures after the Second World War. Great Britain, for example, restricted TV imports on the BBC to a maximum of 14 per cent of total broadcast time. France, West Germany, and Italy established similar barriers to entry. The European Economic Community's plans for a unified Europe in 1992 promised to abolish most trade barriers and make pan-European television a reality. The thinking went that if only a portion of the potentially available television channels were to begin operation, Hollywood imports would increase in volume and in price.

But European unification did not proceed as planned, so that the largest single source of revenue for Hollywood in Western Europe remained home video. The spread of VCRs in Western Europe demonstrated that, given a choice, consumers preferred entertainment with greater appeal and more variety than their state broadcasting monopolies provided. In 1978, VCR sales totalled around 500,000; by 1987, sales topped 40 million, or nearly one-third of all households. Like their counterparts in the United States, European VCR owners not only wanted to time shift programming to suit their own schedules, but also to enjoy different kinds of programming, particularly Hollywood movies. The message was clear; the demand for more entertainment on television had been left unsatisfied. By 1990, video sales in the European Economic Community totalled nearly $4.5 billion, with the lion's share generated by Hollywood movies (Watson 1992).

Western Europe's video business was likewise fuelled by theatrical exhibition. By 1990, the major American film companies collected around $830 million in film rentals from Western Europe, which came to about half of the film rentals they earned in the United States (Illist 1991). Overall, all overseas markets accounted for 43 per cent of their total theatrical revenues by 1990, an increase of 10 per cent over the decade (Fabrikant 1990b).

Two factors helped sales: more and better theatres and more effective advertising outlets. Going into the 1980s, nearly every market outside the US was under screened. Western Europe, for example, had about one-third the number of screens per capita as the United States, despite having about the same population (Illist 1991). And most of its theatres were old and tired. To rejuvenate exhibition and to encourage movie going, American film companies and European exhibitors launched a campaign during the 1980s to rebuild and renovate theatres on the continent. In Great Britain alone, new construction and refurbishment were responsible for 500 new multiplex screens, which had the effect of nearly doubling theatre attendance by the end of the decade (Fabrikant 1990c; Iliot 1993). Similar results were found in Germany, Italy, Spain, and France, as well as in Japan.

Taking advantage of the advertising opportunities created by commercial television, Hollywood pitched its wares as never before. Whole markets, such as West Germany, were opened up to television advertising. And new channels, such as MTV Europe which reached between 15 to 20 million homes, offered opportunities for niche marketing (Groves, 1990). Spending lavishly on advertising, the majors were able to bolster their ultra-high budget pictures in theatrical and in ancillary markets and overwhelm smaller, indigenous films that could not compete in such a high-stakes environment.

GLOBALIZATION

Urges to merge

Hollywood's first response to globalization was to shift operations from vertical integration (e.g. studios acquiring theatre chains) to horizontal integration (e.g. studios partnering with other producers and distributors) (Logsdon 1990: 4). The shift departed significantly from the merger movement of the 1960s, which ushered the American film industry into the age of conglomerates. During the 1960s, motion picture companies were either taken over by huge multifaceted corporations, absorbed into burgeoning entertainment conglomerates, or became conglomerates through diversification. The impetus behind this merger movement was to stabilize operations by creating numerous 'profit centres' to protect against business downturns in a specific area (Balio 1985: 443). Acquiring theatre chains in the 1980s was an extension of this philosophy. Horizontal integration was designed to strengthen distribution and represented a new way of controlling the world entertainment market. As film industry analyst Harold Vogel put it,

> Ownership of entertainment distribution capability is like ownership of a toll road or bridge. No matter how good or bad the software product (i.e., movie, record, book, magazine, tv show, or whatever) is, it must pass over or cross through a distribution pipeline in order to reach the consumer. And like at any toll road or bridge that cannot be circumvented, the distributor is a local monopolist who can extract a relatively high fee for use of his facility.
>
> (Vogel 1989)

A survey of the strongest companies in the industry illustrates how they protected their entrenched positions while assuring themselves access to all the turnpikes and bridges. Rupert Murdoch's acquisition of 20th-Century-Fox in 1985 triggered the recent merger movement. Murdoch's goal was nothing less than to create 'the world's first global television, publishing and entertainment operation' (Cohen 1990: 31). The head of News Corp., an Australian-based publishing conglomerate, Murdoch owned newspapers and magazines in Sydney, London, New York and Chicago valued at over $1 billion. Acquiring a controlling interest in 20th-Century-Fox for $600 million, Murdoch announced his intention to create a full-blown fourth TV network, Fox Broadcasting, to challenge the three entrenched television networks, ABC, CBS and NBC. He did this with the tacit approval of the US's Federal Communications Commission (FCC), which wanted to foster more competition in television broadcasting.

Murdoch made his first move by acquiring Metromedia Television, the largest group of independent television stations in the country. Purchased at a cost of $2 billion, the stations formed the core of his network. (In order to comply with FCC regulations governing the ownership of TV stations, Murdoch became a US citizen.) Murdoch then waged a costly three-year battle to assemble a network of over 100 independent stations capable of reaching nearly all TV homes. Developing counter-programming aimed at young adults to supply those stations, Fox Broadcasting lost hundreds of millions the first three years, but in 1989 it staged a turnaround as a result of two hit series – *America's Most Wanted* and *Married with Children* (*Variety* 1991a).

Next, Murdoch turned his sights on Great Britain, where he launched Sky Television, a four-channel satellite service in 1989 at a cost of about $540 million. By then, News Corp. had become the world's second largest communications company after Time Warner. The Sky Television venture marked the beginning of a push into the newly-privatized television markets of Europe, Asia and the Americas that would involve Murdoch in new satellite services, the production of programming for China and India, the co-financing of soap operas in Mexico, and the development of pay-TV in Germany, among other ventures (Stevenson 1994b).

Paramount Communications and Warner Communications, two of the strongest companies in the business, responded to globalization by 'downsizing' to concentrate on a core group of activities. Paramount Communications was the successor company to Gulf + Western, a multifaceted conglomerate that had acquired the studio in the 1966. Active in a range of unrelated industries such as sugar, zinc, fertilizer, wire and cable, musical instruments, real estate, and dozens of others, G + W became too unwieldy to manage and decided to do an about face. Under the leadership of Martin Davis, G + W shed over fifty companies during the 1980s and created a new identity for itself by becoming a global communications and entertainment giant known as Paramount Communications. Thereafter, the company pursued two lines of business: (1) entertainment, consisting of Paramount Pictures, Paramount Home Video, movie theatres, Madison Square Garden, the New York Knicks basketball and New York Rangers hockey teams, and MSG cable network; and (2) publishing and information, consisting mainly of Simon & Schuster, the nation's largest book publisher (Gulf + Western 1987).

Under the direction of Steven J. Ross, Warner Communications had evolved into a diversified entertainment conglomerate involved in a wide range of 'leisure time' businesses such as film and television, recorded music, book publishing, cable communications, toys and electronic games, and other operations. In 1982, Warner decided to restructure its operations around distribution. Sold were Atari, Warner Cosmetics, Franklin Mint, Panavision, the New York Cosmos soccer team, and Warner's cable programming interests including MTV and Nickelodeon. (In several cases, Warner retained partial interests in the former subsidiaries as investments.)

The 'downsized' Warner Communications emerged as a horizontally-integrated company engaged in three areas of entertainment: (1) production and distribution of film and television programming; (2) recorded music; and (3) publishing. In addition to owning one of Hollywood's most consistently successful studios, a formidable film and television library, and the largest record company in the world, Warner had acquired the distribution systems associated with each of its product lines, including Warner Cable Communications, the nation's second biggest cable operator with 1.5 million subscribers. Warner added considerable muscle to its distribution capability when it merged with Time Inc. in 1989 to form Time Warner, the world's pre-eminent media conglomerate valued at $14 billion (Time Warner 1989).

Time Warner touted its merger 'as essential to the competitive survival of American enterprise in the emerging global entertainment communications marketplace' (Gold 1989: 5). It had in mind not only the takeover of 20th-Century-Fox by Australia's News Corp., but also the anticipated acquisition of Columbia Pictures Entertainment (CPE) by Japan's Sony Corporation, which actually occurred later in 1989 at a cost of $3.4 billion. Sony had previously entered the US entertainment software business in 1987 when it purchased CBS Records for $2 billion. Columbia Pictures Entertainment had 'bumped along on a downhill path' and experienced frequent management turnovers under its previous owner, Coca-Cola Co. But Sony considered the CPE acquisition, which included two major studios, Columbia Pictures and TriStar Pictures, home video distribution, a theatre chain and an extensive film library, as a means of creating synergies in its operations (Kipps 1989). As *Variety* put it, 'The hardware company's strategists had concluded that all their fancy electronic machines would have souls of tin without a steady diet of software' (Gold 1989: 5). To strengthen CPE as a producer of software, Sony spent lavishly to acquire and refurbish new studios and to hire Peter Guber and Jon Peters to set a course for the company.

The third takeover of an American media company by a foreign firm occurred when Japan's Matsushita Electric Industrial Company, the largest consumer electronics manufacturer in the world, purchased MCA in 1990 for $6.9 billion. Like its rival, Sony, Matsushita 'thought the entertainment "software" business could provide higher profit margins than the intensely competitive, and now largely saturated, consumer electronics appliance business' (Pollack 1994: C1). And like Sony, Matsushita thought that synergies could exist between the hardware and the software business.

The parent of Universal pictures, MCA, had relied on television production and distribution for stability. Year in and year out, MCA's profitable television operations accounted for over a quarter of the company's revenues. In 1985, MCA had more network shows on prime time than any other producer. Among them were *Magnum P.I.*, *Miami Vice*, and *Murder She Wrote*. Afterwards, MCA saw its share of the television market shrink as stations stopped buying one-hour action programmes, MCA's strength, in favour of half-hour comedies. And because MCA's share of the US box office had also declined, the company altered its course by going on an acquisitions binge in 1985. In two years, the company spent $650 million to acquire toy companies, music companies, a major independent television station, and a half interest in Cineplex Odeon Theatres. The diversification strategy was designed to strengthen MCA's existing positions and to extend the company into contiguous businesses. MCA purchased New York's WWOR-TV, for example, to ensure that its old programmes were aired in the largest television market in the country. And MCA acquired LJN Toys Ltd to acquire the capability of manufacturing and marketing toy lines tied-in with its movies (Wallach 1988: 3–10). MCA's investment showing the greatest promise was the $500 million Universal Studios Tour near Disney World in Orlando, Florida, which opened in 1990.

Partnering domestically

Hollywood's second response to globalization was to compete for talent, projects and product for their distribution pipelines. After the breakdown of the studio system during the 1950s, the majors regularly formed alliances with independent producers to fill out their rosters and to create relationships with budding talent. A deal might involve multiple-pictures, complete financing, worldwide distribution and a fifty-fifty profit split. Deals like these are still common, but partnerships with the likes of Carolco, Castle Rock and Morgan Creek departed from traditional film industry practice in certain key respects: they typically involved partial financing, domestic distribution and lower distribution fees. Partnerships took this form because the majors needed not only more pictures to increase market share but also a means of sharing the risks and potential benefits of distributing ultra-high budget pictures (Hlavacek 1990; Natale 1991).

After aligning with TriStar, Carolco delivered three big-budget blockbusters in a row, *Total Recall* (1990), *Terminator 2: Judgment Day* (1991) and *Basic Instinct* (1992). To raise financing, Carolco originally made a public offering of stocks but later sold stakes in the company to Japan's Pioneer Electronics, France's Canal Plus, Britain's Carlton Communications and Italy's Rizzoli Corriere della Sera (Kissinger 1991). Carolco's strategy was to cover as much of the production costs for a picture as possible by pre-selling the ancillary rights piece by piece, country by country. In this manner, Carolco was able to acquire $91 million of the $94 million production cost, including Arnold Schwarzenegger's $12 million fee, for *Terminator 2*, one of the most expensive pictures on record. TriStar Pictures paid Carolco $4 million for domestic distribution rights and had first call on the rentals until the advance was recouped, after which it levied a smaller-than-usual distribution fee. Thus the partnership lowered the risks of production financing for Carolco and enabled TriStar to share in the profits of an ultra-high budget picture without much of an investment (Stevenson 1991).

Columbia's relationship with Castle Rock differed in that Columbia functioned as an equity partner as well as a distributor. Organized in 1987 by former 20th-Century-Fox producer Alan Horn and film director Rob Reiner, Castle Rock also produced television shows. Rather than going public for funding, Castle Rock sold stakes in the company to Columbia, Westinghouse Electric, Credit Lyonnais and other investors (Weinraub 1992). Castle Rock turned out hit movies just about every year, including *When Harry met Sally* . . . (1989), *Misery* (1990), *City Slickers* (1991), *A Few Good Men*, (1992) and *In the Line of Fire* (1993). Its hit television shows included *Seinfeld* for NBC and *Sessions* for Home Box Office (Weinraub 1992b).

Warner's deal with Morgan Creek provided substantial advances for production and advertising in return for domestic distribution rights. Like Carolco's deal with TriStar, Warner had first call on the receipts until all advances were recouped after which it collected a reduced distribution fee. Founded in 1988 by James Robinson, a West Coast Subaru importer, Morgan Creek's strategy was to produce big-name 'event' films to compete in the risky overseas market. The company's biggest blockbuster was Kevin Costner's *Robin Hood: Prince of Thieves* (1991), which grossed more than $400 million worldwide (Brennan and Eller 1993; Alexander 1994).

Partnering with a group of independents that specialized in foreign art films and off-beat American fare, Walt Disney Co. and Turner Broadcasting System (TBS) moved aggressively into the independent field. Disney had built an entertainment empire based on the family trade in which motion pictures accounted for only about one-third of its business. Going into the 1980s, about half of the company's revenues and most of its profits came from Disneyland. The balance came from other entertainment activities, such as television, music and records, publications, and character merchandising such as Mickey Mouse watches. When wholesome family entertainment lost some of its box office draw, Disney hired a new management team headed by Michael Eisner to energize the studio. Setting a new course, Eisner transformed Disney into a motion picture heavyweight by forming Touchstone Films in 1984 and by aiming at the young adult market (*Business Week* 1986). As a result of a string of hits that included *Down and Out in Beverly Hills* (1986), *Ruthless People* (1986), *Three Men and a Baby* (1987), *Stakeout* (1987), and *Who Framed Roger Rabbit?* (1988), Disney captured an incredible 20 per cent share of the domestic theatrical market in 1988.

Branching out further into the adult market in 1993, Disney linked up Merchant-Ivory and Miramax Films, two of the most successful art film companies in the business. According to Peter Bart of *Variety*, Disney's strategy was 'to foster an eclectic slate of projects':

> While rival entertainment companies pursue the Time Warner model to become diversified, albeit debt-ridden, hardware-software conglomerates, Disney is determined to become the largest producer of intellectual property in the world. As such, the studio is committed to an astonishing sixty-films-a-year release schedule starting in 1994.
>
> (Bart 1993)

31

In addition to *Howards End*, Merchant-Ivory had made thirty-one films in as many years, including its breakthrough hit *A Room With a View* (1986), based on another E.M. Forster novel, which cost $3 million and grossed more than $68 million worldwide (Weinraub 1992a). The Disney deal was for three years and provided 50 per cent financing for any film the team developed with a budget up to $12 million in exchange for domestic rights. For pictures over that amount, Merchant-Ivory needed Disney's approval. In distributing a picture, Disney agreed to pay all marketing costs and at least $5 million for prints and advertising. The arrangement freed Merchant-Ivory from having to raise substantial sums for financing and enabled it to take advantage of Disney's considerable distribution might. The arrangement provided Disney with prestigious films aimed at adults that carried little financial risk (*ibid.*)

Disney's deal with Miramax consisted of a $90 million buy out in which Disney acquired Miramax's library of 200 art films and agreed to finance the development, production and marketing of Miramax's movies. Founded as a distribution company by Harvey and Bob Weinstein in 1982, Miramax had 'become a logo that brings audiences in on its own'. Adopting a straight acquisition policy from the start, Miramax rose to the front ranks of the independent film market in 1989, when three of its pictures drew critical and commercial attention: *My Left Foot*, which starred a then relatively unknown Daniel Day-Lewis (who went on to win an Academy Award for best actor) and grossed nearly $15 million at the box office; Steven Soderbergh's *sex, lies and videotape*, which garnered a Palme d'Or at Cannes and grossed $25 million; and Giuseppe Tornatore's *Cinema Paradiso*, which won an Oscar for best foreign film and grossed $12 million to become the year's highest-grossing entry in this category (Frook 1992).

Expanding its roster to over twenty-five pictures a year in 1992, Miramax released *Mediterraneo*, which won an Academy Award for best picture and became the top foreign-language import of the year, and Neil Jordan's *The Crying Game*, which won an Academy Award for best screenplay and became a crossover hit by breaking into the mainstream market and grossing more than $50 million (Fleming and Klady 1993). In 1993, Miramax had two more big hits, Alfonso Arau's *Like Water for Chocolate* and Jane Campion's *The Piano*. A Mexican import, *Like Water* grossed over $20 million to become 'the all-time foreign language box office champ' in the United States, surpassing the record of $19 million held by the Swedish import *I Am Curious (Yellow)* since 1969 (Karlin 1993). Produced at a cost of $2.5 million, this award-winning Mexican romance returned its investment in a remarkably short time thanks to Miramax's aggressive marketing campaign.

An international co-production, Jane Campion's *The Piano* was financed by France's Ciby 2000 and filmed in New Zealand by a native-born writer-director with a multinational cast, that had an Australian nationality by dint of its Sydney-based producer, Jan Chapman. (Groves 1993). Miramax acquired *The Piano* only weeks before it was shown at Cannes and shared the festival's top prize with another Miramax pick up, Chen Kaige's *Farewell My Concubine*. At home, *The*

Piano won a record eleven Australian Film Institute awards and in the United States, eight Academy Award nominations and three Oscars, including best original screenplay. (*Farewell My Concubine* received four Academy Award nominations.) As a fully-autonomous division of Disney's distribution arm, Miramax sustained its position in the independent film market by releasing Quentin Tarantino's *Pulp Fiction* in 1994 (Frook 1993b).

Turner moved into the independent film market by acquiring New Line Cinema and Castle Rock Entertainment in 1993 at a combined cost of $700 million. The founder of superstation WTBS in Atlanta and the owner of one of the largest film libraries in the business, Turner had become a principal programme supplier to cable. Described by a Turner executive as 'a preemptive strike', the New Line and Castle Rock acquisitions fit neatly into Turner's plans to become a major motion picture producer (Robins and Brennan 1993).

Castle Rock made its reputation producing top-shelf pictures, as previously mentioned. In contrast, New Line made its fortune during the 1980s producing and distributing genre pictures aimed at adolescents – the *Nightmare on Elm Street* horror series, *Teenage Mutant Ninja Turtles*, and two *House Party* films. Under the leadership of Robert Shay and Michael Lynne, New Line branched out from its traditional slate of inexpensive niche films and created a division called Fine Line Features in 1990 to produce and distribute art films and off beat fare. Within two years, Fine Line rose to the top independent ranks by backing such American ventures as Gus Van Sant's *My Own Private Idaho* (1991), James Foley's *Glengary Glen Ross* (1992), and Robert Altman's *The Player* (1992) and by releasing such English-language imports as Derek Jarman's *Edward II* (1991) and Mike Leigh's *Naked* (1993) (Weinraub 1994a). Fine Line initially steered away from foreign-language entries, but subsequently released Maurizio Nichetti's Italian import, *Volere Volare* in 1992 (Stevenson 1992). With Turner's financial backing, Castle Rock and New Line announced plans to sharply increase production beginning in 1994, the expectation being that TBS would soon rival Paramount and Warner as motion picture suppliers.

Partnering internationally

Hollywood's third response to globalization was to seek an international base of motion picture financing. To reduce its debt load, Time Warner restructured its film and cable businesses and created Time Warner Entertainment as a joint venture with two of Japan's leading companies, electronics manufacturer Toshiba and trading giant C. Itoh. The deal netted Time Warner $1 billion (Laing 1992). This strategy was unprecedented. Following the tack of independent producers, 20th-Century-Fox pre-sold the foreign rights to two high-profile 'event' films, Danny De Vito's *Hoffa* (1992) and Spike Lee's *Malcolm X* (1992), to reduce its exposure (*Variety* 1991b). Another common practice was to seek out co-production deals to take advantage of film subsidies in overseas markets. Studios chose this option mostly with 'unusual material' – which is to say a picture that was not a sequel, that did not have a major international star, or that did not have an 'unflaggingly high-concept' – such as Universal's *Fried Green Tomatoes* (1991) and Paramount's *1492* (1992) (Natale 1992b).

To finance television programming, the majors invested in foreign media industries. When the European Economic Community decided against removing trade barriers and tariffs on movies and television programmes in 1992 as anticipated, Time Warner, Turner, Disney, Viacom and NBC re-evaluated their relationship to this market. No longer did these companies think of Western Europe only as a programming outlet: instead they considered it as another investment source and formed partnerships with European television producers, broadcast stations, cable and satellite networks and telecommunications services. Time Warner, for example, invested in satellite broadcasting in Scandinavia, FM radio in the UK, and pay-TV in Germany and Hungary. Disney formed joint ventures to produce children's programming in France, Germany, Italy and Spain. And Rupert Murdoch's News Corp. purchased a controlling interest in British Sky Broadcasting, Europe's largest satellite-delivered service, and in Star TV, Asia's first satellite TV network (Stevenson 1994b).

AFTERMATH

Signalling a resurgence in the merger movement, Paramount Communications, one of the two remaining major studios besides Disney not to change ownership during the 1980s, was acquired by Viacom Inc. for $8.2 billion in 1993. Spearheading the second-largest merger ever in the media industry after Time Warner's, Viacom's 70-year-old chairman Sumner Redstone united Viacom's MTV and Nickelodeon cable channels, Showtime pay-TV service, television syndication companies, and a string of television stations with Paramount's formidable holdings in entertainment and publishing (Fabrikant 1993). The following year, Viacom acquired Blockbuster Entertainment, the world's largest video retailer with over 3,500 video stores and various side businesses – purchase price, $7.6 billion. Commenting on his acquisitions, Redstone said, 'The new Viacom not only controls many of the world's most recognisable entertainment and publishing brands, but also has the distribution, size and scope to drive these brands into every region of the world' (Flint and Dempsey 1994:)

Aside from the belief that bigger is better to compete in the international market, the motivation for these combinations was a faith in synergy, a belief that one plus one could equal three. Described another way synergy was supposed to function as follows: 'As in a good marriage, each partner would bring qualities that when combined would magically create something better than either could achieve alone' (Sims 1993). The long-term prospects for Viacom looked good, especially after the company succeeded in selling off its Madison Square Garden sports and entertainment empire to reduce its debt load. And the long-term prospects also looked good for News Corp. and TBS. Murdoch moved his Fox Broadcasting closer to equal status with the Big Three television networks in 1994 by stealing away the rights to broadcast National Football League games that CBS had held for four decades and by signing up twelve new affiliates, including eight of CBS's (Carter 1994). Acquiring New Line Cinema and Castle Rock Entertainment, Turner Broadcasting moved into the front ranks of Hollywood and positioned itself for global expansion.

The prospects for the other mergers are uncertain. Burdened with $11 billion of debt after the merger, Time Warner lost money two years in a row and was plagued by clashing corporate styles among its top management. Sony and Matsushita fared worse. After spending billions to acquire CBS Records and Columbia Pictures Entertainment, Sony lavished money 'on hiring executives at enormous salaries and giving golden handshakes to others, on bonus pools reaching into the millions, on perks and for rebuilding the studios to make offices and dining rooms the sleekest in Hollywood' (Weinraub 1994). Signing the Peter Guber–Jon Peters production team alone cost Sony $700 million and was one of the most expensive management acquisitions ever.

Sony performed reasonably well under the new regime until 1993, but afterwards, Columbia and TriStar struggled to fill their distribution pipelines. Virtually all of Sony's hits had been produced by its independent producer affiliates, Carolco and Castle Rock. But when the Carolco deal lapsed and Castle Rock hooked up with Turner, Sony lagged behind the other majors in motion picture production and market share. Some industry observers claimed Sony lacked 'a clear strategy' for taking advantage of the rapid shifts in the entertainment business (Bates and Duktar 1994). After top production executives left Columbia and TriStar in 1994, Sony took a $3.2 billion loss on its motion picture business, reduced the book value of its studios by $2.7 billion, and announced that 'it could never hope to recover its investment' in Hollywood (Sterngold 1994).

The Matsushita–MCA marriage foundered as well, but for different reasons. By producing a string of hits that included two Steven Spielberg blockbusters, *Jurassic Park* (1993) and *Schindler's List* (1993), MCA become a financial bright spot in the Matsushita empire as it confronted the recession in Japan and the rising value of the yen. For its part, MCA hoped the merger would provide it with the financial leverage for expansion, specifically by acquiring Virgin Records, by investing in the NBC television network, and by building a Universal Studios theme park in Japan. Matsushita rejected the proposals and created a rift with MCA's top management, chairman Lew Wasserman and president Sidney Sheinberg. Convinced that MCA's Japanese owners 'did not understand either the corporate nuances of MCA or the dynamic change of the United States media business', Wasserman and Sheinberg threatened to resign unless they were given more autonomy (Fabrikant 1994b).

The second surge of mergers that started with the Viacom takeover of Paramount Communications will continue and probably involve the three major American television networks. The reason is that the FCC's financial interest and syndication rules are due to expire in November 1995. In effect for two decades, the rules precluded ABC, CBS and NBC from owning most of the prime time programming they broadcast, which in effect deprived them of the significant profits hit shows earned in syndication. Since the networks would likely reduce the number of programmes they ordered from outside producers and rely more on in-house projects after the expiration of the 'fin-syn' rules, big suppliers like Time Warner and Disney might be hard hit. To avoid this, conventional wisdom had it that the majors would work to control the networks to 'assure themselves of a guaranteed outlet for their product' (Fabrikant 1994a).

The globalization of motion picture industry has significant film policy implications for the following reasons: (1) it has resulted in the growth of giant media companies in Germany, Italy, France, Holland, Australia and Japan, as well as in the United States; (2) it has occurred with the consent of foreign governments, the same entities that formulate national film policy; (3) it has resulted in ownership changes of Hollywood studios either through takeovers by foreign companies or through partnerships with overseas investors; and (4) it has created more demand for 'software', to the benefit of talent, and more entertainment options, to the benefit of consumers.

REFERENCES

Alexander, Max (1994) 'Under construction', *Variety*, 25 April–1 March: 4.

Balio, Tino (1985) *The American Film Industry*. Madison: University of Wisconsin Press.

Balio, Tino (1990) *Hollywood in the Age of Television*. Boston: Unwin Hyman.

Bates, James and Dukta, Elaine (1994) 'Guber leaves Sony Pictures to form own firm', *Los Angeles Times*, 30 September: A1.

Bart, Peter (1993) 'Mouse gears for mass production' *Variety*, 19 July: 1, 5.

Brennan, Judy and Eller, Claudia (1993) '"Event" pics power o'seas success' *Variety*, 15 February: 45, 72.

Business Week (1986) 'Michael Eisner is leading Disney back to the magic kingdom' 10 February: 33.

Carter, Bill (1994) 'Fox will sign up 12 new stations: takes 8 from CBS', *New York Times*, 24 May: A1.

Cohen, Roger (1990) 'Rupert Murdoch's biggest gamble', *New York Times*, 21 October: 31.

Cohn, Lawrence (1990) 'Only half of indie pics will see the screens in 90", *Variety*, 30 May: 7

Fabrikant, Geraldine (1990a) 'The hole in Hollywood's pocket', *New York Times*, 10 December: C1

Fabrikant, Geraldine (1990b) 'Hollywood takes more cues from overseas', *New York Times*, 25 June: C1.

Fabrikant, Geraldine (1990c) 'Studios look to foreign markets', *New York Times*, 7 March: C1, C8.

Fabrikant, Geraldine (1990d) 'French TV giant turns global', *New York Times*, 20 June: C1

Fabrikant, Geraldine (1993) 'A success for dealer on a prowl', *New York Times*, 13 September: A1.

Fabrikant, Geraldine (1994a) 'Media giants said to be negotiating for TV networks', *New York Times*, 1 September: A1.

Fabrikant, Geraldine (1994b) 'At a crossroads, MCA plans a meeting with its owners', *New York Times*, 13 October: G13.

Fleming, Michael and Klady, Leonard (1993) 'Crying all the way to the bank' *Variety*, 22 March: 1, 68, 69.

Flint, Joe and Dempsey, John (1994) 'Viacom, b'buster tie $7.6 billion knot', *Variety*, 3–9 October: 13, 16.

Frook, John Evan (1992) 'Mirimax paradiso', *Variety*, 21 September: 101, 105.

Frook, Evan (1993a) 'Castle Rock's solid bid for financial freedom', *Variety*, 26 July: 9, 13.

Frook, Evan (1993b) 'Call Harvey and Mickey Mouth', *Variety*, 29 November: 11.

Gold, Richard (1989) 'Sony – CPE union reaffirms changing order of intl showbiz', *Variety*, 27 September–3 October 1989: 5

Gold, Richard (1990) 'No Exit? Studios itch to ditch exhib biz', *Variety*, 8 October: 8, 84.

Goldman, Debra (1989) 'Indie boom turns bust', *Premiere*, May: 30–4.

Groves, Don (1990) 'U.S. pix tighten global grip', *Variety*, 22 August: 1, 96.

Groves, Don (1993) '*The Piano* wins 11 Oz film honors', *Variety*, 15 November: 11.

Gulf + Western (1987) *1987 Annual Report*

Hlavacek, Peter (1990) 'New indies on a (bank) roll', *Variety*, 24 January: 1, 7.

Iliot, Terry (1991) 'Yank pix flex pecs in new Euro arenas', *Variety*, 19 August: 1

Iliot, Terry (1993) 'Multiplexing still perplexing', *Variety*, 4 January: 52.

Karlin, Susan (1993) 'Sweet shortcut for hot "Chocolate"', *Variety*, 30 August: 1.

Kipps, Charles (1989) 'Sony and Columbia', *Variety*, 27 September–3 October: 5.

Kissinger, David (1991) 'Judgement Day for Carolco', *Variety*, 2 December: 1, 93.

Laing, Jonathan R. (1992) 'Bad scenes behind it, Time Warner is wired for growth', *Barron's*, 22 June: 8.

Logsdon, Jeffrey B. (1990) *Perspectives on the Filmed Entertainment Industry*. Los Angeles: Seidler Amdec Securities Inc.

Natale, Richard (1991) 'Lean indies fatten summer boxoffice', *Variety*, 12 August: 1, 61.

Natale, Richard (1992a) 'Majors on a tear to cut marketing costs', *Variety*, 16 March: 3.

Natale, Richard (1992b) 'Risky pix get a global fix', *Variety*, 28 September: 97.

Noglows, Paul (1992) 'Studios stuck in screen jam', *Variety*, 9 March: 1, 69.

Pollack, Andrew (1994) 'AT MCA's parent, no move to let go', *New York Times*, 14 October: C1.

Robins, J. Max and Brennan, J. (1993) 'Turner may tap SASSA to run film venture', *Variety*, 23 August: 9.

Sims, Calvin (1993) '"Synergy": The unspoken word', *New York Times*, 5 October: C1, C18.

Sterngold, James (1994) 'Sony, struggling, takes a huge loss on movie studios', *New York Times*, 18 September: A1.

Stevenson, Richard W. (1991) 'Carolco flexes its muscles overseas', *New York Times*, 26 June: C1, C17.

Stevenson, Richard W. (1994a) 'Lights! Camera! Europe!', *New York Times*, 6 February: 97.

Stevenson, Richard W. (1994b) 'Mundo Murdoch', *New York Times*, 24 May: E1.

Stevenson, William (1992) 'Fine Line finesses art-house mainstays', *Variety*, 10 August: 40, 44.

The Velvet Light Trap (1991) 'The 1980s: A reference guide to motion pictures, television, VCR and cable', *The Velvet Light Trap* 27, Spring 1991: 77–88.

Time Warner (1989) *1989 Annual Report*.

Variety (1990) 'BSB satellite programming blasts off against Murdoch's year old Sky TV', 21 March 1990: 1.

Variety (1991a) 'Chernin yearning to get Fox some Hollywood respect', 19 August: 21.

Variety (1991b) 'Newest H'wood invaders are building, not buying' 21 October: 93.

Vogel, Harold (1989) *Entertainment Industry*. New York: Merrill Lynch.

Wallach, Andrew (1988) *MCA Inc*. New York: Drexel Burnham Lamber, 25 February: 3–10.

Watson, Geoff (1992) 'Sell-through salvation', *Variety*, 16 November: 57.

Weinraub, Bernard (1992a) 'Disney signs up Merchant and Ivory', *New York Times*, 27 July: B1.

Weinraub, Bernard (1992b) 'Castle Rock raises the stakes', *New York Times*, 20 December: F12.

Weinraub, Bernard (1994a) 'New Line cinema', *New York Times*, 5 June: F4.

Weinraub, Bernard (1994b) 'Turmoil and indecesion at Sony's film studios', *New York Times*, 24 October C12.

2

EVOLUTION AND COMPETITION IN THE AMERICAN VIDEO MARKETPLACE

Jonathan D. Levy[1]

INTRODUCTION

In the last twenty years, the range of choices available to US television viewers has expanded substantially. Competition has increased both within the traditional off-air broadcasting sector and between broadcasting and new video delivery media. These new media are generally multi-channel in scope and draw on two revenue streams – advertising and subscription fees – to finance their programme acquisitions and operations. Although these competitive developments have been most pronounced in the US, many other countries have experienced, or will experience, increased competition in video distribution.

This chapter reviews the evolution of video distribution systems in the US since 1975, suggests the direction of future developments, examines some responses of regulatory authorities to the changing video marketplace, and identifies some tentative international implications of the US experience. The second section reviews the availability and use of the various media as well as trends in financing, focusing on broadcast television, cable television, and the direct-to-home satellite services. The third section employs those trends in conjunction with a discussion of technological changes to make some projections about the future of the non-broadcast media and the impact on traditional broadcasting of developments in those media. The discussion suggests that broadcast networks and television stations are most likely to succeed in the new environment by stressing their skills in packaging and scheduling programming, in assembling advertisers and in developing local programming.

The fourth section briefly reviews US public policy towards the video media. Promoting competition among video delivery media is a cornerstone of US communications policy. However, where effective competition is absent, as is currently the case with most cable television systems, some regulation is appropriate. On the other hand, increased competition has led the Federal Communications Commission (FCC) to re-examine some of its longstanding regulatory structure for television broadcasting.

The last section contains some international implications and conclusions. Channel capacity expansion has increased the demand for programming, while additional competition and the attendant audience fragmentation have increased

39

the importance of foreign programme sales. Although the US experience and approach to video competition cannot necessarily be mechanically transplanted on to foreign soil, the march of technology, coupled with consumer demand, makes increased intermedia competition inevitable.

EVOLUTION OF US VIDEO MEDIA SINCE 1975

Since 1975, video media competition has expanded both within broadcasting and from rival media. As Table 2.1 indicates, the number of commercial television stations has increased steadily between 1975 and 1993, from 701 to 1,145. Most of the growth has occurred in the UHF band, and most of the new stations have been 'independents', that is, stations not affiliated with one of the three major commercial television networks – ABC, CBS and NBC. Reflecting the strength of the network-affiliate distribution system, many independent stations have become affiliated with Fox, the fourth commercial broadcast network, which began operations in 1987. Moreover, two new networks, the WB network and the United Paramount Network (UPN) started up in January 1995.

Table 2.1 Numbers of television stations, 1975–93

	1975	1980	1985	1990	1993
Commercial stations total	701	756	919	1,098	1,145
VHF	511	519	522	547	561
UHF	190	237	397	551	584
Affiliates*	615	627	657	766	795
Independents	86	129	262	332	350
Noncommercial stations	259	282	316	361	367

Note: *Affiliates equals commercial stations total less independents
Sources: Warren Publishing (1994: I–41) for all but affiliates and independent stations. Data are for 1 January of the next year.

Independent stations data for the years 1975–85 are for November (Setzer and Levy 1991: Table 3). Independent stations data for 1990 and 1993 are for January of the next year. (Broadcasting Publications, Inc. 1991: C-96; R. R. Bowker 1994: C–112).

The expansion of cable television, outlined below, has also increased 'intra-broadcast' competition. Stations in the UHF band, on which most of the newer stations are located, have a smaller signal coverage area than those in the VHF band. Cable retransmission has increased the reach of UHF stations, thereby reducing the 'UHF handicap'.

The number of non-commercial (also known as public) television stations also increased between 1975 and 1993, rising from 259 to 367. While public television attracts a relatively small audience share (see Table 2.4 below), this expansion has also contributed to increased competition within television broadcasting.

Table 2.2 provides information on the availability of broadcast television and various rival media to US households. Over 98 per cent of US households have television, and over 75 per cent of television households have videocassette recorders. In 1976, only 32 per cent of US television households had access to cable television (and only 17 per cent subscribed), while in 1993, over 95 per cent of television households were 'passed' by cable and over 60 per cent of those households chose to subscribe.[2]

Table 2.2 Households with video equipment and services, 1976–93 (percentage of US television households unless otherwise noted)

	1976	1980	1985	1990	1993
Television sets*	97.4	98.1	98.1	98.2	98.3
Multiple sets	44.8	51.2	56.6	64.5	70.2
Sets per household**	1.6	1.7	1.8	2.1	2.2
Videocassette recorders	na	1.1	20.9	68.6	77.1
Homes passed by cable	32.4	43.7	75.3	92.4	96.2
Cable subscribers	16.6	24.0	42.7	55.5	60.7
Home satellite dish systems	na	0.1	1.6	2.9	3.8
Wireless cable subscribers	na	na	na	na	0.4

Notes: *Percentage of *total* US households.
**Average number of sets per household.
Sources: TVB (1994b: 3–6) for television sets, multiple sets, average number of sets, videocassette recorders (VCRs), and total television households figures used to calculate percentages for cable, home satellite dish (HSD) and wireless cable. For 1980-93, data are for January of the next year, except for videocassette recorders, which are for February of the indicated year. 1976 data are for September of that year.
PKA (1994a: 9) for cable homes passed and subscribers; data are for end of year.
PKA (1994d: 4) for wireless cable (also known as MMDS-multichannel multipoint distribution service) subscribers.
FCC (1987: Table 2) for HSD 1980, 1985. *Satellite Business News* (1991: 5, 1994:1) for HSD 1990, 1993. HSD figures are cumulative US system sales.

Direct-to-home satellite services are, by a wide margin, the second most widely available multi-channel video distribution medium. In 1993, almost 4 per cent of US television households had C-band home satellite dish (HSD) systems. These systems, with dish antennas six to ten feet in diameter, receive the same satellite feeds that programmers use to distribute their networks 'wholesale' to commercial customers such as cable television systems, master antenna systems, wireless cable systems, hotels, or other commercial establishments. In addition, in June 1994, the first Direct Broadcast Satellite (DBS) services, using smaller, cheaper antennas, began serving subscribers. Currently two such services, DirecTV and United States Satellite Broadcasting, offer a total of over 150 channels from a single orbital slot. They utilize the Ku band spectrum that has been internationally designated for direct-to-home service. Primestar, which commenced operations in 1990, also offers direct-to-home service, but does not utilize the DBS spectrum.[3]

By the end of 1994, there were 349,000 DBS subscribers, 242,000 Primestar subscribers, and 2.2 million C-band direct subscribers (Hillebrand 1995: 21; *Satellite Business News* 1995: 1).[4]

Table 2.3 details the availability and usage of cable television, highlighting the fact that while cable is widely available, a substantial number of households choose not to subscribe. Cable television has traditionally been divided into 'basic' service and 'premium' or pay services. Basic service is a package of channels sold for a single fee. It includes retransmitted broadcast stations, locally originated public, educational and government access channels, and a variety of advertiser-supported non-broadcast channels, some of them specialized by subject matter (e.g. news, sports, music, children's programming). Many cable systems divide these services into more than one package or 'tier' of service. Under the Cable Television Consumer Protection and Competition Act of 1992 (1992 Cable Act), which amended the Communications Act of 1934, the term 'basic' has been reserved for the tier of service to which all subscribers must subscribe and which includes at least the retransmitted local broadcast signals and public, educational and government access channels. Other packages of services, which once were called 'expanded basic', are now referred to as 'cable programming service' tiers.

Premium services are those sold on a per-channel or per-programme basis. They generally do not contain advertising. Programme material sold on a per-event basis is also referred to as 'pay-per-view' programming. The figures in Table 2.3 indicate that approximately 46 per cent of cable subscribers chose to subscribe to a

Table 2.3 Television households, cable subscribers and homes passed (millions, unless otherwise noted)

	1976	1980	1985	1990	1993
Television households	71.2	79.9	85.9	93.1	94.2
Homes passed by cable	23.1	34.9	64.7	86.0	90.6
Basic cable subscribers	11.8	19.2	36.7	51.7	57.2
Television households without cable*	59.4	60.7	49.2	41.4	37.0
Homes not passed*	48.1	45.0	21.2	7.1	3.6
Homes passed but not subscribing*	11.3	15.7	28.0	34.3	33.4
Pay households**	na	13.8***	21.8	23.9	26.4
Subscribers as percentage of television households*	16.6	24.0	42.7	55.5	60.7
Subscribers as percentage of homes passed*	51.1	55.0	56.7	60.1	63.1

Notes: *Calculated from first three rows of this table.
**Households purchasing at least one premium channel (i.e., paid for on a per-channel basis).
***1981
Sources: PKA (1994a: 9) for 1976–1990, PKA (1994d: 4) for 1993, for homes passed, basic cable subscribers, pay households; end-of-year data.
TVB (1994b: 3) for television households. Data are for January of subsequent year, except for 1976 figure, which is for September 1976.

premium service in 1993. Pay-per-view, while frequently highlighted as a potential source of substantial revenue, is a relatively small business now. (See Table 2.7 below.)

In 1993, monthly per-subscriber rates for basic service averaged $19.39. The average additional charge for expanded basic was $6.75. A single premium channel cost, on average, an extra $9.11 per month (PKA 1994a: 9).

Part of the increase over the years in cable penetration – that is, the share of homes passed that subscribe to cable – can surely be explained by the expansion in programming availability and channel capacity. In 1983, 48.7 per cent of cable subscribers were served by cable systems with thirty or more channels, while in 1993, over 95 per cent of subscribers had access to thirty or more channels (Warren Publishing 1983: 1548, 1994: I-69). The increase in channel capacity has been accompanied by an increase in the number of national cable video networks from forty-three in 1983 to ninety-nine in 1993 (National Cable Television Association 1994: 7-A). There is also a substantial number of regional non-broadcast services, many of them specializing in sports programming.

As the number of video distribution outlets has increased, the viewing audience has become more fragmented. Broadcast television has lost audience share to cable television and affiliates of the three major commercial networks have lost share to independent television stations, which include affiliates of the newer Fox network.[5] Table 2.4 shows a relatively steep decline in all-day viewing shares[6] of network affiliates between 1984–5 and 1989–90 in all households and in cable households. Between 1989–90 and 1992–3, the decline was more gradual.

For all television households, the decline in viewing of network affiliates is almost exactly balanced by the increase in cable viewing.[7] By 1992–3, at least

Table 2.4 All day viewing shares, all households and cable households

	All households			Cable households		
	1984–5	*1989–90*	*1992–3*	*1984–5*	*1989–90*	*1992–3*
Network affiliates*	63	52	49	53	43	42
Independents	21	19	20	20	15	15
Local	12	13	na	8	9	na
Other**	9	6	na	12	6	na
Public	3	3	4	3	3	3
Cable	14	26	28	24	39	40
Basic	8	20	23	14	30	33
Pay	6	6	5	10	9	7
Total	101	100	101	100	100	100

Notes: The figures in this table are percentages of total viewing, not the more commonly reported household shares. Total viewing shares account for viewing of more than one channel at a time on different receivers in the same household. Some columns do not sum to 100 due to rounding error.
*Affiliates of the three major networks–ABC, CBS and NBC.
**Other Independents are superstations (independent television stations retransmitted by satellite to cable systems) and other distant broadcast signals, generally delivered to cable systems by microwave and not available locally off-air.
Sources: Calculated from CAB (1994: 20, 1991: 6, 1986: 14).

28 per cent of viewing hours were accounted for by non-broadcast programming.[8] In cable households, cable viewing has increased at the expense of independent stations as well as network affiliates. Non-broadcast programming accounted for at least 40 per cent of 1992–3 viewing hours in cable households. The increased viewing shares of cable networks in cable households suggest that the overall growth in cable viewing shares has been caused not only by increased availability of cable over time (i.e. increases in the number of homes passed, leading to increased subscribership), but also by a trend towards heavier viewing of cable networks in cable households. Prime time viewing data for all television households show a similar pattern of rising cable shares (Setzer and Levy 1991: 28; CAB 1994: 22).[9]

Broadcast television revenues derive entirely from advertising, while cable television is supported by subscription revenues as well. In 1993, total video advertising amounted to $30.6 billion, 22.1 per cent of total advertising volume (TVB 1994c: 1). Video's share of the total has been roughly constant since 1982. Total advertising volume was 2.16 per cent of gross domestic product (GDP) in 1993, having fallen from a 1987 peak of 2.42 per cent (TVB 1994a: 1). Video advertising expenditures are correlated with GDP, but they also have a cyclical component. They tend to be lower in times of recession, other things being equal. Video advertising also is higher in years with national elections or Olympic Games competitions (e.g. 1984, 1988, 1992). Broadcast television accounted for 91.6 per cent of total video advertising in 1993; cable television accounted for the remainder (see Table 2.5 below).

Total video advertising revenues have increased steadily in nominal terms since 1975, except for a recent drop in the broadcast network category.[10] However, as Table 2.5 indicates, after adjustment for inflation, total video advertising revenues peaked in 1990, broadcast network revenues peaked in 1984,[11] and television station advertising revenues peaked in 1988. Television station advertising revenues in 1993 were above their 1991 minimum, both in total and on a per-station basis.[12] Inflation-adjusted cable television and national syndication advertising revenues have grown steadily in magnitude and share since 1984.

The broadcast network figures in Table 2.5 are for the three major commercial networks. National syndication consists of national distribution and advertising sales for programming that is not necessarily part of a larger network schedule and that may not necessarily be carried in the same time slot on every station exhibiting it.[13] Advertising on the Fox network is classified as national syndication; it accounts for a substantial portion of this category. Table 2.5 indicates that the rapid growth of this category coincides with the decline in inflation-adjusted network advertising revenues. National syndication has some characteristics in common with network distribution, so the relatively modest decline in inflation-adjusted network plus national syndication revenues[14] suggests that nationwide distribution remains a valuable and efficient delivery mechanism. The 1995 launch of two new part-time broadcast networks (see below) also supports this conclusion.

44

Table 2.5 Inflation-adjusted video advertising revenues (millions of 1982–4 US$)

Year	Total	Broadcast network*	National syndication	Broadcast network plus national syndication	Television stations	Average revenue per station	Total television	Cable
1975	9,783	4,286	na	4,286	5,496	7.8	9,782	na
1984	19,103	8,006	404	8,410	10,175	11.5	18,585	518
1985	19,537	7,491	483	7,974	10,890	11.9	18,864	673
1986	20,877	7,611	547	8,159	11,938	12.3	20,097	780
1987	21,042	7,482	671	8,153	12,041	11.7	10,195	848
1988	21,713	7,753	762	8,515	12,187	11.5	20,702	1,011
1989	21,686	7,347	1,039	8,385	12,069	11.1	20,455	1,231
1990	21,733	7,179	1,216	8,395	11,969	10.9	20,364	1,369
1991	20,119	6,559	1,360	7,919	10,775	9.6	18,694	1,425
1992	20,962	6,806	1,475	8,282	11,140	9.8	19,422	1,540
1993	21,165	6,484	1,672	8,156	11,235	9.8	19,391	1,774

Notes: *Advertising revenue of ABC, CBS and NBC.
Sources: TVB (1991: 4–5, 1994c) for video advertising in current dollars. Economic Report of the President (1994: 335) for consumer price index figures (1982–4=100) used to adjust revenues for inflation. Warren Publishing (1994: I–41) for numbers of commercial stations used to calculate average revenue per station.

Television station revenue derives primarily from the sale of advertising,[15] though broadcast networks also pay 'network compensation' to their affiliates as an inducement to 'clear' (i.e. retransmit) as much of the network's programme schedule as possible. In 1993, gross television station advertising revenues were $16.2 billion, while network compensation was $370 million (TVB 1994b: 11–12).[16]

Table 2.6 provides data for affiliates and independent stations on inflation-adjusted profits as a percentage of net revenues.[17] Fox affiliates are included in the independent station category except as noted. The data show that overall, television station ownership is a profitable business, with margins that compare favourably to those of the Fortune 500 top industrial corporations. Affiliates have, on average, significantly higher profit margins than independents, although profits have been rising in both categories since a 1991 trough. The aggregate profit figures do, however, mask some variations in performance (NAB 1994: 2, 3, 22, 23, 32, 33). For example, in 1993, the median station in the top ten markets had profits equal to 31.7 per cent of net revenues, while the comparable figure for markets 101–110 was 0.8 per cent. In markets 176 and above, the figure was 11.2 per cent, perhaps reflecting the relatively small number of stations in those markets. Moreover, even within size categories, there is substantial variation around the median. In the top ten markets, at least 25 per cent of independent stations had losses in 1993 (NAB 1994: 149).[18]

Table 2.6 Profits of commercial television stations as a percentage of net revenues, 1975–93

	Affiliates*	Independents*	500 largest industrial corporations**
1975	26.2	8.1	na
1980	29.1	17.1	4.8
1985	29.9	13.3	3.9
1986	27.9	–0.6	4.1
1987	26.4	–1.8	5.1
1988	25.0	–3.2	5.5
1989	21.8	1.5	4.7
1990	22.6	6.4	4.1
1991	17.7	5.7	3.1
1992	23.0	12.9	2.4
1993***	26.1	17.5	2.9

Notes: * average for all reporting stations;
** median return on sales;
*** For 1993, independents do not include Fox affiliates. Their profits were 23.1 per cent of net revenues in 1993.
Sources: Affiliate and independent stations data from FCC (1975, 1981) and NAB (1986–1987, 1989–1994).
500 largest corporations data from US Department of Commerce (1994: 559) and Teitelbaum (1994: 217).

Cable television advertising includes sales by cable networks and by local cable television operators, which receive the right to sell advertising on some cable networks in full or partial compensation for carriage of those networks. In 1993, roughly 80 per cent of cable advertising was sold by networks (TVB 1994a: 1). Cable's 8.4 per cent share of 1993 total video advertising remains dispro- portionately low compared to its 25 per cent share of all-day viewing of advertiser- supported programming, i.e. programming other than pay cable or public tele- vision (calculated from Table 2.4). This suggests that cable has great potential to increase its share of the advertising pie at the expense of broadcasters.

Cable suffers from some disadvantages in the advertising market. The larger audiences of broadcast television, and particularly broadcast networks, have two consequences. First, broadcast television remains a more efficient advertising purchase because it permits access to a larger, unduplicated audience. Purchasing advertising on several cable networks could provide exposure to a total audience as large as that of a broadcast network or station, but, unless the cable advertisements all run at the same time, the same person could view the advertisement more than once. In this case, the cable advertisements would reach fewer people. Second, the transactions costs of buying broadcast advertising are probably lower, since the advertiser needs to negotiate with only one entity in order to get the desired exposures, rather than deal separately with several cable networks or systems. On the other hand, specialized cable networks may offer advantages to advertisers, particularly if narrow demographic targeting is import- ant. The small share of cable in total video advertising revenues suggests that, thus far, cable has not significantly reduced broadcasting advertising revenues.

Table 2.7 provides data on cable operator revenues. Subscription services – basic and premium – are the primary sources of revenue, accounting for 86.7 per cent of total cable operator revenues in 1993. Advertising and pay-per-view contribute only small shares of total revenue. Advertising, however, accounts for a large share of cable network revenues, the funds that cable networks use to acquire programming rights. In 1993, gross advertising revenue was 60 per cent of total cable network revenues (PKA 1994c: 1–2).[19]

Table 2.7 Cable operator revenues (US$ millions)

	1975	1980	1985	1990	1993
Total	804	2,549	8,938	17,855	22,863
Basic*	764	1,615	4,443	10,664	15,193
Pay	29	765	3,727	5,105	4,633
Pay-per-view	na	na	25	253	512
Advertising	na	8	139	628	984
Other**	11	161	604	1,206	1,540

Notes: *Includes expanded basic.
**Includes installation and home shopping revenue.
Sources: PKA (1994a: 9) for all but 1975. PKA(1994b: 9) for 1975.

The past twenty years have seen a substantial increase in the availability of non-broadcast media, particularly cable television. Concomitantly, broadcast viewing shares have declined significantly, although the reductions in the past few years have been small. While broadcast network and station advertising revenues have declined proportionately and in real terms, cable television's advertising share remains disproportionately small compared to its audience share. The rise of the Fox network and the launch of the UPN and WB networks suggests the continuing viability of networking, while the high average profit margins for television stations suggest that they can withstand some additional competitive pressures.

THE FUTURE

The next five years will see a continued gradual expansion of the non-broadcast media at the expense of broadcast television. Technological change will make it possible for subscribers to have much more control over the timing of pay-per-view movies and to access some interactive services. Television broadcasters are likely to respond to these pressures by continuing their efforts to cut programming costs, by further exploiting the efficiencies of network distribution, and by seeking new revenue streams. Network responses are and will be driven in part by an important regulatory change – relaxation of the syndication and financial interest rules.

Expansion of non-broadcast media

Although over 95 per cent of television households are now passed by cable, the share of homes passed is likely to rise slightly over the next five years. Moreover, the range of satellite alternatives now available, from C-band to DBS, means that virtually all television households now have access to a direct-to-home service. Wireless cable (a microwave delivery system also known as multichannel multipoint distribution service or MMDS) is poised for some expansion from a small base (Brown 1995: 16, 18). Telephone companies will also be in the business of delivering video programming, either transporting it on a common carrier basis under the FCC's video dial tone (VDT) rules or providing it directly.[20] Thus, most television households will have access to more than one multichannel video programming distributor. Competition among programming distributors will likely benefit consumers by reducing prices and improving service quality.

While cable will remain the preponderant multichannel provider, with sub-scribership continuing to rise, satellite and other media will exert competitive pressure on it. Competition will be based not only on price, but on the menu of programming and services offered. Thanks to the programme access provisions of the 1992 Cable Act (Section 19, codified at 47 USC §548), rival delivery media are generally guaranteed nondiscriminatory access to cable programming. The following discussion concentrates on satellite services, because they are currently the primary competitor to cable.

The penetration of satellite services will be determined primarily by the cost of the equipment, the price of the programming and the range of services offered. C-band system prices have been falling gradually. These systems are widely available for around $2,000 plus installation (Adams 1995: 31), though high-end systems may cost considerably more. The basic DBS home system retails for $699 plus installation. The price is likely to fall, but the magnitude of the decline is unclear. The small size of the DBS dish (18 inches) compared to that of the C-band system (6–10 feet) suggests that the former will be suitable for a wider range of subscriber locations than the latter.

A wide range of programme packages is available to the C-band subscriber, with prices generally comparable to or lower than those of cable. DBS packages are somewhat more expensive than C-band packages. Depending on the choice of DBS package, the rate for basic cable programming may be above basic cable rates. While satellite prices for premium services are nominally a bit higher than cable prices, the satellite providers offer multiple feeds of these services, providing the same programming, but at different times, for added flexibility.

Currently, satellite services have greater channel capacity than virtually any cable system, which permits them to offer a wider selection of sports and movies than cable. Satellite providers also claim to provide superior signal quality to cable or terrestrial broadcast transmissions. On the other hand, satellite services do not carry local broadcast signals, which account for a large share of viewing, even in cable households. Some television stations are retransmitted via satellite, but those that are network affiliates are available only to households without terrestrial access to the relevant broadcast network. Because the satellite video services are one-way (i.e. there is no return channel), their interactive capabilities are limited. Combining satellite equipment with a telephone line can support simple inter-active services such as impulse ordering of pay-per-view movies. However, if substantial demand develops for more complex interactive services, satellite providers will be at a significant disadvantage *vis-à-vis* delivery systems that can offer two-way broadband transmission capability (cable, telephone, wireless cable). These technological considerations are discussed below.

Technological change

The single most important technological change for video distribution is digital signal compression. Digital compression, which is applicable to all video media, will increase substantially the capacity of the non-broadcast distribution media and concomitantly reduce the distribution costs facing new programming net-works. While current transmission standards for television broadcasting do not permit compression, these regulations may be changed. Increased use of optical fibre in cable television systems will also increase capacity.

The increased capacity will be available both for new programming services and for providing additional time diversity for existing services. As cable systems and other terrestrial delivery systems expand their channel capacity, some of the services and packages now only available via satellite will likely be offered via terrestrial systems as well. A leading example of time diversity that expanded capacity would permit is near video on demand (NVOD). As applied to pay-per-view movies, this would involve transmitting the same movie on several different channels with staggered starting times. For example, a hit movie could be transmitted on ten different channels, starting every fifteen minutes. Prospective viewers would never have to wait long for a showing to begin and would have some flexibility to interrupt viewing for an interval by switching from one transmission to another one that began later.

Pay-per-view movie purchase, including NVOD, is one example of an interactive service. Other simple examples are home shopping, banking and bill paying. These services can be performed with a low-capacity return channel, e.g. a telephone line. Provision of substantial two-way capability in a distribution system is quite expensive in the case of cable and not technically practical in the case of DBS (although, with appropriate ground equipment, satellites can be used for two-way broadband communications). The substantial investment required for two-way capacity for interactive applications will have to be justified by services with significant revenue potential. While many in the industry believe that the potential of interactive services is immense, industry opinion is divided on when it will become economical to build two-way broadband digital networks for more than experimental use (Andrews 1995: C16).[21]

The FCC is poised to approve a digital broadcast transmission standard for advanced television (ATV). Non-broadcast media are, of course, also free to provide ATV services, including high definition television (HDTV). HDTV may increase the demand for video services, but it is not clear how it will affect the competitive position of broadcasting *vis-à-vis* the other media. Television broadcasters are hoping that the new regime will permit them some flexibility in the use of their spectrum, leaving them the option of providing services other than or in addition to HDTV (Farhi 1995: D10; Jessell 1995b: 8, 12). Other services could include multiple 'standard definition' digital television signals.

Broadcaster responses to technological and competitive development

The spread of non-broadcast media and the technological changes outlined above will continue the fragmentation of the US viewing audience. Moreover, even though the total number of television households is growing slowly, inflation-adjusted broadcast revenues are not, and network revenues are declining (see Table 2.5). Possible broadcaster responses fit into two broad categories – cutting costs and increasing revenues.

Television broadcasters can cut costs either by shifting their programming mix towards less costly genres or by acting directly to reduce the acquisition costs of the traditionally costly genres of drama and comedy series. The increase in the number of less expensive 'reality' programmes on television is an example of the first category of cost reduction (Farhi 1994: A1; Carter 1992: D9). Apparently

50

successful network efforts to hold down licence fees for prime-time programming illustrate the second category. Techniques to increase revenues include exploiting the efficiencies of network distribution and expanding into non-broadcast distribution. Television networks and stations have employed these tactics over the last few years and the trend is likely to continue.

The three major commercial television networks have long been able to provide advertisers with access to all television households. In order to supply the national reach that many advertisers value highly (Setzer and Levy 1991: 118-26), the three major commercial networks have traditionally exhibited mass-appeal programming and attracted roughly similar audience shares. The advent of Fox as the fourth commercial network in 1987 and of the part-time UPN and WB networks in January 1995 suggests the continuing value and efficiency of nationwide distribution.

Fox and the two new entrants all began by targeting narrower demographic groups than the three major commercial networks. Fox initially aimed its programming at younger audiences, although, as it has expanded its hours, it has moved more recently to appeal to the somewhat older audience than the three major commercial networks have generally sought to attract.[22] Concurrently with its efforts on the programming front, Fox has upgraded its affiliate lineup, in part by investing in minority shares of television station groups. Fox now claims to reach 97 per cent of US television households, almost as many as the three major commercial networks (*Broadcasting and Cable* 1994: 68).[23]

The new network UPN, a joint venture of Paramount and television station owner United Broadcasting, transmits two nights of programming per week, and Time Warner's WB Network has begun with one night per week.[24] UPN is targeting men between 18–49, while WB is targeting the 18–34 age group. Both networks plan to add blocks of daytime children's programming later in 1995 and to expand their schedules in the years ahead. There are not enough local television stations available to provide UPN and WB with the same level of coverage that the other broadcast networks have. Each has begun with approximately 80 per cent coverage. In the case of UPN, 13 per cent of its coverage comes from 'secondary' affiliates. These affiliates, many of them also Fox affiliates, will carry the UPN programming at different times than its primary exhibition. WB will rely on cable subscriber reception of WGN, a local broadcast station retransmitted throughout the country via satellite, for 18 per cent of its total coverage.

In addition to providing the national exposure that many advertisers value, the new networks are also apparently striving to create 'brand identities,' associating the *network* in viewers' minds with a particular type of programming. In this way, each programme benefits from more than just its own individual appeal. As the number of video programming channels and options expands, the importance of brand identity increases.

The relaxation of the FCC's syndication and financial interest rules is having a major effect on network distribution and programme production. These regulations prohibited the three major commercial networks from acquiring a financial interest in the programming that they purchased, prohibited them from syndicating programming (i.e., selling it to stations on a market-by-market basis), and sharply limited the amount of prime-time programming that they could produce in-house. In essence, the rules restricted the networks' ability to integrate vertically. The FCC recently eliminated most of these regulations, and the remaining rules, which relate to syndication, will sunset in 1995 unless the FCC takes specific action to extend them (FCC 1993c).[25]

As these constraints have been relaxed, the networks have moved to produce more of their own programming, and the trend is likely to continue (Lippman 1994: B5). Networks do not necessarily have the ability to produce prime-time programming at lower cost than the movie studios that have historically produced most such programming. Indeed, one way that broadcast networks have expanded their production activities is to form joint ventures with independent producers.[26] While these joint ventures do not reduce programming costs *per se*, this type of vertical integration may be valuable because it can reduce the uncertainty regarding programme distribution, permit an efficient sharing of risk between network and producer, and, in some cases, prevent the expected licence fee for a hit programme from ballooning in the later years of its run. The licence fee 'containment' can be important to a television network (Tobenkin 1994: 6, 10).

The increase in 'in-house' production of prime time programming by the networks has given major producers reason to be concerned about continuing access to the networks for distribution of their product (Carter 1994b: D6). Thus, the launch of the WB and UPN networks may be seen in part as defensive moves by two major producers to ensure distribution of their programming. The same considerations probably explain the interest of firms with major programme production subsidiaries, such as Time Warner, Disney and Turner Broadcasting, in purchasing a broadcast network, now that the penalties in terms of syndication business forgone are eliminated (Carter 1995: C15).

The networks have also sought new revenue streams by expanding into non-broadcast distribution, thereby using more intensively their expertise in assembling programme packages and marketing them to advertisers. ABC owns 80 per cent of ESPN, the leading national sports cable network, and NBC owns CNBC, a cable business news service. Additionally, ABC, NBC and Fox all have taken advantage of the retransmission consent provisions of the 1992 Cable Act[27] to get channel space for new cable networks – ESPN2, America's Talking, and fX, respectively (Carter 1994a: D7).

Television stations have followed some of the same strategies that the networks have adopted. In addition to cutting back on programming costs where possible (Foisie 1994a: 59; Tobenkin 1995b: 22), stations have moved to affiliate with the new networks and have benefited from the competition for affiliates among networks. As the Fox network sought to improve its affiliate lineup, a kind of 'bidding war' erupted in which many stations changed affiliation and the three major commercial networks substantially increased their compensation payments, to the benefit of affiliated stations (Jensen 1994: A1).

At least one of the new affiliation agreements, that of CBS and Group W, also calls for joint programme production activity (Zier 1994: 14). This is consistent with the network trend, identified above, towards integration of programme production and distribution. The role of affiliates in the new WB network is also consistent with this trend. Unlike the other commercial networks, WB does not pay network compensation. Rather, its affiliates must pay back to WB a share of their additional profits from affiliation (Lieberman 1995: 1B). This makes the WB network more like a joint programming venture.

Like the networks, some stations and station groups have used the retransmission consent mechanism of the 1992 Cable Act to acquire the right to provide programming on cable channels (McClellan 1993: 16–17; Brown 1993: 32–64). In this way, they extend their programme production and packaging skills into the non-broadcast area and potentially access an additional revenue stream. As television broadcasting in particular and video delivery in general moves into the digital era, local broadcasters hope for the opportunity to utilize their spectrum more flexibly, perhaps to provide multiple video transmissions of standard quality instead of or in addition to HDTV. This might make over-the-air broadcasting more comparable to a multichannel distribution system, with subscription revenues from these multiple video transmissions providing a potential second revenue stream.

US PUBLIC POLICY TOWARDS THE VIDEO MEDIA

This section briefly sketches some of the FCC's public policy goals for the video media. Guided by the Communications Act of 1934, as amended, the FCC has sought to promote competition and diversity in video media. That is to say, the FCC has been concerned with creating a structure within which a reasonable number of independent video providers are contending for the patronage of the public. Such a structure is expected to generate a menu of programming that satisfies, to the extent possible, the diverse tastes of viewers and provides a reasonably competitive market within which advertisers can purchase time. Moreover, a structure with many independent voices will ensure that a wide range of views on matters of public interest will be aired. These goals have led the FCC to adopt numerical limits for television station ownership at both the local and national levels.

In distributing broadcast channel allocations across geographic areas, the FCC has followed a statutory injunction to ensure that local service is available in all areas of the country (47 USC §307(b)). The goal has been not only to ensure that all citizens have access to television broadcast services, but that those services address local issues and concerns.

The 1992 Cable Act amended the Communications Act of 1934 to provide for substantial regulation of the cable industry in order to restrain cable market power and address related issues. Important provisions of the 1992 Act include: (1) authority to regulate rates for basic and cable programming service tiers of cable systems not subject to effective competition (while affirming a preference for competition over regulation);[28] (2) requirements that vertically integrated cable programme networks provide their services to rival delivery systems on non-discriminatory terms (programme access regulations); and (3) broadcast signal carriage regulations for cable systems and other multichannel video programme distributors (including the retransmission consent provisions referred to on p. 52). (See 47 USC §§325, 534, 535, 536. 543, 548.)

To implement the cable rate regulation provisions of the statute, the FCC first determined, based on a statistical analysis of a large sample of cable systems that, on average, cable systems subject to effective competition had rates 17 per cent lower than similar systems not subject to effective competition. With certain exceptions, the FCC required cable operators to reduce their rates by that per centage.[29] The FCC has also instituted 'going forward' regulations, designed to permit cable operators to raise rates as they add new channels to their basic or cable programming service tiers. The goal of these regulations is to provide appropriate incentives for cable operators to add new services and invest in new capacity, while still restraining the exercise of market power by cable operators. Cable operators are also permitted to introduce 'new product tiers,' packages of new services, on an unregulated basis and may justify rates in 'cost of service' proceedings, using traditional public utility regulation procedures. Services offered on a per-channel or per-programme basis are exempted by the 1992 Cable Act from rate regulation.

The advent of cable television and other multichannel media has undoubtedly advanced the FCC's public policy goals by significantly increasing the diversity and quantity of programming available to virtually all television households. The more than 60 per cent of television households that subscribe to cable benefit from access to this programming in addition to broadcast programming. However, the fragmentation of the viewing audience caused by the expansion of the multi-channel media may be cause for concern. Fragmentation might reduce the quantity or diversity of broadcast programming to the disadvantage of those who do not now subscribe to a multichannel programme distributor.

Non-subscribers may be divided into two broad categories: (1) people who could afford a subscription but do not place a high value on video programming or are satisfied with the range of services available off-air; and (2) people who cannot afford to subscribe. If broadcast television deteriorates, some viewers may respond by subscribing to cable or other multichannel video programme distrib-utors. This would expand their programming menu, but they might be made worse off by virtue of having to pay for something that used to be free. On the other hand, they might end up better off, even accounting for their subscription fees, if the deterioration of broadcast television were accompanied by a sufficient increase in the range and quality of non-broadcast programming. People who cannot afford to subscribe to cable and place a high value on video programming would be harmed by deterioration in broadcast service because they would lose a service that they previously enjoyed.

This discussion has two policy implications. First, it is important for the FCC to re-examine its television broadcast regulations as market conditions change in order to ensure that television broadcasters are not unduly constrained from responding to competition from the newer media. The relaxation of the financial interest and syndication rules reflects such a re-examination, as does the recently opened rulemaking proceeding to relax television broadcast national and local ownership limits (FCC 1995). In that rule making, the FCC also announced its intention to review certain television network regulations, in particular the 'dual networking' rule, which, in effect, prohibits any company from providing more than one television broadcast network. If television stations acquire the ability to transmit more than one video programme simultaneously, perhaps via digital signal compression, the broadcast networks would be an obvious source of additional programming.

The second implication is that restraining the growth of the multichannel media in order to protect television broadcasters is not the way to solve the problem. With 60 per cent of households choosing to pay in the aggregate almost $20 billion annually for cable, it is clear that cable and other multichannel distributors provide a very valuable service. In the event that the quantity or diversity of television broadcast programming fall below an acceptable level,[30] a targeted subsidy to those who cannot afford non-broadcast programming appears preferable to restrictions on the availability of additional services.

INTERNATIONAL IMPLICATIONS AND CONCLUSIONS[31]

International considerations are looming larger in the television industry. The expansion of channel capacity, fuelled by increasing use of satellite distribution, spreading cable television penetration, and digital signal compression, has increased the demand for programming. The attendant audience fragmentation has put pressure on exhibition revenues. To compensate, US programme producers, including the television networks, are attempting to enlarge the revenue stream from international exhibition of their programming. (The networks became eligible to participate in foreign syndication of programming when the financial interest and syndication rules were relaxed.) For this reason, US producers and the US government are concerned about foreign restrictions on imports of US programming. Currently, the European Community limitations are the most pressing concern, with a lower emphasis on Australia (Levy 1994: 16–19).

The expansion in US demand for programming has also created opportunities for foreign producers to sell into the US market, but the cable networks, rather than the broadcast networks, are probably the most likely buyers. While little foreign programming appears on network television,[32] some cable channels are carrying substantial amounts of imported programming. Because the US domestic broadcast market is very large, the tastes of that market are likely to drive production values and decisions. Foreign producers seeking to reach the US market may, of course, choose to emulate the US style of programming in hopes of reaching the broadcast network market, and, indeed, some US programming is produced 'offshore' for cost reasons. An alternative strategy that may be more successful in the multichannel US marketplace is for foreign producers to concentrate on what they do best and aim for the more narrowly focused cable channels in the US. Indeed, Levy (1994) provides several examples of co-productions between US cable channels and Australian television producers. It is worth noting that the Australian broadcast audience and the audience for the most popular US cable networks are of similar sizes.[33] The expected share of revenues from Australian exhibition of such a co-production is therefore far greater than would be the case in a (hypothetical) co-production for US network television. For this reason, the Australian partner in a cable co-production is likely to have greater control over the creative decisions made.

Just as programme producers want and need wide distribution, including international distribution, of their products in order to finance production, so viewers generally want more variety and choice in programming. The use of satellite technology for distribution of programming, either wholesale or retail (i.e., direct-to-home), is increasing in the US and around the world. This combination of technology and consumer demand will challenge any government efforts to limit choices. The US experience with video competition will not be duplicated precisely in foreign countries. In the US, cable television was widely available before direct-to-home satellite television became technically and economically feasible. Moreover, the US has historically relied more heavily on market forces to provide video than have most other countries. The US regulatory approach cannot and should not be mechanically applied to other countries. However, advancing technology, along with broad trends of consumer demand for services, are likely to make increased intermedia competition inevitable.

NOTES

1 Office of Plans and Policy, Federal Communications Commission, Washington, DC 20554, USA. The opinions expressed herein are those of the author and should not be construed to represent those of the Federal Communications Commission or any other member of its staff. This chapter is based in part on Setzer and Levy (1991). The author appreciates the helpful comments of Patricia Forsythe, Robert Pepper, Florence Setzer and Donnajean Ward. They bear no responsibility for any errors in the chapter.
2 Paul Kagan Associates (PKA), the source of the homes passed data in Table 2.2, provides the only consistent set of estimates over time of that figure. However, other sources suggest that there are fewer homes currently passed by cable. For example, a direct-to-home satellite provider estimates that 10 million homes are not passed by cable (Brown 1994: 26), while PKA places homes not passed at 1.3 million.
3 DBS spectrum is in a portion of the Ku band internationally designated for the 'Broadcast Satellite Service' (BSS). Primestar's Ku band service, as well as the C-band services described in the text, are part of the 'Fixed Satellite Service' (FSS), which is designated for point-to-multipoint rather than direct-to-home use. Primestar is planning to migrate to the DBS band.
4 Approximately 1.8 million HSD owners do not subscribe to any services. (See *Satellite Business News* 1995: 1.)

5 Fox provides fewer hours per week of programming than the three major commercial networks, so its affiliates need to acquire more of their own programming than affiliates of the other networks do. In this respect, Fox affiliates bear some resemblance to independent stations.

6 All viewing data presented here are percentages of total viewing, rather than the more commonly reported household viewing shares. Household shares include multiple set viewing and hence sum to over 100 per cent. The viewing percentages in this chapter are usually calculated from source data expressed as household shares.

7 Some of the apparent increase in basic cable viewing between 1984–5 and 1989–90 is due to the fact that WTBS, a 'superstation' (i.e., a television station transmitted by satellite and delivered to cable systems and other distributors), is counted in the 'other independent' category in the earlier year and in the basic cable category in the later year.

8 This figure is the sum of viewing shares for basic cable and premium, or pay cable, services. It is a lower bound on the share of programming not available locally off-air because some of cable households' independent station viewing is of superstations and other distant broadcast signals. While these are television broadcast stations, they are only available via cable in distant markets.

9 These data are for a full 12-month year. Generally, the 12-month period includes the fourth quarter of one year and the first three quarters of the next. Figures for the 1993–4 television 'season', which runs roughly from September to April, indicate that the three-network prime-time share was up for the first time in sixteen years (Foisie 1994b: 14–15). The 1993–4 season three-network total viewing share is 54 per cent, an increase of less than one percentage point over the previous year, so it is premature to declare that the long-term decline in three-network viewing shares has ended. The impact of the Fox network is suggested by its 9.7 per cent share of total viewing in 1993–4.

10 The data cited in the text cover the period up to 1993. Additional data, which are not comparable to the figures cited in the text, indicate that broadcast television advertising revenues (in current dollars) increased significantly from 1993 to 1994. This pattern holds for all categories, including network advertising revenues. See Jessell (1995a: 56).

11 In 1993, inflation-adjusted broadcast network advertising revenues were 19 per cent below their 1984 peak.

12 The average revenue per station in Table 2.5 is calculated as television station advertising divided by total number of stations. Changes in this quotient reflect both changes in the demand for advertising time and increases in the number of commercial television stations.

13 Network programming is generally exhibited in the same time slot on all affiliated stations, except for systematic differences across time zones.

14 The share of broadcast network plus national syndication in total video advertising was 39.2 per cent in 1988 and fell only to 38.5 per cent in 1993. See Table 2.5.

15 Television station advertising includes local sales and 'national spot' advertising sold by individual stations to national advertisers.

16 While most network compensation goes to network affiliates, in a limited number of cases, independent stations receive compensation for clearing network programming that the local affiliate declines to carry.

17 Net revenue includes network compensation and net advertising revenues (i.e., gross advertising revenues less commissions paid to advertising agencies for time sales). The Table 2.6 data are thus conceptually different from the gross advertising revenue data in Table 2.5.

18 These reported losses must be interpreted with caution. Accounting profits and losses may differ from economic profits and losses. An analysis of NAB financial data shows that over time, a large fraction of stations in certain categories report losses each year

(Setzer and Levy 1991: 37–8). However, the number of stations in those categories has risen from year to year. This suggests that profit data such as those reported in Table 2.5 are more reliable as an indicator of trends in profitability than as a precise measure of the level of profitability in any given year.

19 The importance of advertising revenues in financing cable *network* operations, coupled with the fact that cable advertising has apparently not reduced broadcast advertising revenues significantly, suggests that it might have made sense to permit Australian pay TV providers to accept advertising from the start.

20 For a discussion of VDT, see FCC (1994b). The statutory prohibition on telephone company-cable cross ownership in the same area (47 USC §533(b)) currently prevents direct provision of video programming by telephone companies in their service areas, but the situation may change. Some lower federal courts have struck down this prohibition, but the issue has not reached the Supreme Court. Moreover, the prohibition may be repealed by Congress.

21 After some delay, Time Warner began its 'Full Service Network' demonstration project in Orlando, Florida in December 1994. Initially available to five households, it is now expected to reach 4,000 households in 1995 (Shapiro 1994: B1).

22 Fox began with only two nights per week of programming and now offers prime-time programming seven nights a week. Unlike the three major commercial networks, it does not programme the 10:00–11:00p.m. period, so it offers fifteen rather than twenty-two hours per week of prime-time programming. In the past year, Fox added sports programming by outbidding CBS for the rights to some very popular National Football League programming and by acquiring national broadcast rights to a package of National Hockey League games. Recently, as part of an effort to expand its presence in news, another staple of the three major commercial networks, Fox has entered into an agreement with the Reuters news service. Over the years, Fox has also added daytime children's programming. For information on the Fox Network, see Jensen and Carnevale (1994: B1), McClellan (1994a: 28), Flint (1994: 14, 22), and Coe (1995: 25).

23 This coverage applies to Fox's National Football League programming. Some of its affiliates are 'secondary'. They do not necessarily carry the full Fox programming schedule and may carry some Fox programming out of pattern (i.e., not at the same time that Fox affiliates normally carry it).

24 For information on these new networks, see Tobenkin (1995a: 30–6) and Lieberman 1995: 1B–2B.

25 Consent decrees between the US Department of Justice and each of the three major networks, signed in 1978 and 1980, contained restrictions parallel to some of those in the financial interest and syndication rules. These restrictions were lifted in 1993 (*US v. NBC et al.* 1993).

26 Hollywood studios have frequently produced programming jointly with independents, but the scope of co-operation appears to be increasing. See, for example, the description of the ABC agreement with the new Spielberg, Katzenberg, Geffen Studio in McClellan (1994b: 18).

27 The 1992 Cable Act directed the FCC to implement broadcast signal carriage rules that, in certain circumstances, require cable operators to obtain the consent of television broadcast stations before transmitting their signals. Television broadcasters may negotiate compensation in exchange for that consent. See FCC (1993a and 47 USC §325).

28 Congress is currently (mid-1995) considering telecommunications legislation that would reduce the scope of the cable rate regulation. See Stern (1995: 6, 10).

29 For a more detailed discussion of the FCC's cable rate regulation regime, see FCC (1994a, 1994c).

30 How to determine the minimum level of video services that should be available to

everyone and how to structure a targeted subsidy are beyond the scope of this chapter. The first question may well end up being addressed as part of a larger debate about universal service in an environment where cable operators, telephone companies and others provide a mixture of video, voice and data services.

31 Among the important events that occured since the paper was completed and could not be incorporated in the main text are the following. First, the Telecommunications Act of 1996 became law. The 1996 Act eliminated the restriction on the number of television stations that a single entity can own, repealed the statutory prohibition on telephone company–cable crossownership, repealed the FCC's video dialtone rules, provided a new regulatory framework for telephone company provision of video programming services,a dn reduced the scope of cable television rate regulation. Second, Disney acquired Capital Cities/ABC and Westinghouse acquired CBS. Third, the FCC's syndication and financial interest rules expired. Fourth, Echostar launched a new DBS service, while Primestar, having failed to acquire a DBS orbital slot, remains a medium power service.

32 Currently there is one foreign-produced series on a US television broadcast network, the Canadian-made *Due South* (De Santis 1994: B6). Some foreign movies have also been exhibited on network television.

33 In the fourth quarter of 1994, the prime-time audiences for the five top-rated cable networks ranged from 784,000 to 1.6 million *households* (*Broadcasting and Cable* 1995: 72). Australian data for February–June 1994 indicate that the audiences for the top 100 commercial programmes ranged from 1.3 to 3.1 million *viewers* (Federation of Australian Commercial Television Station 1994: Appendix 1). The Australian figures are for the five major cities and so slightly understated the true total audiences for these programmes.

BIBLIOGRAPHY

Adams, J. (1995) 'Where do you go from here? – The 9th Annual Business Forecast', *TVRO Dealer*, January: 26 *et seq.*

Andrews, E. (1995) 'Forward, but how fast, in interactive TV?', *New York Times*, 3 January: C16.

Broadcasting Publications, Inc. (1991) *The Broadcasting Yearbook* 1991 Edition. Washington, DC: Broadcasting Publications.

Broadcasting and Cable (1994) 'In brief', 2 May: 68.

Broadcasting and Cable (1995) 'In brief', 2 January: 72.

Brown, R. (1993) 'Headline news gets retrans boost', *Broadcasting and Cable*, 8 November: 32, 64.

Brown, R. (1994) 'MSOs take direct approach', *Broadcasting and Cable*, 27 June: 26.

Brown, R. (1995) 'MMDS (wireless cable): a capital ideal', *Broadcasting and Cable*, 1 May: 16, 18.

CAB (Cabletelevision Advertising Bureau) (1986, 1991, 1994) *Cable TV Facts*. New York, NY: CAB.

Cable Television Consumer Protection and Competition Act of 1992 ('1992 Cable Act'), Pub. L. No. 102-385, 106 Stat. (1992), amending the Communications Act of 1934. Codified at 47 USC §151 et seq.

Carter, B. (1992) 'Prime time's growing hit? That's news', *New York Times*, 6 April: D9.

Carter, B. (1994a) 'Networks' new cable channels get a big jump on the competition', *New York Times*, 14 March: D7.

Carter, B. (1994b) 'ABC's ownership of big slices of its fall lineup is raising eyebrows in Hollywood studios', *New York Times*, 16 May: D6.

Carter, B. (1995) 'Television in flux: networks for sale, new ones in wings', *New York Times*, 3 January: C15.

Coe, S. (1995) 'Reuters joins Fox in news deal', *Broadcasting and Cable*, 30 January: 25.

De Santis, S. (1994) '"Due South" crosses a boundary for TV production firm', *Wall Street Journal*, 8 September: B6.

Economic Report of the President Together with the Annual Report of the Council of Economic Advisors (1994), Washington, DC: US Government Printing Office.

Farhi, P. (1994) 'Advertisers, suitors zoom in on TV networks', *Washington Post*, 31 October: A1.

Farhi, P. (1995) 'HDTV: high definition, low priority?', *Washington Post*, 23 March: D10.

Federation of Australian Commercial Television Stations (FACTS) (1994) *Submission to the Review of Australian Content Program Standards of the Australian Broadcasting Authority* September, Sydney.

Federal Communications Commission (FCC) (1976) *Public Notice: TV Broadcast Financial Data*, 2 August.

FCC (1981) *Public Notice: TV Broadcast Financial Data*, 10 August.

FCC (1987) *Report and Order* in Gen. Docket 86–336, 2 FCC Rcd 1669.

FCC (1993a) *Report and Order* in MM Docket No. 92-259, MM Docket No. 90–4, and MM Docket No. 92-295, 8 FCC Rcd 2965.

FCC (1993b) *First Report and Order* in MM Docket No. 92–265, 8 FCC Rcd 3359.

FCC (1993c) *Second Report and Order* in MM Docket 90–162, 8 FCC Rcd 3282.

FCC (1994a) *Second Order on Reconsideration, Fourth Report and Order, and Fifth Notice of Proposed Rulemaking* in MM Docket No. 92–266, 9 FCC Rcd 4119.

FCC (1994b) *Memorandum Opinion and Order on Reconsideration and Third Further Notice of Proposed Rulemaking* in CC Docket No. 87–266, 10 FCC Rcd 244.

FCC (1994c) *Sixth Order on Reconsideration, Fifth Report and Order, and Seventh Notice of Proposed Rulemaking* in MM Docket No. 92–266 and MM Docket No. 93–215, 10 FCC Rcd 1226.

FCC (1995) *Further Notice of Proposed Rulemaking* in MM Docket No. 91–221 and MM Docket No. 87–8 (released 17 January 1995) FCC 94–322.

Flint, J. (1994) 'Fox to pitch older viewers', *Broadcasting and Cable*, 3 January: 14, 22.

Foisie, G. (1994a) 'TV station operators keeping eye on costs', *Broadcasting and Cable*, 21 February: 59.

Foisie, G. (1994b) 'Big three rebound, gain in share', *Broadcasting and Cable*, 25 April: 14–15.

Hall, J. (1994) '4 broadcast networks set a record with advertising sales', *Los Angeles Times*, 13 September: B7.

Hillebrand, M. (1995) 'DBS companies look backward, forward', *Satellite Business News*, 18 January: 1, 21.

Jensen, E. (1994) 'Many TV stations switch networks, confusing viewers', *Wall Street Journal*, 7 October: A1.

Jensen, E. and Carnevale, M. (1994) 'Fox proves it's ready to play in the big leagues', *Wall Street Journal*, 25 May: B1.

Jessell, H. (1995a) 'Broadcast TV posts double-digit gains', *Broadcasting and Cable*, 27 February: 56.

Jessell, H. (1995b) 'Hundt proposes 2nd-channel freedom', *Broadcasting and Cable*, 17 April: 8, 12.

Levy, J. (1994) *Implications of Content Regulation for Trade in Television Programs: A US Perspective*, Communications Research Forum, Bureau of Transport and Communications Economics Sydney.

Lieberman, D. (1995) 'Two ventures enter race for prime time', *USA Today*, 5 January: 1B–2B.

Lippman, J. (1994) 'Prime-time targets: studios covet networks as a source of rerun riches', *Los Angeles Times*, 2 September: B5.

McClellan, S. (1993) 'Retrans plans: programming the new channels', *Broadcasting and Cable*, 11 October: 16–17.

McClellan, S. (1994a) 'Fox: the puck stops here', *Broadcasting and Cable*, 19 September: 28.

McClellan, S. (1994b) 'ABC makes high-profile production leap', *Broadcasting and Cable*, 5 December: 18.

NAB (National Association of Broadcasters) (1986–1987, 1989–1994) *Television Financial Report*. Washington, DC: NAB.

National Cable Television Association (1994) *Cable Television Developments, April*. Washington, DC: NCTA.

Paul Kagan Associates (PKA) (1993a) *Cable Television Programming*, 22 March.

PKA (1993b) *The Cable TV Financial Databook*, Carmel, CA.

PKA (1994a) *Cable TV Investor*, 31 March.

PKA (1994b) *The Cable TV Financial Databook*, Carmel, CA.

PKA (1994c) *Cable TV Programming*, 30 September.

PKA (1994d) *Marketing New Media*, 19 December.

R.R. Bowker (1994) *The Broadcasting and Cable Yearbook* 1994 Edition. New Providence, NJ: R.R. Bowker.

Satellite Business News (1991) 'US satellite system sales', 9 January: 5.

Satellite Business News (1994) 'Satellite system sales', 12 January: 1.

Satellite Business News (1995) 'Satellite system sales', 18 January: 1.

Setzer, F. and Levy, J. (1991) *Broadcast Television in a Multichannel Marketplace*. (Working Paper 26, Office of Plans and Policy). Washington, DC: Federal Communications Commission.

Shapiro, E. (1994) 'Time Warner's Orlando test to start – finally', *Wall Street Journal*, 7 December: B1.

Stern, C. (1995) 'Dereg rolls in Senate: 81–18', *Broadcasting and Cable*, 19 June: 6, 10.

Teitelbaum, R. (1994) 'The largest U.S. industrial corporations; hats off! It was a heck of a year', *Fortune*, 18 April: 210 *et seq.*

Tobenkin, D. (1994) 'Production big business for big 3', *Broadcasting and Cable*, 12 September: 6, 10.

Tobenkin, D. (1995a) 'New players get ready to roll', *Broadcasting and Cable*, 2 January: 30–6.

Tobenkin, D. (1995b) 'Syndicators see tough times for first-run', *Broadcasting and Cable*, 30 January: 22.

TVB (Television Bureau of Advertising) (1991) *Trends in Advertising Volume*, New York: TVB.

TVB (1994a) *Trends in GDP, Ad Volume, TV Ad Volume*, New York: TVB.

TVB (1994b) *Trends in Television* New York: TVB.

TVB (1994c) *Trends in Advertising Volume* New York: TVB.

U.S. v. National Broadcasting Company, Inc. et al. (1993) 842 F. Supp. 402.

US Department of Commerce (1994) *Statistical Abstract of the United States*, Washington, DC: US Government Printing Office.

Warren Publishing, Inc. (1983) *Television and Cable Factbook* (Cable and Services Volume) 1982–3 Edition. Washington, DC: Warren Publishing.

Warren Publishing, Inc. (1994) *Television and Cable Factbook* (Services Volume) 1994 Edition. Washington, DC: Warren Publishing.

Zier, J. (1994) 'CBS, Group W form historic alliance', *Broadcasting and Cable*, 18 July: 14.

3

SELLING TELEVISION

Manuel Alvarado

INTRODUCTION

Fundamentally, 1992 for Europe exposed questions and problems about political sovereignty and political interrelationship. Within the broad parameters of the tensions of that duality, this chapter focuses on three key areas – the economic, the legal and the cultural.

Historically, 1992 marked a culminating stage in the process of uniting twelve countries of Europe which was a process initiated in the 1950s with the creation of the so-called European Common Market.

This initiative was designed purely to ease trade agreements between six European countries, each of which possessed large boundaries with a neighbouring state. However, from the beginning, the logic of the organization was the eventual political union of the six countries. The UK was not one of these, partly because the Labour government of the day would not countenance the concept of the eventual loss of political sovereignty and partly because a large and dominant country in that grouping – France – did not relish losing the preeminent and dominating political role that it enjoyed in the Common Market. However, Britain did need to make trade agreements within Europe – the 'advantages' and 'privileges' enjoyed as a result of having both an Empire and a Commonwealth were clearly not going to last for ever – and the country was thus one of the seven founding countries of a 'rival' group EFTA (European Free Trade Association). This was purely a trading association with few political ramifications.

The UK eventually joined the European Economic Community, and the addition of Spain and Portugal in 1986 increased the membership to twelve, including five of the large West European powers – West Germany, France, Italy, UK and Spain. These countries are specifically mentioned because they are important for later comments about European television.

In January 1995 Austria, Sweden and Finland joined the European Community (EC), which brought its membership to fifteen. Switzerland, a small, rich and traditionally politically neutral country is still debating whether to join the EC or to maintain relative economic and political independence from the rest of Europe.

However, it does not maintain a cultural independence because all the countries of Europe, together with one or two which are more substantially part of another continent (e.g. Turkey) belong to another transnational organization i.e. the Council of Europe. This council consists of twenty-three member states and focuses on matters of cultural, educational and legal significance.

The reason for offering this thumbnail sketch is to indicate that the development of Europe-wide broadcasting initiatives involves not only national governments, but also both the major transnational European organizations. Furthermore, there are not clear divisions between the organizations when it comes to discussions of the mass media. Just because the EC has traditionally been concerned with economic and political questions does not mean that cultural and legal policies are not of equal significance while the reverse holds true for the Council of Europe.

THE STRUCTURES OF EUROPEAN BROADCASTING

A crucially important point to remember about all European broadcasting is that from its inception it has always been based on the principles of public service broadcasting. Obviously, this is in total contrast with TV broadcasting in the USA which was fundamentally based on commercial principles, with PBS not being introduced until the early 1960s.

The UK claims to have established the world's first regular daily television service in 1936. This was run by the BBC – a public corporation established by Royal Charter and almost totally financed by licence fee – for three years, then it was closed down due to the onset of the Second World War. It re-opened in 1946, and the other European countries were quick to follow suit. All of them followed the British lead of establishing broadcasting on a public service principle, funded totally by licence fees. Quite apart from other considerations, the close proximity of many relatively small countries, with a weak history of inter-nation harmony, made state regulation and protection crucial political priorities.

The UK was the first European country to take the plunge into commercial television in 1955. However, it is important to note three things that are sometimes overlooked by non-European observers of European broadcasting:

1) Commercial TV in the UK was also totally structured on the basis of public service broadcasting. Furthermore, it still is – that is why commercial TV programmes and schedules look little different from their BBC counterparts.
2) Similarly, the introduction of commercial TV in the rest of Europe followed this path. The first break from it was made over twenty years later by Italy in 1976 when deregulation of TV was instituted.
3) Two countries in Europe still have TV which does not carry advertising.

So what have the links between European broadcasting been like? The simple

63

answer is, not particularly strong. There is an administrative organization to which they all belong – the European Broadcasting Union (EBU) – and all the countries belong to the Eurovision Network which basically provides the technological links between the broadcasters. This system enables news footage to be pushed around Europe and facilitates occasional anodyne and banal competitions such as the *European Song Contest* and the now defunct *Jeux Sans Frontières*.

In terms of actual mainstream programming there is relatively little flow between countries. In fact, it is only over the last fifteen years that money has been used in the European TV markets. Before that, a complex non-financial bartering system was used. Admittedly, the UK is the worst offender here, with virtually no European programming being scheduled on British TV, but all the countries suffer or gain from a substantial scheduling of US product.

So what are the anxieties and fears both European governments and European broadcasters have about the future of broad and narrow-casting in Europe?

THE INTERNATIONAL EXCHANGE OF TV PROGRAMMES

Fundamentally, the fears are about national sovereignty and its preservation. European governments increasingly recognize that their future economic prosperity depends upon collective production activity combined with collectively aggressive international marketing. Only in this way, they believe, can the economic power of the USA and Japan be combated.

At the same time there is the fear of the erosion of cultural difference, historical specifities and linguistic uniqueness. It is the preservation of these national identities which most concerns all European countries in the face of the anglophone 'swamping' of the television and radio systems and record and tape markets by North American media corporations.

Thus it is in this ideological sphere that the Murdochs, Turners and Maxwells are viewed with suspicion and even fear by European governments. When it comes to the financial orbit, it is European broadcasters who are the most concerned. However, traditional economic theories of commodity production do not help us to understand the domestic and international circulation of television programmes. What is required, is a re-conceptualization of the international TV models if we are going to better understand film and television programming in Europe post 1992.

The basic thesis of this chapter therefore is the fundamental proposition which can be expressed in one sentence: the international exchange of TV programmes is not based on the conventional principles of commodity valuation (i.e. assessing the marginal cost of production), but instead has to be analysed in terms of the political and economic position of the buying country.

In most countries the financial organization of television is a complex business.

On the one hand, it is highly sophisticated in terms of governmental statutes, forms of funding, market research, audience research, scheduling patterns, international sales. On the other, it is a highly imprecise affair.

In the case of the UK, for example, the operations of the main broadcasting organizations are complexly structured and controlled; their TV productions are, for the most part, meticulously and expensively crafted; their audience research is detailed and thorough; their scheduling strategies skilful and imaginative; and their activities on the international markets are apparently increasingly successful. However, both in terms of the organizations' own accounting systems and in terms of media research, the actual value of particular programmes is almost impossible to determine. This might seem a surprising assertion to make, but the facts of the financial operation (particularly in terms of the international circulation of TV programmes) of British broadcasting organizations are as follows.

Value

A fundamental problem is that broadcasters are unable to have a precise concept of the value of a television programme. The difficulty generally with a cultural commodity is that, whilst it undoubtedly has both an exchange value and a use value, neither are quantifiable in precise terms. Nor can there be an accurate assessment of market saturation. The reasons for this level of ignorance will be made clear as I proceed, but for the moment I will simply assert that all TV companies can do with precision is: balance the books; produce an accurate set of annual accounts; and make a profit. What they cannot do – and probably never will be able to do – is to put a meaningful price tag on any one product!

Production

Production costs – the seemingly most precise area of costing – are in fact very difficult to estimate, as can be demonstrated by looking at the different accounting systems adopted by the BBC, the ITV companies and Channel 4 in the UK. In the case of the ITV companies, only above the line costs are budgeted. All below the line costs – plant, equipment, land, building, salaries of permanent staff, etc. – are simply totalled for the year and spread across all programmes. Such a practice clearly adequately meets the corporate needs of the ITV companies but would provide some bizarre costings (were they available) for individual programmes which range from cheap studio based children's and current affairs discussion programmes through to expensive, on location historical drama productions.[1]

The BBC, on the other hand, attempts to produce a total budget (encompassing both above and below the line costings) for each production. This would seem to provide more precise figures, but that is no more than a façade. First, the below the line costings must be fairly rough – if they were to be accurate, far more precise and regular estimates of land and property values, depreciation costs, inflation, etc. would have to be made. Second, one wonders if all sections of the BBC are taken into account – for example the audience research department or BBC Enterprises.

Channel 4 would seem to provide the opportunity for a more clear analysis of programme costs because they commission nearly everything they transmit from the ITV companies and from independent TV producers. However, the structure of the financial operation of C4 is such that the cost or value of the programmes it buys are still highly problematic. The situation has changed since the beginning of 1993. Prior to that, because it received an annual lump sum in the form of a subscription payment from the fifteen ITV companies (in exchange for which they have the sole right to sell advertising time on C4), and is required to buy a certain proportion (60 per cent) of its programming from those companies, Channel 4 did not pay a market rate but rather proportionately dispensed its money to those producers who were prepared to provide product at a price the company said it could afford. It is likely that C4 paid significantly less for its product than what would be considered to be the true cost of production (were it known). The ITV companies (grudgingly) accepted this state of affairs not least because it enabled them to use up spare studio capacity, and small independent producers operated special union rates and accepted the money offered them because there was virtually no other outlet for their work. Since 1993 the commercial companies have grumbled because of the new competitor in the market place! (This did not mean, as the Tory government pre-Peacock hoped, that C4 offers an economically more efficient system of broadcasting – all that it meant was that it slotted into the total structural ensemble that constituted British broadcasting.)

Maybe the accounting departments of the BBC, the ITV companies and Channel 4 are far more precise and knowledgeable about production costs than is here being suggested, but until they reveal this to be the case, this account will have to work on the hypothesis that even professional broadcasters have a hazy sense of actual programme cost.

Domestic distribution

Unlike the TV system of the USA, European TV programmes have no exchange value in their domestic markets. In Britain, the BBC (like all the other state broadcasting organizations of Europe) primarily produces programmes that are paid for directly through the licence fee system for domestic transmission. The ITV companies do exchange programmes with each other but, given the federally organized system of commercial TV in Britain, they use an intricate points system – money does not change hands. In effect what they do is write off the costs of production on first transmission. Thus repeat screenings and foreign sales are seen as almost pure profit.

International distribution

Given the imprecise production costings and the fact that it is only possible to financially value a cultural artefact in terms of estimated demand, it is impossible to place a precise figure on any particular programme. Furthermore, given the huge disparities in the wealth of TV companies and organizations around the world, every programme will have a different price tag according to the country to which it is being offered.

What is at stake is not so much the wealth of the TV companies – in most countries TV companies occupy the wealthier strata of industry – but the size of the population. State broadcasting organizations are limited in size, spending power and production capacity by the number of people who pay the licence fee, and the commercial TV companies are limited by the size of the audience possessing significant disposable income that they can sell to advertisers. This is an important factor to consider when analysing the trans-global aspirations of TV Globo, Rupert Murdoch, Bertlesman, Silvio Berlusconi, Turner, Marinho, Azcarraga *et al*.

Thus it is necessary to think not in terms of exchange *value* but in terms of exchange *values* – ones that are susceptible to high degrees of fluctuation. And the definitions of these values are infinitely more complex than, for example, an equally complex area of production such as a motor car. Whilst a motor car and a TV programme share certain attributes – they both require huge initial capital investment, design costs, large labour forces with diversified and specialist skills, mass production line methods, a unit cost of production which falls dramatically in expanding markets and a high level of consumer desirability – there is a striking area of divergence. A motor car will always have a certain basic price determined by its unit (or marginal) cost of production below which it can never fall. In the case of a TV programme the marginal cost of production is irrelevant. A programme which is made for £1 million could be sold for £100,000 to the USA but to Burkino Faso for £100! In fact, in both cases, the eventual price of the programme is more likely to be determined *by the cost of selling it than by the production cost*.

To use the same example, if a British company has an important and expensive drama production to sell, it is likely to invest a considerable amount of money in the attempt to persuade an American broadcasting organization (whether a network, a network affiliate, a syndication chain, or PBS) of a sale success. This investment could involve substantial advertising, international travel and hospitality, screenings and even, in the case of Thames TV, the experiment of block purchasing one week's broadcasting time in Los Angeles and New York as they did in the 1980s. In the case of Burkino Faso, the price may be dependent on not much more than the cost of correspondence via telephone and fax, and the cost of tape or film duplication. At least this is what the companies would claim.

Audience size

It is clear then that the powerful and dominant television exporters on the international markets are in a strong position, which they maintain because of the very low prices they are able to charge for a product that has written off its costs in the domestic marketplace. Furthermore they are able to do this despite the fact that television production that has the highest international currency is television drama – the most expensive product to produce. What are the implications of these facts? For example, is the USA the world's major TV exporter because the American companies are following the well-worn trade routes trodden by Hollywood in previous decades? Clearly American product is highly desirable but this doesn't provide a good answer because it doesn't explain how both Britain and Brazil have become major world players in the global flow of television. Neither country has a particularly strong record in the export of cinema films.

There are, of course, a number of factors that have to be taken into account, such as, in the case of Britain, government legislation, quota restrictions and working in the language that the Americans have already established as almost a world. The crucial element is the size of the population of the dominant TV nations or, more precisely, the size and proportion of domestic television ownership. Whilst a large population obviously can't ensure a powerful television culture *per se*, I would argue that the lack of such a population will make it virtually impossible for a broadcaster to be a major player in the world's markets.

First of all it doesn't matter whether a TV organization is state run through a licence fee system or a commercial company financed through the sale of advertising time – in either case a large audience is required either to pay the tax or to be sold to the potential advertisers. A large audience will ensure a large revenue which will enable the creation of television's most expensive area of production – television drama.

In actual fact there are very few countries with such large audiences. In the case of Western Europe there are only four, perhaps five, such countries. They are Germany, with a population of 80 million and a domestic TV ownership of 30 million receivers; Italy, with 57 million people and 14.5 million TV sets; the UK, with 56.5 million and 19 million sets; and France, with 55 million and 27.5 million sets. Spain is the next largest country, with a population of 39 million owning 13 million receivers. All these countries can afford to write off the costs of production in the domestic market, although the UK is the only country to do so consistently and successfully. Italy, for example, has a rather low TV ownership figure and has a highly fragmented system since deregulation in 1976. Germany has the problem that few other countries share its language and its TV system is fragmented in federal terms. France too has organizational problems and when these countries wished to try and compete with *Dallas* head on they did so through a co-production deal between five countries to produce the not terribly successful *Chateauvallon*.[2]

All the other Western European countries have populations too small to be able to finance large-scale drama productions on their own and hence the current desire to set up all kinds of co-production deals – something in which the smaller British commercial companies are also keen to engage. A good example is the case of HTV (a middle-sized company serving the more sparsely populated regions of Wales and the West Country) which set up an offshot to provide for such possibilities.

Of course, a large population is not enough in itself to generate TV organizations wealthy enough to engage in large-scale production. India has a population of over 750 million and the world's largest film industry, but there are only 2 million TV sets in the sub-continent. A large domestic population is an absolute prerequisite for the success of a company, like TV Globo. With a population of over 135 million and over 30 million TV receivers there are only four countries with higher TV set ownership figures than Brazil – Japan (31 million), China (71 million), the CIS (93 million) and the USA (145 million).

Thus the fact that Brazilian TV is internationally far more successful than its Latin American rival, Mexico, has to do with programme quality. (It is highly questionable as to whether qualitative and aesthetic judgements can be made when analysing the international circulation of cultural commodities.) In fact Mexico is far better placed to be successful (Spanish is the third most widely spoken language in the world; the large Hispanic communities in the USA enjoy Mexican programmes etc.) and with the second largest population in Latin America – nearly 80 million people – Mexico has potentially a large enough domestic audience. However, when there are only 13 million TV sets in a relatively poor country it is an uphill struggle for both the commercial and state broadcasters, as was evidenced by the television coverage of the 1986 soccer World Cup when the two organizations had to combine forces. This is why Azcarraga's internationalist aspirations are so important.

Thus, with the harsh realities of population size being such a determining force when it comes to the successful international marketing of television, it is not surprising that the dominant countries find it relatively easy to maintain their ascendant position. As Collins, Garnham and Locksley (1988) state:

> Given the advantages of the dominant producers and their potential for charging near to marginal costs for exported material it is rational for other countries to import acceptable programmes that are available at prices substantially below the costs of indigenous products. Since television programmes are relatively imperishable and not exhausted in consumption, consumers across the world are potentially able to benefit from the low marginal cost of production of television programmes and enjoy cheap high budget products from the existing dominant producers.[3]

Whilst it might be 'rational' in business terms for countries to import programming which is vastly cheaper than it would be to make, these authors are, of course making a highly contentious statement which is hotly debated by small 'TV nations'!

CONCLUSION

Thus, it is within the context of the imprecision with which TV programmes are financially valued, and economically circulated, that the introduction of the new delivery systems of cable, satellite and video and the appearance of the international media moguls create such problems for European governments and broadcasters.

Apart from in Belgium and Holland cable is not the success it has been in the US. There are a number of possible reasons for this.

1 The requirement that all broadcasters provide a wide range of programming obviating the need for a greater range of more specialist channels.
2 The lack of attraction of uninterrupted movies – HBO – to nations which already have channels without adverts.
3 The earlier established success of video.
4 The financial risks to potential cable operators due to the above factors plus the additional risks resulting from additional governmental legislation.

The fundamental fear here is due to the fact that no government could or would ever be prepared to countenance spending tax payers' money to the tune of nearly US$200 million a year for five years as Murdoch – or News Corporation – are prepared to do. However, the situation is changing and needs careful monitoring. Murdoch's BSkyB has long turned the corner in making a profit and offering eighteen channels, all but two of which are encrypted thereby requiring the payment of a significant monthly subscription.

Where, then, does this leave us with regard to our assessment of 'the anticipated changes in film and television programming under the sweeping European Trade and Communications Agreements after 1992'? The European Parliament has invested a great deal of time and money in the attempt to formulate a media policy. This has resulted in the huge Green Paper – Television Without Frontiers – and some equally substantial responses from many individual European parliaments. At the same time national broadcasting systems and structures are high on the political agendas of all European parliaments. Thus, for example, the British government restructured the operation of British broadcasting.

In the long term these governmental initiatives will have a smaller significance than many politicians seem to realize in the free market conditions and philosophies which increasingly underpin European media operations. It is consumer and audience responses – and the success with which they are wooed by all media organizations (whether run by state broadcasters or international media moguls) – which will determine what television in Europe looks like by the turn of the century.

NOTES

1 Alvarado, Manuel and Stewart, John (1985) *Made for Television – Euston Films Limited*. London: BFI/Methuen.

2 Silj, Alessandro *et al.* (1993) *East of Dallas – The European Challenge to American Television*. London: BFI.
3 Collins, Richard, Garnham, Nicholas and Locksley, Gareth (1988) *The Economics of Television: The UK Case*. London: Sage.

4

THE CRIME OF
MONSIEUR LANG

GATT, the screen, and the new international division of cultural labour

Toby Miller

The diversity of European cultures and ways of life, . . . roughly translated, means the need to protect the sector from U.S. competition.

(Stern 1994a:18)

It's a war to protect art, say the French. What art, ask the Americans.

(Cohen 1994: H1)

We're going to ruin your culture just like we ruined our own.
(Jay Leno, 1994 promotional spot for the pan-European NBC Super Channel)

By the time you read this chapter, the General Agreement on Tariffs and Trade (GATT) will be dead. In January 1995, the World Trade Organisation (WTO) came into being, replacing the agreements and buying the bureaucrats that had been foremost amongst the international institutional voices of laissez-faire economics since Bretton Woods. The last gasp of the GATT came with the 20,000 page protocols, weighing 850 kilogrammes, that were agreed in Geneva in December 1993, signed in Marrakesh in April 1994, and ratified domestically by its 125 members and fellow-travellers over the next eight months. But its effects will be felt – through the work of the new organization – beyond its life. Although the audiovisual market was extremely prominent in these deliberations, in keeping with the shift in emphasis from trade in goods to trade in services (TIS), the US attempt to proscribe cultural protectionism was opposed by virtually every other nation, and cinema and television were finally excluded from the agreement. This chapter traces the history to that debate and the forms of life that generated it, via an examination of the new international division of cultural labour (NICL). But first, some background to the GATT and American audiovisual export, before we return to the cultural politics of the Uruguay Round.

THE GATT

Who can be blind today to the threat of a world gradually invaded by an identical culture, Anglo-Saxon culture, under the cover of economic liberalism?

(François Mitterrand quoted in Brooks 1994: 35)

This is a great and beautiful victory for Europe and for French culture.
(Alain Carignon, French Minister for Communications
quoted in *Facts* 1993: 931)

Since its emergence in the late 1940s as part of a range of new international financial and trading protocols, the GATT has embodied in contractual form central aspects of the First World's rules of economic prosperity: nondiscrimination, codified regulations policed outside the terrain of individual sovereign-states, and multilateralism. It was born under the sign of North American growth evangelism, whereby standardized methods, vast scales of production and an endless expansion of markets would be the engine of economic recovery and development for the West European detritus of the Second World War, although initial plans for an independent organization were shelved because the US Congress resisted any ceding of individual sovereignty (an ironic history, as we shall see).

GATT stood for the paradoxically bureaucratic voice of neoclassical economics, dedicated beyond the call of parochial national interests and state intervention to the higher service of promulgating free trade. Officials of the organization worked like puritans ordered by some intellectual manifest destiny to disrupt trading blocs and restrict distortions to the putative natural rhythms of supply and demand as determined by consumer sovereignty and comparative advantage. Such pristine forms of theorization routinely enunciate quite specific and partial material interests; in this instance, the agenda of the United States, which was suited by such arrangements until Japan and the European Community (EC) became powerful economic agents that were able to make some rules of their own. In any case, by the 1980s, there were serious doubts inside the US about the utility of free-trade absolutism. The seemingly transcendental nature of marginalist economics, which set up good/bad antinomies in the form of liberalism versus mercantilism, became a conditional argument, to be used as and when it suited the purposes of its self-interested enunciators (the US was extremist in one direction over cinema and television, in another on agriculture). The highly moral mode of the GATT itself became its legalistic ruination, as new forms of protectionism appeared via non-tariff implements and industry policy to match the varied positions of member states. At the same time, we should acknowledge that the seven rounds of negotiations conducted since 1948 have seen a reduction in official tariffs on manufacturing from 40 per cent to 5 per cent, noting that global trade increased over that period by a factor of four (Lang and Hines 1993: 46). On balance, the GATT has functioned most effectively for the First World, such that 20 per cent of the world's population currently conducts over 80 per cent of its international business.

The services sector in particular has expanded massively over the last decade, to the point where it now comprises 70 per cent of gross domestic product in the industralized nations and 50 per cent in much of the Third World, accounting for US $1 trillion a year in trade, perhaps a fifth of the global total (Drake and

Nicolaïdis 1992: 37; *Economist* 1994: 55). The GATT was slow to notice this growth, in part because the tenets of neoclassical dogma, and the technological limitations of the 'human' side to the sector (restaurants, for example) were not especially amenable to conceptualizing and enumerating its frequently object-free exchange. But as the great and powerful nations of the free world saw capital fly from their manufacturing zones, and sought to become net exporters of textuality, they discovered ways of opening up the area to bureaucratic invigilation. TIS was found to comprise, *inter alia*, film, television, and broadcast advertising production and distribution (Sjolander 1992–3: 54n. 5; Grey 1990: 6–9). The Punta del Este Declaration of September 1986 put TIS at the centre of GATT debates, because of pressure from the US (always the main player in negotiations) in the service of lobbyists for American Express, Citibank and IBM. And the entertainment sector was equally significant. As Daniel Toscan du Plantier, president of the French government's film marketing body, put it recently: 'cinema used to be side salad in world commerce. Now, it's the beef' (du Plantier quoted in Cohen 1994: H23). And the illegal copying of electronic texts was estimated at US $70 billion in 1994 – a further copyright incentive in the area of intellectual property (Hills 1994: 185; Mayrhofer 1994: 137). The final agreement struck to end the seven year Uruguay Round was negotiated by a small number of industrialized nations and then delivered to a hundred other countries with a weekend to ponder the final draft (Childers 1994: 5).

The GATT's institutional legacy, the WTO, will have a legal personality, a secretariat and biennial ministerial conferences. This new machinery will make it easier for multinational corporations (MNCs) to dominate trade via the diplomatic services of their home government's representatives, to the exclusion of environmental and other matters of public interest, which will no longer have the entrée that GATT gave via recognition of non-government organizations. Multinationals will fnd it easier to be regarded as local firms in their host countries, and Third World agricultural production will be opened up further to foreign ownership (Lang and Hines 1993: 48–50; Dobson 1993: 573–6). Continuation of work on TIS should be amongst the first tasks of the new body. But despite its high-theory commitment to pure/perfect competition, political pressures mean the WTO will need to devote a great deal of care to archaeological, artistic and historic exemptions to free-trade totalizations, as even the GATT routinely did (Chartrand 1992)

AMERICAN AUDIOVISUAL EXPORT

Unrestricted advertising encourages the growth of the type of fast-moving, cheaply produced programming ('satellite slush') evidenced on Super Channel, with its bland mélange of Dutch football, world gold sponsored by Korean air, re-run ads for Kelloggs cereals and Clausthaler beer, third-rate Australian movies, *Flipper* and other old Hollywood standbys, American college football and corporate-sponsored news and weather in slow, tedious English.

(Keane 1991: 82)

Entertainment is one of the purest marketplaces in the world. If people don't like a movie or record they won't see it or buy it. The fact that the American entertainment industry has been so successful on a worldwide basis speaks to the quality and attractiveness of what we're creating.
(Robert Shaye, Chair of New Line Pictures quoted in Weinraub 1993: L24)

The fact that de-industrialization has left the US the most indebted nation in world history is mitigated by its surplus in aerospace and the screen, and by its immense internal audience of film goers and TV stations which is matched by a growing global market, following deregulation abroad of public-service broadcasters and the decline of state-socialist cultural and communication systems. Unacceptable barriers to a balance of screen trade that is even more favourable to the US include local media content quotas, restrictions on foreign ownership of the press, subsidies to screen industries, and subvention and diplomacy designed to assist audiovisual bourgeoisies in exporting their product. The GATT has been the space for playing out these desires.

After the US failed to have cultural industries incorporated in the 1988 Free Trade Agreement with Canada, its foreign-service and trade officials were concerned to thwart EC plans for import quotas on audiovisual texts. The Community's 'Television Without [intra-European] Frontiers' directive drew particular ire for its 50 per cent limit on imported texts. But attempts to have the Uruguay Round of the GATT derail such policies were almost universally opposed, with significant participation from India, Canada, Japan, Australia, all of Europe, and the Third World in the name of cultural sovereignty. This position equated cultural industries with environmental protection or the armed forces, as beyond neoclassicism. Of course, American negotiators argued that the GATT must 'agree to disagree on motives – cultural sovereignty or business opportunity – and then start negotiating.'[1]

Despite this coalition of forces, everyone saw the French as the true bulwarks against open audiovisual trade. Hence my title's troping reference to Jack Lang, initially French Minister for Culture and then with added responsibility for Communication (and finally Education) over most of the decade up to the conclusion of the GATT. He vigorously contested American dominance in the area, and his conservative successors, including Communications Minister Carignon, were just as nationalistic over the issue.[2] Lang ran a dualistic policy divided between the promotion of cultural industries, such as film, and the conservation of national heritage. The expansion of his portfolio responsibilities to include communications was a recognition of the significance of TV in both these areas. In the audiovisual sphere, he wanted to build French audiences, to draw them from Hollywood by following a producer- and writer-led model of industry development. At the 1993 Venice Film Festival, he outraged an audience that included Steven Spielberg and Martin Scorsese with a splenetic diatribe against American film (Hayward 1993: 383–4; Weinraub 1993: L24). Meanwhile, US government agencies were pressuring distributors, exhibitors, and politicians around the world to open up the audiovisual sector to additional imports, leading to bizarre acts of resistance such as Korean film-industry people releasing snakes into theatres during screenings of *Fatal Attraction* (Adrian Lyne,1987) to scare audiences away (Buck 1992:129).

Some crucial facts are forgotten in this terpsichory of diplomatic and business hypocrisy. The US government endorses trust-like behaviour overseas, whilst prohibiting it domestically. And its local film industry has been aided through decades of tax-credit schemes, film commission assistance, state and Commerce Department representation, the Informational Media Guaranty Program's currency assistance, and oligopolistic domestic buying and overseas selling practices that (without much good evidence for doing so) keep the primary market essentially closed to imports on grounds of popular taste (Guback 1987: 92–3, 98–9; Schatz 1988: 160; Thompson 1985: 117–18, 122–3; Guback 1984: 156–7). After the Second World War, Hollywood's Motion Picture Export Agency even referred to itself as 'the little State Department', so isomorphic were its methods and contents with US policy and ideology. Meanwhile, the Justice Department is authorized to classify all imported films, which it can proscribe as 'political propaganda' (as it has done with Canadian documentaries on acid rain and nuclear war, for instance) (Sorlin 1991: 93; Parker 1991: 135, 137).

And too much is made of the barriers to American exports. Western Europe, the target of so much American concern in this area, has 10 per cent of its TV airtime filled by American materials, which amounts to two-thirds of US trade in TV. By contrast, the total of all foreign imports to the US is perhaps 2 per cent of its programme schedule. Washington/Hollywood/New York preside over the most closed television and cinema space in world history. In any case, the EC is clearly an expanding market for imports, despite its cultural protectionism: US film revenue from members of the Community increased throughout the 1980s, to 90 per cent of total sales there by 1990. If we consolidate TV, film and video textual traffic, the balance of screen trade is clearly lopsided. As at mid-1994, the American industry relied on exports for US $8 billion of its annual revenue of US $18 billion, with 55 per cent of that coming from Western Europe (*Daily Variety* 1994:16). Europe imported US $3.7 billion in 1992, compared to US $288 million in reciprocal sales; and the disparity is increasing. Overseas hard-top exhibition is now a more significant source of US revenue than domestic receipts, as the new multiplexes have massively increased attendances throughout Europe over the 1990s (Hill 1994a: 2, 7 n. 4; *Film Journal* 1994: 3). The top-ten grossing Hollywood films of 1992 all made more money overseas than at home, while screen exports totalled US $6.7 billion in 1991, up 13 per cent on the previous year and double the figure from a decade earlier. Film rentals amounted to US $4 billion in 1993, more than half from outside the US. Between 1988 and 1993, international box office receipts increased by 14 per cent, domestic ones by just over half that figure (Miller 1993: 102; Groves 1994: 18). What are the industrial implications of this increasingly global nature of the screen?

THE NEW INTERNATIONAL DIVISION OF CULTURAL LABOUR

During the months leading up to the signing of the GATT protocols in 1993, production of the TV series *White Fang* in New Zealand was halted, and workers left unpaid, because French finance was in disarray awaiting the outcome.

(*On Film* 1993: 1)

We have created a product that by, say, putting the name of Warner Brothers on it is a stamp of credibility. But that could be an Arnon Milchan film, directed by Paul Verhoeven, starring Gerard Depardieu and Anthony Hopkins, and shot in France and Italy, and made with foreign money.
(John Ptak, Creative Artists Agency of Hollywood quoted in Weinraub 1993: L24)

The idea of the NICL echoes the retheorization of economic dependency theory that emerged from West Germany in the late 1970s after the unprecedented chaos of that inflationary decade. In place of the classical division of labour models, the opportunity provided by new markets for labour and sales and the shift from the spatial sensitivities of electrics to the spatial insensitivities of electronics pushed businesses away from treating Third World countries as suppliers of raw materials. They came to be regarded instead as shadow-setters of the price of work, competing internally and with the First and Second Worlds for employment opportunities. Manufacturing practices were not only divided within the plant, but across the globe. This process has broken up the prior division of the world into a small number of industrialized nations and a majority of underdeveloped nations. In its place, the life of production is split across continents (Fröbel, Heinrichs and Kreye 1980: 2–8, 13–15, 45–8). How far can this trend go, away from the assembly of infinitely substitutable heavy-industry parts? How well does it sit with a services domain of de-industrialized states? Will they once more lose jobs to the periphery whilst retaining super-profits for their own ruling elite?

Unlike the vertically integrated studio system of the classical Hollywood era, most US film production is now undertaken by small editing, lighting and rental studio companies that work with independent producers and sell their services across a variety of audiovisual industries. Films are shot across the world, but central decisions and post-production facilities are concentrated as much as ever in Los Angeles in a hybrid complex of entertainment sectors. This is efficient for an industry where standardization is important to keep costs down, but innovation remains critical as a hook for audiences. The market functions as a site for the numerous transformative moments in the life of US production in a way that never occurred in the vertically integrated period prior to the 1950s. A combination of

77

anti-trust decisions and the advent of television at that time made for legal and economic forces compelling change. In the decade from 1946, there was a decrease of a third in the number of locally made films and more than a doubling of imports. Production went overseas from the 1950s as the world audience grew, location shooting became a means of differentiating stories, and studios purchased facilities across the globe to utilize cheap labour. Between 1950 and 1973, just 60 per cent of Hollywood films in production began their lives in the US (Christopherson and Storper 1986). This was in keeping with the film industry's advice to Congress in the 1950s that the aim of rebuilding Europe so that it could buy American goods was best achieved through overseas equity investment by US firms, rather than dollar loans (Guback 1974: 9).

American financial institutions are long-practised in the ways and means of purchasing foreign theatres and distribution companies and sharing risks with local businesses. By the end of the 1980s, overseas firms were crucial suppliers of funds invested in Hollywood and loans put up against distribution rights in their countries of origin (Buck 1992: 119,123). Joint production arrangements are well-established between US studios/producers and French, British, Swedish and Italian companies, with connections to theme parks, cabling and home video. These are far from being straightforward instances of a unilateral exercise of power. For instance, when Congress was inquiring into the ownership of Hollywood by Japanese, French and Australian companies in the late 1980s, Milos Forman expressed concern that if a German corporation bought Fox, all the war films could be 'slightly corrected'. The American Film Institute is anxious about any loss of cultural heritage, and others either question what is happening to local US drama that may now be scripted with special attention to foreign audiences, or worry that the importation of 'understated drama and subtle entertainment' from Europe crowds out space for local production. The 'quality' versus 'entertainment' arguments may be shifting – tremulously but marginally – into reverse (Briller 1990: 75–8; Forman quoted in Briller 1990: 77; Quester 1990: 56–7).

But this is not a serious problem to anybody looking in from the outside. Like the scenery and convenience aspects to service industries such as tourism, the international screen has some peculiarities that do not apply to manufacturing. First, it is risky on all but a huge scale: the vast majority of investments are complete failures, a pain that can only be borne by large competitors. Second, whilst new technology problematizes the necessity for the co-location of shooting, editing and financing, it also reduces the need for 'authenticity'. The tide of co-production is clearly towards the NICL, with host governments working together against or with American power. But the overall trend is still for the US industry to attract talent that was originally developed as part of national-cinema policies: expected to compete with North America, not be absorbed by it. This is what Michael Apted recently referred to as a 'Europeanizing of Hollywood' (quoted in Dawtrey 1994: 75). Peter Weir's post-production might take place in Australia, to keep local technicians in work and satisfy off-screen indices of localism in order to obtain state financing, but does that make for a textual disinvestment away from Hollywood?

CULTURAL POLITICS: EUROPE = CIVICS, US = COKE

FBI + CIA = TWA + Pan Am – graffito written by Eve Democracy in
One + One

(Jean-Luc Godard, 1969)

Think of the Mexican entertainment market, with its young population and
fast-growing middle class, as a teenager out looking for a good time after
being cooped up for too long. For economically emerging peoples all over
the globe, Hollywood speaks a universal language.

(Gubernick and Millman 1994: 95)

Worried that free trade is making their indolent lifestyle less viable, the
French are blaming sinister conspiracies and putting quotas on American
movies.

(Brooks 1994: 34)

If the European Commission governments truly care about their citizens'
cultural preferences, they would permit them the freedom to see and hear
works of their choosing; if they are really concerned about a nation's cultural
heritage, they would encourage the distribution of programming reflecting
that heritage.

(Jack Golodner, President of the Department for Professional Employees,
AFL-CIO, 1994: H6)

The 1993 GATT agreement on services, seven years in the making, was at risk
until the last. Agriculture had long drawn the headlines in the business press, but
the final obstacle – and the one that really made the negotiations subject to intense
general interest – was the dispute enacted between Western Europe and North
America, effectively France against the United States, over these questions of film
and TV. The Americans sought a stop to all EC subsidies and quotas, arguing
from the precepts of neoclassical economics for an untrammelled play of
comparative advantage inside laws of supply and demand. Conversely, the French
argued from an entirely other set of precepts, which accepted that cultural products
are public as well as private goods, with an historic and national significance
inimical to the calculus of utilitarian individual maximization. These were
fundamentally different forms of debate: one justifying monopolistic competition
on the grounds of the fabled sovereign consumer, the other justifying state support
in the name of the fabled sovereign citizen. Where the consumer was a fully
formed subject making a rational choice in favour of entertainment and distraction,
the citizen was an insufficiently knowing subject in need of education in civic
presence and fealty.

Both positions are the outcome of contingent moralisms. For example, the
Office of the United States Trade Representative placed Australia on its 'Priority
Watch List' in 1992 because of state assistance to local television content, at the
same time as it was granting Australian dairy, beef and sugar producers access to

79

between 0 and 4 per cent of its domestic markets (Miller 1993: 117). And US governments have often been alarmed at the very international, arriviste nature of their own industry (French 1994: 37). For its part, the EC's process of unification has been four decades of disagreement over the primacy of state sovereignty over supranationalism, internal economic competition versus cooperation, and centralized as opposed to demotic decision-making (Hainsworth 1994: 9). The abiding logic of the Community's audiovisual policy is commercial: it clearly favours existing large concerns that can be built upon further. And the NICL has served to bring into doubt the opposition US – entertainment, Europe – education, with art cinema effectively a 'Euro-American' genre in terms of finance and management, and, as was noted earlier, much of Hollywood itself owned by foreigners (Lev 1993). In this sense, the seeming discontinuity with earlier concerns, when the EC had a primarily economic personality, is misleading: a notion of cultural sovereignty underpins concerns vis-à-vis the US, but so too does support for monopoly capital and the larger states inside its own walls (Burgelman and Pauwels 1992). Meanwhile, the old notions of state cultural sovereignty that were so crucial to Europe's political traditions are being attenuated by the twin forces of 'bruxellois centralization' from outside and separatist ethnicities from within (Berman 1992: 1515).

For a long period towards the end of the Uruguay Round, Bill Clinton's team of negotiators seemed to be indefatigably opposed to the French. His administration was indebted to Hollywood for political and financial aid, and subject to prolonged campaigns by studio heads, producers and directors as well as on-the-spot lobbying in Geneva by Jack Valenti, head of the Motion Picture and Motion Picture Export Associations of America (Grover and Lewyn with Javetski 1994: 35). Early in December 1993, Clinton's principal delegate, Micky Kantor, accepted continued state subvention of cultural production in Europe and elsewhere, whilst remaining committed to the removal of levies on cinema admissions and video hire and purchase. But a week later, even this was gone in the interests of achieving some outcome at the GATT for the many years of effort (Hill 1994a: 1).

It would be a mistake to regard the exclusion of audiovisual trade from the Marrakesh accord as a conclusion to the debate, however. As Jaques Attali (1994), founding President of the European Bank for Reconstruction and Development, has said, an agreement to disagree is no zero signified. Not only will the WTO address what was left undecided, but the advent of new cultural and communications technologies will further complicate our understanding of the audiovisual sector and make protectionism – and copyright – increasingly complicated. It may even be that part of the European taste for Hollywood is formed, paradoxically, by exposure to its own production; in other words, the US is an entertainment 'other', alluring precisely because it has the weight of Europe against it, and hence benefiting from competition that would not be present without the subsidised screen. For to be left with a monopoly in inessential items – which is what Hollywood desires – is ultimately to run out of stimulus, difference and appeal. In addition, local production encourages increased consumption, which serves the interests of all producers, especially with the growth in video-cassette recorder ownership, whilst also creating new story ideas for Americans to feed on (Brooks 1994: 46–7). On the negative side of the ledger, the WTO is unlikely to do much for screen growth in Africa, where local film industries are in any event hampered by the International Monetary Fund's insistence on severe currency devaluations (building on the monopolistic conduct of the legally validated American Motion Picture Export Company (Africa)) (Ukadike 1994: 306; Guback 1984: 157).

Inside the US, doubts are being expressed about the entire GATT process. Although the outcome will ultimately benefit the great and powerful, in the first instance it must eliminate tariffs of its own. Legislation means that this loss of revenue, potentially US $12 billion, has to be offset by increased taxes or decreased spending. The Commerce Department immediately turned towards broadcasting – the one domain that had lost out at the GATT – as a wealthy area that could afford a spectrum tax. This brought predictable condemnation (Wharton 1994: 6).

From the other side, the British, for instance, have remained dubious about French notions of culture. As one official put it, 'we can't expect viewers to watch Jacques Tati films the whole time' (quoted in Collins 1994: 92). And US firms are negotiating on a country-by-country basis over most communications issues, regardless of the European bloc's stance at the GATT (*Emmy* 1994: A17). Sony Entertainment published a report in mid-1994 that argued against EC quotas as inimical to the very producers they are designed to assist. The Community itself makes both hostile and friendly sounds, with many commercial TV networks failing to observe national production quotas, while Valenti is claiming that the film and television industries should be conceptually disaggregated in policy making, as the latter is clearly growing of its own accord (Stern 1994b: 39; Zecchinelli 1994: 13; Stern 1994c: 1). Meanwhile, France and the US have announced informal bilateral talks, and Spielberg is being reinvented by Paris. After *Jurassic Park*, he was derided in Europe for rampant commercialism, drawing particular opprobrium from French Culture Minister Jacques Toubon. And Spielberg was among the Hollywood directors who argued against the European position in the GATT. But less than a year later, *Schindler's List* was being hailed as a triumph of serious filmmaking, and he was invited to meet Mitterand to discuss both the Holocaust and the film industry. He left the Élysée Palace full of support for the continuation of local film making and the maintenance of cultural heritage (*Daily Variety* 1994: 1; Williams 1994: 55–6).

As a further complication, the TV–film nexus continues to be critical. In true NICL fashion, Turner Broadcasting, Time Warner, Disney, Viacom, NBC and others are jostling their way into the centre of the vast and growing Western European industry as sites of production as much as dumping-grounds for old material. And Carignon is now referring to US satellite programming as 'a genuine war machine'. Meanwhile, the new stations throughout the continent invest in local programming with cost savings from scheduling American fillers (Stevenson 1994: 6). And the US Department of Commerce continues to produce policy materials on media globalization for Congress that run lines about both economic development and ideological influence, problematizing claims that Hollywood is pure free enterprise and that its government is uninterested in blending trade with cultural change (Ferguson 1992: 83–4).

The head-to-head confrontation of December 1993 is, clearly, the apex of a far from symmetrical, in fact a quite scalar, form of life. But this is not to argue against the significance of such debates. If the day comes when the United States complains that Japan's ideological objections to organ transplants are non-tariff barriers to the export of the American heart, or takes issue with the French for prohibiting patents on DNA maps on the grounds that they represent an inalienable human heritage, we shall see this debate played out again on less entertaining terrain. For this is the crowded hour of the first instance of economic versus cultural determinations; an hour we should all spend contemplating Daniel Singer's splendid oxymoron: 'GATT culture, that is to say, the resistible reign of merchandise' (1994: 56).

Notes

1 From 1915 to 1952, films were just business in US case-law, with no right to First Amendment protection because the Supreme Court found that they were 'business, pure and simple'. But not by 1993 (Miller 1993: 100; Kuhn 1988: 30)!

2 Two phrases from this section – a directive on television and a minister of communications – indicate the indivisibility of TV, video and film for our purposes here, despite the overall remit of this volume. Television funding accounts for well over half the finance of contemporary European film production, and for its part, the American Film Marketing Association recently opened up membership to TV producers (Hill 1994b: 54; Weiner 1994: 18).

REFERENCES

Economist (1994) 'A disquieting new agenda for trade', 332(7872): 55–6.
Daily Variety (1994) 'After GATT pique, pix pax promoted'; 8 June: 1, 16.
Film Journal (1994) 'Deja vu', 97(6): 3.
On Film (1993) 'GATT quota row puts muzzle on White Fang', 11: 1.
Emmy (1994) 'Superhighway summit', 16(2): A1–69.
Attali, Jacques (1994) 'Hollywood vs Europe: the next round', *New Perspectives Quarterly*, 11(1): 46–7.
Berman, Nathaniel (1992) 'Nationalism legal and linguistic: the teachings of European jurisprudence', *New York University Journal of International Law and Politics* 24(1): 1515–78.
Briller, Bert R. (1990) 'The globalisation of American TV', *Television Quarterly*, 24(3): 71–9.
Brooks, David (1994) 'Never for GATT', *American Spectator*, 27(1): 34–7.
Buck, Elizabeth B. (1992) 'Asia and the global film industry', *East–West Film Journal*, 6(2): 116–33.

Burgelman, Jean-Claude and Pauwels, Caroline (1992) 'Audiovisual policy and cultural identity in small European states: the challenge of a unified market', *Media, Culture and Society*, 14(2): 169–83.

Chartrand, Harry Hillman (1992) 'International cultural affairs: a fourteen country survey', *Journal of Arts Management, Law and Society*, 22(2): 134–54.

Childers, Erskine (1994) 'Old-boying', *London Review of Books*, 16(16): 3, 5.

Christopherson, Susan and Storper, Michael (1986) 'The city as studio: the world as back lot: the impact of vertical disintegration on the location of the motion picture industry', *Environment and Planning D: Society and Space*, 4(3): 305–20.

Cohen, Roger (1994) 'Aux armes! France rallies to battle Sly and T. Rex', *New York Times*, 2 January: H1, 22–3.

Collins, Richard (1994) 'Unity in diversity? The European Single Market in broadcasting and the audiovisual, 1982–92', *Journal of Common Market Studies*, 32(1): 89–102.

Dawtrey, Adam (1994) 'Playing Hollywood's game: Eurobucks back megabiz', *Variety*, 7–13 March: 1, 75.

Dobson, John (1993) 'TNCs and the corruption of GATT: free trade versus fair trade', *Journal of Business Ethics*, 12(7): 573–8.

Drake, William J. and Nicholaïdis, Kalypso (1992) 'Ideas, interests and institutionalisation: "trade in services" and the Uruguay Round', *International Organisation*, 46(1): 37–100.

Facts on File (1993) 53(2768): 931.

Ferguson, Marjorie (1992) 'The mythology about globalisation', *European Journal of Communication*, 7(1): 69–93.

French, Philip (1994) 'Is there a European cinema?', in John Hill, Martin McLoone and Paul Hainsworth (eds) *Border Crossing: Film in Ireland, Britain and Europe*. Belfast: Institute of Irish Studies.

Fröbel, Folker, Heinrichs, Jürgen and Kreye, Otto (1980) *The New International Division of Labour: Structural Unemployment in Industrialised Countries and Industrialisation in Developing Countries*. Trans. Pete Burgess. Cambridge: Cambridge University Press; Paris: Éditions de la Maison des Sciences de l'Homme.

Golodner, Jack (1994) 'The downside of protectionism', *New York Times*, 27 February: H6.

Grey, Rodney de C. (1990) *Concepts of Trade Diplomacy and Trade in Services*. Hemel Hempstead: Harvester Wheatsheaf.

Grover, Ronald and Lewyn, Mark with Javetski, Bill (1994) 'Sunset Boulevard for Jack Valenti?', *Business Week*, 3354: 35.

Groves, Don (1994) 'O'seas B. O. power saluted at confab', *Variety*, 356(4): 18.

Guback, Thomas H. (1974) 'Cultural identity and film in the European Economic Community', *Cinema Journal*, 14(1): 2–17.

Guback, Thomas H. (1984) 'International circulation of U.S. theatrical films and television programming', in George Gerbner and Marsha Seifert (eds) *World Communications: A Handbook*. New York: Longman.

Guback, Thomas H. (1987) 'Government support to the film industry in the United States', in Bruce A. Austin (ed.) *Current Research in Film: Audiences, Economics and Law*. Vol. 3. Norwood: Ablex.

Gubernick, Lisa and Millman, Joel (1994) 'El Sur is the promised land', *Forbes*, 153(7): 94–5.

Hainsworth, Paul (1994) 'Politics, culture and cinema in the New Europe', in John Hill, Martin McLoone and Paul Hainsworth (eds) *Border Crossing: Film in Ireland, Britain and Europe*. Belfast: Institute of Irish Studies.

Hayward, Susan (1993) 'State, culture and the cinema: Jack Lang's strategies for the French film industry', *Screen*, 34(4): 382–91.

Hill, John (1994a) 'Introduction' in John Hill, Martin McLoone and Paul Hainsworth (eds) *Border Crossing: Film in Ireland, Britain and Europe*. Belfast: Institute of Irish Studies.

Hill, John (1994b) 'The future of European cinema: the economics and culture of pan-European strategies', in John Hill, Martin McLoone and Paul Hainsworth (eds) *Border Crossing: Film in Ireland, Britain and Europe*. Belfast: Institute of Irish Studies.

Hills, Jill. (1994) 'Dependency theory and its relevance today: international institutions in telecommunications and structural power', *Review of International Studies*, 20(2): 169–86.

Keane, John (1991) *The Media and Democracy*. Cambridge: Polity Press.

Kuhn, Annette (1988) *Cinema, Censorship and Sexuality, 1909–1925*. London: Routledge.

Lang, Tim and Hines, Colin (1993) *The New Protectionism: Protecting the Future Against Free Trade*. New York: New Press.

Lev, Peter (1993) *The Euro-American Cinema*. Austin: University of Texas Press.

Mayrhofer, Debra (1994) 'Media briefs', *Media Information Australia*, 74: 126–42.

Miller, Toby (1993) *The Well-Tempered Self: Citizenship, Culture, and the Postmodern Subject*. Baltimore and London: Johns Hopkins University Press.

Parker, Richard A. (1991) 'The guise of the propagandist: governmental classification of foreign political films', in Bruce A. Austin (ed.) *Current Research in Film: Audiences, Economics and Law*. Vol. 5. Norwood: Ablex.

Quester, George H. (1990) *The International Politics of Television*. Lexington, Mass.: Lexington.

Schatz, Thomas (1988) *The Genius of the System: Hollywood Filmmaking in the Studio Era*. New York: Pantheon.

Singer, Daniel (1994) 'GATT and the shape of our dreams', *The Nation*, 258(2): 54–6.

Sjolander, Claire Turner (1992–3) 'Unilateralism and multilateralism: the United Sates and the negotiation of the GATTS', *International Journal*, 48(1): 52–79.

Sorlin, Pierre (1991) *European Cinemas, European Societies 1939–1990*. London: Routledge.

Stern, Andy (1994a) 'Euro TX/Film confab indecisive: A/V protectionist policy sought, but no solution in sight', *Daily Variety*, 1 July: 18.

Stern, Andy (1994b) 'Film/TV future tops confab agenda', *Variety*, 27 June–3 July: 39.

Stern, Andy (1994c) 'Valenti denies Euro TV crisis', *Daily Variety*, 23 June: 1, 17.

Stevenson, Richard W. (1994) 'Lights! Camera! Europe!' *New York Times*, 6 February: 1, 6.

Thompson, Kristin (1985) *Exporting Entertainment: America in the World Film Market 1907–1934*. London: BFI.

Ukadike, Nwachukwu Frank (1994) *Black African Cinema*. Berkeley and Los Angeles: University of California Press.

Weiner, Rex (1994) 'AFMA welcomes non-film media', *Variety*, 356(4): 18.

Weinraub, Bernard (1993) 'Directors battle over GATT's final cut and print', *New York Times*, 12 December: L24.

Wharton, Dennis (1994) 'GATT tax buzz wavers: White House not firm on broadcaster levy', *Daily Variety*, 27 June: 6.

Williams, Michael (1994) 'Euros bury dinos, fete "list" auteur', *Variety*, 7–13 March: 55–6.

Zecchinelli, Cecilia (1994) 'Gaps seen for EU TV meet', *Daily Variety*, 26 June: 13.

5

EUROPEAN CO-PRODUCTION STRATEGIES

The Case of France and Britain

Anne Jäckel

The 1993 GATT talks and the vociferous campaign led by the French to exclude audiovisual productions from the GATT Agreement in the name of culture focused the world's attention on France's capacity to retain both a specific film culture and a relatively prosperous film industry. The survival of French cinema in a world dominated by American movies was largely explained by France's protectionist attitude towards its domestic film industry. Little mention was made of the international aspects of French film policy, a policy which, regardless of nationality, has benefited many individuals who, for various reasons, have found it difficult to make films in their own country. In the past, France has welcomed and supported, amongst others, directors such as Losey, Wajda, Kurosawa and Tarkovski. No one would deny that France draws as much prestige and status from its international cultural policy as the film-makers it so generously assists, capitalizing on the overtones of excellence such policy implies. However, French patronage in the world of cinema has not been without its critics. It has been argued, for instance, that France's paternalistic attitude towards its former colonies has produced a situation where black and beur[1] film-makers in France seem to be 'too close for comfort' to the funding bodies (Blackwood and Givanni 1988: 116). Nevertheless, French artistic patronage remains impressive: in 1993, France produced 152 films, sixty of which were directed by non-French film-makers.

Of the 101 'French-initiated films', six were shot in languages other than French, and ten were made by non-French directors. These figures do not include the thirty-six cinematographic co-productions where France was a minority partner (half a dozen of which were in English with a British partner), nor the fifteen films shot by film-makers from the former Eastern bloc and supported by ECO, the special fund set up by the French Ministry of Culture in 1989 (see Table 5.1).

In the early 1990s, the number of films co-produced with a foreign partner remained fairly stable and equal to the number of 100 per cent French films.

Co-productions are by no means a new or a French phenomenon. Efforts by film producers and distributors to extend their influence beyond their national boundaries date back to the beginning of the century. In the aftermath of the First World War, politicians encouraged initiatives trying to establish coalitions with

Table 5.1 French cinematographic production, 1987–93

	1987	1988	1989	1990	1991	1992	1993
Total number of films registered	133	137	136	146	156	155	152
Number of 'French-initiated' films	113	115	101	106	108	113	101
Number of 100 per cent French films	96	93	66	81	73	72	67
Number of co-productions (French majority)	17	22	35	25	35	41	34
Number of co-productions (French minority)	20	22	35	37	36	31	36
Total number of co-productions	37	44	70	62	71	72	70
ECO films				3	12	11	15

Source: CNC Info, 1994

foreign partners. The 1920s were a period of fertile activities by Scandinavian, British, French, Italian and German film companies to establish European film concerns in order to combat the economic and cultural dominance of Hollywood on the world market. For a variety of reasons, all those attempts collapsed in the 1930s (Vincendeau 1988: 29). They were revived in the late 1940s with the negotiation by national governments of international co-production treaties. France and Italy were the first countries to sign a co-production agreement in 1949. The Franco-Italian Agreement was a response by the two governments to bring back production to pre-war levels and to offset the damaging effects of the invasion of American films (Guback 1969: 39).

Within a few years the aims and objectives of the Agreement were fulfilled. The Italian and French industries had substantially increased their production, employment figures had risen, French and Italian actors had achieved international stardom, and many of the co-produced films were not only popular in both their domestic markets but also in the rest of Europe and beyond. The Treaty marked the beginning of a long partnership between the two countries. Today, well over 1,500 films have been made under the Franco-Italian Agreement. On the negative side, anecdotes on abuses abound and the Agreement has not always been successful in preventing Americans taking advantage of French and Italian subsidies. One can hardly claim that all Franco-Italian films are masterpieces, but many of the Classics of European cinema were developed as co-productions: Visconti's *Rocco and his Brothers*, Jean Luc Godard's *Contempt*, Alain Resnais's *Last Year in Marienbad*, and many of Fellini's films were made under the official Agreement. The system worked well because co-producers came from countries with cultural affinities, a similar industrial and institutional framework, comparable schemes of incentives and markets which could claim, until the 1980s, a more or less equal potential. Such fruitful cooperation not only led the two countries to sign agreements with other partners, but encouraged other countries to follow their example. Today, France has co-production agreements with almost forty countries and co-productions have become a way of life for the smaller countries of Europe.[2] Both co-productions within the EU and European partnerships with North America, Australia and the Far East are on the increase.

Britain entered the field of co-productions relatively late in the day and, for a long time, the number of films co-produced under its official agreements remained insignificant, even those made with France, the first and the most productive of its European partners. Linguistic and cultural differences, as well as opposing film policies and practices, made it difficult for the two film industries to cooperate under the Anglo-French Agreement. During the first twenty-five years of its existence, the Agreement signed by Britain and France in 1965 barely produced an average of one film per year.

The first registered co-productions include a forgotten Brigitte Bardot vehicle (*Two Weeks in September*), and two of the most expensive productions made in the late 1960s, *The Night of the Generals* and *Mayerling*. Anatole Litvak's film about the plot to assassinate Hitler was shot in Poland with Peter O'Toole and

Omar Sharif. For his version of the tragic love affair between Prince Rudolf of the Austro-Hungarian Empire with Maria Vetsera, Terence Young used Viennese locations and an international star-laden cast led by Omar Sharif, Catherine Deneuve, James Mason and Ava Gardner. On the whole, the films co-produced under the aegis of the Anglo-French Agreement laid little claim to British or French culture. Least of all *Moonraker*, the most expensive and the most successful James Bond movie of the 1970s, a film shot on location in France, Italy, Brazil, Guatemala, the United States and in outer space. Several Anglo-French films had record budgets in their times, such as *Moonraker* in 1978, Fred Zinnemann's adaptation of Frederick Forsyth's novel, *The Day of the Jackal*, Roman Polanski's *Tess*, and in the late 1980s, Axel Corti's *The King's Whore* and Milos Forman's *Valmont*. A James Bond film, a thriller made by a Hollywood studio director in 1972, a film made by the Paris-born Polish director of *Rosemary's Baby* and *Chinatown*, costume dramas directed by an Austrian and a Czech living in California. How did those films come to qualify for co-production status?

Before establishing nationality criteria, the Anglo-French Agreement states that 'films of high quality, capable of enhancing the reputation of the film industries of the two countries, should benefit from the provisions of the Agreement'. In the past and particularly at times when the respective domestic film industries were facing a slump, high quality often came to mean films with an international appeal, usually backed by foreign (American) investment. In the case of *Moonraker*, with three major French studios fully occupied for months and special effects offering a new challenge to British studios,[3] who was to complain if the Board of Trade or the Centre National de la Cinématographie (the French film body) were to ask for a few more 'nationals' to be included in the film credits?

In the early 1980s, only a trickle of commercially unsuccessful British–French films whose official status was left unconfirmed by the authorities were made. After 1985, cultural, institutional and political differences prevailed. With, on the British side, a producer/scriptwriter approach, close links with Hollywood and a lack of incentives under a Conservative government which appointed a new Minister for the Arts almost every year, and, on the French side, a directorial approach and the introduction of a new system of tax-shelter by a socialist government whose flamboyant Minister of Culture, Jack Lang, was openly committed to a programme of state intervention in the film industry, little wonder co-productions between France and Britain came to a halt for three years.

In the late 1980s, however, the prospect of a unified Europe, combined with the deteriorating situation of theatrical admissions for the domestic products in France, led to the resurrection of the Anglo-French Agreement. Lacking incentives in Britain, and under pressure from their American partners to find ways to enter a market which promised to be twice as large as the American one, British producers began to look to the other side of the Channel for co-producing partners. They found French producers eager to endorse the statement made by a Unifrance official that 'the international appeal of films shot in English such as *The Bear* or

The Big Blue seemed to bear out the logic of France producing a handful of costly international pictures a year'. For French producers, making films under the official Agreement was a safer option in a country inclined to legislate in favour of national quotas and prone to defend and promote the French language, even though the evidence shows that the 'competent authorities' were often willing to ignore blatant irregularities.

The three British–French co-productions made in the late 1980s were all large-budget movies with high production values which included American stars and directors. These were Richard Lester's *The Return of the Musketeers*, Jerry Schatzberg's adaptation of Fred Uhlman's novel *Reunion*, a story of friendship set in Germany in the 1930s, and *Valmont* with Colin Firth in the title role and two American actresses playing the devious Marquise de Merteuil (Annette Bening) and the virtuous Madame de Tourvel (Meg Tilly). Forman was allowed to shoot his version of Choderlos de Laclos's *Dangerous Liaisons* in authentic Baroque locations such as the Opera Comique and the Chapel of Versailles. In terms of themes, cast, locations and marketing, the three films bear striking similarities with the first films made under the Anglo-French Agreement in the late 1960s. The choice of British and French producers to base their renewed collaboration upon a common European heritage of history and high culture seemed a safe commercial proposition but, unfortunately, neither the old recipe of a sequel to a swashbuckling adventure shot almost twenty years earlier – with the same but now older stars – nor the high production values of *Reunion* and *Valmont* worked with domestic or international audiences.[4]

The following years proved even worse for the large-budget British–French co-productions. *The King's Whore*, the first film to fly the European banner at Cannes in 1990, was booed by the festival audience. Directed by the late (Paris-born) Austrian film-maker Axel Corti and scripted by French director Daniel Vigne, the film claimed a much criticized multinational cast in which a British actor played an Italian king who falls in love with a French countess (played by an Italian-born American actress) married to an Italian count (played by a French actor). *The King's Whore* was cited as 'the classic Euro-pudding of all time' (*The Guardian*, 18/6/90: 36), a label also bestowed upon another Franco-British film, *Mister Frost*, although two of the stars were American (Jeff Goldblum and Kathy Baker)! Yet neither critical rebuff nor commercial failure dented the enthusiasm of the British or the French producers and, by 1991, a fully-fledged programme of large-scale films had gone into production. Six of the eight most costly productions started in France that year were registered under the Anglo-French Agreement. The use of the English language and the size of the investments involved had traditionally set British–French films apart from other European co-productions, but the budgets of *1492, Conquest of Paradise* (over $43m), *The Lover* ($30m) and *City of Joy* ($27m) reached unprecedented levels. On the one hand, the film-events of Ridley Scott, Jean Jacques Annaud and Roland Joffe responded to the demands of distributors for spectacular films and reflected the ambitions of their entre-preneurial producers, Canadian-born Jake Eberts of Allied Film Makers, Claude

Berri of Renn Productions and Alain Goldman, the French producer of *1492*, all prepared to engage in risky projects with or without American backing. On the other hand, the European directors' endeavours to shoot 'unfilmable' stories in 'impossible' locations represented a challenge few financiers were prepared to take.[5]

All British–French co-productions made between 1988 and 1992 were shot in English, even 80 per cent French films such as *Valmont* and *The Lover*. The British partners responsible for raising finance often proved unable to fund their side of the deal from UK sources.[6]

Despite the lack of British finance and the fact that the films were shot in far-away locations where costly sets had to be built and hundreds of extras hired (in India for *City of Joy*, in Vietnam in the case of *The Lover*, in Costa Rica for *1492*), and that, in the case of the majority French film *The Lover*, the main principals were non-French nationals, the films were registered under the official co-production Agreement.[7] That the films were made under the terms of the Anglo-French Agreement in spite of such obvious irregularities is highly informative on how far European – notably French – policy-makers were prepared to go to let European films have a chance to compete with American products.[8] A 'glossy style', high production values, a massive distribution and a mixed – not to say a poor – critical domestic reception were characteristics *The Lover* and *1492* shared with Roman Polanski's *Bitter Moon* and Louis Malle's *Damage*, another two British–French co-productions released in 1992.

Although disappointing, their overall performance was still far better than that of indigenous British or French films that year. Snubbed by British audiences, *The Lover* and *1492* were the only two 'French films' to enter the Top Ten Chart in France. *1492* was the best performing domestic film in Spain and *The Lover* and *Damage* did particularly well in Japan. In North America, the better performance of *City of Joy* (at no. 90 in *Variety's* top rentals with $14m)[9] seemed to confirm that, in order to access the US market, a significant degree of American input was a prerequisite.

The use of the Anglo-French Agreement to make English-language films with global appeal was not the sole prerogative of well-established European directors in the early 1990s. Non-European filmmakers who were attracted to Europe where they felt directors were able to enjoy artistic freedom and recognition, did not find the official Agreement obstructive. In 1990, Australian director Ben Lewin had filmed *The Favour, the Watch and the Very Big Fish* in Paris. The following year, New Zealander Vincent Ward made *The Map of the Human Heart*, a Canadian–Australian–French–British film, and Argentine Luis Puenzo shot his adaptation of Camus's novel, *The Plague*, in Buenos Aires. 1993 saw the release of *Friends*, Elaine Proctor's South African drama, and *Orlando*, an adaptation of Virginia Woolf's novel, Sally Potter shot on location in Russia in a deal with Lenfilm studios. In 1994, came *A Business Affair*, a smart comedy about a romantic triangle set in literary circles, scripted and directed by Charlotte Brandstrom, a French, Swedish-born LA-based filmmaker, *The Prince of Jutland*, an historical drama shot in Denmark by the Oscar-winner director of *Babette's Feast* (Gabriel Axel), and *Before the Rain*, a film directed by the Macedonian-born director, Milcho Manchevski.

By choosing a story that needs a large canvas, filmmakers from smaller countries – in terms of their film industry – are 'condemned' to work with foreign partners. Some found that, in Europe too, the logistics of a story spanning several decades (*The Plague, Orlando*) and/or several continents (*The Map of the Human Heart*) can be problematic, particularly for the less experienced filmmaker who must also learn how to control a multinational cast and crew and cope with the conflicting demands of producers involved in a multiplicity of deals (thirty-five in the case of Ward's film). They also lacked the machinery available to Annaud, Ridley Scott, Polanski or Malle to launch their large-scale film-events, a handicap they shared with the less-experienced French and British nationals directing more modest pictures.

Curiously, whilst the large-budget films of the 'global players' tend to ignore contemporary issues, the co-productions made by both non-European filmmakers and the British and French directors working with small budgets, attempt, with varying degrees of success, to confront and negotiate cultural differences.[10] *Prague*, for example, deals with both the European experience of the Holocaust and the possibility of a new relatedness within Europe. In Britain, Ian Sellar's whimsical portrayal of a Westerner obsessed with his past and confronted with Eastern Europeans living in the present was found so 'contrived' that a reviewer wondered 'if it had been funded by an obscure EC grant encouraging Czech/ Scottish cultural exchange' (*Empire*, no. 41, November 1992: 36). By contrast, French film critics appreciated 'the way the film successfully combined British sense of humour and comedy in a true Eastern European tradition' (*Positif*, no. 378, July/August 1992). Reviewing the film at the Cannes film festival and admiring the way *Prague* skilfully incorporated into the script communication problems and misunderstandings between people who do not speak the same language, *Positif* hailed *Prague* as a paradigm of European Cinema. The strong continental feel of a film like Sellar's *Prague* may have won its director the appreciation of cinephiles and screenings at film festivals, but it did very little to improve the film's chances of success with distributors. If the intervention of British Screen managed to secure *Prague* a theatrical release in Britain, the film, confined to a limited run on the art circuit, floundered at the box office.[11]

The short theatrical career of a film like *Prague* illustrates the difficulties experienced in the early 1990s by low-budget co-productions with a distinctive European flavour. At the 1992 European Exhibition Conference, the Portuguese representative pointed out that 'market prospects for European films were damaged by audience conception of what constitutes a European film, a pre-conception dating from the Nouvelle Vague'. According to Vasconcelos, European films were dismissed by European spectators as 'films difficult to enjoy' (Hopewell 1992: 13). British–French co-productions were no exception, particularly those which did not benefit from generous production and promotion budgets. In the distribution game, priority is rarely given to films directed by newcomers. Some films did not even get a theatrical release.[12]

On the eve of European unification, the renewed collaboration between Britain and France offered mixed results. If the large-scale film-events directed by well-known filmmakers claiming to be 'citizens of the world' were more successful with audiences than the domestic fare, their ratings did not necessarily benefit from the fact that they often came to be regarded as 'Hollywood movies' (and were even labelled as such in the French and British press). The director and producer of *The Lover* targeted their film to an international audience, but to their surprise, they found that, in South East Asia for example, Annaud's film tended to be received as 'a French film'. The discrepancies between the performance of the British–French–Spanish *1492, Conquest of Paradise* in its co-producing countries emphasize the fragmentation of the European market and indicate that, 'on the Continent', cultural and nationalistic considerations continue to play a part in attracting domestic audiences still used to seeing national films with home-grown stars on their cinema screens. Paradoxically, the reception of Ridley Scott's film in Spain and France and that of Annaud's film in France highlight a blatant irony as far as film policies are concerned. In the two European countries most inclined to protect and promote cultural autonomy and linguistic specificity, the dubbed versions of the films performed better than any other national film on the domestic market in 1992! In France, the validity of a policy which allowed films in the English language and with a minimal French input to qualify as French works came under attack from both the intellectual establishment and the film industry. The French Ministry for Culture did not abandon their policy encouraging the production of large-budget films but the disappointing results of the British–French film-events of the early 1990s were not without incidence on subsequent changes in film policy. In 1992, access to French funds became restricted for films shot with a minimal French input and in a language other than French. As a result, between 1992 and 1994, no film with a budget over $10m was registered under the Anglo-French Agreement and most co-productions were British-initiated. The only exception was the tri-partite majority Canadian *Highlander III*.

Well before November 1994, when the Agreement was finally ratified to allow tri-partite co-productions, Britain and France had entered into multi-lateral co-productions (five European co-producing partners were involved in *Orlando*) and non-English language productions. In 1993, *Before the Rain* was shot in Macedonian, Serbo-Croat, Albanian and English; 1994 projects include two French-language films, *Le Roi de Paris* and *Wind of Anger*, and the Russian-language *Chonkin*.

In 1993, the United Kingdom had joined Eurimages, the Council of Europe's pan-European support fund, of which France was a founding member. It had also signed the European Cinematographic Convention (somewhat uncharacteristically it was the first country to do so). Since then, most registered co-productions have received the support of the British Screen-managed European Co-production

Fund and several small and medium-size budget co-productions have had the backing of Eurimages and/or several of the Media initiatives. If, for Britain, the shift to continental Europe reflected 'both necessity and the inclinations of the management of British Screen' (BFI 1993: 29), the co-productions' modest budgets bear witness to the meagre resources of British producers. French interest did not disappear, but the 1992 regulation changes meant that French producers no longer automatically looked to British partners for their international productions. The major French players such as Bouygues and Canal Plus which had already started to invest in the United States could afford to ignore the Agreement and make films in the production facilities they had set up in Hollywood. Others preferred to take advantage of French incentives and invest in large-budget films directed by French filmmakers.

However, as the 1993 French production figures showed, the protectionist attitude of the French establishment and its obsession with francophony should not be exaggerated. The CNC is known to use discretion in applying the rules. Moreover, whilst the rules for accessing the funds of the Automatic Support Fund were being tightened, changes in the Soficas regulations were introduced whereby the Soficas' possibilities of investing in non-French-speaking films were being enlarged.[13]

Somewhat conflicting in nature, those various changes reflect the dilemma of the French caught between their global ambitions and their desire to retain a policy geared to helping domestic production and to promoting plurality and artistic autonomy. From a French perspective, the Anglo-French Agreement offered enough flexibility to depart from rules which could prevent the wider national strategy from achieving its goal and sufficient rigidity to consider complying with them, should such strategy be altered.

In recent years, the Agreement has played an important part in the effort to produce in Europe large-scale international films which respond to the demand of distributors and cinema audiences for spectacular entertainment. Art cinema is also well represented with *The Cook, the Thief, his Wife and her Lover* (1989), *Prospero's Books* (1990) and *The Baby of Macon* (1992). The sustained popularity of Peter Greenaway's films amongst European cinephiles demonstrates that a personal style can transcend national and linguistic barriers (Porter 1985: 9).

On the whole, few filmmakers have attempted to explore the possibilities of a 'new European cinema' (*Prague, Orlando*) and non-EC citizens (Ward, Puenzo, Manchevski) have explored cross-cultural issues more readily than their French and British counterparts. Nevertheless, one can argue that it is a considerable achievement that, at a time when their countries are in the process of renegotiating their own identity, British and French producers are prepared to invest in new emerging talent from different cultures. Clearly, they cannot be accused of adopting the 'Fortress Europe' approach. The list of creative talent involved in the 1988–93 British–French films attests to Europe's capability to attract the talent on which Hollywood had built its reputation. To a point, the use made of the Anglo-French Agreement in the late 1980s and early 1990s may even serve to testify to the vitality of an economic and cultural Europe open to others. In many ways the efforts of British and French producers, directors and policy-makers to work together and the problems they encountered are symptomatic of the situation faced by Europeans willing – some would say, enticed by incentives and others, forced by necessity – to experiment with a changing form of popular culture.

If an archaic piece of legislation dating back to 1965 (and hardly amended since) allowed such developments to take place on the eve of European unification, partisans of deregulation all over the world need not worry about a stricter enforcement of present and future audiovisual regulations by European bureaucrats. However, the latest strategic changes proposed at national and pan-European levels may give reason for concern to both the local film industries in Europe and the advocates of cultural plurality.

In the late 1980s, the strategies adopted by policy-makers for the various European and pan-European programmes, whether EC- or Council of Europe-initiated, along with an increasing range of private initiatives, seemed to bear witness to the ingenuity and the vitality of Europeans in the audiovisual sector. The number and diversity of the Media projects alone were sufficient to disperse any fear of cultural homogeneity. Yet, few of the current nineteen Media initiatives, and the films they have supported, have succeeded in establishing themselves as viable commercial propositions. As a result, proposals have been made to support only those producers who pay attention to the commercial potential of the films they are backing. In recession-hit France too, financial incentives for film production are to be much more closely linked to the box office performance of films both at home and abroad. Ironically, state support and subsidies for 'potentially commercial films' are likely to be less acceptable than for 'auteur films' or films directed by first-time filmmakers.[14] In a country which calls cinema 'the seventh Art' and where the director is still a highly respected (and often self-indulgent) figure and where commercial success is often frowned upon, such new direction makes the production of low-budget art movies more vulnerable.

On the co-production front, the archaic bi-lateral Anglo-French Agreement has now been replaced by a more flexible arrangement allowing for purely financial participation. If the recently amended Agreement better reflects the economic reality of film production, it offers no guarantee that the new co-productions express the diversity of European cultural identities. Nor does it attempt to define how the international/European 'film of quality' should develop in the future. The Anglo-French Agreement does not carry a cultural remit. By contrast, in 1992, the European Convention on cinematographic co-productions emphasized again the somewhat conflicting aims of the Council of Europe: 'to achieve a greater unity between its members' and 'to defend the cultural diversity of the various European countries.'[15] Article 128 of the Treaty of Maastricht also states that 'the Community shall contribute to the flowering of the cultures of the Member States, while respecting their national and regional diversity and at the same time bringing the common heritage to the fore.' It has been argued that the attempted creation of a truly regional (or European) culture may ultimately be a hollow enterprise because the dominant media organizations are already connected to a web of audiences, finances and missions that extend beyond what those regional (or European) policy-makers have in mind (Strover 1994). However, in to-day's politically-correct Western world, the cultural argument is a political force regional, national and international negotiators can hardly ignore.

European rhetoric continues to stress both unity and diversity despite the marked shift in emphasis from unity to diversity in audiovisual policy measures between 1982 and 1992 (Collins 1994: 99). In 1994, a single European culture and identity is still a non-entity. Close examination of the evidence gathered on the films registered under the Agreement between France and the United Kingdom shows that such identity, as reflected in the English-language international co-productions, is little more than a longing for a mythical bond rooted in a lost past and used to sell Europe to the world markets. On the other hand, it also reveals that, in a small but nevertheless significant way, there are filmmakers in Europe who are able and willing to take up and build on the new challenge of exploring the diversity of cultures in Europe. Their films mark the emergence of new symbol systems giving consideration and value to current European cross-cultural concerns. There is no reason to believe that, given a decent promotion budget and a better distribution schedule, their pictures could not prove profitable. The mixed results of the high-budget co-productions can hardly be used to justify the recent move – at national and European levels – to support producers committed to large-scale projects geared to reaching a wide audience.[16] The new proposals, in sharp contrast with earlier priorities given to low-budget productions and the promotion of artistic freedom and creativity, run the risk of cutting short the very experiments that stood a chance of supporting Europe's claim to offer an original and healthy alternative to Hollywood. In December 1993, the notion of fair trade in 'the international image markets' seemed to gain more credibility and to prove more appealing than the old concept of free trade. Large media concerns – whether American, Japanese or European – found it difficult to convince the rest of the world that they were the victims and the small countries of Europe the villains. Within Europe, the GATT negotiations revealed the patently uneven playing field on which European film industries operate. Several countries have shied away from direct government intervention in their rapidly disappearing film industries. Today, European legislators have become more vigilant. A stricter quota enforcement may do little to slow down the internationalization of film production but it will ensure that the proper conditions for indigenous productions are met and that the cultural specificity of the sector is recognized and safeguarded. If the present confusion over issues of artistic autonomy, nationality and popularity reveals a lack of confidence on the part of European policy-makers in both cultural revival and economic recovery, such lack is not reflected in the high level of activity and creativity amongst European producers even though investments in co-productions are declining. There are signs that in Europe, what may have begun as a necessary form of film financing can turn into the production of symbol systems that contribute to the fostering of both cultural pluralism and international unity and understanding. On the ability of such forms to develop depends not only the survival of the cultural specificity Europeans are anxious to defend, but the very possibility of the globalization of cultures.

NOTES

1 Filmmakers of North African origin.
2 Arguably, the most successful collaboration comes from Scandinavia where in 1988, nordic consensus declared *Pelle the Conqueror* best Swedish film in Sweden and best Danish film in Denmark.
3 *Moonraker* was filmed at the Boulogne, Billancourt and Epinay studios near Paris and in Britain, at Pinewood and Shepperton studios (London).
4 *Valmont*, released shortly after Stephen Frears's Oscar winner, *Dangerous Liaisons*, did not arouse much interest in France and its delayed release in Britain did little to help its theatrical performance. In its director's native land, however, *Valmont* was extremely popular.
5 It took four years for producer Jake Eberts and director Roland Joffe to raise finance for *City of Joy. The Lover*'s cast and crew, being the first French team to go back to Vietnam, encountered numerous problems on location. For *1492*, the French producer partly financed his Colombus project by selling its foreign rights. Paramount committed almost 20 per cent of the film budget in exchange for North American rights.
6 Along with *The Lover*, Timothy Burrill co-produced another two Franco-British films, Eddy Matalon's *Sweet Killing* (with Canada) and Polanski's *Bitter Moon*, but the British producer declared he had not been able to raise finance in the UK for all his 1991 projects! Ridley Scott was reported as saying that 'not a penny of British money was forthcoming for *1492*'. It qualified as an English co-production only because he and many of the technicians were British.
7 *1492* was registered as a tri-partite Anglo-French and Spanish co-production in France and Spain but as a 50/50 British–French film in Britain where tri-partite arrangements had not been ratified.
8 Official involvement by both the Spanish and the French Ministries of Culture was acknowledged in the film credits of *1492*. On the Spanish side, despite fierce criticism from domestic filmmakers indignant at the fact that 20 per cent of the Ministry's budget was to go to a film with a nominal Spanish interest, *1492* was awarded 200m pesetas (just under $2m) and its director given permission to shoot in authentic locations in Salamanca and Seville, an official decision very similar to that of the French authorities to allow, in 1988, the shooting of the wedding scene of *Valmont* in the Royal Chapel of Versailles.
9 Taking $3.4m, *1492* only came at no. 111 whilst *The Lover*, grossing $1.5m, reached no. 137 in the North American Chart. Source: *Variety*,11/1/93: 24.
10 Interestingly, in 1985, *Nanou*, the first film of Conny Templemann, a National Film School graduate, about an English girl's involvement with a young French political extremist, was probably the Anglo-French film which could lay more claim than any other to 'addressing the reality of the relation between the two national cultures involved' (Porter, 1985).
11 In the UK, *Prague* only grossed $30,000 and was screened on BBC2 four months after its theatrical release. Its one-week screening at an Art & Essai theatre in Paris only attracted 711 spectators.

12 *Shuttlecock* had its UK premiere on Channel 4 in 1994, *Sweet Killing* went straight on video and to date, *The Plague* and *Turn of the Screw* have not found a British distributor.
13 The Soficas are a production investment tax shelter for cinema and television financing companies (which buy rights in films on future receipts). The Companies are private investment companies (agreed by the Ministry of Finance and the Ministry of Culture) and only films agreed by the CNC can be channelled through the Soficas.
14 Of the 101 'French-initiated films' produced in France in 1993, thirty-nine were films directed by first-time filmmakers.
15 Neither does the amended British–French Agreement include 'a special aid based on artistic merit'. Such aid is part of the co-production agreements France has signed with Algeria, Belgium, Brazil, Canada, Germany and Italy.
16 The poor results in 1994, in terms of box office performance, of the large-budget French films in France also cast some doubt upon a policy privileging large-scale productions.

BIBLIOGRAPHY

BFI Film and Television Yearbook 1994 (1993). London: BFI.
Blackwood, M. and Givanni, J. (1988) 'Black film-making in Europe', *Screen*, 29(4), Autumn.
Bonnell, R. (1989) *La vingt-cinquième image*. Paris: Gallimard/FEMIS.
Collins, R. (1994) 'Unity in diversity? The European Single Market in broadcasting and the audiovisual, 1982–1992', *Journal of Common Market Studies*, 32(l), March.
Dale Martin, (1992) *Europa, Europa*. France: Media BusinessSchool/Académie Carat.
Drummond, P., Paterson, R. and Willis, J. (1993) *National Identity and Europe*. London: BFI.
Durie, J. (1993) *The Film Marketing Handbook*, Media Business School Publication. London.
Farchy, J. (1992) *Le cinéma déchaîné*. Paris: CNRS.
Finney, A. (1993) *A Dose of Reality*, London: EFA & Screen International.
Guback, T.H. (1969) *The International Film Industry: Western Europe and America Since 1945*. Bloomington: Indiana University Press.
Hill, J., McLoone, M. and Hainsworth, P. (1994) *Border Crossing, Film in Ireland, Britain and Europe*. London: BFI.
Hopewell, J. (1992) *Report on the European Exhibition Conference* held in Cork, Madrid: Media Business School Publication.
London Economics (1993) *The Competitive Position of the European and US Film Industries*. London: Media Business School Publication.
Mattelart, A., Delcourt, X. and Mattelart, M. (1984) *International Image Markets*. London: Comedia.
Petrie, D. (ed.) (1988) *Screening Europe*. London: BFI Working Papers.
Porter, V. (1985) 'European co-productions: aesthetic and cultural implications', *Journal of Area Studies*, 12 (1995): 6–10.
Strover, S. (1994) 'Institutional adaptations to trade: The case of US-European co-productions', unpublished paper presented to the 'Turbulent Europe: Conflict and Identity' EFTSC Conference, London.
Vincendeau, G. (1988) 'Hollywood Babel', *Screen*, 29(2), Spring.

Part II

NATIONAL
FILM
POLICIES

6

BRITISH FILM POLICY

John Hill

Fears for the future of the British film industry have a long history and stretch back to at least the 1920s when British film production came close to extinction (Hartog 1983). However, during the 1990s such fears have been aired with increasing frequency. The reasons for this are plain enough. UK feature production has been in decline (and well below other European countries such as France and Italy), the level of budgets has been falling and US films have increasingly dominated British screens and video outlets (accounting for over 90 per cent of theatrical box-office in 1992). A significant factor in these developments has been the role played by government. What this policy has been and what issues it has raised are examined below.[1]

The key event in the evolution of recent film policy was undoubtedly the arrival of a new Conservative government, led by Margaret Thatcher, in 1979. Although it was not until its second term of office that the government's solitary white paper on the industry *Film Policy* (1984) finally appeared, its approach to the film industry was nonetheless apparent from an early stage. The Films Act was due for renewal in 1980 and it had been generally expected that a Labour government would increase state support for film in recognition of its cultural, and not just commercial, worth. With the arrival of the new Conservative administration, however, these plans were immediately put to rest.

This was not surprising of a government whose approach towards the arts in general involved cutbacks and the encouragement of business sponsorship and economic self-sufficiency. However, in the case of film, the new Conservative government was reluctant to conceive of it in artistic and cultural terms at all, with the result that its policies were almost entirely concerned with the commercial aspects of the industry. As such, film policy corresponded to the government's more general economic attitudes: in particular, an unflagging belief in the virtues of the free market, a commitment to the minimization of state intervention in the economy and a corresponding wish to reduce public expenditure and privatize public assets (Gamble 1988). These concerns quickly manifested themselves in a Board of Trade review of the industry, written shortly after the election of the new government, which queried what role, if any, the state should have in supporting the film industry (Department of Trade 1979: 1). The answer was obviously much

101

less than previously and *Film Policy* explained how the government planned to do away with 'the paraphernalia of Government intervention' in order to set the film industry 'free' (Department of Trade 1984: 12). What this meant, in practice, may be seen in relation to the three main planks – or 'props' as the White Paper puts it – of government support for films up to this point: the quota, the Eady levy, and the National Film Finance Corporation (NFFC).

GOVERNMENT POLICY

The quota dates back to the Cinematograph Films Act of 1927 which, in response to the decline in the number of British films in British cinemas, had required distributors and exhibitors to handle a minimum percentage of specifically British films. The government did initially extend the life of the quota but in January 1982 reduced the quota of 30 per cent for feature films by half before suspending the quota altogether from 1 January 1983.

Abolition was also the fate of the Eady levy. This was originally devised by the Treasury official, Sir Wilfred Eady, and was introduced on a voluntary basis in 1950 before being made compulsory under the Cinematograph Films Act of 1957. Designed to return a proportion of box-office takings back to production, it consisted of a levy upon exhibitors' earnings and was administered by the British Film Fund Agency. The government initially extended the life of the levy but, in a plan designed to reduce public expenditure, required the BFFA to allocate a proportion of its funds to the NFFC as well as the BFI and Children's Film Foundation. The 1985 Films Act which followed, however, abolished the levy completely. As the preceding White Paper explained, the levy – like the quota – represented 'an unreasonable burden on the cinema exhibition industry' and was not seen by the government to provide 'an efficient way of encouraging an economic activity that should be essentially oriented towards the market' (Department of Trade 1984: 11, 12).

Similar reasoning was applied to the NFFC. Originally designed as a temporary measure to help alleviate the then crisis in British production, the National Film Finance Corporation was established in October 1948 as a specialized bank to make loans in support of British film production and distribution. Subsequent legislation ensured a continuing role for the NFFC and by the end of the 1970s the NFFC had invested in over 150 British feature films. Largely as a result of growing financial difficulties, the NFFC's activities during the 1970s had become limited and between 1972 and 1979 it was involved with only twenty-nine features. However, with the appointment of a new managing director of the NFFC in January 1979 it looked as if Labour was preparing to increase the organization's funding as well as extend its cultural remit.

In contrast, the Conservatives sought to put the NFFC on an even more commercial footing than before. It ended its support for the Corporation (other than through Eady), encouraged greater reliance on commercial borrowing and, when it was decided to abolish the Eady levy, it effectively 'privatized' the organization. This involved the replacement of the NFFC by the British Screen Finance Consortium (subsequently British Screen Finance Limited). According to the White Paper, British Screen was to continue to fulfil 'the positive functions of the NFFC, while at the same time being enhanced by the dynamic of private enterprise' (*ibid.* 1984: 15). To encourage private investment in the new company, the government agreed to provide £7.5 million over a five-year period, at the end of which it was expected that the company should have become self-supporting. Three private investors – Channel 4, Cannon and Rank – agreed to provide further capital (in the form of loans) and Granada committed later. However, at the end of five years, only Channel 4 had renewed its investment.

In assessing these measures, it would be wrong to regard them as simply destructive. For, in the case of the quota and the Eady levy, it was not so much their abolition which presented a problem as the absence of any alternatives to them. It was already evident in the 1970s, for example, that the quota was not being enforced and that a number of cinemas, especially independents, were failing to meet their quota of British features. One of the reasons for this was the decline in British feature production, such that the number of films registered as British for purposes of quota fell by over half, from ninety-eight to forty-eight, between 1971 and 1979. If the original purpose of the quota had been to stimulate British film production the evidence suggested that it was now failing to do so and that its objective might be better fulfilled by other means.

This was also true of the Eady levy which, by the 1980s, represented in real terms only one-seventh of its original value. Moreover, it had been a recurring criticism of the levy since its inception that its allocation on the basis of box-office success characteristically rewarded those least in need of it. This was amply demonstrated when the details of the levy's distribution were made public from 1979 onwards and revealed the extent to which the most commercially successful 'British' films such as *The Wild Geese*, *Superman*, *Alien* and *Flash Gordon* accounted for the lion's share of the pay-out. Moreover, with the decline in cinema attendances which was a feature of the late 1970s and early 1980s there was certainly some justice in the exhibitors' claims that the levy was not only an increasingly onerous burden upon them but also an unfair one given the extent to which films were increasingly viewed on television and video. As a result, many accepted that the Eady levy should go, but felt that it should be replaced by a different form of levy, either on television or videotape. Indeed, in April 1985, the House of Lords went so far as to pass an amendment to the Films Bill in support of such a move. The government, however, remained resolutely opposed to levies of any kind and it was this unwillingness to find means to support British filmmaking, rather than the abolition of the quota and the Eady levy in themselves, which represented the real problem for the production sector of the British film industry.

This reluctance to support production was also evident in the government's approach to fiscal matters. In 1979 the Inland Revenue ruled that films could be treated as 'plant' and were thus eligible for 100 per cent capital allowances in the first year. As a result of this ruling the financing of film production became more attractive to City institutions which, through the operation of leaseback deals, became increasingly involved in the support of British films (including, for example, *Chariots of Fire*, *Educating Rita* and *Local Hero*). However, despite the encouragement to production which these tax incentives provided, the Conservatives refused to maintain them. A number of amendments to the scheme were introduced and then it was phased out altogether in 1986. Although the White Paper argued that this was designed to 'encourage efficiency and enterprise', the evidence suggested otherwise and investment in film, which had been rising steadily during the early 1980s, fell dramatically in the years which followed (1984: 12).

The major form of state support for film production to survive, in this respect, was the annual allocation of £1.5 million to British Screen. Despite the low levels of funds at its disposal, the company managed to defy the gloomy forecasts of its early critics. Indeed, in both the quantity and range of the films which it supported, it actually did rather better than the NFFC had done during the early 1980s. Thus, while the NFFC was involved in only seventeen completed features between 1980 and 1985, British Screen had a stake (in the form of investments and guarantees) in forty-four features in the period 1986 to 1989. However, although British Screen achieved a generally respectable return on its investments and won some notable commercial success (as in the case of *Scandal*), it failed to succeed as a profit-making enterprise and did not, as the government had intended, become self-supporting by the end of the decade. As a result, a postponement of loan repayments due to the initial investors in 1989 had to be re-negotiated and, in the same year, the Department of Trade and Industry was prevailed upon to provide further funding until 1994 (subsequently extended to 1996).

British Screen, in this respect, benefited from the government's apparent reluctance to follow through fully its commitment to the logic of the marketplace. A part of this reluctance may have derived from a belated recognition of the almost impossible demands which had been made upon the organization. For, while British Screen was required to be run on a commercially successful basis, it was not free to operate as a purely commercial enterprise, obliged as it was to encourage specifically British film production and foster British talent. Moreover, what must also have become apparent was how important a role British Screen had come to play in this regard. In 1984 the White Paper had expected the contribution of the company to British film production to be no more than 'modest'. However, by the end of the decade, British Screen had become the main source of British production finance, outside of television. As such, even a Conservative government must have had reservations about simply abolishing it, especially given the failure of its other policies to stimulate film production in the way that had been promised.

One measure of this failure is provided by the 'Films Minister' Norman Lamont's speech to the Commons in November 1984 when he declared his confidence in the industry's ability to prosper without government assistance. In support of his argument, he cited three 'notable examples' of successful film financing: Thorn EMI, Goldcrest and Virgin (*Hansard*, 19 November 1984, vol. 68, col. 29). However, less than two years later all three companies had ended their involvement in production. The collapse of Goldcrest was particularly dramatic in this respect. It had not only come to symbolize the 'renaissance' of British film-making which was so much celebrated during the early 1980s but had also succeeded in attracting a substantial number of City institutions to invest in film production. The failure of the company, however, reminded the City of the high risk character of film investment and, with capital allowances also ended, City funding for film production virtually dried up. In the absence of other sources from within the industry, it was therefore television which was destined to become the most stable and significant source of UK production finance. The role of Channel 4, in this respect, was critical.

CHANNEL 4

Channel 4 was launched as the fourth national television channel on 2 November 1982. The origins of the channel lie in the Annan Committee's report on the future of broadcasting in 1977 and although Labour plans for the channel, as with those for the film industry, were altered by the succeeding Conservative government, these changes were not as radical as might have been expected of a government committed to market-orientated, deregulatory policies. Most importantly Channel 4 was provided with a clear 'public service' remit as well as a secure financial base. Under the Broadcasting Acts of 1980 and 1981, the Channel was obliged to appeal to tastes and interests not generally catered for by the existing television services and to 'encourage innovation and experiment in the form and content of programmes' (Broadcasting Bill, 1981: 13). Its programme-making was to be financed by advertising, but indirectly, in the form of a subscription paid by the ITV companies as a percentage of their net advertising revenues in return for which they sold and collected the income from Channel 4's own advertising time. This arrangement provided particularly important financial protection for the Channel in its early years as it was not until 1987 that Channel 4's advertising revenue exceeded its income from the television companies. The most notable innovation in the context of British broadcasting, however, was that the Channel, unlike the existing BBC and ITV companies, did not itself operate as a production house but either purchased or commissioned work from independent production companies, the ITV companies or abroad.

It was within this context that Channel 4's contribution to the film industry took place. Drawing on the example of German television (most notably that of ZDF and WDR), the channel embarked upon a major policy of investment in films, intended not simply for broadcast but also proper theatrical release. The results of this policy were impressive in terms of both the number and range of films with which the Channel were involved. In its first twelve years, the company invested over £90 million in 264 films, including many of the most distinctive features of the 1980s and 1990s (such as *My Beautiful Laundrette, Letter To Brezhnev, The Draughtsman's Contract, Caravaggio, Distant Voices, Still Lives, Mona Lisa, Riff-Raff* and *Life is Sweet*). The success of the channel's experiment also encouraged other television companies to follow its example. The BBC became increasingly involved in film production (*Truly, Madly, Deeply, Enchanted April, Edward II, The Snapper*) and, following the experience of distribution problems due to pressures for early television transmission, committed itself, in 1994, to an annual slate of about five films per year intended for a proper theatrical and video release. A number of ITV companies were also tempted to invest in feature film. These included Thames (*A Month in the Country, Dealers, The Courier*), Central (*Wish You Were Here, Prick Up Your Ears, Paris By Night*) and Granada which scored notable successes with *My Left Foot* and *The Field*. Altogether, ITV companies were involved in twenty productions between 1985 and 1989. As a result the number of films dependent upon television finance rose dramatically during the 1980s, increasing from only 4 per cent of all UK productions in 1982 to 49 per cent by 1989, a figure which would be even higher if it did not include the nominally British off-shore productions of the US majors (Lewis 1990).

However, while a number of Channel 4's films proved surprisingly profitable (as illustrated most recently by the enormous successes of *The Crying Game* and *Four Weddings and a Funeral*), the ability of the company to succeed when other sections of the British film industry failed did not derive from any superior financial acumen on its part. On the contrary, the Channel's success in film production, in large measure, depended upon its insulation from purely commercial considerations. Due to the funding of both television generally and Channel 4 in particular, the production of films by and for television does not depend upon direct financial returns in the same way as conventional film production with the result that Channel 4's film policy has not been driven by purely commercial considerations and very few of its films have made them a profit. Moreover, film production, within the channel, has enjoyed something of a privileged status in so far as the relatively high percentage of the channel's overall budget (6–7 per cent) devoted to feature film investment has not been matched by the number of programme hours or audience ratings which the resulting films have provided. The channel, in this respect, has been committed to a 'subsidy' of film production on the grounds of its cultural worth and importance in a way in which government film policy has not.

CHANGING INDUSTRIAL STRUCTURES

What this tells us about the government's film policy is significant. For despite the government's belief in the restorative powers of the free market, it was apparent that the traditional commercial sector of the industry did not benefit from its actions and that what stability the industry enjoyed was the result of a continuing dependence upon the state – either directly in the form of financial support provided to British Screen (as well as to the British Film Institute

Production Fund, the Scottish Film Production Fund, the Arts Councils, and Regional Arts Associations) or indirectly through television, and Channel 4 in particular, for which, through licence and regulation, the government possessed a statutory responsibility.

Indeed, that the industry continued to remain dependent upon state support of one form or another illustrates one of the major shortcomings of the government's commitment to free market economics. For as a number of commentators have observed of the government's economic policies more generally, a reliance on the free play of market forces does not in itself reverse industrial decline. It only reinforces existing market strengths and weaknesses (Leys 1985). This was particularly so in the case of the film industry where state intervention has historically been based upon a recognition that the British film industry did not, and could not, compete on equal terms within the international film market. The withdrawal of government support was therefore unlikely to revive the industry, only enfeeble it further.

The basic weakness of the British film industry, in this respect, derives from Hollywood's commanding position within the world market. Within the West it is only the Hollywood majors which have been able to spread the financial risks of film production in such a way as to make filmmaking, more or less, consistently profitable. This is the result of a number of factors: their scale of production; the concentration of resources and deal-making activity in Los Angeles; the size of the US home market and the ability to amortize costs within it; the ownership or control of an international network of distribution and exhibition interests; and, most recently, an ability to take advantage of 'ancillary' markets such as video and pay-TV. These factors provide the Hollywood majors with such an overwhelming economic advantage that British producers have little prospect of competing on equal terms with them even in their home market. Hollywood domination of British screens has, of course, been a persistent problem for Britain but, in recent years, it has become especially so.

This is the result of two main trends: the decline of the domestic theatrical market and the divorce of production from distribution and exhibition interests. Since their peak of 1,635 million in 1946, cinema admissions in Britain had been steadily declining and reached an all-time low of 58.4 million in 1984. Although this figure has risen consistently since then (reaching over 100 million in 1991) it is nonetheless clear that the returns which a British film could expect from the domestic market were considerably lower than in previous decades. Thus, whereas it was once possible for a British film to recoup its costs on the home market, this was virtually impossible to achieve during the 1980s, even on a low budget. In the face of a similar decline in audiences in the US, the Hollywood majors were able to sustain profitability through income from video and pay-TV. In Britain, however, this has proved impossible and the US domination of the video market is even greater than the theatrical market (with UK releases accounting for only 4.6 per cent of video rentals in 1991).

The diminishing profitability of film production resulting from this decline in the home market has therefore encouraged major British companies to abandon production in favour of distribution and exhibition and other non-film interests (as has been the case with Rank). During the 1930s and 1940s, the British film industry moved steadily towards an integration of production, distribution and exhibition interests with the result that two organizations, Rank and ABPC, dominated all aspects of the industry by the end of the Second World War. This led to a modest domestic version of the Hollywood studio system whereby each company ensured a regular supply of films for its cinemas through production in its own studios, although from the 1950s onwards responsibility for actual production was increasingly devolved on to independent producers. This process reached its conclusion in the mid-1980s when the withdrawal of Rank and Thorn-EMI from production led to an almost complete divorce within the industry between producers on the one hand and distributors and exhibitors (primarily devoted to showing Hollywood films) on the other. This meant that the increasingly risky business of production was left in the hands of independent production companies who put together projects on an irregular or one-off basis (often involving quite labyrinthine funding arrangements as a result of the absence of any one major source of finance). As a result, no less than 342 production companies were involved in film production during the 1980s and, of these, 250 participated in only one film (Lewis 1990).

This growth in the independent sector is, of course, an example of the way in which media production more generally has been increasingly re-structured along what has been characterized as more flexible, 'post-Fordist' lines (Harvey 1989; Storper and Christopherson 1987). The diversification of activity which this represents, however, has been largely confined to production and has not extended to distribution and exhibition (Aksoy and Robins 1992). In 1983 the Monopolies and Mergers Commission found against both Rank and EMI, and their aligned distributors, which they estimated controlled some 60 per cent of the film exhibition market and an even greater share of the film distribution market in Britain. Despite its commitment to the free market, the government was reluctant to take remedial action and it was another six years before even quite modest remedial action was taken over arrangements for exclusive showings. In the meantime the two main circuits extended their control of exhibition even further so that when Cannon took over the ABC chain (as part of its acquisition of Thorn-EMI) the two groups accounted for two-thirds of all UK box-office revenue. This control was subsequently weakened by the opening of multiplex cinemas, mainly by US exhibitors, in the later half of the 1980s. Nonetheless, three exhibitors – MGM Cinemas (as Cannon became following its acquisition by MGM Pathé), Rank and UCI (the leading UK multiplex operator owned by Paramount and MCA/Universal) – still accounted for over 65 per cent of box office receipts in 1993. In the case of distribution, the five leading distributors – all Hollywood subsidiaries – accounted for over 80 per cent of theatrical revenues.

This situation was documented by the Monopolies and Mergers Commission (1994) when it found evidence of both a 'scale monopoly' in the case of MGM Cinemas and a 'complex monopoly' in the case of the main distributors and exhibitors. As a result, it recommended the ending of alignments and a further limiting of exclusive runs. Although the Commission was reluctant to link this monopoly situation to the low percentage of British films on British screens there can be little doubt that the continuing concentration of interests in exhibition and distribution at a time when the UK majors had withdrawn from production inevitably added to the problems of film producers. British films no longer had the security of a guaranteed outlet which a vertically integrated industry had once provided and, due to the alignments of the main exhibitors with the major US distributors, often struggled to achieve a circuit release. Thus, even two such successful films as *My Beautiful Laundrette* and *Letter to Brezhnev* were turned down by both Rank and EMI. Moreover, while the UK majors may have dropped out of production, the internal pricing structures which had been a feature of a vertically integrated industry remained (Relph 1990). These arrangements had been designed to accelerate returns from exhibition and distribution rather than production. Hence, when the UK majors left production they were able to hold on to the most profitable sector of the film business while pushing the greater financial risks on to the producer and production financier.

In such a situation it is not difficult to see how the British film industry of the 1980s became dependent upon television and what state support remained. The shrinkage of the domestic theatrical market combined with the withdrawal of the UK majors from production created a crisis in the provision of production finance which only television and semi-state bodies were in a position to overcome with any reliability. This reliability, moreover, derived from their relative insulation from the demands of the strict commercial environment which made other financial sources – US independent distributors, video and satellite companies – so vulnerable. Thus while the video market in the UK is now substantially larger than the theatrical market there has been virtually no investment in film production from the video sector. The Parkfield Group did invest successfully in *The Krays* but its collapse in July 1990 has deterred other video companies from following its example. Similarly the merger of British Satellite Broadcasting (BSB) with Sky in 1991, one year after its launch, brought to a halt its programme of investment in British film production although, under pressure to meet the European Commission's directive on European programming *Television without Frontiers*, BSB did reach an agreement with British Screen in 1994 to make a modest investment in British productions in return for pay-television rights.

DOWNING STREET SEMINAR

The problems facing British film production came to a head in 1989 when the number of films produced fell to thirty. This appeared to lead to some rethinking of government policy and, in June 1990, Margaret Thatcher herself chaired a one-day seminar at Downing Street on the future of the British film industry. She was apparently sympathetic to the case put to her and as a result of the meeting a number of promises were made: financial support for European co-production; a commitment to MEDIA 92 (subsequently 95), the audio-visual programme of the European Community; a review of policies designed to stimulate overseas investment in UK film production and to market and promote British films abroad; and, finally, the establishment of two working parties on the structure of the industry and related fiscal matters.[2] However, having been belatedly converted to the cause of the British film industry, Mrs Thatcher was, somewhat ironically, replaced as prime minister by John Major only five months later.

The early Major years did, nonetheless, see a modest retreat from the Conservatives' original stance of aggressive non-intervention. A British Film Commission was established in May 1991, a European Co-production fund to be administered by British Screen was also set up and, after a futile attempt to attract private finance, the subscription to Eurimages, the Council of Europe's production and distribution support fund, was finally paid (but only to be withdrawn again in 1995). Following the 1992 general election, film was also reorganized, along with the arts and sport, into a new Department of National Heritage which seemed to suggest that a greater degree of recognition was being given to the cultural importance of film than hitherto.[3] Other initiatives, however, faltered. Plans for an export agency were dropped and the recommendations of the working party on fiscal matters were rejected. This group reported at the end of 1990 and made three main proposals: tax relief for foreign artists working in the UK; accelerated write-offs against tax; and the establishment of a new tax vehicle modelled on the French Sociétés de Financement de l'Industrie Cinématographique et Audiovisual (Soficas). All three ideas were dismissed by the then Chancellor of the Exchequer, Norman Lamont, although, in 1992, he did announce a small measure of accelerated tax relief. As for the other working party, this found itself unable to report at all. The group was initially composed of representatives from the production sector and there was some agreement regarding the introduction of levies on videotape and the use of incentives to distributors to reinvest in British production (Stevenson 1994). However, when the group was joined by representatives from the distribution and exhibition sectors it proved impossible to reach agreement.

During this period, television's involvement in film production also underwent some changes. For whereas a number of European countries have formalized (sometimes through legislation as in France) the relations between television and film, the support for film by television in Britain during the 1980s was a largely unplanned, and possibly unexpected, consequence of government film and broadcasting policy. As such, the delicate ecology between film and television which evolved in the UK during the 1980s was always vulnerable to financial pressures. This became evident in 1988 when the government altered the way of collecting the ITV levy (in effect a tax paid by the ITV companies for the right

110

to broadcast). The levy, originally on profits, was now to be on advertising revenues and this had the effect of closing off a form of 'tax shelter' which had allowed ITV companies to write off up to 30 per cent of their production costs. As a result, the making of features became much less attractive than before and ITV involvement in feature production fell by one-third between 1989 and 1990 and virtually dried up thereafter. The ITV companies' retreat from film production was also related to the uncertainty surrounding the allocation of television franchises in 1991 which led to two companies involved in film production – Thames and TVS – losing their licences. The now notorious system of competitive bidding, used to decide the new franchise-holders, also reduced the amount of money available for programme-making which meant that, given its high cost, feature production was destined to become less attractive to the ITV companies. Disputes over the involvement of Granada Television in film production were, for example, one of the factors which led to the resignation of Granada Chairman David Plowright in February 1992 (*Screen International*, 14 February 1992: 4).

This new commercial climate in broadcasting also affected Channel 4 which, from 1993, became responsible for selling its own advertising. So far it has done so with such success that it is has ended up in the peculiar position of subsidising the ITV network. Nevertheless, this change has meant that the channel has had to become more commercial and that its commitment to high cost programming such as feature film production will inevitably depend on its ability to compete effectively for both ratings and advertising revenue. Indeed, some evidence of the channel's increasingly commercial orientation has already been provided by the the decision of the Department of Independent Film and Video to end its support for the workshop sector and move away from film features. This department has traditionally funded more unorthodox features (such as *The Gold Diggers*, *The Last of England*, *Rocinante* and *The Passion of Remembrance*) than the Drama Department which has had the responsibility for 'Film on Four'. As a result of its decision, the range of films produced by Channel 4 is destined to narrow (Hill 1996).

CONCLUSION

A recent discussion of British government policy towards broadcasting suggests that it has failed to achieve either a coherent market-based system or a clearly regulated practice of public service broadcasting (Prosser 1992). Something similar may also be said of the government's policy towards film. Its commitment to the 'free market' failed to lay the basis for a commercially successful film industry and, as with broadcasting policy, this led to something of a retreat from full-blown market rhetoric. This did not, however, generate support comparable with other European countries or encourage any rethinking of the cultural role which a cinema in Britain might play. Elsewhere, I have argued for the importance of a 'national cinema' which is capable of registering the lived complexities of British 'national' life (Hill 1992). The feasibility of such a cinema, however, depends upon the kind of political and cultural support for film which the Conservative government has chosen not to provide. Without a more substantial and coherent policy for film, and its relationship with television, the quantity and range of British film production is bound to suffer.

NOTES

1 This article is a revised version of a previous paper (Hill 1993). I should also like to acknowledge the financial assistance of the British Academy, London in the research of this article.
2 A significant feature of the Downing Street proposals was their emphasis on Europe and Mrs Thatcher is believed to have been motivated by a vision of Britain as the centre of European filmmaking in the post-1992 European market. For a discussion of the issues which the British cinema's re-orientation towards Europe raises, see Hill (1994).
3 While the establishment of the DNH was generally welcomed, the development of a coherent film policy was obstructed by a quick turn around of ministers. The first minister, David Mellor, was generally sympathetic to the film industry but was forced to resign in September 1992. His replacement, Peter Brooke, announced a series of discussions on the future of the industry in 1993, but he too was replaced before these reached a conclusion. His successor, Stephen Dorrell, came from the Treasury. He was responsible for the appearance of the first policy document to appear since the White Paper on film in 1984, *The British Film Industry*, but departed the DNH soon after to be replaced by Virginia Bottomley (see Department of National Heritage 1995).

REFERENCES

Aksoy, A. and Robins, K. (1992) 'Hollywood for the 21st century: global competition for critical mass in image markets', *Cambridqe Journal of Economics*, 16: 1–22.
Broadcasting Bill (1981), London: HMSO.
Department of National Heritage (1995) *The British Film Industry*, Cm 2884, London: HMSO.
Department of Trade (1979) *Review of Policy on Film Finance* London: HMSO (mimeo).
Department of Trade (1984) *Film Policy*, Cmnd. 9319. London: HMSO.
Gamble, A. (1988) *The Free Economy and the Strong State*. Basingstoke and London: Macmillan.
Hartog, S. (1983) 'State protection of a beleaguered industry', in J. Curran and V. Porter (eds) *British Cinema History*. London: Weidenfeld & Nicolson.
Harvey, D. (1989) *The Condition of Postmodernity*. Oxford: Basil Blackwell.
Hill, J. (1992) 'The issue of national cinema and British film production', in D. Petrie (ed.) *New Questions of British Cinema*. London: BFI.
Hill, J. (1993) 'Government policy and the British film industry 1979–90', *European Journal of Communication*, 8: 203–24.
Hill, J. (1994) 'The future of European cinema: the economics and culture of pan-European strategies', in J. Hill *et al.* (eds) *Border Crossing: Film in Ireland, Britain and Europe*. London/Belfast: BFI/Institute of Irish Studies.
Hill, J. (1996) 'British television and film: the making of a relationship', in J. Hill and M. McLoone (eds) *Big Picture, Small Screen: The Relations Between Film and Television*. Luton: John Libbey Media/University of Luton Press.
Lewis, R. (1990) *Review of the UK Film Industry: Report to BSAC*. London: British Screen Advisory Council (mimeo).

Leys, C. (1985) 'Thatcherism and manufacturing', *New Left Review*, 151: 5–25.

Monopolies and Mergers Commission (1994) *Films: A Report on the Supply of Films for Exhibition in Cinemas in the UK*. London: HMSO.

Prosser, T. (1992) 'Public service broadcasting and deregulation in the UK', *European Journal of Communication*, 7(2): 173–93.

Relph, S. (1990) *A Review of UK Film Production*. London: British Screen Advisory Council (mimeo).

Stevenson, W. (1994) 'Regenerating Britain's film industry: what are the policy options?', in A. Moran (ed.) *Film Policy: An Australian Reader*. Brisbane: Griffith University.

Storper, M. and Christopherson, S. (1987) 'Flexible specialization and regional industrial agglomerations: the case of the US picture industry', *Annals of the Association of American Geographers*, 77(1): 104–17.

7

POLICY RHETORICS OF AN IMAGINARY CINEMA

The discursive economy of the emergence of the Australian and Canadian feature film

Michael Dorland

Times have changed ... [L]arger production companies and software houses ... and the publicly listed production houses are leaving town and beating the competition at their own game rather than circling the wagon. It's time to export or die rather than protect or die.

(Ellis 1994)

THE CANADIAN CONTEXT

Very early on in the institutionalization of the contemporary Canadian feature film, whose initial mechanisms of support were in place by the late 1960s, an astute observer of the cultural scene, a novelist, essayist and filmmaker in his own right, made the following observation. 'The establishment of a feature film industry', wrote Jacques Godbout in 1968, 'is a mirage in our desert.' And it was a mirage not least because of the contradiction between the *discourses* of Canadian filmmakers, who had been lobbying government for the previous half-decade for feature film production and assistance policies, and their own film making *practices*:

for the last five years they have all been clamouring and working for a traditional feature film industry, in which they will never participate themselves and against which, in fact, they have made their films. It is an avant-garde determined to create its own rear-guard – which is a very ironic situation indeed.

(in Paquet 1968: n.p.)

Eight years later, i.e. eight years after the establishment of the Canadian Film Development Corporation in 1968 (and since 1982 Telefilm Canada), the principal federal state agency set up to fund feature film production, a public investment of $21 million by 1977 representing continual annual losses averaging 86 per cent over the period, André Lamy, the National Film Board commissioner, soon himself to head the CFDC in the early 1980s, would come to a conclusion

114

remarkably similar to Godbout's. The entire enterprise, he wrote, of attempting to create a feature film industry in Canada was founded upon an illusion; namely, the presumption that a feature film industry actually already existed in Canadian reality (as opposed to being a long-term objective of both cultural and economic policy). 'The problem of the feature film industry in Canada,' Lamy wrote, 'is precisely that it is not an industry in the classical sense of the word. And any policy based on the *presumption* that such an industry exists can only produce catastrophic results, economically or culturally' (NFBC Archives, Film Policy Box 262, Lamy to Litwack, 13 April 1977, my translation).

The end of the 1980s witnessed various attempts within the Canadian film 'industry' to provisionally assess what some twenty years of public funding of Canadian feature film production had brought about. In one such assessment, Connie Tadros, then editor of *Cinema Canada*, took the occasion of the magazine's 150th issue (of an eventual 169 before its demise in 1989) to review a course of development succinctly summed up in her title, 'From community to commodity'. Until the mid-1970s, she argued, the developmental options had seemed clear: 'One either participated in a communal adventure toward the creation of a national cinema, or one was reduced to a commodity in the American marketplace' (Tadros 1988: 9) If the Canadian industry had grown phenomenally since 1972, 'fed by tax shelters and a weak dollar', it had not become 'an independent industry, despite the rhetoric'.

> The producers who seem most solid today are those working with Americans on projects for the U.S. market. Paradoxically, the film makers we show off at festivals have nothing to do with this part of the industry.
>
> (Tadros 1988: 8)

But instead of 'a truly national Canadian film industry', Canada had ended up with a bifurcated production infrastructure, 'working in the American marketplace, or working within the confines of government subsidy in Canada' (Tadros 1988: 13). In Tadros' analysis, an initially articulate national cultural vision – integrating 'production, distribution, information and promotion supported by government policy' – had resulted instead in a subsidized industry 'so dependent upon public funds and tax measures that divergent points of view find no expression'.

> Without the financial backing of the government, the Canadian film and television industry would wither . . . having used up all the funds available yet having failed to secure its own market to support its efforts.
>
> (Tadros 1988: 13)

In Tadros' account, Canada's bicephalous production 'industry' consisted of a dominant component which as a result of identifying with, and working with, the American entertainment industry, had made considerable economic strides. 'Never has there been so much money circulating nor so many people at work. Never have there been so many foreign sales of Canadian programs, nor so many companies which seem solidly structured to persevere.' But the apparent wealth of the 'industry' had been secured at the expense of a national ideal of cultural production. Instead, that ideal had been replaced by a dominated production component, a subsidised creature of government policies, whose efforts produced 'not the industrial products of a healthy, private industry,' but the independently produced authors' films that 'the government takes on the festival circuit to impress the world with our ability'.

Tadros went on to make various attempts to explain how Canada's two-headed production 'industry' had come into being. A key factor was the ambiguous role played by federal government film policies and agencies that 'had delivered the Canadian industry into the hands of the American marketplace' (Tadros 1988: 12). Attempting to explain why Canadian policies had taken their particular form, in turn, raised the tempting, but problematic, conspiracy thesis in which the 'final arbiters' of policy would be not the Canadian state, but Hollywood Canadians who had 'convince[d] our government that economic independence for the Canadian film/television industry is unnecessary' (1988: 9–10). However, Tadros would conclude that the ultimate pressures on the course of Canadian film policy development were not external, but were, in fact, internal to the Canadian national 'psyche', in the form of a weakness of will – the will to independence, both individual and governmental, most notably. In the end, Tadros was left with the following explanation of the vicissitudes of Canadian film policies: they were reflections of the phantasms of a local production milieu characterized 'by a phenomenal ability to deceive itself' (Tadros 1988: 8). The self-deceptive discourse of the Canadian production milieux, articulated more by what it does not say than by what it does, thus developed in interaction with a state apparatus functioning in response to this deluded discourse. As a result, for Tadros, Canadian policy development consisted in a dialogue of illusions, between, on the one hand, a production milieu given to massive self-delusion as to its own capacities, and, on the other, a state apparatus given to 'totally misguided readings of the industry workings' (Tadros 1988: 8). The interaction between the two would produce film policies she characterized as 'the great lie' (Tadros 1988: 9).

Between 1968–88, then, three different readings, but all attempting to circum-scribe an identical phenomenon: namely, the illusory or imaginary dimensions of feature film policy in the Canadian context. However, to employ such terms as 'illusionary' or 'imaginary' serves not to minimize the reality of the phenomenon: on the contrary, it is to emphasize that one is dealing here with a complex form of language-game whose discursive contours it behoves us, as analysts of film policies, to better understand.

THE AUSTRALIAN CONTEXT

Assessments of Australian cinema since that country's feature film revival beginning in 1968 identify many of the same questionings as found in the Canadian context. What have over two decades of the development of a government-assisted film industry amounted to? What has been the fate of the dream of an Australian national cinema, of the desire to found a film industry whose films would speak of 'the national' as well as 'the local', fusing the workaday world with that of the imagination? From the perspective of the late 1980s, 'the ideal of a[n Australian] national cinema has looked increasingly naive and anachronistic' (Dermody and Jacka 1988b: 117). Australian cinema of the late 1980s was 'safe and respectable', 'middle-class and middle-aged', 'subdued and tame' (Dermody and Jacka 1988b: 68, 74).

> Australian cinema is in a limbo, poised between a past which is a history of the attempt to found a national cinema, or perhaps only a local industry, and a future which is uncertain and only dimly imagined by those who work with this local industry. There is a loss of vision, a failure of nerve . . . in spite of all the surface busy-ness.
>
> (Dermody and Jacka 1988b: 127)

What dynamism was visible stemmed less from the films than from the business side of 'the industry' as a result of changing funding-regime policies. But the point, the touchstone, the justification for this activity remained the ambiguous 'history of the attempt to found a national cinema, or perhaps only a local industry'. In other words, Australian cinema remains positioned within 'the complex set of discourse and institutions in which cinema exists' (Dermody and Jacka 1988b: 128). Put slightly differently, Australian cinema constitutes one aspect of 'a formidable level of government regulation, the purpose of which is to preserve the Australian character of various forms of cultural production, including cinema' (Dermody and Jacka 1988b: 117). Above all, what characterizes this discursive apparatus, of which cinema is but one locus, is the consistency of the rhetorical positions expressed. This is particularly evident in the 'representative policy documents that span the period 1969 to 1988 and which *exhibit a remarkable consistency of rhetoric*' (Dermody and Jacka 1988b: 118; emphasis added). While the specific thematic of this rhetoric need not concern us in detail here – suffice it to be described as 'a realistic aesthetic combined with a unitary conception of Australia's national identity' (Dermody and Jacka 1988b: 120), two principal traits do need to be clearly identified. First, it is a policy rhetoric that consists in the repetition of well-worn formulae ('remarkably short on critical interrogation of the terms in which the debate is couched and the underlying philosophy of a national cultural policy' [Dermody and Jacka 1988b: 120). Second, these formulae, by the late 1980s, remained significantly unchanged since the 1960s and 1970s. As a result, the discourse of Australian cultural policy retains a high degree of autonomy both from changing historical circumstances and practices, is largely impervious to cultural critique (Cunningham 1992), and derives its efficiencies from a political nationalist discourse which 'in spite of its inadequacies . . . does have . . . a *strong rhetorical effectiveness* . . . and is the easiest . . . to legislate for' (Dermody and Jacka 1988b: 120; emphasis added).

DISCURSIVE ECONOMIES

In the case of both Australia and Canada, readily comparable countries in their constitutional and institutional histories as former, predominantly white, British colonies, with similar cinematic pasts and comparable government–film institutions (e.g. the role played by John Grierson), discovering – or rediscovering – the feature film at approximately the same time, in a process of mutual institutional and policy exchange, we are dealing, then, with equivalent semi-peripheral political economies (Alexander 1979). More to the point, however, from the perspective of film policy history, is that the problematic of the discontinuous film industries of countries such as Australia and Canada (or New Zealand) is posed within a shared contextual paradigm of ambivalent decolonization, as Sylvia Lawson (1979) pointed out a number of years ago. Such countries, while post-colonial within the English-speaking world, were emphatically *not* post-revolutionary. In such contexts, the difficulty of film history in the English-speaking ex-colonies is that it is confronted with a double form of continuous colonization, both practical and intellectual, to be recouped into conscious knowledge: 1) for the 'industry', not so much a struggle against American cultural imperialism as (often desperate) strategies of survival *in spite* of Hollywood; and 2) perhaps more importantly, for academics and policy makers, to have to overcome 'the political and cultural apathy of their own societies' (Lawson 1979: 66). Because the ex-colonies were 'politically divided, socially and culturally fragmented' (and in the case of Canada, linguistically fragmented as well), a number of specific knowledge-effects had been produced that would have to be compensated for, not the least being the disarticulation (notably between technology and social structure) characteristic of peripheral economies. Principal among these, for our purposes here, would be the *dualistic* structure of film industry organization. The term semi-peripheral is used here with considerable circumspection. (For an informed discussion of its problematic conceptual status when applied to both the Australian and Canadian contexts, see Resnick 1990.) On the one hand, this entailed the integration since the 1920s of portions of the local industry within the dominant Anglo-American media, in which Australia and Canada would play important roles as junior members of the Anglo-American team, act as markets for media exports, as competitive broadcast programming importers, and as offshore centres of production in which a growing portion of the local industry would be increasingly integrated within transnational production. And, on the other hand, though belatedly, the configuration of Canadian, Australian (or for that matter, British) cinema in the form of what Dermody and Jacka have termed 'displaced national cinemas' (1987: 10). Thus, the ensuing disjunction of film industry organization between the exhibition-distribution-consumption of an *imported cinema* in Canada and Australia, and the chronic scarcity of resources allocated to the *production of* Canadian or Australian films. The fundamental structural disarticulation of industry organization would, in turn, systematically disequilibrate not only the subsequent development of national policies with respect to the local 'industry', but as well the reception context of movie-going (or TV watching) audiences for whom the norm has historically been determined by the audiovisual output of (highly selected) other countries. Among other relevant displacement effects that should be mentioned is the consistently problematic and chronic belatedness of the development of the academic study of the history of displaced national cinemas: not until the early 1980s in Britain, the mid-1980s in Australia, and the early 1990s in Canada, has serious study of each respective national cinema been much more than wishful. As for the study of policy, suffice it to mention, especially in the Canadian context, the perennial difficulties of gathering basic industrial information that have prefaced every official report on the Canadian film industry ever produced.

The point here is that, in the context of displaced national cinemas, of intermittent 'film industries' undergoing the major organizational and capitalistic upheaval represented by the transition towards increased private production of feature-length films – in the growing contradiction between economy and culture that crystallized by the late 1970s in the development of cultural industries policies – discourse, and the various forms of discourse, comes to play an increasingly central function in providing the semblance of coherence making the transition possible. Crucial to the possibility of historical understanding of the intermittent film industries of Canada and Australia is their discursive interaction within what Sylvia Lawson so brilliantly termed 'the polemic for the revival of feature film production' (Lawson 1979: 62). This is, then, to foreground the primarily discursive or imaginary nature of the emergence of a feature film industry in the Canadian and Australian contexts, not as an economic object, but as the discursive articulation of a public idea, an imaginary construct upon which another imaginary construct, national identity, is seen substantially to rest and become manifest. As Dermody and Jacka proposed in their path-breaking study of the Australian feature film revival of the 1970s, this public idea – in effect, the rhetorical project of the constitution of a civil society (Dorland 1994) – is produced by, and constituted as, 'talk' – the rhetoric of lobbyists and journalists, the speeches and statements of politicians, the annual reports of government bodies, the pamphlets and documents of contending interest groups within the industry, and, finally, in the films themselves.

> As a result of all that talk and declamation, 'the industry' was already an over-determined and even fetishized object *before* it had any claim to material existence.
>
> (Dermody and Jacka 1987: 26; emphasis added)

In the historical polemic for feature film revival, the 'overdetermined and fetishized object' that survived over time, since the collapse of an originary, pre-sound 'film industry' in the 1920s, would not be a film industry *per se*, but at least certain elements of a peripheral film production infrastructure sufficiently established to support the periodic emergence of discursive formations (among critics, filmmakers, producers, or government bureaucrats, for instance) that produce

119

'talk' about an imaginary or potential industry. In displaced national cinema contexts, it is the survival of these production elements that made possible the continuation of the polemic. In this sense, the 'film industry' both exists *and* does not exist simultaneously. If its existence in the economic reality of the 1960s and 1970s was small-scale and precarious – as Dermody and Jacka put it succinctly, 'In economic and industrial terms, the [Australian] film industry is small, uncertain, insecure, seasonal, fragmented, artisanal and entrepreneurial' (1987: 23) – its existence in the *discursive economy* constituted by the public talk of its protagonists, in 'the verbal force field in which the industry has been conceived, argued and legislated for, and put into public existence' (Dermody and Jacka 1987: 197), is of another order of reality altogether. It is on this largely imaginary, discursive level that the perhaps naive, but honourable *dream* of a national cinema, and a film industry of one's own, of the desire for cultural independence, of the *aspiration* to cultural modernity particularly as signified in the 1960s by cinema's various 'New Waves,' appealed with especial force to the wishes and vanities of aspiring feature filmmakers, of journalists and editorial writers, of producers sensing new business opportunities, and the politicians of the welfare state's unprecedented expansion into cultural domains that had not hitherto been the object of state attention. In other words, the distinction between economic and discursive realities becomes blurred, particularly in times of heightened cultural nationalism, and in periods of the emergence of new discursive formations, and the legislative and institutional forms by which these emerging discourses will be given more concrete incorporation.

However, as Dermody and Jacka would demonstrate in their study of the Australian feature film revival, the discursive economy of the emergence of the contemporary Australian feature would be formed from the combination of the two major discourses of Australian cinema. Industry-1, the discourse of a national cinema, as articulated by the producers (but also many directors, writers, actors and union-leaders) who became established in the 1970s, represented

> a certain style of film making (modest, artisanal, democratic); a certain style of film (socially concerned, gentle, humanistic, sometimes didactic, but non-confrontational and often aesthetically timid), and a certain politics of Australian film culture – against the monopolies, somewhat distrustful of America and its cultural domination of Australia, in favour of government regulation and safeguards on the Australian character of the industry.
>
> (Dermody and Jacka 1987: 198)

Industry-2, the discourse of initially the traditional distribution/exhibition interests and latterly of the film financiers, packagers, brokers and producers who emerged with the tax incentive legislation of 1980, is, on the other hand, 'reactionary':

> anti-intellectual, anti-film buff, anti-art, anti-government regulation of the industry, scornful of Australian nationalism and the concern about US domination, concerned with the mass audience, bums-on-seats, box-office

dollars and the *business* of film (as against film as art or communication).
(Dermody and Jacka 1987: 199; emphasis in original)

This somewhat caricatural opposition between the two discourses conceals the extent to which each functions as the *alter ego* of the other, structuring a discursive field of binary oppositions – art/industry, national/international, culture/commerce – articulated as 'a melodrama that depended for its sense upon the convention of the absence of a middle-ground' (Dermody and Jacka 1987: 197). 'The life of this industry as a *double personality* is especially striking', for it structures both an operational discursive space and at the same time establishes the limits of this discursive space. Thus, it allows, first, 'the industry *at any one time* to say one thing and be the other', which produces, second, an oscillation over time that evens out

> into an uneasy, uncertain, unconfident status, leaving the industry neither one thing nor the other, neither a repository of the values of a potential national cinema nor an aggressively successful business, pushing into foreign territories. Between these two projections lies a zone of inertia, in which the past is being replayed for an audience that seems to have lost interest, patience, and any remnant of loyalty.
> (Dermody and Jacka 1987: 201; emphasis added)

Third, it establishes the aesthetic – indeed, discursive – patterns that define the limits of Australian feature production (and its discourses) as 'a narrow field of conservative aesthetic choices [i.e. the repetition of well-worn formulae], repeated over and over' (ibid.: 201).

THE DISCURSIVE ECONOMY OF THE EMERGENCE OF THE CANADIAN FEATURE FILM

If the duality of the emergent film industry as a double personality is an especially striking characteristic of the Australian context, it will be even more pronounced in the Canadian case. Because of the linguistically differentiated enclave represented by Quebec, not only would the dualistic structuration prevalent in film 'industry' organization common to the political economy of displaced national cinemas be a decisive element of emergence, but in the Canadian context it would be multiplied and reinforced by the environing social and political organization of Canada as a cultural duality. Not only would dualism bear upon contextual organizing structures, it would apply as well to the political economy of language in Canada, particularly in the 1960s and 1970s politicization of language from an instrument of communication to a symbol of membership in an increasingly self-conscious collectivity that by the 1970s would distinguish itself from the rest of Canada by the use of the descriptor 'Québécois'. Thus, the problematic of feature film emergence in the Canadian context takes place diachronically in not one but *two* languages at a time of rising contestation and renegotiation of the political, economic and cultural relations between Canada's two founding language groups. In this sense, the Canadian feature film is, as much as the Australian, an over-determined and fetishized object, but additionally is the designator of a range of unresolved (constitutional, ideological and cultural) contestations, designating the historical sedimentation of existentially contrived values and norms in search of institutional *denouement*. In this sense, the emergence of the Quebecois feature film has been viewed as part of the larger ideological continuum of the struggle for Quebec's affirmation of its 'national' identity, both prior to and since Confederation (1867) (Véronneau 1987).

Complicating matters here, however, is the fact that the emergence of the Quebecois feature – postulated on the aesthetic, technological and social continuity between made-for-television documentary and fictionalized series production of the late 1950s and the documentary shorts of the 'direct cinema' – took place institutionally within the film agency of the federal state, the National Film Board (as a result of the move of its headquarters from English-speaking Ottawa to largely French-speaking Montreal in 1956). Indeed, the role of federal institutions is paradoxically central to the emergence of French-language versions of the discourses of Industry-1 and Industry-2 in the Canadian context. In the first instance, a francophone version of Industry-1 as the emergence of the desire to make feature-length films (and in some instances to actually do so, as in *A Tout Prendre* in 1963 or *Le Chat dans le Sac* in 1964) identifiably occurs within the National Film Board in the early-mid 1960s. However, this discourse, in the context of its emergence in the National Film Board, is predominantly conceptualized, not as in English-Canada as a private film industry, but initially as a public service cinema (Caughie 1986). In the second instance – indeed, within approximately four years – the creation of a second federal cinematographic institution, the Canadian Film Development Corporation, to support private-sector, commercial feature film making, would be both the result, and the principal institutional embodiment of, the emergence of an Industry-2 discourse that some Quebecois film critics would see as the politically motivated (not to say culturally genocidal) move by Ottawa to 'exterminate the Quebecois cinema that at the beginning of the 1960s had given birth to all the new [forms of] cinema throughout the world' (Staram n.d.: 37; my translation), in order to preserve the American film monopoly in Canada. The difficulty with this view – with Quebecois nationalist accounts of the emergence of the Quebecois feature film – is that the events do not respect linguistic compartmentalizations, but reflect instead the emergence of two cinematic discourses, whose boundaries are far from clearly delimited. Thus, for example, the dualistic institutional role played by Guy Roberge, on the one hand, the first French Canadian to be appointed Commissioner of the NFB (1957–66), but, on the other hand, one of the principal institutional brokers in the creation of the CFDC. One could note the fact as well that the first French-language, feature film makers to come out of the Board (G. Groulx, J. Dansereau, B. Gosselin, D. Arcand, M. Brault, G. Carle and A. Lamothe) will rapidly leave it for an embryonic private sector as hostile to the continuing role of state institutions in film and television production as a counterpart, emergent private sector in English Canada. In other words, if there are two linguistic sites of the emergence of an Industry-1 discourse, one French, one English, their institutionalization will be defined in emergent Industry-2 forms. Indeed, one could say that, in the Canadian context, an embryonic Industry-1 discourse articulating an aesthetic or cultural desire to make feature-length films emerges from within the state film making (and television) apparatus, but, given the reluctance – or for that matter, inability – of the state agencies to alter the dominant (i.e. Industry-2) political economy of audiovisual circulation, of which they are now an integral component, the Canadian Industry-1 discourse has also to seek institutionalization in the form of an Industry-2 discourse, but in the claim to be the embodiment of an emergent Canadian *industry*, thus proposing a shift in the political economy.

This claim itself is partly real, and partly imaginary: it is real to the extent that the advent of television in the Canadian context of the early 1950s had created the infrastructure of a private production industry that had never existed before (see details in Dorland 1991a: 113–15). But it is also imaginary, to the extent that the development of the alternative political economy being proposed is not only contingent upon the reduction of existing state structures, but its future growth was, at that point in time, purely speculative: in other words, from where would the growth of the emergent Canadian private sector come? There were only three possibilities: 1) from the downsizing of the state sector; 2) in co-operation with another cycle of expansion into the Canadian market by American (now television) production companies; and 3) from the actions of the Canadian capitalist state in support of an emergent form of Canadian private industry. In this sense, the dualistic role of the Canadian state would be that of coordinating the first and second options, of inversing the historical predominance of the state sector in favour of the emergent private sector by integrating the development of the latter into that of more developed private industries, that of France principally through the mechanism of co-production (the first co-production treaty between France and Canada dates from 1963); and that of the United States through proposed mechanisms of continental economic integration modelled on the US–Canada Auto Pact (1964)

In this sense, too, the role of the liberal capitalist state, as that of the other actors, is also dual: on the one hand, the development of *Canadian* forms of capitalist enterprise in film, which is a cultural as much as an economic objective, and on the other hand the *economic* development of those forms through their integration within the dominant *capitalist* structures, those of the American (or global) industry. This paradox will be embodied in the discursive ambiguity of the notion of a Canadian film industry as an object of discourse. In other words, within the verbal force field of the late 1950s and early 1960s, in which the 'industry' would be conceived, argued and legislated for, and put into public circulation, the emergence of the Canadian feature film sees the discursive encryption of three intertwining processes of emergence: 1) a *Canadian* film industry; 2) within it, the publicly financed but privately produced commercial feature film; and 3) within this, contemporary Quebecois cinema in its own forms of 1) and 2). However, rather than each process of emergence being the differentiation of a respective object – say, the feature as an aesthetic object and the industry as an economic object – we find, instead, the emergence of a still largely un-differentiated discursive field across which are dispersed conflations of ideological polemics within a bi-nationalism (Canada/Quebec, but also Canada/US) conceived in greater part industrially yet also cultural in its general articulation, but whose individual components within the discursive field are not themselves sufficiently articulated to be articulated into discrete objects. In the period of its emergence (1957–68), the Canadian discursive economy remained disarticulated (consistent with the disarticulations of a peripheral economy). But, contrary to Dermody and Jacka's model of the Australian feature film emergence, the discursive economy of the Canadian feature film in the period of its emergence established a verbal force field in which the dominant discourse is an Industry-2 discourse. If it contained embryonic elements of an Industry-1 discourse, these would affirm themselves in more vocal form subsequently, but not until the early 1970s and then largely in reaction to the predominance of the Industry-2 discourse and its economic non-performativity in particular. In other words, the 1960s witness the emergence of the discursive economy in which an Industry-2 discourse is predominant. In the first half of the 1970s, an Industry-1 discourse develops that, among other reasons, since it is internally divided by the increasingly vocal claim to difference of Quebec filmmakers, will remain marginal to the Industry-2 discourse that, as of mid-decade, is reinforced by 1) the governmentalization of Quebec cinema that follows with the entry in 1975 of the previously abstinent Quebec state as co-ordinator of a replica discursive economy, and 2) as of the same year, the 'industrialization' of feature film capitalization that results from modifications to tax legislation. The 1980s, following the largely self-inflicted collapse of the capital market as a result of the economic inexperience of the emergent private producer 'class', will as a result see the incorporation, by state policy, of the broadcasting system into the discursive economy. Throughout, it should be strongly emphasized, the dominant discourse remains an Industry-2 discourse, constant in its demands for the creation of a private industry oriented towards world markets as the dominant force in Canadian audiovisual production (or 'entertainment software industry', as it currently calls itself) (see Dorland, Saint-Laurent and Tremblay 1993).

SECOND CINEMA FILM POLICY

The discursive economies of the emergence of the Australian and Canadian feature film were dualistic in the sense of being *both* discourse and economy, of both a public idea and an economic *telos*. Their emergence meant that, henceforth, the possibility of *more* speech about an object-field had been institutionalized; but this could not guarantee the coherence of that speech, nor even that it meant what it said about itself; on the contrary, a discursive space had been established that would, at best, allow the emergent industry to continue to be able 'at any one time to say one thing and be the other'. If one can generalize from the Canadian–Australian experience, that experience would seem to suggest that the study of 'second cinema film policy' might constitute a discrete object of knowledge with particular problematics, structures, etc. of its own that would warrant more systematic preoccupation than it has so far received. Indeed, it might be possible to argue that the notion of 'second cinema', in post-colonial contexts, would appear to be a more productive one than that of 'national cinema', to the extent that the latter conceptualization has been so over-determined by the problematic notion of nationality (Buscombe 1980; Straw 1991; a useful typology of the varieties of national cinema is provided by Crofts 1993). The notion of second cinema, as Dermody and Jacka have suggested (1982, 1988), by foregrounding secondariness, acknowledges realistically, on the one hand, the primacy held in theatrical exhibition and distribution in peripheral national contexts by the 'first cinema' of Hollywood; but, on the other hand, at the level of the imaginary, also acknowledges the double dream of not only establishing a film (or television) industry of one's own, but one that also dreams of being able to compete with Hollywood either at home (as in Australia), or, failing that, as in Canada, since the one need not imply the other, abroad. The acknowledgement of secondariness, I would suggest, opens up the study of film policy to dimensions that have been previously either ignored or downplayed. For instance, the acknowledgement of the imaginary dimensions of second cinema film policy makes possible the realization that one is dealing with an historical phenomenon, albeit one that is fragmented and discontinuous, but which has been widely shared by the film cultures of respective English-language contexts (particularly Britain, Australia and Canada) since the 1920s. It further makes possible the realization of the extent to which the dimensions of the imaginary have been the touchstone of various national policies in film, not to mention the larger field of mass communication in post-colonial contexts. This entails inquiry in greater detail into how the dream/desire of a second cinema takes on material/textual form. How has it been 'translated' into, on the one hand, institutions; into, on the other, film-texts; and, thirdly, into policies? How, finally, have these various forms of a specific organization of writing practices formed themselves into history? But, most broadly perhaps, the acknowledgement of secondariness entails the recognition, in the study of film policy, of the complexity of the transition from disarticulated elements of (a state-supported) production infrastructure to the beginnings of capitalist forms of the internal economic organization of film production, of which the emergence of the commercial feature film signifies the highly condensed expression.

Not only is the transition to a capitalist economy always cataclysmic – this hardly bears repeating – but, simplifying considerably, the transition to an economy of generalized exchange is also accompanied by conjunctural transformations in the realms of subjectivity, aesthetics and discursive articulations. In this perspective, one might look again at the Canadian and Australian discourses on national identity as experimental forms of 'currency' (nodes of sociability) attempting to establish a civil economy of symbolic exchange. Such a perspective would make it possible to better understand the various shifting grammars that come into play in the transition to commodity exchange in the political economy of culture. The emergence of the feature film in the Australian and Canadian contexts thus represents particular articulations of the complex tensions between the spheres of economy and culture that all industrializing countries have historically experienced. They are, as I hope to have indicated, far richer moments for the academic study of film policy than has been acknowledged heretofore.

REFERENCES

Alexander, M. L. (1979) 'The political economy of semi-industrial capitalism: A comparative study of Argentina, Australia and Canada, 1950–1970', Ph.D. dissertation, McGill University, Montreal.

Buscombe, Edward (1980) 'Film history and the idea of a national cinema,' *Australian Journal of Screen Theory*, 9 and 10: 141–53.

Caughie, John (1986) 'Broadcasting and cinema', in Charles Barr (ed.) *All Our Yesterdays: 90 Years of British Cinema*. London: BFI.

Crofts, Stephen (1993) 'Reconceptualising national cinemas', *Quarterly Review & Film*, 14(3).

Cunningham, Stuart (1992) *Framing Policy: Criticism and Policy in Australia*. Sydney: Allen & Unwin.

Dermody, Susan and Jacka Elizabeth (1982) 'Second cinema: first principles', unpublished paper read at the 1982 Society for Cinema Studies Conference, Los Angeles.

Dermody, Susan and Jacka, Elizabeth (1987) *The Screening of Australia: Anatomy of a Film Industry*. Sydney: Currency Press.

Dermody, Susan and Jacka, Elizabeth (1988a) *The Screening of Australia: Anatomy of a National Cinema*. Sydney: Currency Press

Dermody, Susan and Jacka, Elizabeth (1988b) *The Imaginary Industry: Australian film in the late '80s*. North Ryde: AFTRS Publications.

Dorland, Michael (1991a) 'The Discursive economy of the emergence of the Canadian feature film: discourses of dependency and the governmentalisation of a displaced national cinema, 1957–1968', Ph.D. dissertation, Concordia University, Montreal.

Dorland, Michael (1991b) '"We of the never never": Second cinema film policy as an historiographical problem', paper read at the Griffith University Film Policy Conference Brisbane, Australia, 27–29 November.

Dorland, Michael (1994) 'The expected tradition: Harold Innis, state rationality and the governmentalisation of communication: towards a theory of Canadian civil society', paper read to the Harold Innis and Intellectual Practice for the New Century Conference, Concordia University, Montreal, 13–15 October.

Dorland, Michael, Saint-Laurent, Michael and Tremblay, Gaétan (1993) 'Téléfilm Canada et la production audiovisuelle indépendante: la longue errance d'une politique gouverne-mentale', Communicaùtion 14:(2) 101–36.

Ellis, David (1994) quoted in Pamela Cuthbert, 'CRTC opens the gates'. *Playback*, 26 September.

Godbout, Jacques (1968) 'A trap: the script', in André Paquet (ed.) *How To Make Or Not To Make A Canadian Film*. Montreal: Cinémathèque canadienne.

Lawson, Sylvia (1979) 'Towards decolonization: some problems and issues for film history in Australia', *Film Reader*, 5: 63–71.

National Film Board of Canada, Archives, Film Policy, Box 262.

Paquet, A. (1968) 'The script: a trap' in André Paquet (ed.) *How To Make Or Not To Make A Canadian Film*. Montreal: Cinémathèque canadienne.

Resnick, Philip (1990) *The Masks of Proteus: Canadian Reflections on the State*. Montreal and Kingston: McGill-Queen's University Press.

Straram, Patrick (n.d.) 'Fragmentations, citations à propos d'un génocide', *cinécrits*, 3: 37–40.

Tadros, Connie (1988) 'From community to commodity: tracing the path of the industry between 150 covers', *Cinema Canada*, 150, March: 5–14.

Straw, Will (1991) 'The myth of total film history' in Ron Burnett (ed.) *Explorations in Film Theory: Selected Essays From Ciné-Tracts*: Bloomington: Indiana University Press.

Véronneau, Pierre (1987) 'Résistance et affirmation: la production francophone à l' ONF, 1939–1964', Ph.D. dissertation, Université du Québec à Montreal.

8

FILM POLICY IN LATIN AMERICA[1]

Randal Johnson

In the 1990s, Latin American film industries face an uncertain future. Perhaps they have always faced an uncertain future. In Argentina, Brazil and Mexico, the countries with longest and strongest cinematic traditions, film industries have developed in a cyclical pattern in which moments of success have been followed by periods of decline and crisis. In smaller countries filmmaking has tended to be sporadic at best (Table 8.1). Political turmoil, economic instability, high inflation rates and debt crises have contributed to the instability of national industries. But they are not the only factors.

Table 8.1 Latin American film production (selected countries)

Country	1970	1975	1980	1985	1991
Argentina	28	34	27	24	21
	...	1[1]	–	...	6
Bolivia	...	...	...	2	1[2]
Brazil	72	90	103	86	9[3]
	...	1	...	...	...
Columbia	...	2	5[4]	9	3[5]
	...	–	–	1	...
Cuba	1	8	6	10	6
	–	–	–	3	3
Ecuador	...	...	...	...	1
Mexico	124	162	109	101	32
	2	...	48	5	1
Peru	...	1	1	4[6]	1
	...	–	1	2	1
Venezuela	3	9	12	16	7
	3	1	4	1	1

1 *Source*: UNESCO, Statistical Yearbook 1994. Bottom figure indicates international co-production. Hyphen = no production. Three dots (. . .) indicates that no information is available.
2 1989 figure.
3 The 1991 figure for Brazil is an estimate. Fewer than ten films were produced in that year.
4 1982 figure.
5 1989 figure.
6 1986 figure.

During the last three decades television has consolidated itself as what Thomas Elsaesser calls the 'hegemonic force' in most national contexts (Elsaesser 1993: 123). With the ready availability of recent feature length films on video cassette, the home has replaced the movie theatre as the preferred venue for film viewing (Table 8.2). The increasing availability and diversity of cable and satellite networks will likely reinforce that preference. While Hollywood has adapted well in the television age, attaining a mutually beneficial financial co-existence, Latin American film industries have by and large failed to do so. In countries such as Brazil, which possesses the fourth largest commercial television network in the world, TV Globo, there is little integration between the two media.

During a film festival held recently at the Museum of Image and Sound in São Paulo, one of the participants in an organized debate suggested that 'film and video are things of the past' (Coelho 1994: 13). This suggestion – perhaps hyperbolic – is a recognition of the rapidly changing world of audiovisual communication in the 1990s. New technologies – ranging from the continued growth of home video to the rapid expansion of cable and satellite systems – radically augment spectator viewing options and seemingly transform traditional media into dinosaurs. In many cases, established exhibition circuits have been unable to hold their own, much less modernize facilities, resulting in the dramatic decline of theatrical markets throughout Latin America. Transnational cultural products, including, besides the cinema, the programming of broadcasters such as ESPN, HBO, MTV and CNN, transmitted – in English, Spanish and Portuguese – via cable and satellite delivery systems, have become even more ensconced as a significant part of the daily fare of audiences throughout the hemisphere.

The new conjuncture, in which neo-liberal economic policies and increased international pressure for free trade coincide with the explosion of new technologies, presents policy makers with new challenges. Film policies have developed over time and with different configurations – depending on the specificities of the national context and the structure of the industry – in order to guarantee at least a modicum of stability for future development and to ensure the production of culturally serious or aesthetically experimental filmmaking which might not survive if subject to exclusively commercial measurements. The old paradigms, however, based by and large on corporatist support of at least a portion of the production sector, often at the expense of other sectors of the industry, have revealed their limited effectiveness. Theatrical markets continue to decline, films continue to be unprofitable (with some felicitous exceptions). In some cases existing structures of film policy have been abolished (Colombia), revived and strengthened (Argentina, Venezuela), transformed (Mexico), or have simply imploded (Brazil).

In this chapter I will attempt to outline some of the challenges facing film policy in contemporary Latin America by examining the traditional strategies governments have used in their support of national industries as well as some recent developments whose ultimate success has yet to be determined. A major focus of the essay will be Brazil, which has seen both great success and dismal failure over

Table 8.2 Home video in Latin America

	Argent.	Brazil	Chile	Colom.	Mexico	Peru	Uruguay	Venez.
VCR households (in millions)	2.7	7.5	0.6	1.3	5.28	0.4	0.25	0.6
Video outlets (rentals/sales)	8,000	6,000	800	1,800	8,300	800	700	470
Colour TV households (in millions)	8.5	38	2.8	5.5	15.5	1.6	0.64	3.3
PRVC* wholesale price (US$)	50	45	43	25	35	32	50	23
Overnight rentals (US$)	2.35	1.60	1.30	1.00	1.70	1.25	1.50	1.00
Theatrical admission price (US$)	2.32	2.32	4.70	2.46	0.94	1.91	5.60	1.60
No. of screens	290	1,550 [1]	135	485	1,467	196	39	308
Monthly video releases (ave.)	160	80	84	60	85	15	90	80
Est. piracy level (%)	40	30	27	40	38	80	65	45
Annual video releases	1,924	7,000	500	8,000	4,000	60	400	1,000
Population (millions)	33	155	13.2	34	84.4	22.4	3.1	19.9

Source: Variety, 29 March 1993, p. 62.
*Pre-recorded videocassette.
1 The figure for Brazil is clearly overstated, even if it refers to the number of screens rather than theatres. In 1984 there were slightly over 1,400 theatres in the country and the number was declining steadily. An article in this same issue of Variety (p. 60) cites one Brazilian distributor as saying that 'About 360 theaters bring in 88% of revenues.' In its 1994 issue on Latin America (28 March–3 April), Variety reports only 800 'screens' in operation. My estimate would be that there were around 1,000 theatres in the country in 1992.

the last thirty years, but since Brazilian film policy parallels that of many other Latin American countries, at least in some of its particulars, the article will attempt to trace the commonalities in different national contexts.

OCCUPIED MARKETS

Any discussion of film policy in Latin America must be set within the context of the US film industry's historical domination of national markets. This situation is well known and has been widely discussed and analysed by critics and film industry professionals alike. A lengthy discussion of the matter here is thus unnecessary. Suffice to say that American cinema accounts for well over half of all films distributed throughout Latin America (Table 8.3). The expansion of home video has only served to reinforce this almost absolute domination. Unable to depend even on home markets for a return on investments, and lacking access to significant ancillary markets, unprotected Latin American film industries have lacked the capital necessary to sustain continuous production on a large scale. Inevitably, the result has been the underdevelopment of most such industries, despite short-lived moments of success (e.g. the 'Golden Age' of Mexican cinema, the Brazilian *chanchada*).

Throughout Latin America, furthermore, the film going public historically has been conditioned by the standards of European and American cinema, which dominated local markets as early as the first decade of the century. These films displayed levels of technical perfection impossible for incipient national industries, and with that perfection they imposed certain cultural models of the 'proper' or preferred form of cinematic discourse. Audiences became accustomed to that form and have been reluctant to accept alternative forms, even if produced locally. Latin American cinema has found itself in a double bind. On the one hand, it has not had the economic resources to equal the technical achievements of advanced industrial countries, and on the other, it has often lacked audience support for introducing different modes of filmmaking.

In discussing the decline of the alternative, political or 'avant garde' cinematic movements that emerged throughout Latin American and elsewhere in the 1960s, Thomas Elsaesser quite precisely points to the resiliency of American cinema in maintaining its domination of local markets in much of the world:

> By the mid-1970s, most of the (alternative) initiatives . . . had all suffered setbacks with the remarkable recovery of commercial Hollywood. Indeed the self-consciously national cinemas of Latin America saw themselves courted mostly at international festivals, where they became part of a European radical chic. Much the same happened to the New German cinema: a modestly successful export item on the art cinema circuit, it was massively supported by government funds and government agencies, but showed no signs of rallying domestic audiences to its own films.
>
> (Elsaesser 1993: 121)

Table 8.3 Origin of feature films imported (country of origin (%))

Country	Year	Total	US	France	Italy	USSR	UK	Ger.	Japan	Others
Argent.	1988	164	56.7	7.3	13.4	1.2	3.7	2.4	0.6	14.6
	1989	200	63.0	5.0	13.5	0.5	6.5	1.5	–	10.0
Bolivia	1988	183	68.9	2.7	6.0	1.1	1.6	1.1	1.1	17.5
	1989	189	69.3	1.1	5.3	–	2.1	2.1	–	20.1
Columb.	1988	429	60.6	3.5	8.2	1.2	0.7	–	0.2	25.6
	1989	418	67.2	4.5	9.1	0.2	0.5	1.7	0.2	16.5
Cuba	1989	124	17.7	4.0	6.5	14.5	1.6	0.8	0.8	54.0
	1990	61	31.1	3.3	1.6	8.2	–	1.6	3.3	50.8
Ecuador	1987	320	88.1	–	0.6	0.6	0.6	0.3	–	9.7
Mexico	1990	317	53.0	4.7	9.8	0.6	2.8	3.2	1.6	24.3
	1991	241	69.3	0.8	10.0	5.8	4.6	0.8	0.4	8.3
Peru	1988	263	66.5	4.2	8.7	0.8	1.5	1.1	0.8	16.3
	1989	211	81.0	0.5	4.7	0.5	0.9	1.9	0.5	9.9
Venez.	1990	211	86.7	0.9	0.9	–	2.8	0.9	–	7.1
	1991	203	84.7	4.4	1.5	–	2.5	–	–	6.9

Source: UNESCO, Statistical Yearbook 1994.

Elsaesser goes on to say that the independent cinemas that had emerged, often with a politically or aesthetically radical thrust, faced the option of either coexisting with Hollywood on Hollywood's terms, or virtually ceasing to exist. This situation, in which the marketplace assumes paramount importance, exacerbates the dilemmas of government policies toward national film industries.

CINEMA/STATE

Outside of the United States, direct government support of national film industries is the rule rather than the exception.[2] Industries in Europe, Africa, the Middle East, Asia, Latin America, as well as Canada and Australia, are supported in one way or another by the state. Even India, which has one of the largest and most successful commercial film industries in the world, producing over 700 films per year, has a government sponsored Film Finance Corporation which makes the production of alternative, experimental, or less commercially oriented films possible.[3]

In Latin America, periods of success, however relative, have by and large been accompanied by considerable state support. When state support has waned, as in Argentina after the fall of Peron in 1955 or during the López Portillo administration in Mexico (1976–82), the strength of the industry has also declined (Schnitman 1984: 39–40; Maciel 1993: 33). Feature films in Colombia were almost non-existent until the establishment of the Fondo de Promoción Cinematográfica (FOCINE) in 1978. Film production in Venezuela increased steadily in the 1980s after the creation of the Fondo de Fomento Cinematográfico (FONCINE) in 1981.[4] The strongest period in the history of Chilean cinema coincided with the Unidad Popular years and Allende's election to the presidency, when the cinema became incorporated into government policy. The state has been heavily involved in the re-emergence of a culturally and politically significant Argentine cinema in the post-dictatorship period – what has been called a 'cinema of redemocratization' – through the activities of the Instituto Nacional de Cinematografía (Newman 1993). The same has occurred in relation to the recent resurgence of Mexican cinema, which has been supported by revigorated policies of the Instituto Mexicano de Cinematografía (IMCINE). To a very large extent the hopes of Brazilian filmmakers rest on the promise of renewed investments in the film industry by recently elected president Fernando Henrique Cardoso.

The modes of film production, distribution and exhibition are shaped by a variety of industrial, economic, cultural, aesthetic and ideological factors. As an industry, the cinema in Latin America is affected by state measures in ways not affecting other art forms. Since in most instances it depends largely on imports for virtually all production equipment, as well as raw film stock, it is sometimes dramatically affected by changes in import or exchange policies. Ticket prices are often set by government agencies, so the production sector has virtually no say in determining the market value of its product. Development has been hindered by foreign trade accords in which, bowing to pressure from Hollywood, governments have agreed to the principle of free flow of motion pictures across international boundaries. In fact, in Brazil trade accords have made it less expensive to import foreign prints than film stock. In short, even without direct government protection of intervention, Latin American cinema is in many ways dependent on or shaped by the state and its policies.

Film policies are normally but one facet of broader cultural policies. Government support of diverse modes of cultural production has existed for centuries and continues to exist in countries throughout the world, including advanced industrial democracies. Cultural policies in different national settings by necessity vary according to the set of cultural and social values at stake. Rationales for state cultural policies are often cast in terms of the notion that culture is an integral part of development and that as the ultimate guarantor of a nation's cultural unity and identity, the state has a legitimate responsibility to protect society's cultural memory and heritage, to defend its cultural values, to stimulate cultural production, and to ensure that culture is not defined exclusively by market criteria. In other words, cultural policies are frequently designed to preserve the nation's cultural, artistic and historical patrimony and to mitigate what many see as the deleterious effects of the commercial mass media and the privately owned culture industry. To say that the state has a legitimate role to play in relation to culture, however, is a far cry from reaching a consensus about the nature and goals of that role.

In its relationship to cultural production, the state may well act, to use Octavio Paz's apt phrase, as a 'philanthropic ogre'. Its relative emphasis on the philanthropic or the 'ogreish' varies at different historical moments according to specific national characteristics and conjunctures. Governments have their own interests and their own reasons for intervening – or not intervening – in support of different sectors of cultural production, and those interests may not always coincide with those of the cultural producers. By its very nature, the state determines the parameters within which artists may act, and in most cases they have relative freedom as long as they stay within these parameters.

The state, Weber suggests, has a monopoly on legitimate coercion and violence, which inevitably functions as a component of its policy towards culture. Although they can and often do control the distribution of cultural goods through censorship and repression, most states would normally prefer to control by indirect constraints and consensus. Thus the existence, even in periods of repressive authoritarian rule, of governmental boards, agencies, commissions and institutes designed to support different sectors of cultural production. Cultural policies are never simply a question of 'defending' a national identity or 'supporting' certain forms of cultural production.

Cinema–state relations are a two-way street. Since at least the 1920s industrial groups or professionals in different Latin American countries have requested state protection and aid, and governments have responded in accordance with their own priorities and designs. For a thorough analysis of film policies in specific national contexts, which is beyond the scope of this chapter, one should examine the internal tensions and the diverse articulations between cinema and state. Such an analysis clearly transcends the purely economic and the impact of foreign cinemas on the national film industry.

PROTECTIONIST POLICIES

Octavio Getino suggests that approaches to film practice and film industry development in Latin America have been shaped by two opposing strategies, one based on 'economism', which sees the film industry and its products in purely economic terms, the other based on what Getino calls 'ideologism', or a privileging of the ideological and cultural aspects of the cinema over commercial potential (Getino 1987: 9–11). One need not endorse Getino's terminology to recognize the underlying truth of his observation. The fundamental opposition between commercial and cultural interests is often at the root of tensions which have arisen within Latin American cinema over the last few decades and has often shaped state policies of support of local industries.

By its very nature a film industry produces objects which are both symbolic goods and economic commodities. In most contexts the cinema's viability as a form of artistic expression depends on the availability of production financing, which in turn depends on the film's potential to attract a fairly wide audience and attain success in the market. The artistic and economic aspects are often intricately intertwined. In ideal terms, one might suggest that state policies towards national film industries have as their goal the creation of a situation in which the production of artistically or culturally relevant films is guaranteed through measures designed to strengthen the industry as a whole. The ideal, however, rarely becomes reality.

Jorge Schnitman distinguishes between restrictive, supportive and comprehensive protectionist policies. A restrictive policy, which includes such measures as screen and import quotas as well as import tariffs and customs duties, is designed to give the local industry some breathing room by impeding a complete takeover of the local market by foreign concerns. A supportive policy includes direct state support of the industry in the form of bank loans and credit, prizes, production subsidies and other forms of film financing, assistance in reaching foreign markets, and training of film industry technicians. Restrictive policies provide indirect support of the industry while supportive policies lend direct financial support. A comprehensive state policy would include both restrictive and supportive measures (Schnitman 1984: 46).

In Latin America, some kind of protectionist legislation is in effect in Argentina, Brazil, Colombia, Cuba, Mexico, Nicaragua, Peru and Venezuela (Getino 1987: Table 46). Most of those countries have also imposed screen quotas – the compulsory exhibition of national films – which have often been the backbone of film policies in Latin America.[5]

Screen quotas have taken various forms, including the forced exhibition of national short films in each programme of foreign films, the establishment of a certain number of days per year of compulsory exhibition, the stipulation of a percentage of films exhibited which must be locally produced, or the setting of a proportion of national films to be exhibited in relation to numbers of foreign films released. In addition, it is not uncommon for cinematic legislation to stipulate precisely how long a national film must be kept in exhibition, either in absolute terms or in terms of attendance figures in relation to average attendance in the same theatre.

In Latin America, compulsory exhibition legislation first began to appear in 1932, when the Brazilian government implemented a policy mandating the exhibition of a national short film with every programme of foreign films. The Mexican screen quota dates from 1939, when the Cárdenas government (1934–40) made the exhibition of one domestic film per month mandatory. In Argentina, compulsory exhibition legislation was first implemented in 1944. Screen quotas in Colombia, Peru and Venezuela are more recent, dating only from the 1970s.[6] The most substantial screen quotas have been those of Brazil, which attained the figure of 140 days per year in 1980, and Mexico, which reached 50 per cent of screen time in the country.[7] However, after the bottom dropped out of the Brazilian film industry in the late 1980s and early 1990s, the quota became a dead letter, and in Mexico, following new legislation inspired by neo-liberal, free market ideas, the quota will be gradually phased out over the next few years, the idea being that Mexican cinema must become competitive in its own marketplace by 1998 (29 *Variety* 1993).[8]

The major benefit of the screen quota is that it does guarantee some space in the market for national production which otherwise might not find exhibition outlets because of the almost total domination of domestic markets by foreign films. In this sense, it may well be a necessity for the continued existence of national filmmaking in some contexts. Nevertheless, screen quotas have not been totally effective, and they also have revealed major drawbacks.

First of all, whereas governments can legislate the compulsory exhibition of national films, they cannot legislate compulsory attendance by a public long conditioned by the products of Hollywood. Second, quotas have been difficult to enforce, since exhibitors have long seen them as an unwanted (and unwarranted) government imposition. In some cases, exhibitors have simply refused to fulfil the quota. In Brazil, for example, non-compliance reached the point where one cinema in Rio de Janeiro had a deficit of 668 days in relation to the 140 day quota. In other words, this particular cinema had gone almost two years without exhibiting a single Brazilian film. Numerous others owed between 350 and 550 days (Souza 1993: 52). Getino has suggested that the implementation and enforcement of the Colombian screen quota was also difficult, especially in light of the instability of local production (Getino 1987: 121).

In one sense – and this has long been at the crux of exhibitors' arguments against screen quotas – compulsory exhibition forces one sector to risk a potential financial loss for the benefit of another. Exhibitors have tended to respond in two ways: through the courts and by producing their own 'quota quickies,' that is, low cost films made exclusively to fulfil compulsory exhibition obligations. In Brazil, production by exhibitors gave rise to the soft-core pornochanchada in the 1970s and to hard-core pornography in the 1980s. Judicial action has emerged especially when other measures are combined with a screen quota to the detriment of the sector as a whole. One contributing factor for the decline of FOCINE in Colombia, for example, is that exhibitors revolted when the government attempted to increase a tax on box-office receipts – FOCINE's major source of income and, consequently, Colombian cinema's major source of production financing – from 8.5 per cent to 16 per cent. Exhibitors refused to pay, filed suit, and boycotted films produced by FOCINE. Such situations clearly result in an increase of tension and hostility between the production and exhibition sectors.

THE GOOD, THE BAD, AND THE UGLY

In Brazil, this tension (if not outright antagonism) goes back to the very beginnings of film production in the country. In the early 1900s producers and exhibitors were normally one and the same. The development of independent distributors drove a wedge between producers and exhibitors, and the exhibition sector began to function almost exclusively for the benefit of foreign cinemas. In the 1930s, exhibition groups fought legislation initiating a timid screen quota for Brazilian short films, just has they have fought every attempt to expand the quota until today, arguing free trade and open markets in opposition to state intervention and manipulation of the rules of the marketplace.

Without a screen quota and other protectionist measures, Brazilian cinema very likely would exist only on the most crass commercial basis, if at all. At the same time, state policy towards the film industry has clearly led to a loss of profits for exhibitors and is at least partially responsible for the current decline of the exhibition sector, which has been pernicious for the Brazilian film industry as a whole. It is thus a difficult question to deal with, for both sides are obviously correct in their arguments.

The relationship between the state and the exhibition sector deteriorated steadily over the last two decades, primarily because of exhibitors' resistance to increasingly interventionist government policies. In 1974, *O Estado de São Paulo* ran an article with the headline 'The great duel of national cinema', referring to the duel between exhibitors and state-supported producers as analogous to a Western movie, with the producer as hero, the exhibitor as villain, and the state as sheriff. The 'duel' would by 1980 become a 'war', fought largely in the courts, as exhibition groups, sometimes in conjunction with distributors, continually filed suits and frequently obtained at least temporary injunctions against various aspects of state policy, especially the compulsory exhibition law. In its report for the second half of 1988, Concine lists suits filed by thirty-two exhibition companies (not counting multiple co-litigants) representing over 10 per cent of the total number of theatres in Brazil (Concine1988: 314–17).

As of the late 1980s, Brazilian cinematic legislation stipulated that exhibitors must show national films at least 140 days per year, regardless of the number of

Brazilian films produced in a given year or the quality of those films. Although exhibitors could negotiate with distributors of foreign films, they were obligated to pay a minimum of 50 per cent of net income for Brazilian films. They were also obliged to show a national short subject as part of each programme of foreign films, purchase standardized tickets and box-office income recording sheets from Embrafilme at inflated prices, and keep Brazilian films in exhibition as long as the average of total spectators for two weeks or more equalled 60 per cent of the previous year's weekly average.

In return, exhibitors received virtually nothing from the state except the disdain which has long characterized producers' attitudes towards the sector. Although it was among Embrafilme's attributes to attend to the needs of the sector, it refused to divert funds from production and did not even provide subsidies or low-interest loans to help them renovate their equipment and theatres. The result of the authoritarian imposition of unwelcome measures was a decline in income and a deteriorating sector which led to the closing of many theatres, especially in the interior of the country, and to the current crisis of Brazilian cinema. The permanence of the 'quota mentality' in the Brazilian film industry is evidenced by repeated – and repeatedly unsuccessful – attempts to impose a screen quota on television and on the home video market. The proof of the failure of the Brazilian government's policy towards the exhibition sector – and towards Brazilian cinema as a whole – is the dramatic decline in the number of theatres in operation in the country, now under 1,000 for a country of 150 million. Few films can cover costs in such a small market. Thus foreign films have an additional advantage since they have normally covered costs and made a profit prior to entering the Brazilian market.

Perhaps recognizing the dangers involved in the failure to resolve this dilemma, other countries have attempted different solutions. In Venezuela, for example, the government has offered financial incentives to exhibitors for showing national films, including an increase in ticket prices, which had been frozen for several years, in exchange for 6.6 per cent of profits from foreign films. It has encouraged cooperation with the sector, by providing, for example, an additional 6.6 per cent of receipts for Venezuelan films. All of this led to increased revenues for financing local production. Public support of national films has also led some distribution chains to invest in Venezuelan film production (King: 1990 219–20). In Argentina the government, while seeking increased access to the exhibition market, has offered to pay for the opening week's expenses at first-run movie theatres when national films are shown (*Variety* 1993). In Mexico, which has long been the most statist of all Latin American countries with regards to the cinema, at one time holding a virtual monopoly of distribution and exhibition outlets, the state exhibition sector is being privatized and the state is phasing out the screen quota, forcing Mexican cinema to sink or swim in the marketplace. The point is that the kind of clientelism which has led to such one-sided policies as that of Brazil no longer seems to offer a viable solution.

In terms of supportive policies, Latin American countries have tended to act within the same range of possibilities: financing credits, low-interest loans, state-backed co-productions, various kinds of subsidies and subventions, advances on distribution, and co-productions between the state and private producers or between the state, private producers and foreign concerns. To finance such programmes, countries have resorted to taxes on box-office receipts, which puts a primary burden on the exhibition sector, taxes on profit remittances by foreign distributors, taxes on the production sector (e.g. in Brazil there existed a mandatory 'contribution' for film industry development paid by producers), and even direct budgetary appropriations. It is beyond the scope of this chapter to go into detail about each individual situation.

Latin American film industries have discovered, however, that even comprehensive state policies – combining restrictive and supportive policies – are insufficient to truly guarantee stability. In some cases, such as Colombia and Venezuela, among others, when filmmaking got underway the domestic market had already been divided up among foreign interests. Competing in such a market, based on a precarious cinematographic infrastructure, is virtually impossible. Carlos Alvarez reveals that the small size of the Colombian market also works against the success and stability of the national industry, since very few films can recover costs in the domestic market alone (Alvarez 1989: 174). Mexico and Argentina reveal similar problems. Although many films from the two countries have in recent years been highly acclaimed by critics both at home and abroad and garnered numerous awards in international festivals, by and large they have been unable to gain a strong and secure foothold on their respective domestic markets (Newman 1993; Maciel 1993; Torrents 1993). Brazil is another case in point. Despite the existence of restrictive policies (notably a screen quota of 140 days per year) and increasingly aggressive supportive policies, Brazilian cinema, long one of the strongest in Latin America, is back to square one, with production levels lower than any time since the 1930s. The reasons behind this dramatic decline are the subject of the next section of this chapter.

FILM POLICY IN BRAZIL

The Brazilian film industry has, in the last decade, faced the most severe crisis of its history, a crisis that threatens its very existence. Never has a Latin American film industry experienced such a rapid climb and such a precipitous fall. Its experience illustrates the pitfalls of film policies throughout Latin America and may well represent a lesson to be learned by other governments as well as by the current Brazilian administration, which has shown signs of a willingness to invest once again in national producers.

In the late 1970s, it seemed that Brazilian cinema, supported by the state film agency, Embrafilme (Empresa Brasileira de Filmes), would finally take off and reach an unprecedented level of stability and prosperity. Between 1974 and 1978 the total number of spectators for Brazilian films doubled from 30 million to over 60 million, and total income increased by 288 per cent, from $13 million in 1974 to over $38 million in 1978. Brazilian cinema's share of its own market increased from around 15 per cent in 1974 to over 30 per cent in 1978.

Despite such success, the 1980s witnessed a downturn that reversed the economic growth of the previous decade. The number of theatres in the country dropped from 3,276 in 1975 to slightly over 1,500 in 1984 to less than 1,100 in 1988. In 1994, *Variety* reported the number of screens in the country to be only 800. The occupancy rate for all theatres dropped from 19 per cent in 1978 to a mere 12 per cent in 1984, and annual attendance per capita went from 2.6 times in 1975 to 0.8 in 1983. Attendance figures for Brazilian films dropped from the 1978 high of 60 million to less than 24 million in 1988 and has continued to plummet, as national film production declined from 102 films in 1980 to eighty-four in 1983 to less than ten in 1991 (which represents an improvement on the previous year). But until the bottom dropped out, the crisis was perhaps less apparent in the number of films produced than in their quality. Between 1981 and 1985, hard-core porn accounted for an average of almost 73 per cent of total production, a trend which continued at least through 1988, a year in which twenty of the thirty top-drawing Brazilian films were pornographic (*Jornal da Tela*, March 1986: 3).

On one level, of course, the crisis of Brazilian cinema in the 1980s reflected the larger crisis of the national economy in a period when the so-called economic 'miracle' of the 1967–73 period, characterized by high growth rates and relatively low inflation, was replaced by an economic nightmare with a 100 billion dollar foreign debt and near hyperinflation. The economic crisis forced the government to impose severe restrictions on imports, making film production costs rise dramatically and accentuating what is often called the 'dollarization' of the film production process. Film production costs increased rapidly at a time when the market was shrinking, thus accelerating the process of decline, and ticket prices, which have long been controlled by the government, did not keep pace with inflation, further reducing the industry's income. High inflation rates have made film-going a luxury for much of the Brazilian population.

Television, which was so successful during this same period (due in part to considerable infrastructural public sector investments in the telecommunications industry), provided Brazilians with inexpensive yet generally high-quality entertainment in the comfort of their homes. At the same time, unlike the US and Western Europe, television did not provide the national film industry with a significant additional source of income since historically there has been little integration between the two media. In addition, the rapidly expanding video market caused the home to replace the movie theatre as the venue of choice for viewing films. In 1987, film and video distributors in Brazil both had revenues of around $90 million; by 1991 video revenue had increased to around $490 million, while theatrical revenues had increased only slightly, to around $125 million (a decrease of $13 million from the previous year) (Nery 1991).

But the crisis goes beyond mere economic considerations. It represents the bankruptcy of the state-supported model of film production that led Brazilian cinema, in the mid-1970s, to truly remarkable levels of success. It is a crisis of a questionable policy that did not derive from a far-sighted vision of the future of Brazilian cinema, and that was authoritarian in many of its particulars, especially in relation to the exhibition sector. Although the policy made viable many important film projects, including most of the Brazilian films distributed in the US in the1980s and early 1990s, it ultimately failed to reconcile the state's cultural and industrial responsibilities vis-à-vis the cinema and led to the meteoric fall of the Brazilian film industry during the last several years.

The policy failed largely because of its corporatist and clientelistic nature, which led it to respond to the demands of clients who occupied dominant positions in the cinematic field rather than provide infrastructural support which could have strengthened the industry as a whole. Although the state claimed that its goal was to make the cinema more competitive in its own market, the screen quota and the various forms of financial assistance it provided in fact suspended the rules of the marketplace for national films, which ceased to compete against foreign films in the domestic market and began to compete against each other in the reserve market. Embrafilme became the major source of production financing and it itself became a marketplace where filmmakers competed against each other for the right to make films, thus exacerbating tensions within the industry and creating a situation in which the play of influences was often more important than the talent of the filmmaker or producer. In this sense, the situation in Brazil became similar to that of Mexico during the López Portillo administration. As Alberto Ruy Sánchez has convincingly written, state support of the Mexican film industry during that period, sustained by a complex play of personal and political interests, was essentially pernicious, creating a situation in which the film itself was the least important aspect of the industry (Sánchez 1981: 46).

To put the discussion in historical context, a brief overview of the development of state policy towards the film industry is in order. State support of the film industry dates from the early 1930s, when Getúlio Vargas' government implemented the first of what would turn out to be a long series of protectionist measures, most in the form of a screen quota for national films, designed to give the industry a modicum of stability for future development in a market long dominated by foreign films. Since the 1930s, and especially after the 1964 military coup d'état, the state role evolved from that of regulator of market forces to active agent and productive force in the industry, especially through its various programmes of film production financing (low-interest loans, advances on distribution and co-production with private companies).

The Brazilian government began its direct financial support of the film industry in 1966 with the creation of the Instituto Nacional do Cinema (National Film Institute). The Institute, created by an executive decree of the military regime, was the result of a long struggle by most sectors of the film industry (Johnson 1987: 107–12). It administered three major programmes of support: first, a subsidy programme providing all national films exhibited with additional income based on box-office receipts; second, a programme of additional cash awards for 'quality' films, selected by a jury of critics and film industry professionals; and, third, a film-financing programme in which the Institute administered co-productions between foreign distributors and local producers using funds withheld from the distributor's income tax. These three programmes were available to all interested filmmakers and thus tended to support the production sector as a whole.

The co-production programme ended in 1969 with the creation of Embrafilme, which was originally intended to promote the distribution of Brazilian films in foreign markets, and the funds withheld from the distributor's income tax became a major source of the agency's budget. As early as 1970 Embrafilme began granting producers low-interest loans for film production financing. Between 1970 and 1979,when the loan programme was phased out, Embrafilme financed over 25 per cent of total national production in this manner.[9]

As initially formulated, decisions to grant production financing were ostensibly made on purely technical grounds, taking into consideration the size of the company, its production history, the number of awards it had won in national and international festivals, and its experience. Such a policy may seem reasonable for most economic sectors or most industries, but the film industry is different in that its product transmits cultural, social, and ideological values, and such 'neutrality' was seen as unacceptable by many segments of Brazilian society. The influential newspaper *O Estado de São Paulo*, for example, editorialized on 28 January 1972 that Embrafilme should *not* be a merely technical agency, but rather should finance only films of high quality which contribute to the 'moral foundations' of Brazilian society. Since a 'neutral' policy designed to foster Brazilian cinema as a whole led to the production of films deemed undesirable by many social sectors, including the military – and here I am referring to the rash of *pornochanchadas* (erotic comedies) which began to appear in the early 1970s, many partially subsidized by the state – a reformulation of Embrafilme's production policy became inevitable.

In 1975, Embrafilme was reorganized and at that time absorbed the executive functions of the now-defunct INC. The Conselho Nacional do Cinema (Concine) was created the following year to assume INC's legislative role (Mello 1978: 11–29, 53–8). In 1973 Embrafilme had created its own nationwide distributor, long a goal of Brazilian producers, and in 1974 it initiated a programme of co-production financing that gradually replaced the loan programme. As initially formulated, the enterprise participated in selected film projects with up to 30 per cent of total production costs. With an advance on distribution of another 30 per cent, the state could cover up to 60 per cent of a film's production costs. In the late 1970s, Embrafilme began providing up to 100 per cent of a film's financing in some cases.

The co-production programme described above marked a fundamental re-direction in state policy towards the industry. With this programme, the granting of production financing became much more selective. When the state decides to co-produce a limited number of films, it must inevitably decide which Brazilian cinema it will support. This causes the state, on the one hand, to enter into competition with non-favoured sectors of the industry and, on the other, to become a site of contention for competing groups. The reorientation of the state's financial assistance to the industry exacerbated conflicting positions among film makers.

Another effect of the shift in policy was, it is often said, to 'socialize losses and privatize profits' (Schild 1986). Since the state assumed the lion's share of the financial risk involved in film production, many directors and producers tended to be less concerned with keeping costs down and, at least to some extent, with public acceptance of their films. Embrafilme's co-production programme undeniably improved the technical quality of Brazilian cinema, but by doing so it allowed production costs to be inflated to levels far above the market potential for return in the domestic market. At the same time, Embrafilme did little to improve and strengthen the industry's infrastructure. Its focus, at least in terms of financial support for the industry, was almost exclusively on production and its own distributor. In many ways, dependence on the state caused the film industry to cease having an autonomous life of its own, and its modes of production, distribution and consumption became mediated and bureaucratized by the state.

By the mid-1980s, it become clear that the existing mode of state-supported cinematic production was obsolete and transformation of the relationship between cinema and the state was necessary. The urgency of the restructuring became clear, and Embrafilme once again the object of severe public criticism and debate, when the *Folha de São Paulo* published, throughout the month of March 1986, a series of articles on the enterprise's management. In an editorial titled 'Cine catástrofe' (20 March 1986), the newspaper referred to Embrafilme's activities as a 'moral, economic, and artistic disaster'. Increasing numbers of film industry professionals recognized the need for a re-evaluation of the relationship between cinema and the state.[10] Despite another attempt at transformation which took place during the Sarney administration (1985–90), Embrafilme's fundamental orientation – the clientelistic support of individual film projects rather than the industry as a whole – remained unchanged, and the general situation of the Brazilian film industry continued to deteriorate. In March 1990, in one of his first actions as recently inaugurated President of Brazil, Fernando Collor de Mello abolished Embrafilme and Concine and reversed a governmental cultural policy that had been evolving irregularly in the country since the 1930s. Collor's action – inspired by neo-liberal, free market economic theories – represented the coup de grâce to a poorly formulated film policy which had largely ceased to be recognized as socially legitimate.

NEW DIRECTIONS

After Collor's elimination of government financing of the film industry in 1990, other agencies, mostly at the state and local level (e.g. BANESPA, the state bank of São Paulo), initiated limited programmes of support which has kept at least a small number of films in production. More recently, Brazil's new president Fernando Henrique Cardoso has announced plans to develop an 'industrial policy'

143

towards the cinema which will studiously avoid the Embrafilme model. The idea is to use government policy to attempt to make films profitable in the marketplace, with a combination of public and private investments. The announced policy will also attempt to strengthen interchange with other countries as a means of assuring an international market for Brazilian films (*Folha de São Paulo*,15 November 1994). The change in policy direction, if indeed implemented, signifies the end to the clientelistic and paternalistic policy which had dominated Brazilian film policy since the early 1970s and may represent a new beginning for Brazilian cinema. At the same time, signs exist that the exhibition sector may be on the rebound, especially through the construction of multiplex sites in urban shopping centres (*Variety* 1994). In the Brazilian case, cautious optimism may be in order, although it appears unlikely that the national cinema will again attain the levels of the 1970s, unless there is a concerted effort to reach some kind of accommodation with the exhibition sector.[11]

Changes have also occurred in other Latin American countries. Government financing of production in Argentina increased dramatically in the early 1990s due primarily to a controversial measure in which the National Film Institute extended a 10 per cent tax on box office receipts to home video and television revenues. The measure – opposed by home video distributors, television stations, video clubs and the MPEAA – doubled the agency's revenue from $4.3 million in 1991 to close to $8 million in 1992. The institute has used the increased funding to finance production and promotional campaigns. The agency has also attempted to reach some kind of agreement with exhibitors, offering to foot the bill for the first week's expense when national films are shown (*Variety* 1993).

In 1993 the Venezuelan government increased funding of FONCINE from $810,000 to $4.5 million. Additional funding was expected from a new tax, approved in 1992, on home video sales. This increased funding has permitted FONCINE to begin financing new productions and to dedicate more efforts towards promoting Venezuelan cinema abroad. Besides these measures, the government has attempted to reach some sort of accommodation with exhibition circuits, permitting them to use their accumulated debt – overdue payments for exhibition of FONCINE's products – in the renovation of their theatres and in production financing (*Variety* 1994). In Colombia, events have not been quite so felicitous. A 1992 decree abolished FOCINE, which had unsuccessfully attempted to define its role in the promotion of Colombian cinema. During its fifteen year history, FOCINE produced some 200 features, medium-length films, shorts and documentaries. The government absorbed FOCINE's funds and will act as their adminstrator (*Variety* 1993). The ultimate outcome of such developments remains to be seen.

The most recent success story has been that of Mexico, especially in the wake of the international success of films such as *Danzón*, *Cabeza de Vaca* and *Like Water for Chocolate*. The success is due in part to changes made in national film policy during the administration of Carlos Salinas de Gortari (1988–94). In 1991 the government film agency, IMCINE, was restructured and transferred to the jurisdication of the National Council for Culture and the Arts. At the same time, a process of privatization was initiated, with the closing of state production companies such as Conacite 2 and Conacine. IMCINE focused on stimulating the production of films which were not exploitatively commercial, financing a new generation of young filmmakers and investing in quality projects (*Variety* 1991). In 1992 new film legislation was implemented, accelerating the privatization of such firms as the government distributor Cotsa, the Churubusco Studios and Los Estudios América. The legislation also deregulated ticket prices, allowing them to find their own place in the market, to debureaucratize and deunionize the industry, and to phase out the screen quota for national films. Implicit in this legislation is that the days of protectionism are over, and that, although the government will continue to support production on a limited scale, by and large filmmakers will need to fend for themselves (*Variety* 1993). Despite the success of such films as *Like Water for Chocolate*, it remains to be seen whether the recent surge of Mexican cinema can be sustained.[12]

One of the major lessons learned from the situation in Brazil is that without social legitimacy a successful government policy of film industry support is impossible. Such legitimacy is not automatic; it must be earned, and without authoritarian impositions on one sector (e.g. exhibition) in order to support the corporatist interests of another. Unless governments are willing to simply write off investments in the film industry – and they seem increasingly unwilling to do so – a substantial portion of the financial risk must shift to the private sector. In the neo-liberal context in which most Latin American cinemas now operate, film industries will be forced, even with the odds stacked against them, to deal more effectively with the marketplace, both domestic and, where possible, international. Although it can certainly aid and assist, the state cannot, by itself, replace the private sector and ensure the future of film industries in Latin America.

NOTES

1 This chapter develops arguments made in 'The rise and fall of Brazilian cinema, 1960–1990', *Iris: A Journal of Theory on Image and Sound*, no. 13 (Summer 1991); 'Regarding the philanthropic ogre: cultural policy in Brazil, 1930–45/1964–90', in *Constructing Culture and Power in Latin America*, Daniel H. Levine (ed.) (Ann Arbor: University of Michigan Press, 1993); and 'In the belly of the ogre: cinema and state in Latin America', in *Mediating Two Worlds: Cinematic Encounters in the Americas*, John King, Ana M. López and Manuel Alvarado (eds) (London: BFI, 1993).

2 One should not assume that there is no state support of film production in the US, no matter how secondary. Numerous films have been produced with funds from the NEA and PBS. Close links have also long existed between the American film industry and diplomatic policies.

3 In *Third World Film Making and the West*, Roy Armes (1987) describes diverse forms of state support of film industries throughout Latin America, Asia, Africa and the Middle East.

4 See Getino (1987) for a brief discussion of these organizations and their modes of film industry support, especially pp. 55–71. For more detailed accounts, see Aguirre and

Bisbal (1980) on Venezuela, Alvarez (1989) and Lenti (1993) on Colombia. Schnitman (1984) discusses the situation in Argentina and Mexico in some detail. For Brazil, see Johnson (1987). On the situation in Cuba, see Chanan (1985). For a good overview of Latin American cinema as a whole, see King (1990).

5 Import quotas have been much more problematic. Argentina tried to impose a reciprocity system on American imports in the late 1940s (i.e. the number of films allowed into the country was tied to the number of Argentine films accepted in the foreign market), but the attempt ultimately fell through due to intense pressure from the Motion Pictures Export Association of America (Schnitman, 1984; 34–6). Brazil briefly attempted something similar with newsreels in 1946, with an equal lack of success.

6 Getino (1987), King and Schnitman (1984) are the best sources for information on screen quotas in different Latin American contexts.

7 The evolution of the screen quota in Brazil was the following: 1932: one short for each programme of foreign films;1939: one feature per year; 1946: three features per year; 1951: one feature for every eight foreign films; 1959: 42 days per year; 1963: 56 days per year; 1969: 63 days per year (provisional); 1970: 77 days per year (provisional); 1970: 112 days per year (not implemented); 1970: 98 days per year (not implemented); 1971: 84 days per year; 1975: 112 days per year; 1978: 133 days per year; 1977: compulsory exhibition of one Brazilian short subject with each programme of foreign films; 1980: 140 days per year (Johnson 1987: 185,188).

8 In March of every year, the trade magazine *Variety* publishes a special section on Latin American cinema. Issues cited in this article date from 25 March 1991, 29 March 1993, 28 March–3 April 1994. Subsequent references will include only the year.

9 Among films financed under the co-production programme were Joaquim Pedro de Andrade's *Macunaíma* (1969), Carlos Diegues's *Os Herdeiros* (The Heirs, 1968), and Nelson Pereira dos Santos's *Como era gostoso o meu francês* (How Tasty Was My Little Frenchman,1971). For a complete listing, see Johnson (1987: 202–4).

10 Cinema Novo veteran Carlos Diegues (*Bye Bye Brasil*), for example, referred to the enterprise as a 'cultural Medicaid system that treats cancer with Band-aids', and Embrafilme director Carlos Augusto Calil (1985–87) asserted that the state could no longer attempt to substitute for private enterprise and that the existing model was simply no longer viable. Diegues's remark came in an interview to the *Jornal do Brasil*, 23 February 1985, and Calil's in an interview to that same paper on 23 March 1986.

11 Two recent films reveal the problem. In March 1995, André Luiz Oliveira's *Louco por cinema* (Crazy about Cinema, 1995) was released in a single art-house location in Rio de Janeiro, Estação Botafogo, with a seating capacity of less than 100. Luiz Alberto Pereira's *O efeito ilha* (The Island Effect, 1994), screened in the 1995 Riverside Film Festival in California, has yet to be exhibited in commercial circuits.

12 It is worth noting that Alfonso Arau, director of *Like Water For Chocolate*, is currently working in Hollywood. His first American feature, A *Walk in the Clouds*, was released in late 1995.

BIBLIOGRAPHY

Aguirre, Jesús María and Bisbal, Marcelino (1980) *El nuevo cine venezolano*. Caracas: Editorial Ateneo de Caracas.

Alvarez, Carlos (1989) *Sobre cine colombiano y latinoamericano*. Bogotá: Universidad Nacional de Colombia.

Armes, Roy (1987) *Third World Film Making and the West*. Berkeley and Los Angeles: University of California Press.

Chanan, Michael (1985) *The Cuban Image*. London: BFI.

FILM POLICY IN LATIN AMERICA

Coelho, Teixeira (1994) 'Sensibilidades', *Imagens* (Campinas), 1 (April): 8–13.

Concine (Conselho Nacional de Cinema) (n.d.) *Relatório de Atividades: Segundo Semestre 1988*. Rio de Janeiro.

Elsaesser, Thomas (1993) 'Hyper-, retro- or counter-cinema: European cinema and Third Cinema between Hollywood and art cinema', in John King, Ana M. López, Manuel Alvarado (eds) *Mediating Two Worlds: Cinematic Encounters in the Americas*. London: British Film Institute.

Getino, Octavio (1987) *Cine latinoamericano: Economía, y nuevas tecnologías audiovisuales*. Havana: Fundación del Nuevo Cine Latinoamericano; Mérida: Departamento de Cine, Universidade de los Andes.

Johnson, Randal (1987) *The Film Industry in Brazil: Culture and the State*. Pittsburgh: University of Pittsburgh Press.

King, John (1990) *Magical Reels: A History of Cinema in Latin America*. London: Verso.

Lenti, Paul (1993) 'Colombia: State role in film production', in John King, Ana M. López and Manuel Alvarado (eds) *Mediating Two Worlds: Cinematic Encounters in the Americas*. London: Verso.

Maciel, David R. (1994) 'El imperio de la fortuna: Mexico's contemporary cinema, 1985–1992,' in Chon A. Noriega and Steven Ricci (eds) *The Mexican Cinema Project*. Los Angeles: UCLA Film and Television Archive.

Mello, Alcino Teixeira de (1978) *Legislação do cinema brasileiro*. 2 vols. Rio de Janeiro: Embrafilme.

Nery, Mário. (1991) 'No trono doméstico', *Veja*, 14 August.

Newman, Kathleen (1993) 'Fernando Solanas's *Sur* and the Exiled Nation'. John King, Ana M. López, Manuel Alvarado (eds) in *Mediating Two Worlds: Cinematic Encounters in the Americas*. London: British Film Institute.

Paz, Octavio (1979) *El ogro filantrópico: Historia y política*. Mexico: Joaquín Mortiz.

Sánchez, Alberto Ruy (1981) *Mitología de un cine en crisis*. Mexico City: Premia.

Schild, Susana (1986) 'Embrafilme, um modelo falido', *Jornal do Brasil*, 23 March.

Schnitman, Jorge (1984) *Film Industries in Latin America: Dependency and Development*. Norwood, N.J.: Ablex Publishing Corporation.

Souza, José Inácio de Melo. (1993) 'A morte e as mortes do cinema brasileiro', *Revista USP* 19 (September–November): 50–7.

Torrents, Lisa (1993) 'Mexican Cinema comes alive', in John King, Ana M. López, Manuel Alvarado (eds) *Mediating Two Worlds: Cinematic Encounters in the Americas*. London: British Film Institute.

9

INDIA'S NATIONAL FILM POLICY

Shifting Currents in the 1990s

Manjunath Pendakur

The relationship between the film industry and the state in India can be characterized as a patron–client relationship, the foundation of which was built by colonial authority. The post-Colonial State maintains elitist attitudes towards popular culture in general and cinema in particular. The government of India's intervention into the film industry, until the end of British colonial rule in 1947, was limited primarily to censorship of films. It was aimed at preventing the nationalists from employing the power of cinema to mobilize the masses. When political power passed on to the Indian rulers, censorship was kept intact and, under the rubric of development of indigenous arts, the central and state governments expanded their powers over the film industry. Documentary and newsreel production was monopolized by the central government and theatre owners were compelled under the law to exhibit them.[1] Furthermore, when the country was reorganized into states based on language in the early 1950s, it gave rise to language chauvinism on the one hand, but on the other helped promote local languages and various art forms, including cinema. This chapter is concerned mainly with the complex relationship between the state and the fast changing film industry in the country by examining the institutional mechanisms through which the state exercises its power.

Despite the expansive power of the state and its apparatuses, film production, distribution and exhibition in India are primarily the domain of private capital. Some 830 feature films are censored in the country every year out of which only a handful are financed by government institutions. What is striking about film production in India is that films are made in more than twenty-one languages (even in Sanskrit which is not spoken any more!). Hindi language cinema, however, dominates, not only because more films are produced every year, but because of the fact that it has national distribution and has been able to develop audiences around the world, limited though they are to regions where Indians have migrated. Films are produced in several cities – Bombay, Madras, Calcutta, Hyderabad, Bangalore, Mysore, Trivandrum and Cuttack – of which Madras turns out more films than any other centre. The constant influx of new producers with little experience in the complexities of production and distribution of films has resulted in extravagant budgets, often chaotic production conditions where a popular star is juggling shooting dates between twenty films that he/she has signed to do. With the growth of 'black money' (untaxed profits) and corruption in government, film production has become a relatively easy way to convert money made illegally into 'white' money. There are too few theatres, some 12,900 in 1992, for a population of nearly one billion people. They are unevenly spread out in big cities and towns, leaving rural areas, where almost 80 per cent of Indians live, unserved. Uneven development, chaotic production conditions, a high level of publicity generated about the stars and their extravagant lifestyles and excessive violence and sex in films attracts attention from political parties and state institutions. As we will see in this chapter, failures in self-regulation on the part of the industry cry out for reform by the state, thereby enhancing the role and power of the state in India's film industry.

NATIONAL FILM DEVELOPMENT CORPORATION

In the last twenty years, the central government has played a major role at the national level in the film industry, including financing, distribution, promotion of films at home and abroad; subsidies for theatre construction; censorship; taxation; limiting entry to foreign companies; and awards to filmmakers. The institutional mechanism to implement several of central government policies was the National Film Development Corporation (NFDC) which was organized in 1980, amalgamating two earlier institutions – the Film Finance Corporation and the Film Export Corporation. The government initially set up the NFDC as a tool to develop 'good cinema' as opposed to the commercial fare. NFDC's powers and activities have, over the years, grown considerably. They include nearly all the important activities of filmmaking and marketing at home and abroad. Its screening, subtitling, duplicating and other facilities, which have been added in the last ten years, are impressive.

The NFDC encourages good scriptwriting by holding national competitions and helps produce the chosen few either by co-financing or fully financing them. In less than nine years since its inception, NFDC has co-financed over 200 feature films, several documentaries and fully funded twelve feature films (Chandran 1989). Its own productions include Satyajit Ray's *Ghare Bhaire* (1984) and his last film *Ganashatru* and many other international award winners such as Ketan Mehta's *Mirch Masala* (1986) and Utpalendu Chakravorty's *Debshishu* (1986). It is not possible to assess how many of these feature films have actually returned their investment or made a profit because those data are not available.

Basically, the NFDC provides 'interim' financing to filmmakers who make substantial investments in a project to complete their film, charging them interest on the loan. The loan is advanced on the basis of a collateral, just as a bank does. Only since 1984 has the NFDC started to fully finance a few films a year. As the banks have been reluctant to get involved in financing movies, the NFDC's role even as a co-financier is crucial to many filmmakers.

The NFDC has also become involved in international co-production of features and television programmes, most notably *Gandhi* (1984) and *Salaam Bombay* (1988), both of which brought many prestigious awards. The latter was directed by Mira Nair, winning her the famed Caméra d'Or at Cannes in 1988. With the expansion of television, NFDC has started to collaborate with India's government-controlled, national television network, Doordarshan, in making TV movies.[2]

Under its theatre financing scheme, where private entrepreneurs receive low interest loans and a subsidy, the NFDC financed 127 theatres, of which eighty-two are operational in fifteen states of India, thereby adding a total of 65,801 seats (see Table 9.1). This policy helped alleviate the severe shortage of theatres in general, although it is hard to tell whether it has resulted in building theatres in rural towns with populations under 50,000 where such entertainment facilities are sorely needed.

Table 9.1 Theatres completed under NFDC's theatre financing scheme, as of 1989

State	Number of theatres	Seating capacity
Andhra Pradesh	11	8,446
Assam	2	2,010
Bihar	1	772
Gujarat	2	1,724
Karnataka	10	7,183
Kerala	7	6,098
Madhya Pradesh	12	10,708
Maharastra	5	4,187
Manipur	1	1,326
Orissa	6	4,756
Pondicherry	1	971
Rajasthan	1	1,163
Tamilnadu	8	6,256
Uttar Pradesh	11	6,286
West Bengal	4	3,915
Total	82	65,801

Source NFDC News (1988: 6)

The NFDC acts as a distributor and exhibitor for feature films. In the 1980s, it imported about fifty to sixty films a year, a wide variety coming from different parts of the world to be screened in the few non-commercial theatres in various cities (Chandran 1989). It claims to have first option on playing time at the theatres built with its assistance. However, it is not known to what extent that has been used. Generally speaking, theatre owners are not enthusiastic about providing playing time to off-beat films because they claim that audiences are not interested in such films. However, there are many examples of successes, once given access to theatres. Govind Nihalani's *Ardh Satya* (1983), produced at a cost of Rs. 1.6 million, grossed at least double that in its theatrical release.[3] In 1985, Amol Palekar's *Ankahee*, not an NFDC production, ran for more than thirteen weeks in three theatres in Bombay (Palekar, Personal interview, Bombay, 1985). Despite those 'hits' the overall performance of the off-beat film has been poor in terms of attracting audiences and building a base. The NFDC's efforts to expand the markets domestically for India's new cinema appear discouraging.

Some filmmakers have complained that their films have not been promoted well by the NFDC, as it tends to concentrate its efforts on a few big-name directors such as Satyajit Ray and Mrinal Sen (Palekar, Personal interview, Bombay, 1985). That controversy aside, participation by Indian filmmakers at international film festivals appears to have grown. Indian films have historically been popular in various parts of the Middle East, Africa, Asia, USSR and Latin America. These markets expanded throughout the 1970s in conjunction with the rise in the number of Indians living abroad. Gross revenues from export of feature films grew from Rs. 55 million in 1973 to Rs. 150 million in 1980, which was the peak year, and started to decline.[4] The NFDC has grappled with this problem by setting up a regional office in London and by organizing film bazaars during various international film festivals as well as at the New Delhi International Film Festival. Although video piracy is blamed as the main cause for the decline in export revenues, between 1981–8 (for which data were available) the sale of video rights through the NFDC has grown considerably. That, however, does not offset the losses incurred by the decline in sale of theatrical and television rights of films. That point is dramatically made if we compare the total revenues in 1981 and 1988, which shows the overall decline to be more than half.

NFDC appears to be concentrating on the traditional markets for Indian films abroad to increase sales. The Arabian Gulf, the USSR and Indonesia used to be the biggest markets for Indian films. The UK and USA markets have grown in size in the last ten years. In the Gulf countries and in many parts of Africa, video markets are probably larger than theatrical and television broadcast markets. Video piracy, however, makes it difficult for the copyright holder to gain much from that growing market. In the US market, the diasporic audiences have not only grown in size but have returned to theatres. In major cities such as New York, Chicago and San Francisco Hindi films are regularly shown at least in one theatre operated by a South Asian-owned company. The Bombay film industry's organized attempt to delay the release of videos in 1995 may have helped because distributors advertised major films in the South Asian media stating that the film would not be available on video for quite some time. Perhaps more importantly, the poor quality of the videos and the possibility to socialize with one's friends in a theatre are attractive propositions to South Asian audiences. Going to the movies with family and friends is a pleasurable reminder of the audiences's past in South Asia.

NFDC has not yet tapped into the North American market well. It has been planning to open a regional office in New York to have a presence in this most important but tough market. It needs to promote and market Indian films to various kinds of markets in the US and Canada including art cinema houses, video outlets, and non-theatrical markets such as the universities and colleges.

IMPORTATION OF FILMS

Foreign imports entered the Indian market via four legal channels: (1) Motion Picture Export Association of America; (2) Sovexport Film; (3) the NFDC; and (4) non-resident Indian importers. Pirates of foreign film/video materials circulate widely, although clandestinely, coming into the country probably through the Gulf countries of the Middle East. It is estimated that the American Majors alone lose an estimated $10–15 million annually due to video piracy in India (MPEAA 1989).

Foreign distributing companies were not allowed into India without an operating agreement with the NFDC. Due to foreign exchange shortages, the government has historically used this policy to limit the number of imports into the country and thereby the earnings of foreign distributors. It has also attempted to impose limits on remittances of hard currency by those companies as well as on the uses of non-repatriated earnings (Pendakur 1985: 52–72). The MPEAA and the Sovexport Film each had bilateral agreements to operate in India. Under the terms of those agreements, the MPEAA was allowed to import about 100 titles and the Sovexport Film twenty titles a year (Chandran 1989). The MPEAA members, who together earned about $5 million annually from India, could remit no more than $700,000 in 1989, $1 million in 1990 and $1.4 million in 1991.

Foreign corporations licensed as importers had to pay the NFDC a canalizing fee of 15 per cent on the cost of prints, insurance and freight of films, trailers, stills, etc., that were brought into the country. This fee did not amount to much given the quota being around 120 films total per year. However, it was a guaranteed source of hard currency for the NFDC. Soviet imports did not receive as wide a release as the MPEAA imports, which were shown in about 100 theatres in large and medium size cities (Pendakur 1985: 52–72).

In the home video distribution market, all but the MPEAA companies were restricted to sell and distribute their titles through the NFDC. It runs the only film-to-tape transfer and video duplicating technology centre in the country. The NFDC claimed that it had acquired rights to over 100 'good' films from all over the world and released high quality cassettes (NFDC 1988). Although technically not barred from the home-video market, the MPEAA companies ran into a clever rule devised by the government to limit their profits. For all titles that the MPEAA companies imported into India prior to 1 August 1988, video tapes had to be imported through the NFDC (MPEAA 1989). This policy effectively made the NFDC sole agent for the Hollywood majors' large libraries of film titles in the Indian market. The MPEAA argued that without sufficient quantities of previously released titles, its member companies could not operate profitably.

RELAXATION OF IMPORTS

The tight control exercised over the import of feature films from abroad meant, among other things, Indian audiences interested in foreign films had to wait a long time to see some of the best films from abroad. As the MPEAA member companies were seldom interested in distributing films from all over the world, unless they owned copyright to those films, what Indian audiences saw was mostly the Hollywood popular films with severe cuts imposed by the Censor Board. These patterns of the past thirty or so years are in the process of being changed some what in this decade.

The first radical shift in policy came when the central government modified its import policy in the late 1980s by licensing several distribution companies owned by non-resident Indians to import feature films from abroad.[5] The policy broke the monopoly of the MPEAA and immediately some fifteen to twenty companies came into being and started importing feature films. They were, however, mostly 'B' grade, action/adventure genre films, which promised a lot of sex and stunts on their large hoardings but left the audiences dissatisfied after the Censor Board went to work on them.

The next major revision of the government's policy took place in September 1992 after the policy of liberalization and privatization of the Indian economy were implemented by Prime Minister Narasimha Rao. The Central Board of Film Certification (CBFC) certified sixty imported films between Sept 1992–March 1993, a six month period. In the same period, 165 Indian films were approved by the censors (Nair 1993: 1 and 4)

Since March 1993, many more American imports became available on India's screens: *The Bodyguard* and *Unforgiven* are such examples. Needless to say, the MPEAA member companies were pleased with the new policy. Joe D'Cunha, General Manager of Columbia/Tristar Films of India Ltd predicted that imports of his cartel members would go up to an all time high. By May 1993, MPEAA members had imported forty-seven features of which thirty had been cleared by the censors; the others were waiting certification. D'Cunha declared:

> It is the best phase ever witnessed by film importers in recent times. The clearance of films hardly takes a week, which otherwise used to vary from six months to a year. It is because of this change in scenario that MPEAA members are in a position to import good quality films.
>
> (Nair 1993: 1 and 4)

High 'quality' is not necessarily the principal outcome of this policy. As the MPEAA companies sell in blocks (block booking), there are always marginal films included with 'quality' films. What appears to have occurred is that the MPEAA can quickly exploit a large market of the English-speaking audience through greater efficiencies introduced in censorship and other regulatory bottlenecks of the past.

Mr G. H. Jiten, President of NRI Film Importers Guild, subscribed to a different opinion. He asserted that the scrapping of the canalizing fee will encourage independent importers to bring about fifty films to the country every year. He indicated, 'NRI importers will be trying to import the best quality foreign films available in the world market to give a stiff and – "clean" competition to MPEAA members' (Nair 1993: 4). That was a reference to the earlier times when the NRI importers were criticized for bringing in mostly sex and violence oriented films. It was estimated that importers would bring in 170 films during 1993; an increase of 50 per cent from 1992. The MPEAA planned to import some eighty films, the rest from independents including the NFDC, which planned to import some thirty films from around the world (Nair 1993: 4). It is not clear whether or not the independent distributors have been able to bring in a diverse body of films into the country and become viable in opposition to the MPEAA.

Prior to the September 1992 modifications, import of foreign films was routed through NFDC as it was the canalizing agent for film import and export from India for some time. The Film Import Selection Committee at the NFDC had to clear each film for the country. The reasoning behind this selection process was that a group of experienced filmmakers with the interest of 'educating' film audiences would pick better quality films. It, however, ran into trouble with the MPEAA companies and other distributors rather quickly. The distributors argued that such a policy meant double 'censorship' of their films. Furthermore, after obtaining permission from the NFDC, the film could still be delayed, cut or banned by the Censor Board.

NFDC was paid a canalizing fee by the importers for each film that was brought into the country. They also had to pay a censorship fee. By making the CBFC the sole authority to determine what imports are allowable into India, the central government in one stroke removed the whole obstacle to importers and also reduced their expenses.

The Censor Board appears to have relaxed their attitude towards nudity and violence in certain films. For example, *Schindler's List* was passed without any cuts. This may in the long run encourage US distributors to attempt to import a wider variety of films from within their own supply, but the vagaries of the Censor Board make this a nearly impossible. I will return to film censorship later.

In the liberalizing Indian economy of the 1990s, Hollywood film distributors have discovered a huge pent up demand for movies with glitzy special effects (norm of the high budget, blockbuster genre) and animated features. *Jurassic Park* with its thirty ton, fifty foot-high branchiosaur went on to create history in the Indian market and set two precedents in 1994. Universal Pictures dubbed the film into Hindi, costing some $30,000, and released it simultaneously in eight cities as a wide release. These were unprecedented decisions but they paid off quite handsomely. The film ran in forty-four theatres in the Bombay territory. In large cities such as Delhi, it opened at four theatres but the run expanded to include twice as many theatres. Ticket prices in the black market are often used in India to judge how 'hot' the picture is. Scalpers in some Bombay theatres demanded Rs. 40 per ticket and in Pune they were going for Rs. 150 each. The Indian audiences, just as the mass audiences in the US, had taken to giant size animals of an imagined past. The film was estimated to gross a sum of Rs. 50,000,000, unprecedented for any imported film into India (Chandra 1994: 117).

The other distributors followed Universal's path and planned the release of hit films such as Patrick Swayze's *Ghost* and Jean-Claude Van Damme's *Universal*

154

Soldier and *Double Impact* – all dubbed into Hindi. While this attempt by US and other importers to compete with India's national cinema on its own turf with dubbed versions of mega hits from abroad created jitters in the Bombay filmmaking circles, their fear was premature because Disney's animated feature, *Aladdin*, did not achieve such a high box office success. Mody Enterprises, in which Disney has an equity partnership, dubbed the film into several languages and released it, but it had mixed success. Undaunted, Mody plans to import some eight to ten features every year from the Disney vault as well as the new productions. It is not clear yet if Indian audiences will be as enamoured with humanized animals as they were with the killer animals of *Jurassic Park*.

CENSORSHIP

An interesting discussion on film censorship between B.K. Karanjia, a well-known journalist and editor of *Screen*, the film industry trade paper, and Hrishikesh Mukherjee, a prominent film editor-director and then chairman of NFDC, was published almost ten years ago. It captures the conflicting tendencies that exist among the filmmakers (and other elites) and policy makers in India regarding the role of censorship in Indian society. Karanajia related to Mukherjee how Justice Khosla (who headed the committee which studied censorship back in the early 1960s) called Stanley Kubricks' *Clockwork Orange* an obscene film. Karanjia disagreed with the judge and observed that the film 'is a very violently anti-violent film. It brought out the horror of violence very effectively' (Karanjia 1984: 2). To which Mukherjee replied:

> Justice Khosla was, in my opinion, absolutely correct. What is important is the effect these types of films will have on the Indian audience. Our audiences are still very immature. So we have to take into consideration their receptivity. Justice Khosla's contention was that when sex is coupled with violence it is easily imitated. . . . Justice Khosla told me from his personal experience: Sex – allow; Violence – curb it. Sex, combined with violence – ban it.

> (Karanjia 1984: 3)

If this guideline was followed strictly by the censors, more than half of Hindi films produced in the 1980s would qualify for such a ban. Mukherjee went on to say:

> At the same time in our country we cannot put all the blame on cinema. For in Bengali films you see hardly any violence compared to the amount of violence in Bengal. Which film is responsible for the cement scandal or the Bhagalpur blindings?

> (Karanjia 1984: 3)

Notwithstanding the above statement, as filmmakers, critics, government functionaries and elites, they exhibit contradictory tendencies on the issue of sex and violence in films. On the one hand filmmakers such as Hrishikesh Mukherjee don't

155

want to strengthen the hand of commercial filmmakers by allowing them to do what they want, but on the other, they don't want restrictions on their own art practices. Most telling is their position on the Indian audience whom they hardly consider as 'adults'. Such is the imperial influence on elite minds in India.

While the US film industry avoided government censorship by imposing self censorship in the 1920s, the British colonial administration institutionalized censorship in India. The national government has continued that tradition. The Cinematograph Act of 1918, the first such law to deal with cinema, licensed the safety of theatres and certified films that were suitable for public exhibition. In 1920, boards of film censors were set up in Bombay, Calcutta, Madras and Rangoon whose decisions were valid throughout British India but could be suspended by a provincial authority. General principles governing censorship were borrowed from the British Board of Film Censors in England. Provincial boards of censors had all the power to license films for exhibition, which meant a film allowed in one area of India may be banned in another. This system, cumbersome and costly from the point of filmmakers, was changed with the Cinematograph Act of 1949 when censorship was centralized (Ministry of Information and Broadcasting 1978: 2–3).

The Central Board of Film Certification administers the Cinematograph Act through regional boards of censors located in Bombay, Madras and Calcutta.[6] These boards have the power to recommend cuts as well as ban a film outright. A producer may appeal their decision to higher authority vested in appeals committees, and eventually the Ministry of Information and Broadcasting in New Delhi. If all that fails, s/he could contest their decision in a court of law.

While the 'no kissing' policy has been widely publicized in the Western media, implementation of censorship policy in general is uneven at best. For instance, the Board is supposed to ensure that 'anti-social activities such as violence are not glorified or justified', 'the modus operandi of criminals or other visuals or words likely to incite the commission of any offense are not depicted', and 'pointless or avoidable scenes of violence, cruelty and horror are not shown'. Not only vulgarity and obscenity are forbidden but 'visuals or words depicting women in ignoble servility to man or glorifying such servility as a praiseworthy quality in women are not presented' (Chandran 1989). Commercial cinema is replete with violations of the above guidelines as producers with political clout in the capital have been able to stretch the regulations. Raj Kapoor, a major producer-director who died in 1988, could get away with a lot more sexual imagery in his films, allegedly due to his loyalty to the ruling Congress Party.[7] Amjad Khan, an actor-director, who was frustrated in his efforts to get censor clearance for his film *Chor Police* noted, 'If I am influential enough to know the right man at the right place, I can get things done in ten minutes' (Ramachandran 1985: 542). Filmmakers in Calcutta have long complained that their regional censor office applies the regulations much more strictly compared to the ones in Bombay and Madras.[8]

Despite rules and guidelines, suggestive dialogue, crude sexual exhibition, rape and other violent acts against women are common ingredients in the popular cinema. Several filmmakers have been able to push the limits of allowability by providing morally acceptable endings to the film. For instance, I.V. Shashi's *Her Nights*, the story of a prostitute, contained explicit sex and became a box office hit. He was allowed to release the film only after he agreed to change the ending:

> Originally, the film ended on a tragic note. But the censors refused to give a certificate unless there was a happy ending. They wanted the hero to marry the prostitute, even though it went against the grain of the film and the prostitute's character. I had to oblige them by re-shooting the ending.
>
> (*India Today* 1980: 65)

In another Malayalam block buster, *Dream Niqhts*, a pubescent heroine seduces a fifteen-year-old boy. They are seen passionately making love behind a temple. In a twist, probably provided to appease the censors, she is killed by a snake bite in divine retribution.

In some cases, where the Censor Board ordered the deletion of certain scenes, the producers restored them to the release print after obtaining the clearance. This has come to be known as 'interpolation'. A Kannada film, *Antha* (1985), consisted of extremely violent scenes where a pregnant woman was kicked in her stomach. It drew huge audiences in Bangalore and the press speculated on how such a film could obtain the censor certificate. The Board's response was that it had not permitted those scenes but the producer had interpolated them later. There are some instances when audiences have been totally shocked (or delighted) to find an explicitly sexual scene, clearly interjected after the film made it through the Censor Board.

Besides such gratuitous sex and violence, the overall impact of censorship on Indian cinema is the distorted treatment of sexuality. Adult themes are seldom tackled in a mature way, such as showing sex as a basic human need and how it cannot be fulfilled in a society where young couples have seldom the space, the privacy or the cultural tolerance for it. While the society remains puritanical, the larger-than-life images of sexuality in cinema are highly exaggerated ones, simply fuelling fantasy to millions of young people. One wonders whether any of these fantasies ever come true and whether the Indian moviegoers' psyche is a bank of frustrations.

Censorship has had serious consequences on the political use of cinema. For instance, no filmmaker is allowed to name and criticize the party in power, the Nehru/Gandhi family, or deal with controversial topics such as the Naxalbari revolutionary movement or the scandalous arms deal with the Swedish firm, Bofors, in the 1980s. M.S. Satyu's *Garm Hava* (1974), which went on to win the national award, was held up for nearly a year. It was the first time a filmmaker touched the topic of how a Muslim family felt during the time of India's partition in 1947. In 1975, a year marked by a national emergency, *Kissa Kursi Ka* created history when it was denied censorship.[9] The film made by Amrit Nahata, a member of Parliament, was apparently critical of the ruling party and lampooned its leaders, including the Prime Minister. Its negative as well as the prints mysteriously vanished. It is alleged that they were burnt at the behest of Sanjay Gandhi, the then Prime Minister's son (Bobb 1978: 24–33). A film entitled *Naxalites* (1980), written and directed by the well-known K.A. Abbas, was held up for 102 days before receiving the censor certificate. Anand Patwardhan's documentary film, *Bombay Our City* (1984), which dealt with the suffering heaped on the tenement dwellers in Bombay by the city government and the rich who wanted to beautify the city, was detained by the censors until a public uproar caused it to given in. One Bengali producer-director, Biplab Ray Chaudhuri, told me that his film *Yeh Kahani Nahin* (1985), dealing with the conflict between the caste Hindus and untouchables was unacceptable to the censors unless he made sixty-four cuts. They were all dialogue scenes where the high caste characters revealed their feelings towards the untouchables and, without those dialogues, there was no story left. He fought the case in court and eventually won after agreeing to delete four scenes.

The consequence of such legal battles often damage a film's distribution and thereby its profitability. Shyam Benegal, another major director, who has had his share of the problems with the censors, put it bluntly:

> Litigation could be suicidal for the producer with all his money locked up in the film. The way the economics of the industry works, it is imperative for any producer to get his film released without delay. He cannot afford to take the Censor Board to court.
>
> (India Today 1980: 71)

Any delay in releasing a film is costly, especially if the producer has borrowed completion money at usurious rates of interest, as is common. Even getting an 'A' (adults only) certificate as opposed to a 'U' (all ages) certificate could make a big difference to the producer's profitability.[10] In the particular instance of Ray Chaudhury's film, it could not compete for the national award, thereby affecting its future marketability and profits.

Two significant cases of censorship of the 1990s are *Bombay* (1995) and *Bandit Queen* (1995), which reveal how deeply political the whole exercise has become in post-colonial India. *Bombay*, directed by Mani Rathnam, deals with a love story between a Hindu youth and a Muslim girl set against the backdrop of the high level of tensions that have developed between Hindus and Muslims since 1989. It is an extremely effective film as it draws the viewer's attention to how communities are being split by political parties in the name of religion, and how that has ended up in bloodshed even in cities such as Bombay where Hindus and Muslims have coexisted for decades. The first half of the film develops the tensions between the two families in rural India and the youths' rejection of tradition and their escape to the big, modern city where they encounter prejudice but manage to overcome it by their love and humanity. While their falling in love and the ensuing tensions are not new to Indian popular cinema, what is new is the powerfully evocative imagery of *Bombay* and its music. The second half of the film deals with the couple's life in Bombay where they live with their two little boys in a culturally diverse community. The couple are about to make peace with their stubborn fathers who come to visit them, but all that is suddenly torn apart by political violence. Their friends, family and the whole neighborhood is caught up in the stormy political upheaval resulting from the destruction of the Babri mosque in Ayodhya in December 1992 by thousands of armed Hindus mobilized by a Hindu right-wing political party, known as the Bharatiya Janata Party. Bombay is enveloped in violence for days where neighbours kill neighbours, friends become enemies, families and homes are destroyed. The protagonist in the film, the Hindu youth, is a journalist who defies the order of the day and brings some sense to the politicians behind all the violence and succeeds in having the cycle of revenge stopped. The film had trouble from the beginning.

It is believed that Mani Rathnam had to make a deal to cut a scene lasting some four and half minutes of an inflammatory speech made by Bal Thackeray, the leader of Shiv Sena, an arm of the BJP. He apparently speaks of 'ethnic cleansing' in Bombay and preserving that city only for the Hindus whose ancestry is Maharashtrian. Shiv Sena controlled the city government in Bombay by this time and had sufficient power on the street to prevent the release of the film if the director did not compromise. While the film attempts to be even handed in placing the 'blame' on the opposing Hindu and Muslim political parties, it shows angry Muslims taking to the streets with weapons in hand after the mosque is destroyed as though that is how it happened. After the carnage, all attributed to the warring, faceless Hindus and Muslims supposedly with the help of their political leaders, there is not a single scene in which the police open fire on the crowds. We see them trying to establish order, but not as killers which is what happened by all known accounts.

Despite these important compromises, the historical distortions and half truths, the film ran into trouble with the Censor Board. Portrayal of Thackeray was seen as being too 'strong' by the Censor Board, although the dialogues were apparently lifted straight from his speeches. The chairman of the Censor Board, Shakti Samantha, sought the opinion of the Home Ministry on the film and screened the film for some top ministry officials as well as top police and crime branch officials. The city police commissioner, Satish Sawhney, was reported to have 'felt that the film was not fit for public viewing, and that its exhibition involved risk'. Basically, the Censor Board feared reaction and threat of violence from the Shiv Sena party members according to a senior member of the Censor Board:

> We could have passed the film without the government's involvement, but why take the risk? Tomorrow, if some problem occurs, police might turn back and say we didn't seek their opinion. Though we can stop a film's exhibition if it creates disturbance, we are taking precautions.
>
> (Noorani 1995: 240)

The police authorities in Bombay predictably passed the buck to the Chief Minister, Sharad Pawar of the Congress (Indira) Party. The end result as far as public records go is the deletion of parts of a speech given by Thackeray. What is astonishing in this particular case is not that the Censor Board had any objections in terms of the violence or some other issue, but that it acted with cowardice and failed to carry out its own constitutional role of upholding the law. According to an earlier Supreme Court ruling on a different film, it is impermissible to delay, let alone refuse certification because of the fear of violence. The highest court of the land had held that the state cannot plead its inability to handle the hostile audience problem, if the film is unobjectionable and cannot constitutionally be restricted. The court had asked the question, 'What good is the protection of freedom of expression if the state does not care to protect it?' The court had declared that freedom of expression cannot be suppressed on account of threat of demonstration and processions or threats of violence.[11]

The Censor Board clearly abdicated their duties and functions by passing the buck to the police and then on to the Chief Minister of the State. The Cinematograph Act 1952 (as amended) confers the necessary authority to the Board to set up examining committees, revising committees, and explicit reference is made for outside assistance in the form of advisory panels. They rule out extra constitutional and extra-legal 'assistance' as the Board may consult only these panels which are set up within the purview of the law. In the case of *Bombay*, by playing it safe bureaucratically and passing the buck to the Home Ministry and the Chief Minister of the State, the chairman of the Board abdicated his responsibility to uphold the law.

Bombay eventually was released and has gone on to a successful run of twenty-five weeks. The Telugu version of the film opened all over Andhra Pradesh but has had problems in the twin cities of Hyderabad and Secunderabad, with large Muslim populations. One of the theatres, Devi, received an anonymous telephone call during a late night show that a bomb had been placed in theatres. Immediately the Police Commissioner stopped the screening of the film in the twin cities. Mani Rathnam, the director, flew to Hyderabad to meet with the distributors and the politicians. He was reported to have met N.T. Rama Rao, the Chief Minister, to seek his intervention in this matter. Meanwhile the distributor went to court against the Police Commissioner's order (Sastry 1995: 1). Mani Rathnam has also received death threats and an attempt on his life was made in July. His house in Madras was bombed while people were asleep, but no one was killed. Mani Rathnam escaped the attack with minor injuries. The culprits have not been caught. These incidents prove that no matter how many cuts or compromises, the film would be opposed by somebody or the other and that the role of the state should be to protect free expression and not to second guess how the viewers would respond or which political party would oppose the film.

Bandit Queen was an invited entry at the Young Director's section of the Cannes International Film Festival in 1995 and received rave reviews from international journalists. It has since been featured at other major international venues. The film is based on what its director, Shekhar Kapur, calls the 'true story' of Phoolan Devi, a low caste woman, who suffered the worst humiliations that poor people suffer in certain parts of rural India. Phoolan is married off at age 11 to a much older man who rapes her. She runs away from his house back to her parents, but then becomes an object of men's ridicule and secret desires. She is falsely accused of inviting the village headman's son to bed and the village leaders (all men) throw her out of the village. The police lock her up in a jail where she is gang raped by them before she is let out. She ends up in a gang of bandits and learns survival from them, falls in love with a low caste leader of the dacoits, and becomes the most celebrated bandit in the Chambal Valley in northern India. The poor masses whom she helps with her loot give her the title of 'Devi' (goddess). The caste tensions among the bandits lead to internal warfare and her lover is killed and she gets captured by the rival leader. She is gang raped and dragged through her village naked to show how upper caste men will treat low caste women who aspire to be leaders and what upper caste men can do to 'goddesses of low castes'. She escapes from that gang and joins a rival gang led by a Muslim and regains her notoriety and fame as a leader of the poor, low caste masses. All of these developments reach a high point where they become an embarrassment to the Chief Minister of the State who is up for reelection. The military is sent out to make sure she has no choice but to surrender to the authorities. After all of her friends are killed by the military, Phoolan Devi, with gun in one hand, accepts the terms of the military to surrender in a media event organized to benefit the politicians.

This gritty, political drama has no fantasy elements that are common in most Hindi popular films. It is not the dull 'realism' of India's New Wave either. The narrative is episodic, but builds tension with disturbing accuracy. The technical aspects of the film, particularly its cinematography and sound, are of incredibly high quality. Although the narrative is not in Phoolan Devi's voice, the director does not appear to compromise in any way to tell his story about the caste, class and gender warfare that characterizes much of rural India through a celebrated woman who survived it all.

The film was financed by Channel 4 in England for an estimated $4 million. By now, the real Phoolan Devi had spent eleven years in a jail without 'trial' and received a pardon by Mulayam Singh Yadav, the new Chief Minister of Uttar Pradesh, himself from a low caste origin. Kapur showed the uncensored film to Phoolan Devi who decided to oppose the release of the film. She claimed that it was not the story she had narrated to the writer in the jail at all and challenged several key scenes in the film. The Delhi High Court banned the public exhibition of the film due to the dispute.

The film developed other political problems in India. The Film Federation of India had nominated the film for an Oscar under the foreign film category. The Delhi High Court issued another order in February 1995 to withhold the film from going to the Oscars in the US and the Federation had no choice but to withdraw the film (Burman 1995a: 3).

As was expected, the Censor Board denied a certificate without cuts. Shekhar Kapur, the director, spoke about the impasse with the Censor Board:

> I've said I won't cut, and they said they won't let the film go if I don't cut. I don't have a legal standing. If tomorrow the producer or distributor

decides to release with cuts, I can't do anything. All I will do is take my name off it.

(Roy-Chowdhury 1995: 30)

All the intrigue, political intervention, jealousies in the industry, media hype, the Oscar nomination, and the subsequent withdrawal have made this film an event of the decade. Given the brutally explicit representation of caste and gender conflict in the film through the prism of violence, frontal nudity, gang rape (even while in police custody), it will be a miracle if the Censor Board allows its public screening in India without significant mutilation of the film. The first hurdle to get the certification was removed in July 1995 when Phoolan Devi, now married and living in a wealthy suburb of New Delhi, settled out of court by making a deal with Channel 4 for $60,000 (da Cunha 1995: 32). The producers apparently accepted a few cuts to get the film through the Censor Board in Bombay. Phoolan Devi, however, proved once again that she was a great survivor and that she is still a bandit *par excellence*.

Such clear cut instances of conflict between the producer and the censors, the economic consequences notwithstanding, prove that censorship is inherently coercive. It limits artistic and political expression in Indian cinema. The producers often second guess what may be and may not be allowed and construct ideas and scenes around those conceptions. The net result is a chilling effect on the filmmakers and exclusion of certain themes which might be considered risky by the investors. The government's role in India's cinema is clearly that of patron and police. One cannot help notice how close it is to a feudal overlord who patronizes art and, at the same time, sets serious limits to it.

Members of various boards, who are appointed by the government, are largely treated with suspicion by the industry and its critics. G.D. Khosla, former justice who chaired the 1969 Enquiry Committee on Film Censorship, made the following observation about the board members:

Censorship should be exercised by those who do not live in ivory towers. The films, in the first instance, are shown to a group of morons – the so-called panel advisors on the Censor Board – who are nominated not because they are qualified but because they have influence in the right quarters. They grab the offer to sit on Censor panels so that they may have the thrill of uncensored films free of charge.

(Ramachandran 1985: 540)

At best, the panel members reflect the conflicting tastes and moral standards of a multi-cultural society, which give rise to differences in the way the guidelines are applied to various films. Besides, when they are confronted with a politically charged film, they may worry about what the consequences might be if they displease the politicians in New Delhi. Patronage often works in subtle ways to reinforce the power of the state as the ultimate arbiter of taste, morality and the boundaries of political discourse in Indian cinema.

SELF-REGULATION AND INTERNAL BATTLES

The principal industry organizations in production and distribution of Hindi films – the Film Makers Combine and the Film Distributors Council – attempted to regulate the industry in the 1990s but collapsed due to internal contradictions. The Indian Motion Picture Distributors Association, representing the interests of the distributors in the Bombay circuit, also joined the tug of war in 1994. There were similar developments in the southern film industry as well. Due to space limitations, only the most recent battle is described here and its should be read as representing a historical process at work for almost half a century.

FMC was organized by the producers to exert control over the production and distribution of films in the country including the 'clearance' between theatrical and video releases of feature films. As production costs are seldom under control and Hindi film costs have risen sharply in the 1990s due primarily to the high salaries paid to stars and raw stock prices, the producers decided to organize themselves to curb star power. They introduced a ceiling of sixteen films that any a star could sign up simultaneously and attempted to limit competition for release dates as well by trying to regulate the release of films. The producers had to apply for permission from the FMC after signing up a star in their film and also get their clearance to release it when it is completed. Additionally, video and cable rights could not be sold until the films completed their theatrical run in the country. For a brief period, the FMC also got another industry organization, the Film Distributors Council, to go along with its policies to give them teeth. However, this whole initiative has run into serious problems within a short time as the interests of producers, stars, distributors and exhibitors are not always identical. Even the distributors themselves were not unified on these issues.

Vidhu Vinod Chopra, the producer of *1942, A Love Story* (1994) appears to have precipitated a crisis in FMC which ended in weakening the organization. Chopra's film was a multi-starer with a multi-million rupee investment, starring Anil Kapoor, Manisha Koirala, Jackie Shroff and Anupam Kher. When he applied for permission to shoot, he did not receive immediate action from the FMC. Given that costs mount in this industry as time passes, Chopra decided to go ahead with the shooting of the film which resulted in his suspension from the FMC. Chopra obtained permission from another organization in the industry, the Film Federation of India, and thereby challenged the collective power of the producers vested with the FMC. The distributors, who essentially are investors in film production as they advance large sums of money to feature film producers, rendered another fatal blow to the FMC through their organization, the FDC. Following FMC's inability to stop Chopra from completing his film, the FDC started issuing clearances to certain producers with *Rangeela* starring Jackie Shroff and Aamir Khan, and *Nayak* starring Sanjay Dutt. The producers did not approach the FMC to obtain clearances even to simply follow the convention (Nair 1994a: 1 and 2).

The FMC in retaliation against the FDC called on the producers in May 1994 to stop the release of all films, an action that backfired. While some major producers went along with the FMC resolution, others did not. Two films that featured major stars – *Aatish* and *Mohra* – had been booked into theatres and would have incurred heavy losses to all concerned if the ban was respected by their producers. While some producers simply wanted to avoid confrontation and see a solution to the problem at hand, others were of the opposite view. Dhirubhai Shah, who produced *Vijaypath*, due for release in May, was candid in his breach with the FMC:

> I have to finish the background score for the film and my film will be released as soon as I finish the work, irrespective whether there is an embargo or not. Nobody is going to bear the losses I incur for expressing my solidarity.
>
> (Nair 1994b: 4)

Shah is also a leading video distributor and FMC's embargo against simultaneous release of a film in theatrical and video markets would have hurt his interests. Chopra was also adamant about releasing his *1942, A Love Story* on 3 June 1994 even if the stalemate between the various organizations was not resolved.

The FMC's policy of regulating the release of motion pictures in the video and cable markets also ran into problems. The FMC wanted the video copies to come out two weeks after the release of the film in theatres and the film would then go into the cable market six months after its release theatrically. In the case of successful films such as *Hum Aap Ke Hain Koun* (1994), the delayed video release helped, but not in the case of failures which are most common in the industry.[12] N. N. Sippy, president of Indian Motion Picture Distributors Association (IMPDA) who once was a party to these agreements between the FMC and the FDC found the rules too rigid:

> Video postponement for two weeks or even more is justified if the film is on a successful track. But nobody can hold the release of cable rights for six months, especially those producers who notice that their film is a failing proposition right from the first week. As it is, the moment the video comes out, there are pirated cable versions of the same cassette.
>
> (Deshpande 1995a: 4)

Sippy was referring to the illegal use of copyrighted material in the burgeoning cable industry in India and the film industry's failure to get the government to protect their interests. Apparently, the FDC believed that video rights should not be offered to anyone but the distributors themselves. They also insisted on issuing permissions to producers to start new films, which the FMC believed was their prerogative as they represented the producers.

These differing priorities and interests finally resulted in a month-long strike by the Film Distributors Council over the issue of 'clearance' between theatrical, video and cable runs of motion pictures. This decision of the distributors sent tremors throughout the Bombay film industry as producers got caught in a Catch 22 situation. The FMC declared,

Distributors should restrict their activities to the commercial exploitation of films and should not meddle with production activities by giving clearances and monitoring star ceilings.

(Nair 1994c: 1)

Asked about the possibility of a compromise between the producers and distributors, N.N. Sippy, president of the Indian Motion Picture Distributors Association, put it plainly when he stated,

The producers have been calling us for a meeting. But our question is for what? We don't believe in only convening meetings and passing resolutions. We believe in taking action. Whatever we had decided was for the benefit of the industry and they should accept these facts.

(Deshpande 1995a: 4)

It looked for some time as though only the courts could resolve this dispute. Leading exhibitors were trying to get the distributors to go to court to resolve the dispute or to have the ban lifted.

Within a year, the Film Makers Combine, initiated to unify the producers on a set of issues, began to crack under pressures from both outside and inside the organization. The dissatisfied producers left the FMC to form their own organization called the Association of Motion Picture and TV Programme Producers (AMPTPP), reflecting the new realities of a changed industry as well. Some of the leading producers joined, thereby spelling an end to the FMC. Pahlaj Nihlani, one of the dissidents who formed the new association and became the president, revealed another facet of the power struggle between producers and distributors – the personality conflicts and the struggle for power in these organizations:

The bunglings that the current leadership of FMC has committed will have to be set right. We cannot afford to allow them to continue to do so just because we put them in the seat of power. Drunk with power, they may not be aware of the grievous injury they have inflicted on the industry. But we know that any further injury would spell its doom. So, by resigning, we have shorn them of power and put them in their places.

(Nihalani 1995: 6)

The majority of filmmakers had felt that the bickering, back biting and passing of resolutions which failed to attain self-regulation did not serve the film industry in the long run. Leading producers of Hindi films G. P. Sippy, Kamal Bharjatya, Shyam Benegal, Subhash Ghai, and N. B. Kamath formed the new organization. Sippy declared that the motto of the new association was, 'Live and Let Live'. While it was reported that the AMPTPP contacted organizations representing producers, distributors, studio owners, craft persons, actors, women artists, etc. it has not become clear yet as to what it could achieve in terms of self-regulation of the Hindi film industry (Burman 1995b: 3). The FDC also continued to haemorrhage when some of the provincial distribution organizations affiliated with the FDC began to abandon their national umbrella by summer 1995 (Deshpande 1995b: 1).

There has been a similar struggle in southern India as well with regards to the video and other new markets for movies made in the four southern states in different languages. To limit piracy on cable and video, the producers' association had agreed to vest the rights of their motion pictures with the South Indian Film Chamber of Commerce, a lobby group representing the producers, distributors and exhibitors. The producers had hoped that SIFCC would be powerful enough to not only represent their interests with the cable and video businesses but also with the government. In the meanwhile, the government of Tamilnadu passed rules to govern the cable industry whereby they restricted the telecast of feature films whose rights were not legally bought from the copyright holders. The producers then decided to take back their rights from the SIFCC so that they could negotiate with the cable and cassette industry on their own (*Screen* 1994: 1 and 4).

STATE GOVERNMENTS AND THE FILM INDUSTRY

Several state governments have assisted in developing their own regional film production by way of low-interest loans and subsidies to eligible entrepreneurs for infrastructure such as studios, labs, recording and dubbing facilities, etc. Many states have also instituted cash awards to meritorious films.

In Karnataka, a southern state, which offered the best support scheme in 1985, an art film producer was entitled to a cheque of Rs. 300,000 for a colour feature film if principal photography was done in that state and if s/he obtained a censor certificate (Mysore Math 1985: 1). Commercial films also made within the state were awarded a subsidy of Rs.150,000 for a black and white feature and Rs. 250,000 for a colour film. All films made within the state were further supported by a 50 per cent reduction in the entertainment tax charged on every ticket. The subsidy, first offered in 1967, has clearly boosted production in the state over a thirty-year period: feature film production went up from twenty-six in 1967 to eighty-eight in 1987. A total of 612 feature films had been subsidized between 1967 and 1984 (Subba Rao 1984: 94).

Available data suggest, however, that Karnataka was spending a small portion of what it collected from taxation on tickets. In the eight years between 1977 and 1984, the state's entertainment revenue amounted to Rs. 1,471.30 million, whereas it paid out only Rs. 40.47 million, which amounted to about 27 per cent (Subba Rao 1984: 94). While this policy may have assisted low-budget filmmakers and generally supported overall development of the infrastructure of the industry in the state, the government appears to be the biggest beneficiary, as the taxes from the film industry go directly into the general treasury.

Recently, Veerappa Moily, the Chief Minister of Karnataka, announced some long-awaited revisions to the state's policy towards the film industry. Theatre construction would be considered as 'industry' and would become eligible for tax concessions and other incentives given to industrial development in the state. This may help in the construction of new cinema halls in a state that desperately needs them, particularly in the rural towns. There were several provisions in the new policy to provide substantial tax relief to the industry as a whole. For instance, entertainment tax on each ticket came down to 15 per cent from 25 per cent of gross collection capacity for a minimum of fourteen shows per week. Although this means mandatory payment of the tax whether seats are filled or not, this helps theatre owners directly and producers/distributors indirectly as their slice of the box office pie will grow. Under the new taxation policy, the state removed surcharge on tickets up to Rs. 1.25 for Kannada films. Clearly intended to help the Kannada film industry, it also gives relief to the poorer classes who buy these tickets.

As an added incentive for filmmakers who are interested in taking some risks to make films that may not have commercial appeal but may win recognition in artistic circles, Moily provided an exemption for one year from the entertainment tax to Kannada films invited to the Indian Panorama and international film festivals. Those winning national and international awards and those selected for the Indian Panorama section of Indian festivals would be given a special incentive of Rs. 200,000 over and above the subsidy given to all Kannada films produced in the state. A new subsidy of Rs. 100,000 was provided for each Kannada film and teleserial (minimum theatre episodes) shown on Doordarshan (Kumari 1994: 1 and 4).

The state of Karnataka also added some new awards to the already established cash awards available for 'quality' films in the Kannada language. The best feature film with social relevance would receive Rs. 75,000 and a gold medal. It would also be exempt from the entertainment tax for one year. The best children's film would be awarded a gold medal and Rs. 50,000. Four other new awards are: best art director (Rs. 10,000); best lyricist (Rs. 15,000); best male and female playback singers (Rs. 5,000 each). The state increased the existing cash awards substantially (existing award in parenthesis): best film of the year, Rs. 100,000 (Rs. 50,000); director of the film that receives the best film of the year award, Rs. 20,000 (Rs. 5,000); second best film of the year Rs. 75,000 (Rs. 25,000); director of the second best film, Rs. 15,000 (Rs. 4,000); third best film Rs. 50,000 (Rs. 20,000); its director, Rs. 10,000 (Rs. 3,000); best actor and best actress, Rs. 20,000 (Rs. 4,000); best supporting actor/actress/child artiste, Rs. 10,000 (Rs. 2,000); best story writer, screenplay writer, dialogue, cinematographer, music director, sound engineer, editor, Rs. 10,000 each (Rs. 4,000). These are in recognition of artistic achievement in the industry and is long overdue.

CONCLUSIONS

The relationship between the state and the film industry in India is riddled with complications. At best the state plays the role of a benevolent overlord. While it is necessary for the state to intervene in the industry to encourage young artists by providing grants and subsidies to films which may not get financed by commercial distributors, and also assist in promoting and helping them gain access to the market, its role as a censor is extremely problematic. I have argued that censorship in India is historically connected to its colonial legacy and the Victorian morality persisting even today. The contradictory attitudes in the industry are not only troubling but have proven to perpetuate the power of the state over cinema. In the final analysis, what filmmakers have done is to resort to subversion of the censorship law and its regulations.

Whether any of these supportive mechanisms instituted by the state and central governments in India can be sustained in the face of international pressures is anyone's guess. As India is a signatory to the General Agreements on Tariffs and Trade, and the fact that the Hollywood majors have discovered that there is demand for certain of their films, subsidies and tax relief provided by various states to support local production may be challenged in the near future.

The very nature of how people consume films in India may change before the end of the century, given the recent trends of expansion of national television, emergence of private national and international networks vertically tied to major Hollywood studios, and programming on these satellite channels produced at home and abroad. As film production companies diversify their operations into television and other related media, one will not be able to look at film policy in isolation from these 'new' entertainment industries any longer. The internal battles over self-regulation in the film industry, sketched in this chapter, reflect some of those shifting currents in the industry. These are the seeds of change that will have far reaching implications for how films will be made in India, who will make them, and with what impact.

NOTES

1 The consequences of such state control over documentary production have not been studied well. Independent filmmakers who want to produce documentaries have to raise their own finances and their films may not get screen time at all as the state monopolizes that time. To get government finance, they have to be included in a roster of producers and can only make approved films. The few independents who work outside this system of production, rely principally on exposure at foreign film festivals and sales abroad. For an analysis of such recent independent production see Pendakur (1995).
2 For an analysis of shifts in national television policy away from education and development to popular entertainment see Pendakur (1991: 234–62).
3 The rupee is not converted into dollars because of the possibility that it would create a false impression by diminishing the size and importance of these figures. One US dollar, however, these days is equivalent to 31 rupees. A better figure to use is to compare purchasing power of the Indian masses in relation to the wages paid.
4 These data were compiled from different sources: for 1973–6 see Dharap (1979); for 1977–80 see, *India Today* (1981: 63). For an analysis of the issues related to Indian cinema's export markets see, Pendakur and Subramanyam (1995).

168

5　The category of non-resident Indians was created to allow Indian nationals and their descendants living abroad to invest hard currency in the Indian economy with attractive interest rates. India exported millions of workers to the Middle East after 1973, probably the largest pool of workers of all skill levels in the post-colonial period, and those who cannot remain in those countries on a permanent basis send their hard earned savings home. This population, coupled with the growing number of Indians in North America, the latter with certain lobby power in their home country, may have resulted in these policies related to non-resident Indians.

6　Voluntary censorship along the lines of the Hays Office's Production Code Authority was recommended by a government instituted Film Inquiry Committee in 1952. It had support from the Indian Motion Picture Producers' Association. Those recommendations have never been implemented (Ministry of Information and Broadcasting 1978: 2–3).

7　In *Mera Nam Joker* (1970) and in *Satyam Shivam Sundaram* (1978) he presented his heroines in the nude and convinced the Censor Board to allow those scenes. Before the latter film was released, he declared the market value of female nudity without mincing any words, 'Let people come to see Zeenat's tits, they'll go out remembering the film' (*India Today* 1980: 66).

8　Biplap Ray Choudhury's *Nirbachan* was delayed by the censors in Calcutta in 1995 and was released only after several prominent directors pressured the Minister for Information and Broadcasting by way of a letter writing campaign.

9　For an analysis of the emergency's effect on India's mass media and the political scandal surrounding this film see Pendakur (1988).

10　Producers fear they would lose about 30 per cent of revenue if their film was assigned an 'A' certificate. To avoid it, they may agree to re-shoot, delete the scenes found objectionable by the censors, etc.

11　The case concerned a Tamil film, *Ore Oru Gramathile* (1989), which dealt with the controversial policy of reserving certain number of jobs in state and central governments, and also seats in colleges, to classes of people held by the state as 'backward'. A writ petition was filed against the exhibition of the film and the producer had to go all the way to the Supreme Court to obtain justice. The film won the National Award at the film festival held by the government of India that year. See, Noorani: (1995: 240).

12　Pirated video copies of popular films such as *Hum Aapke Ke Hain Koun* continued to show up on the market but in limited numbers despite the industry's effort to control piracy. Clandestine copies of feature films on video for consumption abroad increased by one account. See Burman (1995c). In the video stores in Chicago, however, such films were not available because the video wholesalers in the US market have realized that the South Asian audiences are returning to movie theatres in greater numbers to view films and there are high returns in that market. Consequently, the video wholesalers are leasing 35mm theatres to show Indian imports on a regular basis.

REFERENCES

Bobb, D. (1978) 'Kissa kursi ka. The case of the missing film', *India Today*, 1–15 June.

Burman, J. (1995a) 'Shekhar Kapur's "Bandit Queen" out of Oscar race', *Screen*, 3 March: 1 and 2.

Burman, J. (1995b) 'FMC split now formal', *Screen*, 24 March: 1 and 2.

Burman, J. (1995c) 'Swift action by Bombay police. Video pirates of "Raja" and "Karan Arjun" arrested, released', *Screen*, 7 July: 1 and 4.

Chandra, A. (1994) 'Jurassic Park: a monster hit', *India Today*, 31 May: 117.

Chandran, M. (1989) *Documents*, National Film Development Corporation, Manager, Promotion and Public Relations, Bombay.

da Cunha, U. (1995) 'Bandit set for Indian pic screens', *Variety*, 20–6 March PAGES?

Deshpande, M. (1995a) 'IMPDA scoffs at FDC's non response', *Screen*, 2 June: 1 and 4.

Deshpande, M. (1995b) 'FDC faces further split. Bihar distributors form rival association', *Screen*, 7 July: 1 and 2.

Dharap, B.V. (1979) *Indian Films 1977 & 1978*, Pune: Motion Picture Enterprises.

India Today (1980) 'Films. Who's afraid of censorship!', 1–51 October.

India Today (1981) 16–31 July.

Karanjia, B.K. (1984) 'In Dialogue', *NFDC News*, March.

Kumari, U. (1994) 'Bonanza for Kannada film industry', *Screen*, 15 April: 1 and 4.

Ministry of Information and Broadcasting (1978) *Film Censorship in India* (A Reference Paper) National Documentation Centre on Mass Communication, Research & Reference Division, Government of India, New Delhi, 16 June.

MPEAA (1989) *Report to the United States Trade Representative: International Trade Restrictions Facing MPEAA Member Companies*, Motion Picture Export Association of America, Washington, D.C., March.

Mysore Math, S.G. (1985) 'Liberal incentives to boost Kannada cinema', *Screen*, Bombay, 9 August: 1.

Nair, P. (1993) 'Boom time for film importers', *Screen*, Bombay, 7 May: 1.

Nair, P. (1994a) 'Confusion prevails in production sector', *Screen*, Bombay, 22 April: 1 and 2.

Nair, P. (1994b) 'Impasse continues. Exhibitors to seek court intervention', *Screen*, Bombay, 13 May: 1 and 4.

Nair, P. (1994c) 'No releases after May 6', *Screen*, 6 May.

NFDC News (1988) National Film Development Corporation of India, Bombay, October-November.

Nihalani, P. (1995) 'Need for an image spruce-up', *Screen*, 10 March.

Noorani, A. G. (1995) 'Police as film censors', *Economic and Political Weekly*, Bombay, 4 February.

Palekar, A. (1985) Personal Interview, Bombay, July 17.

Pendakur, M. (1985) 'Dynamics of cultural policy making: The U.S. film industry in India', *Journal of Communication*, 35(4): 52–72.

Pendakur, M. (1988) 'Mass media during the 1975 National Emergency in India', *Canadian Journal of Communication*, 13(4): 32–48.

Pendakur, M. (1990) 'Indian feature film Industry: current problems and future trends', in John Lent (ed.) *Asian Cinemas: Industry and Art London*. London: Croom Helm.

Pendakur, M. (1991) 'A political economy of television: state, class, and corporate confluence in India', in Gerald Sussman and John Lent (eds) *Transnational Communication: Wiring the Third World*. London: Sage.

Pendakur, M. (1995) 'Cinema of resistence', *Documentary Box*, Yamagata International Film Festival, Tokyo, Summer.

Pendakur, M. and Kapur, J. (1996). 'Think globally, program locally: privatization of Indian national television', in D. Winsek, *et al.* (eds) *Democratizing Communication: A Comparative Perspective on Information and Power*. Hampton Press.

Pendakur, M. and Subramanyam, R. (1996) 'Indian cinema beyond national borders' in J. Sinclair, (ed.) *New Patterns in Global Television: Peripheral Vision*. Oxford: Oxford University Press.

Ramachandran, T. M. (ed.) (1985) *70 Years of Indian Cinema (1913–1983)*. Bombay: CINEMA India-International.

Roy-Chowdhury, S. (1995) 'The shame of men', *India Currents*, 9, 4 July.

Sastry, K. N. T. (1995) '"Bombay" withdrawn in Hyderabad', *Screen*, Bombay, 24 March 1 and 2.

Screen (1994) 'Video rights vested with producers', Bombay, 22 April 1 and 2.

Subba Rao, V.N. (1984) *Kannada Talkies Golden Jubilee, 1934–1984*. Bangalore: Government of Karnataka and Karnataka Film Chamber of Commerce.

10

CINEMA POLIC(ING)Y IN INDONESIA

Krishna Sen

In the 1990s cultural policy and cultural studies more generally has come to be increasingly framed with reference to globalization. Indeed, it has become common sense to name 'consolidation of global media system' (Robertson 1990: 27) as a key characteristic of the current phase of 'globalization'. Symptomatically, a recent (October 1994) issue of the Singapore based journal *Sojourn* sub-titled its volume on the 'mass media' *Local and Global Positions*.

In the theoretical engagement with the media, there is a growing attempt to conceptualize 'globalization' as a process that is different from those described in the 1960s and 1970s under the label of 'dependency' and 'media/cultural imperialism'. Amongst the most frequent citations in this academic discourse are Appadurai's notion of 'mediascape' (alongside all the other 'scapes') and Hannerz's argument about the disjuncture between cultural, economic and political centres of the world. Both work against the 'Western power' versus 'national resistance' paradigm on which the cultural imperialism thesis was predicated. For instance, Zaharom and Yao argue that 'developments relating to the media need to be understood within the wider context of globalization and transnational capitalism', but 'cannot be examined only from the view of local forces and responses – or . . . from the simplistic premiss of nation versus nation, East versus West' (1994: 177).

At the same time, the rhetoric of the national governments in most of Southeast Asia, at any rate, posits media globalizatian as yet another, and particularly pernicious, phase of 'Western cultural domination' of Asia. There are resonances here with the military analogy which Philip Schlesinger evoked to understand media policy in the British context. Schlesinger talks about the 'active mobilisation by states against "invasions" of their communicative space from outside . . . or "subversion" from within'. He suggests that

> notions of strategic and tactical use of communication are far from alien to our understanding of the construction of cultural collectivities and the workings of the media. This is no accident, for the media and the wider cultural fields are indeed conceived of as battlefields, as spaces in which the contests for various forms of dominance take place.
>
> (Schlesinger 1991: 299)

In both the rhetorical/government and theoretical/academic discourse on media, the nation-state appears embattled. In the former, the concrete nation is pitted against another (or a group of more) powerful nation(s). In the latter, the concept of nationhood is threatened by transnational technologies and capital.[1] Into this picture one can paint in the military metaphor of the Asian states seeking to define and secure national cultural borders against incursions.[2]

Against this picture where the global looms large in any discussion of the nation, particularly of national cultural policies, I want to suggest that Indonesian film policy, even in the 1990s, is best understood in relation to contradictions that are primarily located within the putated geographical borders of Indonesia. This is not to argue that the analysis of Indonesian film policy can take place entirely in relation to an 'inside' that can be marked off from the 'outside'. Co-productions and foreign investments in the media are instances where such distinctions become untenable. But the overall trend in Indonesian film policy during the New Order (that is since 1966) suggests that the state is far more anxious to restrict production taking place within Indonesia, than to keep out films coming in from the outside. As such we might think of Indonesian film policy as attempts by the state to police the cultural misdemeanours of its citizens rather than performing the military function of protecting them against alien advances.

THE NEW ORDER

Over the last twenty-five years, there has emerged a substantial body of scholarly and popular knowledge that is highly critical of the way in which the Suharto government came into power in 1965 and the coercive means that it has used to maintain its power.[3] From the point of view of this critical discourse, the foregoing assumption that the New Order government is more anxious about opposition within, weakening its grasp of the state, rather than differences from beyond the national border, is quite unsurprising.

In 1965–6 a brutal civil war brought the army under General Suharto to unquestionable domination in the Indonesian political system. The New Order is the name that Suharto's supporters gave to the new government, signifying the promise of renewal and change from the Sukarno government, now dubbed the 'Old Order'. Anderson sees the New Order as a victory for the state itself (1990 Ch. 3). In Anderson's terms Indonesian history is the unfolding of the struggle between the 'representative' interests of the nation and the 'aggrandizing' interests of the state. While the years of parliamentary and guided democracy are the unfolding of tensions between an old state inherited from the Dutch and the new nation born out of the independence struggle, the 'New Order is best understood as the resurrection of the state and its triumph *vis-à-vis* society and nation' (1990: 109).

Indonesian political scientist Mochtar Mas'oed has commented that the New Order government from the beginning aimed at creating 'a mechanism of "ordered politics"' (1989: 4). I have argued elsewhere that the New Order represented precisely the political foil to the revolutionary excesses of the Old (dis)Order of Sukarno's government. Screaming voices of mass demonstration had to be ordered to silence, or at any rate to well-modulated civil speech. All of public life, including the media, was to be re-ordered (Sen 1994: 157–8).

The army's first step in the establishment of this 'order' was to kill or imprison hundreds of thousands (some estimates of deaths run to half-a-million or more) of suspected communists and radical nationalists. Since then the army has been called in to suppress radical Muslims, students, militant workers, peasant opposition and any opposition to 'development' projects – all in the name of 'order'. With a few exceptions, like the independence movements in East Timor and West Papua, this order-keeping has taken place not at the physical or conceptual border zones of the nation, but in the heartland of the nation, where there is no question about challenges to national integrity, but only questions about the nature of the current regime.[4] In this context, New Order Indonesian film policy is caught between the nationalist rhetoric of protecting 'Indonesian culture' from foreign incursions and the restrictive policing of creative options for Indonesian film-makers.

NEW REGULATIONS AND DEREGULATION IN CINEMA

The political turmoil of 1965–6 transformed most institutions in Indonesian public life, including the institutions of cinema. The changes affected the professional organizations, the economics of film production and the workings of censorship. The transformation was not worked overnight and some of the changes had started before the military coup of October 1965.

The New Order inherited from the previous government the basis of a tightly controlled medium, under the Ministry of Information. Up until 1964, the responsibility for cinema had been divided between four departments: education and culture, information, trade, and industry. In 1964 the Minister of Information became responsible for all aspects of cinema in Indonesia. Cinema was thus treated like the radio and the press, under the information portfolio, while other cultural and artistic activities such as theatre and literature remained the responsibility of the Minister of Education and Culture. In 1978 the Department of Information was placed under the responsibility of the Co-ordinating Minister of Politics and Security (Menko Polkam), while the Department of Education and Culture was under the Co-ordinating Minister of People's Welfare. Thus the positioning of cinema within the state apparatus emphasized its media-information influence and, hence, security and propaganda dimension rather than films' 'artistic' or 'creative' dimension.

Leftist nationalist politics of the Sukarno era had led to anti-Americanism in many aspects of foreign policy. A much publicized element of cultural nationalism was the banning of American films in 1964. In a dramatic reversal of policy after October 1965 the film market was thrown open to foreign imports. By 1967 the number of imported films rose to about 400 for the year and then nearly doubled in 1969. In the fifteen years prior to the banning of US films in 1964, when AMPAI (American Motion Pictures Association in Indonesia) had dominated the market, it had been able to set up a chain of local distributors and theatres. Once it became possible to import again the former local agents of the big American companies were able to re-establish themselves as importers. At the same time, the removal of political constraints on business relations with Hong Kong and Taiwan allowed the Chinese business contacts to be revived so that Chinese films (from these two countries) became a major part of the import sector for the first time since the 1930s. And this was a time when the local industry (with some of its star actors and directors behind bars) was struggling to produce five to ten films a year.

The struggle to produce Indonesian films, for a market where the import sector was historically a lot stronger, had bred a discourse of cultural nationalism. But in 1966 an open door policy of film import could be introduced with almost no resistance because opposition to imports had become associated with left-wing politics. However, as before 1965, so very soon after that traumatic year, film professionals started arguing against unrestricted imports. Towards the end of 1967, then Minister of Information, B. M. Diah, decreed steps to 'rehabilitate national film production' by 'giving protection to artists and workers so that they may commit themselves to the field of cinema' and 'improving the standard and technology of national cinema' (Ministerial Decree No. 71/SK/M/1967). The new measure, frequently referred to as 'SK 71' imposed a flat levy of Rp. 250,000 for each film imported into Indonesia. That amount was then to be made available to a local production and the funding import company regarded as a co-producer. The fund was to be administered by an autonomous Film Foundation, on the basis of recommendations from the Film Council. The system remained in operation, with minor changes, till early 1976.

In 1970 Indonesian film production began to rise. Twenty-two films were produced that year, equalling the average of the early 1960s. In 1971 the number of local productions rose to fifty, and their share of the audience to about 20 per cent. The rise in production by all accounts was not a result of the new scheme (which was fraught with corruption) but was due to the rapid expansion of the Indonesian economy in that period, which made little difference to the annual import of about 750 foreign films.

Producers of Indonesian films had two main complaints about their position in the film market in the early 1970s. First, importers had more films to offer to theatres than did individual producers. As principal suppliers of films to the theatres, importers had preponderant say on when, how many and even which Indonesian films would be shown. This power seemed more odious as importing became concentrated in fewer and fewer hands since each importer came to have a vastly greater number of films to sell than even the largest producers. While the number of theatres was rising too, the expansion was disproportionately greater at the top end of the market. The expensive urban cinemas in Indonesia have historically catered for a section of the society which was mainly interested in

Hollywood films. The new up-market cinemas, therefore, automatically favoured the importers.

The growing political importance of criticisms of foreign cultural and economic influence from around 1972–3 kept the issue of protection for the local film industry on the agenda. Soon after the 'Malari' riots of 15 January 1974 (triggered by increasing dissatisfaction with the Japanese investment in Indonesia), which prompted the government to accommodate economic nationalism (see Robison 1986: Ch. 5), a programme of progressive reduction of film imports was started. The plan was to reduce imports by 100 films each year. Imports were down from 600 in 1972 to 300 in 1976. It was projected that, by 1979, there would be no imports, except for a select few exceptionally good films.

However, hardly anyone in the industry, including one suspects the Minister of Information, Mashuri himself, trusted that projection entirely, since even as he was cutting imports, he was taking steps to shore up the position of Indonesian importers in the international film market. Acting on the advice of some importers that the competition among Indonesian buyers was artificially raising the prices of foreign films, Mashuri decided that importers should form themselves into buying units for negotiations with the foreign film dealers. The argument was in tune with the national economic policy formulated under the influence of the government think tank, the Centre for Strategic and International Studies (CSIS), which was promoting the 'building of "national giants" in an attempt to counterbalance the power of the "foreign giants"' (Robison 1986: 151).

In October 1973 all importers of Chinese films were grouped into a single 'Consortium', whose elected leadership would negotiate the buying and then hand the films to the member companies for distribution. In March 1976, despite opposition from many importers the consortium system was extended to all imported films.

Four consortia were established: one each for Chinese films (Mandarin Consortium) and other Asian films (Asia Consortium), and two for European and American films (Euro-America I and Euro-America II, the latter dissolved two years later). The Minister authorized four companies to head the four consortia, and effectively laid the legal foundation for monopoly control of imports, since there were no real checks on the power of the companies leading each group of importers. The heads of groups treated the entire consortium's quota as their own and employed various means to squeeze out member companies which resisted.

From 1978 on, under General Ali Murtopo, the most prominent member of the New Order regime ever to hold the information portfolio, there was a further strengthening of the import sector. The last vestige of the pre-1965 restrictions on imports, by which only two copies of a foreign film could be brought in, were now removed. Minister Mashuri had raised the permissible number to three. Murtopo raised it to six, then to nine and finally to fifteen in 1982. The old restriction had meant that the imported films could play in only two theatres at the same time and copies normally became unusable by the time they had done the run of the major cities. Indonesian films, therefore had an advantage in the smaller towns and second run cinemas. The ability to import more copies also significantly reduced the unit price per imported film, since the largest element in the cost structure, the royalty, remained fixed in most instances, regardless of the number of copies bought. The changes Ali Murtopo effected thus meant that imported films could now occupy a greater share of the market at a smaller financial outlay.

Mashuri had altered the levy under 'SK' 71', mentioned earlier, to a requirement for each importer to fund the production of at least one film for every three imported. While the majority of film workers remained in support of compulsory production, the industry's financiers were able to orchestrate an argument that compulsory production was leading to a decline in the quality of films. Within weeks of Ali Murtopo becoming Information Minister the compulsory production legislation was replaced by a flat levy of Rp. 3 million (about a tenth of the production cost of a low-budget film in the late 1970s) per imported film. Despite his rhetoric that films must become one of Indonesia's main non-oil export commodities (a rhetoric that has continued into the 1990s), local production declined during Murtopo's ministry from 122 in 1977 to fifty-two in 1982.

In 1983, Ali Murtopo was replaced by Harmoko, a former journalist and editor with huge financial stakes in the press and reportedly also in the television industry, which became open to private investment after 1987. Harmoko returned for a brief period to Mashuri's policy of progressive reduction of import quota, which was down to 160 in 1990, and has since remained fixed at that number. Through the early 1990s he presided over a rapidly shrinking production sector. According to Ministry of Information figures, ninety-five film production companies were active in 1990–1, which declined to fifty-five the followinq year and fifteen the year after, and was down to thirteen in 1994. The most strident critics of the Minister within the film industry see this decline as a direct consequence of the rise of an import monopoly with a stranglehold over the film distribution system which the Minister has been unable or unwilling to stem.

As mentioned above, in line with the government's 1970s economic policy, state protected import monopolies had begun to be established in the film industry. Suptan Film under Sudwikatmono, foster-brother of President Suharto, was appointed co-ordinator of the Mandarin Consortium. Suptan became part of the Subentra group, established in 1980 by Sudwikatmono and Benny Suherman, a prominent Chinese Indonesian businessman. From the very beginning, Suptan under Sudwikatmono was more successful than any of the other consortia in controlling the member companies. Increasingly, through the second half of the 1980s, distribution of all imported films throughout Indonesia came to be channelled through Suptan's agents, who had formerly distributed only Chinese language films. Eventually even the offices of the other two import associations were moved to the Suptan building, so that by the end of the 1980s Suptan was, to all intents and purposes, the only film importer.

Suptan's monopoly was made possible partly through political manoeuvring, but also in large measure through investments by its parent company Subentra in an entirely new development in the Indonesian film market. In 1986 the company established the first of its chain of 'sinepleks' or 'cinema complex' (that is theatres with multiple screens) called '21'. Only a major conglomerate like Subentra could enter into such a bold new venture at a time when audience numbers, especially at the upper end of the market, were dwindling. The experiment worked. The plush new carpets, comfortable seats, clean toilets and the most advanced projection and sound system brought back some of the spectators.

Subentra's rapid expansion in the film industry needs to be seen in part in the context of the changes unleashed in Indonesian economy as a whole in the mid-1980s as a result of the collapse of oil prices and recession. Robison suggests that the government, under pressure from both international and sections of domestic capitalists to abandon the system of protection and state-allocated monopolies, started liberalizing some sectors of the economy (Robison 1992). However, in the film industry (and other sectors where Presidential cronies had substantial interest), the old structures remained firmly in place. Subentra was thus well-placed to take advantage of its protected monopoly in film import, while at the same time moving into the deregulated banking sector, which according to some observers, provided the large business conglomerates with 'a licence to print money'.

In the two years after the establishment of the first cinema complex in 1986, Subentra invested heavily in converting older theatres into new style multi-screen cinemas, initially in Jakarta and then in the other major cities. By 1990 Subentra owned just over 11 per cent of all screens in Indonesia (Ardan 1992: 88), but a far larger proportion of the top quality theatres in major cities.

The new style cinemas further disadvantaged Indonesian films in comparison to imports. A 1975 decree, issued jointly by the Minister of Information and the Ministers of Internal Affairs, and Education and Culture, had made it obligatory for every theatre to screen at least two Indonesian films every month, for at least two days each. This secured Indonesian films some 10–15 per cent of the total available screen-time. Since the quota referred to each theatre, given that the legislation had no way of anticipating the multi-screen theatres more than a decade before their establishment, the new cinema complexes could stay within the law by screening Indonesian films on only one of the three to six screens of the theatre, thereby giving local productions proportionately less screen-time. By the late 1980s, Indonesian filmmakers were so anxious about the market share of local films in relation to imports, that some of them joined the fray against Suptan on the side of the giant American film exporter MPEAA.

Since 1972, when the government started legislating single film import agencies into existence and establishing import quotas, the Motion Pictures Export Association of America (MPEAA), which represents the major Hollywood studios (MGM, United Artists, Warner Brothers, Universal, Disney and 20th Century Fox), had periodically expressed its concern over its reduced access to the Indonesian market. In 1988, for the first time since the expulsion of the American export agency in 1964, the MPEAA demanded the right to distribute its films directly to Indonesian cinemas. In 1989, at the instigation of the MPEAA, Indonesia was included in the US Trade Department's 'watch list' for unfair trading practices. In June 1991, after three years of intense negotiations involving US diplomats and various Indonesian ministers, MPEAA dropped its demand to distribute directly and agreed to work through two Subentra subsidiaries. The policy of progressive reduction of the quota was also dropped in return for concession in Indonesia's textile and plywood exports to the US. The entertainment tax on foreign films was reduced to become equal to that on Indonesian films screening in 'A class' theatres (i.e. the top end, with cinemas classified from 'A' to 'D').

The Indonesian film market then is economically highly regulated but culturally deregulated. Economic nationalism, which legitimized the creation of import monopolies, does not seem to have under-written cultural nationalism. If one looks at the New Order government's film policies, it does not appear to represent a state particularly threatened by foreign cultural incursions, whether that is defined as another nation (or group of nations) or the multinational media institutions. On the other hand its censorship rules suggest a considerable anxiety about the content of locally produced films.

STATE CENSORSHIP

Censorship is the most visible aspect of government control over the form and content of films. Every film must be approved by the Board of Film Censorship (Badan Sensor Film, hence-forth BSF) before it can be released. Until the mid-1980s, when attention shifted to import monopolies, censorship was the most intensely discussed aspect of cinema in Indonesia. Pre-censorship as a condition of production distinguishes Indonesian films not only from their imported counterparts but also from all other local private sector media. Inherited from the Dutch era, the BSF is the oldest and most persistent institution of Indonesian cinema. However, the BSF is only one stage in the sequence of state control that locally produced films have to pass through. The scenario of a film requires approval from the Directorate of Film of the Department of Information before shooting can start. At the completion of the shooting, the rush copy (unedited prints) needs to be submitted to the same authorities for 'guidance' about what may need to be edited out. These additional restrictions were introduced in the early years of the New Order.

Since the abolition in the early 1970s of the government subsidy programme for which the submission of scenarios was originally required, the official justification (which film producers largely accept) for this first step in censorship is that it protects financiers against investing in a film that will ultimately be banned by the BSF. In some instances a scenario may be referred on to other departments with responsibility for issues and subjects contained in the film, as an attempt to make pre-production censorship less arbitrary and more responsive to specialists. It works as a discreet kind of censorship, which affects fewer people, causes little open friction between the government department and those involved in the industry and rarely gets into the press.

The BSF is in law the only agency of film censorship. As mentioned earlier, boards of censorship, with different names, have existed as long as there have been Indonesian films. The first one was set up in 1925 by the Dutch government, before a single film had been made in Indonesia, due to a fear that American films would destroy the natives' respect for the ruling whites. After independence, censorship was placed under the Department of Education and Culture reflecting a new attempt to take cultural and social factors into consideration. Until the early 1960s, the censorship board was responsive to socio-cultural sensitivities and popular pressure. Through the 1970s, however, the BSF's openness to the society at large and its willingness to accommodate pressures apart from those coming from important state functionaries, declined markedly (Sen 1994).

In 1971, some of the members of the BSF made an attempt to open the institution to the wider public. In August 1971, the BSF started a monthly bulletin called *Berkala BSF* intended to allow the public access to the internal workings and discussions of the BSF. The bulletin's first and only issue reported in detail the discussions about three controversial films censored in the preceeding few weeks. Had the periodical not died in its infancy through lack of interest and funding, it would presumably have been abolished or altered in 1973, when measures were taken to make the internal workings of the BSF strictly confidential, so that meetings were no longer minuted but taped and the tapes held at the BSF. Access to them required the special permission of the Director General of Radio, Television and Film. The most recent Ministerial Decree (1994) on procedural matters of the board stipulates strict confidentiality of all discussions during the process of censorship of a film. To enforce confidentiality, names of members who form any particular censorship group are not released. Nor are the details of the film to be examined. Therefore, the members themselves do not know in advance who or what they are dealing with.

The changing composition of the BSF in the 1970s indicates its transformation, to all intents, into an arm of the government's internal security apparatus. The first New Order board, convened in 1965, was made up of twenty-four government representatives and nine from the political parties. The government departments most heavily represented were Information, and Culture and Education with ten members each. In 1968 it was replaced by a much smaller board with a substantially reduced government representation. This relative autonomy of the BSF was eroded quickly after 1973. The BSF was put under the control of the Director of Radio,Television and Film (Dirjen RTF), who was its ex-officio chairperson. The Executive Director, responsible for the day to day working of the BSF, was also drawn from the Department of Information.

Representation of government departments and especially the security agencies was further increased in 1979 by Ali Murtopo, who had himself held several senior positions in army intelligence including the Deputy Chief of the highest internal security agency BAKIN (Intelligence Co-ordinating Body) before becoming Minister of Information. Under Ali Murtopo, the number of BSF members was raised to thirty-seven, including the chair and executive chair. The other thirty-five members were divided into four sections, responsible respectively for Indonesian, European and American, and Asian films, and video cassettes. The heads of these sections, who made up the 'core group', were drawn from the Department of Information, BAKIN and the Attorney-General's Office. BAKIN also had two other representatives on the board, the Attorney-General's office had three others and the police department had four members. Government departments thus made up more than two-thirds of the BSF, over a third of those from its internal security arm.

In 1977 a new *Censorship Guideline* (Pedoman Sensor) was laid down in a ministerial decree to systematize practices that had become the norm since 1965. Soon after two other documents were published – *Kode Etik BSF* (henceforth Censorship Codes) in 1980 and *Kode Etik Produksi Film Nasional* (henceforth Production Codes) in 1981. Together they suggest that censorship is conceived in New Order Indonesia principally in relation to its national cinema.

While the government's public relations pronouncements emphasize censorship of sex and violence, these take up a comparatively minor portion of the regulatory documents mentioned above. For instance, the 1977 *Censorship Guideline* in its list of twenty-four criteria for banning or cutting films has only a single direct reference to sex: a warning to 'films which emphasise sex and violence'. There is another oblique reference to sex and perhaps to foreign cultural incursion in the statement about 'fiims that might damage, endanger and are not appropriate to norms of polite behaviour in Indonesia'. The 'general principles' in the introduction to the *Censorship Guideline* states

> As a consequence of our involvement in international communication, we cannot isolate ourselves from the influence of foreign culture entering Indonesia, through film [among other means], be they foreign or national films containing foreign ingredients. This has both positive and negative elements.

But there is no further reference to foreign culture in the actual list of censorship criteria. Though some of these criteria can be read as referring to Indonesian and foreign films, at least a third of them are much more readily seen as relating to Indonesian films only.

What runs most strongly through the *Guideline* and the two codes of ethics mentioned above is an injunction to avoid all reference to social conflict or tension in Indonesia. Therefore films are to be banned or excised if they are deemed to be able to 'destroy the unity of religions in Indonesia', harm the 'development of national consciousness' or 'exploit feelings of ethnicity, religion or ancestry or incite social tensions' or even 'arouse sentiments (of ethnicity, religion and race) and engender social tension', including those between the 'rich and poor', as one former head of intelligence explained at a seminar at the Censorship Board.[5]

The Production Codes laid down by the Film Council in 1981 recast the BSF proscriptions as positive prescriptions. Accordingly Indonesian films 'need to express' 'the harmonious co-existence of religions' and 'mutual respect for the practice of faith in accordance with the religion and belief of each person'. Films are also urged to show 'how Indonesian people put unity, unification as well as the well-being of the nation and the state above personal and group interests' and particularly to include episodes 'which emphasise the values of . . . national unity'. Further, films are forbidden to 'project scenes which show the conflict of one religion with another'.

Films are expressly forbidden too from expression of dissent against any policies of the government or anything that could cause damage to persons or institutions associated with the state. *The Production Codes* urge films to not include 'any statement which may lead to the decline of the community's trust in the organisations of justice' and specifically forbids mocking of the 'upholders of law and order', and showing police officers being killed at the hands of criminals. Indeed, crimes may only be depicted if they were shown to be punished and in stories involving kidnapping the child must be returned unharmed by the end of the film!

OPEN SKIES AND 'MUTE SONGS'[6]

I have tried to demonstrate that the regulations and the processes of censorship are designed to produce film texts that will speak of a state in total control and of a nation united. Noticeably too the state institutions of particular concern are the justice and police departments – institutions which tame the dissent of citizens. At the same time as the censorship regulations have sqeezed the filmmakers' room to move, the audiovisual market has become increasingly open to foreign products.

More often than not we take for granted that post-colonial Asian states will be anxious to protect the nation from so-called 'Western culture'. Thus, the Indonesian case of increasing openness to foreign cultural products through its film market policies over the last twenty years or so and more dramatically in its 'open sky' policy since the mid-1980s (that is allowing the use of private parabola antenae) begs some explanation. There isn't space here to explore the collective memory of the civil war of 1965–6 which continues to drive those who hold governmental power in Indonesia to a large extent. Suffice it to say that, in that context, local voices on the national media are far more likely to speak of internal contradictions of class and region that did once threaten the existence of the Indonesian nation-state. We might see film policy as one instance of muting that kind of dangerous speech. (I have argued this in some detail in the introduction and Chapter four of my book on Indonesian cinema (Sen 1994).

What is important from the point of view of this chapter is not so much the nature of the New Order state, but the argument that globalization is not necessarily a threat to the nation-state. Nor does openness to global media necessarily represent liberalization or reduction of control by the state. Indeed the chaotic profusion of global cultural products filling the national media space may precisely suit the policy requirements of a state that sees itself as threatened by the cultural work of its own citizens.

This is not, however, a recasting of the cultural dependency thesis. Quite the opposite. Openness to global media no longer means being tied to American cultural (and political) agendas. It means watching Australian science programmes, Brazilian telenovelas, Indian epics, Japanese animation films, Malaysian cooking programmes. (All of which I have watched at homes of Jakarta friends.) Openness to global media in the 1990s does not represent a loss of power of the Indonesian state in relation to a more powerful state, i.e. the US. It represents a further power to drown the conversations of the Indonesians in a cacophony of sounds and images.

NOTES

1 Some theorists of nation and nationalism have defined the modern nation-state as an imperative in the process of globalization, not a contradiction to that process. See Arnason (1990).
2 There may be a case for suggesting that cultural regionalism of a kind that is evident in the European Community's response to global media, may arise also in regional groupings such as the ASEAN. Though Dewi Anwar (1994) has argued that ASEAN is not likely to follow the path of the European Community in making the nation-states within it more pliable to regional concerns.
3 For a summary of these critical positions see Southwood and Flanagan (1983).
4 I am indebted to Ien Ang and Carol Warren for the term 'border zones' where the lines between inside and outside become impossible to separate heuristically or empirically.
5 Seminar was part of the preparatory process to produce the *Production Codes* in 1981.
6 'Mute Songs' refers to the title of Pramoedya Ananta Toer's most recent book, *Nanyi Sunyi Seorang Bisu 'Lonely Songs of a Mute Man'* (1995) Jakarta: Lentera. The book is a personal record by the country's greatest novelist of his fourteen years in prison. It is a testimany too to the brutal suppression of art and politics by the Suharto regime.

REFERENCES

Anderson, Benedict (1990) *Language and Power: Exploring Political Cultures in Indonesia*. Ithaca, NY: Cornell University Press.
Anwar, Dewi (1994) *Indonesia in ASEAN: Foreign Policy and Regionalism*. New York and Singapore: St Martin's Press and Institute of Southeast Asian Studies.
Ardan, S.M. (1992) *Dari Gambar Idoep ke Sinepleks*, Jakarta: GPBSI.
Arnason, ? (1990) 'Nationalism, globalisation and modernity', in Mike Featherstone (ed.) *Global Culture: Nationalism, Globalisation and Modernity*. London: Sage.
BSF (Board of Censorship) (1977) 'Pedoman Sensor' in *Kriterium Penyensoran Film*, Jakarta: Ministry of Information.
Dewan Film (1981) *Kode Etik Produksi Film Nasional*, Jakarta: Ministre of Information
Mas'oed, Mochtar (1989) 'State reorganization of society under the New Order', *Prisma*, no. 47: 3–24.

Robertson (1990) 'Mapping the global condition: globalisation as the central concept', in Mike Fetherstone (ed.) *Global Culture: Nationalism, Globalisation and Modernity.* London: Sage.

Robison, Richard (1986) *Indonesia: The Rise of Capital.* Sydney: Allen & Unwin.

Robison, Richard (1992) 'Authoritarian states, capital-owning classes and the politics of newly industrialising countries: the case of Indonesia', in *World Politics*, 61(1): 52–74.

Schlesinger, P. (1991) 'Media, the political order and national identity', in *Media, Culture and Society*, 13: 3.

Sen, Krishna (1994) *Indonesian Cinema: Framing the New Order.* London and New Jersey: Zed Press.

Siahaan, J.E. and Ryanto, Tony (eds) (1971) *Berkala BSF.* Jakarta: n.p.

Southwood, J. and Flanagan, P. (1983) *Indonesia: Law, Propaganda and Terror.* London: Zed Books.

Zaharom, N. and Yao, S. (1994) 'Preface', *Sojourn*, 9(2): 173–7.

Official documents

1967 Ministerial Decree No. 71/SK/M/1967.
1977 Ministerial Decree No. 03A/KEP/MENPEN/1977 (on Censorship Guideline).
1981 *Kode Etik Produksi Film Nasional.* Jakarta: Film Council, Department of Information.
1994 Ministerial Decree No. 216/KEP/MENPEN/1994.

11

FILM AND CINEMA
IN SINGAPORE

Cultural Policy as Control*

David Birch

MOVIE-GOING AS NATION BUILDING?

When George Yeo opened the fourth Singapore International Film Festival in March 1991 he made it clear that the arts in Singapore were dependent upon the economic success of Singapore. 'For the arts to flourish', he said, 'there must be a critical mass of creative activities and a long-term economic basis for their sustenance' (*The Straits Times*, 23 March 1991). In an unpublished confidential report by the Committee on Performing Arts (November 1988), appointed by the Advisory Council on Culture and Arts to 'recommend strategies to integrate performing arts as a permanent and visible manifestation of Singapore's cultural lifestyle', the brief was to 'assess the progress made in promoting the growth and appreciation of the performing arts', and 'to identify factors and propose measures that will create a conducive environment for sustained growth in the performing arts'. This technocratic language, often used to describe media and performance in Singapore, reached new heights in this report with statements like:

> With a relatively small population, strategising for a potentially vibrant performing arts environment in Singapore is no different from the strategies successfully applied to Singapore's high tech economic activities. In many respects, performing arts in Singapore, apart from being an enrichment experience for the people, will form an integral part of Singapore lifestyle no different from its greenness and cleanliness which together will affirm its position as a centre of excellence and an attractive place in which to invest.
>
> (Report 1988: 58)

In this respect 'culture' is seen as 'a reward for material success' (Report 1988: 64) and is all part of the push to make Singapore the 'hub city' of the region. Philip Yeo, Chairman of the Economic Development Board in Singapore, made the point in *Singapore 1990* that

> responsibility for economic development lies not only with the front line promotional agencies such as the EDB but the whole of Singapore – the

185

government agencies responsible for infrastructure, the workers responsible for labour productivity and the people of Singapore, for social stability.

(Yeo 1990: 5)

'Going to a show', the popular expression for going to the movies, clearly brings with it responsibilities, then, for the Singaporean as loyal citizen in this nation building process, although I doubt that this is the reason cinema attendance is the most popular form of recreation outside of the home in Singapore. Despite the fact that cinema tickets have doubled in price since 1991, there has been a major growth in both the number of cinemas (particularly the growth in multiplex (cineplex) cinemas, with the first ten screen cinema opening in Yishun in May 1992) and in the audiences for those cinemas, since the mid-1980s.[1]. There is also considerable enthusiasm.[2] A good example was the screening of *Batman Returns* in September 1992 at the Yishun cineplex. It opened with a midnight show, followed by a 1 a.m. screening, a 1.30 a.m. screening, a 3.35 a.m. screening and finally a 4.05 a.m. screening, before settling down into its normal daily and evening slots. At all shows it played to a capacity house – and continued to do so for the next twelve weeks. Furthermore, when *Lion King* opened in Singapore in October 1994, it did so with simultaneous screenings of both the English and Mandarin versions – a first for Singapore – and it was screened in markedly upgraded cinemas using a Dolby Digital sound system – a system gradually replacing the THX system currently used in many of Singapore's older cinemas.

Audiences are paying, on average, S$6 or S$7 for a ticket (higher for restricted films), compared to S$26 in Japan, S$16 in London, S$3.50 in Indonesia, S$3 in Thailand, S$1 in the Philippines and S$13 in Australia (based on 1993 prices). This is big business, and in 1993 the Cathay Organisation (fifty-nine years in Singapore) and Golden Village Entertainment (one year in Singapore) linked up to co-operate on film distribution and cinema management in Singapore, leaving the Eng Wah Organisation as Singapore's only independent distributor (Chinese films only, with exclusive rights to Golden Harvest films) with six cinemas and ten screens (approximately 7,000 seats). Eng Wah went public in July 1994 with proceeds of the share float aiming to build more cinemas and upgrade existing ones into cineplexes, and has also joined forces with the Shaw Organisation on a joint venture to lease and operate cineplexes, creating a new company, Shaw Theatres. The move was an important one, signalling as it did the need for companies to consolidate in the very competitive business of cinema operations and the usually more cut-throat business of film distribution rights. With huge organizations like Shaw Theatres teaming up with WyWy Creative Lifestyle, with an investment of S$80 million to develop Singapore's largest cinema-entertainment complex in Suntec City (opened in 1995) and with United Artists Theatre Circuit, one of the largest cinema operators in the world, opening a three screen cineplex at the new Bugis Junction in June 1995, with much bigger plans for Singapore in the future (up to five new complexes) and more for the region overall, competition is fierce.

186

A SINGAPORE FILM INDUSTRY?

What those companies are fighting for, of course, is to make more money, but they are doing it with a product which continually draws attention to itself, in the most obvious of visual ways, as *foreign*. Nevertheless, there is a push for developing Singapore as a centre for the regional film industry (both distribution and production), and this is not just happening willy nilly. The Economic Development Board of Singapore has actively encouraged (and funded) the moves. Scholarships are being offered for Singaporeans to study the film industry abroad. S$7 million has been committed to the development of film, sound and video industry training in Ngee Ann Polytechnic. A multi million dollar theme park (Tang Dynasty Village) has been recently opened, and functions as a major set (with three separate studios) for both television and film productions. Legend Media, an Australian film company, with 30 per cent Singapore ownership, intends to set up a production subsidiary in Singapore, having already established an operational group head office in Singapore in March 1991, with plans to establish a S$22 million studio complex at Changi and the Singapore Broadcasting Corporation, now restructured from a government statutory board to a set of government owned companies known as the Singapore International Media Group of Companies, is currently building Tuas Television World, a S$120 million studio complex. Seven feature films are set to be produced by Legend Media within Singapore each with a budget in excess of US$10 million – three are expected to be shot entirely in Singapore. In April 1993, for example, the government announced that venture capital funds used for film and media projects would attract generous tax incentives and one of the successes, so far, has come from Mandarin Films' (based in Hong Kong) Singapore production of *All's Well, Ends Well II*, doing well at the box office in Hong Kong, Taiwan and Singapore. So far Mandarin Films have invested S$36 million in twelve Chinese movies, with five shot wholly in Singapore (*All's Well, Ends Well II, Insanity, Laughter of Water Margin*, and *Satin Steel*) with plans to invest a further S$24 million on eight new Chinese films to be shot in Hong Kong and Singapore.

Hemdale Asia Pacific, the company responsible for *The Last Emperor, Platoon*, and *Terminator*, have opened an office in Singapore (as well as Jakarta and Kuala Lumpur), with plans to build a post-production studio in Singapore by 1996, justifying the move by stating that it costs 50 per cent less to make a film in the region, even after the costs of flying in crew and equipment. Hemdale expects to make three movies a year, with budgets of approximately US$ 5–10 million. George Cardona, who ran the first film course in Singapore, has set up a local film company, Five Stones Studio, producing its first Singapore made movie *Shirkers* on a budget of S$400,000, and aimed at the European television market. Serene Productions (*Life on a String*, and *Farewell to My Concubine*), established plans in 1992 to set up a sound recording unit, followed by a post production unit in Singapore. The plan was to work with Atlab Film Processing, an Australian processing company who set up a S$4 million laboratory in 1992. Atlab was bought out a year later by a consortium of Singapore companies citing lack of work as the reason for pulling out of Singapore. Other plans in the pipeline include Peter Wang's *A Life Cycle in Four Chapters*, and the makers of *The Last Blood*, Singapore based 'Movie Impact', have plans for at least three more. Warner Brothers have expressed interest in funding film production in Singapore with plans to set up a S$30 million investment fund in Singapore to finance the production of Chinese language movies in the region. Nippon Film Development and Finance Inc. (*Howard's End* and *The Crying Game*) invested S$20 million in September 1993 in its first Asian office outside of Japan. A new company, Orient Films, was also set up with plans aimed at making movies for the North American market, with the first movie to be *The Hawk's Eye*, to be shot in Singapore and Sri Lanka with a budget of US$46 million, and finally Wiseguys, set up in Singapore in 1993, and headed by David Searl, is investing up to US$15 million in two films in 1995 to be directed by David Worth (*Kickboxer, Any Which Way You Can*).

The first commercial film to be locally produced, in recent years, was the S$1.7 million *Medium Rare*, based on the life of ritual killer Adrian Lim who was executed in 1988 with his wife and mistress for the murder of two young children in Singapore. Although independent short film making has been active in Singapore in many years, 1991 saw the first Singapore Short Film Awards, with twenty entries. 1992 had double that amount – though this did include eleven training videos from the National Productivity Board. The 1991 winner, Eric Khoo, probably one of Singapore's most talented (and controversial) independent filmmakers (*Barbie Digs Joe, Pain* – submitted to the 1994 Film Festival but banned by the BFC on the grounds that it was too violent), nevertheless picked up Best Director and a Special Achievement Award in 1994, awarded by an international panel, and gained the singular honour of being Singapore's first filmmaker to have his film (*Carcass*), made with Nazir Hussain, classified 'R (A)'. *Pain* has featured in a number of international film festivals, including screenings at the Rotterdam, Toronto, Vancouver, Calcutta, San Francisco, Brussels and Hong Kong festivals. Local Singapore film company Jaytex Productions also made the highly successful (R(A) rated) *Bugis Street* starring Hiep Thi Le (*Heaven and Earth*), directed by Taiwan director Yonfan. There are also plans from Jaytex to have three or four co-productions with China, Hong Kong and Taiwan in 1995, as well as a Hindi movie. Kingfisher Productions, a Singapore concert promotion company, also have plans with an initial investment of S$5 million to produce four movies in Singapore, with the first, a nostalgic Chinese musical (budget of S$3 million) to be shot in Singapore and Shanghai and aimed at the Chinese regional market.

Cineasia Entertainment Group plans to produce at least six movies in Singapore, and intends to establish production infrastructure in Singapore (partly funded by the government), and there is now an Association of Singapore Film and Video producers with thirty-five members so far. Plans to relocate Flix Animation's technological base to Singapore are also in train with Singapore's first full length locally produced animation film, produced by Animata Productions, a local Singapore company. Moreover, Carrie Ng, a well-known Hong Kong actor, has plans to set up her own film company Carrie Films, with expectations of three Chinese films per year, using mostly Singapore actors. The first film began shooting in November 1994, with a budget of S$3 million. September 1994 also saw the important Motion Picture and Finance Seminar, organized by the Magna group (an investment consultancy company) in order to promote Singapore as a potential investment centre for filmmaking. Similarly, in January 1995, Singapore hosted *Cineasia '95*, the first time this international film and cinema operators' convention has been held outside of the United States. The 1997 convention will be held in Hong Kong.

And it is here where the problems for the Singapore government, anxious to build a nation to a particular model rarely celebrated, or even alluded to, in the hundreds of films coming out of America, Europe, Hong Kong, China, Australia and, to a lesser extent, Taiwan, start to mount. And it is here also where my interests in this chapter really begin. They begin with the tensions that are inherent in a situation where the Singapore population, generally held to be the world's most avid movie-goers, are watching film after film produced in cultures which, in so many ways, appear to represent a number of potential threats to a social fabric which has been carefully constructed by a government anxious to develop a loyal citizenry driven by a culture of self-sacrificing nation building (see Birch 1993a). Not the values, by any means, of most of the films screened in Singapore, or likely to be made in Singapore in the future. So what to do?

CUT!

When Soviet director Kira Muratova went to Singapore to screen her own movie *The Asthenic Syndrome* at the fourth International Film Festival in 1991, she found herself faced with cuts of some scenes which had full frontal nudes. In protest, she withdrew the movie from the festival, but not before making the point, through her translator, that she had fought a life-long battle with censorship in the Soviet Union, and that she had not thought she would be faced with the same thing in 'the free world' (*Business Times*, 27 March 1991).

Censorship has always been a major feature of the media in Singapore (see Birch 1993b). Films would sometimes be screened with large gaps in them, having come under the attention of the Board of Film Censors. Some would never be screened at all – which is still the case – and strict control of certain types of published material (books, journals, magazines and so on) is exercised through the Internal Security Act of 1964, which allows the government to ban the distribution of material which might be considered an incitement to violence, to cause disobedience, a breach of the peace, to promote hostility between races, or prejudicial to the national interest, public order or national security. Specifically, the Undesirable Publications Act of 1967 prohibits distribution of material deemed 'contrary to the public interest'.

Despite some recent relaxation, brought about by a major review of censorship, most particularly for theatre scripts, censorship still exists and, more powerfully, so does self-censorship. The 1964 Emergency (Essential Powers) Act, with the Essential Control of Publications and Safeguarding of Information Regulations of 1966, for example, still ensures strict regulation. As all journalists also have to sign the Official Secrets Act, dissemination of information (particularly if Singapore journalists are out of the country) can be severely restricted. Entrenched civil service practices of not helping the media, in place for many years and a direct legacy of colonial rule, have meant that a climate of secrecy and information control has flourished in Singapore, often on the most trivial of matters.

Things are changing, but entrenched self-censorship practices are considerably harder to change, and indeed, form a part of policy spaces in Singapore which many would not want to change.[3] Parliamentary Secretary for Law and Home Affairs, Associate Professor Ho Peng Kee, for example, speaking in August 1994, said

> Every citizen in Singapore has something that many others want – a place and future in Singapore. This enviable position has been brought about by a winning partnership – a hardworking and cohesive people who have responded positively to an honest and firm government which does not fear implementing correct, long-term policies even though some of these policies may cause initial hardship or adjustment problems for the people. This working formula must continue.
>
> (*The Straits Times*, 11 August 1994)

Part of that formula relies on a population willing, not just to wear the effects of censorship and control, but also to engage in self-censorship. The current difficulty facing the Singapore government is that the willing population appears to be decreasing year by year. Strong voices are now heard engaging with, and critiquing, policies that at one time were hoped, at least by the government, to be unproblematic to a nation building itself in the wake of a reluctant independence in 1965. Two main related themes emerge: control and censorship, and are handled in the main by strategies of supervision (film classification), strategies of effacement (film cuts) and strategies of erasure (banning movies altogether).

Supervision

One of the major moves made in 1991 was the introduction of a film classification system. Previously no films were classified in Singapore (only the Philippines and Indonesia among ASEAN countries classified films) so that no one (of any age) would be restricted from seeing any movie screened in Singapore. As part of the move to 'open up' Singapore as an information hub with a strong regional and global presence, but also as a strategy of appeasement for an increasingly vocal, and expanding, educated middle class (see Birch 1992), film classification was introduced in July 1991, having been announced four months earlier in March

190

1991, just before the opening of the fourth Singapore International Film Festival, but initially mooted in May 1990 by the Board of Film Censors (established in 1953 and currently supervised by the Ministry of Information and the Arts), in consultation with the BFC Advisory Panel (fifty-six members) and the Films Appeal Committee (seven members). The Ministry of Information and Arts announced that censorship guidelines would be relaxed 'because of Singaporeans' growing exposure to that ways of the world' (*Business Times*, 23 March 1991), and due to the fact the 'Many Singaporeans' outlooks change when they are exposed to liberal lifestyles and attitudes during travels abroad (*The Straits Times*, 23 March 1991).

Information flows

This apparent liberalization of the position in Singapore has little to do with a relaxing morality, however, but much more to do with the increasing attempts to situate Singapore as a regional centre on the information highway. Control of information is effectively not only control of the economy, but also control of the means of modernization. The more modern a society becomes, the more complex its structures, and the more reflexive it needs to be to understand those structures – economic and cultural. That reflexivity requires a continuous flow of information, and, that, of course, brings with it considerable dangers, when that information is flowing from potentially 'undesirable' sources which have traditionally seen Asia as 'uncivilized'. Values might be threatened; political and cultural stabilty may be shaken, sovereignty may be challenged.

The increasingly corporatist nature of governments worldwide means that the maintenance of stability is crucial in order not just to ensure competitive advantage, but also to redefine what it means to be modern in Asia. Singapore is spending a great deal of money to do just that. By the year 2005 virtually every home, office, school and factory in Singapore will link their computers. One of the world's most advanced national information infrastructures will be finalized, and Singapore 'the intelligent island' will realize a vision (see Birch 1995a).

Much of the infrastructure is already in place. Telecom, for example, set aside a S$3 billion budget in order to enhance its networks and develop new services. Things are sufficiently established to allow *The World Competitiveness Report* to place Singapore among the top nations in the world in terms of its strategic exploitation of IT, and it has recently been redesignated as a developed nation. A point that the glossy brochures heralding *IT2000 A Vision of an Intelligent Island* produced by the National Computer Board make very clear.

And so they should. This is not an idle vision. It is principally designed to 'bring about new national competitive advantages and enhancements in the quality of life and the people of Singapore'. That quality is unashamedly tied to the success or failure of the Singapore economy. For Singapore to be 'the first developed city of distinction in the tropics, a city of gracious living and a cultured society' (one of the chief goals of Prime Minister Goh's Next Lap strategy), then the economic infrastructure must be there to pay for it.

As a national priority, information is considered to hold the key to this economic infrastructure and the need to become more competitive. So that in the *IT2000 Report* a strategic plan was put in place which will allow IT to 'be pervasively applied to improve business performance and the quality of life'. That pervasion is based on five strategic thrusts.

1 To develop a global hub 'to help turn Singapore into a highly efficient switching centre for goods, services, capital, information and people'.
2 To boost the economic engine 'to help Singapore develop high value-added manufacturing with links to lower cost manufacturing centres in the region and markets around the world'.
3 To improve the quality of life to make work 'more efficient and chores less time consuming' in order to 'increase discretionary time'.
4 To link communities locally and globally 'to help strengthen social bonds among our people by linking like-minded people, or those with a common cause or interest, electronically'.
5 To enhance the potential of individuals because 'In the Next Lap, skills, creativity and knowledge will become even more important for success. Workers will need to be retrained and reskilled continuously to keep pace with changes in their working lives'.

To do this involves a National Information Infrastructure linking people, business and government through a framework involving telecommunication networks, common network services (involving software value-added services), national IT applications, technical standards and a policy and legal framework which will look after the non-technological issues of a social, economic and regulatory nature.

The key word in such a comprehensive approach is *synergy*. The result: to bring together a number of separate agencies so that 'the total effect is greater than the sum of effects of each agency alone'. The master plan for all of this lies with the National Information Infrastructure Division who are actively promoting awareness of the benefits so that the people of Singapore 'will be equipped with IT skills as far as possible to prepare them for life in the Intelligent Island'.

But finding a balance may not always be driven by the economic engine. As recent elections in Singapore have demonstrated, the ballot box is an increasingly sensitive means of giving feedback. And, regardless of how cynical critics may be of the moves by Goh's government to create a more open political culture in Singapore, the voice of the educated and affluent middle classes is being increasingly recognized as important.

At the moment, the rhetoric of persuasion is designed to highlight the responsible role of the Singapore citizen in contributing to the generation of 'a viable and attractive climate for investment by IT corporations'. This can be achieved, the publicity says, by actively accepting the 'new freedom in an IT oriented culture'. What those new freedoms are may not be immediately recognizable. Nor, perhaps, do they need to be. But impact there undoubtedly will be given that the writing is on the wall as far as the planners are concerned. Do not go down this track, and Singapore, as a nation which has always seen its people as its only major resource, will be left well behind in the regional and global thick of things.

'Society', the Information Technology Institute of Singapore quite reasonably asserts, is now judged 'not by what it produces, but by how it manages and uses information'. What that means, of course, is that increasingly politicians, business people and bureaucrats become the cultural managers of a society. Uncomfortable though that idea may be for some, the control and management of information and information flows (and, therefore, the people and cultures associated with that information) is becoming a critical item on the agenda of most governments in the Asia/Pacific region and beyond. And Singapore is leading the way.

Censorship

Despite the seemingly new liberal moves being made, then, censorship still takes place (no frontal nudity or allusions to sexual penetration, for example, even in 'R' rated movies; no films deemed to promote 'unhealthy values, like drug-taking, or religiously or racially controversial movies'). 'Love play and foreplay we'll allow, but penetration we will not', is how one official put it (*Business Times*, 23 March 1991). Films were rated 'G' for general viewing, 'PG' for parental guidance, and 'R' for those 18 years and above. In September 1991 the R category was changed to R(A), raising the age limit to 21 and allowing only those films which were considered to have 'artistic merit' – the '(A)' of the classification. The main censorship guidelines for R(A) films are:

- the film should have a strong storyline and a credible cast;
- the film's theme should not be exploitative of sex or violence;
- scenes of nudity, love-making and violence should form an integral part of the film;
- The film should be critically acclaimed or possibly award winning

No 'X' movies are allowed. As Brigadier-General George Yeo said, as Acting Minister for Information and Arts at the time, 'we must maintain standards against pornography, against excessive violence and against themes which inflame racial, religious hatred in Singapore' (*The Straits Times*, 22 March 1991). The first three 'R' rated movies to be shown were David Lynch's *Wild at Heart*, and two Hong Kong movies, *Erotic Nights* and *Stooges in Tokyo*. They played to capacity houses and created debates, still running in many respects, about the morality of such films, and also about the 'types' of people who go to see them.

Basic Instinct and *The Lover* (based on a Marguerite Duras novel), for example, were screened in Singapore (in September 1992), but with cuts insisted upon by the BFC and approved by the Films Appeal Committee. Both were given R(A) classifications because of sexually explicit scenes, or because, as in the case of

The Lover, a quarter of the two hour film was given over to love scenes. Twentieth Century Fox argued that *Basic Instinct* should be classified PG (its classification in America was Restricted following cuts of thirty-five to forty seconds in order to avoid an X rating there) thus opening the film to much larger audiences in Singapore than the R(A) over 21 rating would allow.

More recently, *Schindler's List* was given an R(A) rating because of forty seconds of nudity and bedroom scenes. If there is nudity of any description the BFC has a clear directive to give the film an R(A) rating (*The Straits Times*, 7 April 1994). Steven Spielberg was given the opportunity by the BFC to cut the nude scenes, thereby allowing a PG rating, and hence extending the audience in Singapore. He refused. Journalist Ravi Veloo called him pig-headed, and argued that if he really cared about the overall message of the film he would cut the scenes to allow more people in Singapore to see such a socially important film (*The Straits Times*, 7 April 1994).

Media attention now (1994), as it was at the introduction of the film classification system in 1991, concentrates mostly on the Restricted (R) classification, although there is now increasing pressure for a more flexible approach allowing some R(A) movies to be 'converted' into PG classification so that at least two audiences could view what would be different versions of the film. But in four years the issues haven't changed very much. The debate is still very much a debate constructed on an 'East–West' values divide, except that in 1994 the politics driving this divide, in Singapore and in the region overall, have become more strident (see Birch, 1995a). The R(A) rated films rate as much attention now as the earlier R rated ones did in 1991, given that a number of supposedly more sexually explicit movies are now being screened in Singapore. Letters to the press, in 1991, heralded the eventual moral breakdown of society under the massive weight of Western decadence. 'Nudity is nudity', wrote Woo Tau How,

> and is obscene, whether it's for art's sake or not. It is well known and studies have substantiated that once our sexual drive is released, it is next to impossible to curb it. Are we then prepared to face the issue of high incidence of teenager pregnancies and abortions, which is plaguing the Western countries?
>
> (*The Straits Times*, 17 April 1991)

Khong Kin Hoong (*The Straits Times*, 27 April 1991), puts the case that: 'We are proud that Singapore dares to challenge the decadence of the West and seeks to maintain a high level of morality. We want to be able to raise our children in a society free from immoral influences.' The very existence of that society is at stake for Jason Dendroff (*The Straits Times*, 27 April 1991), because it is only with the removal of R rated movies that 'our society [will] be an aesthetic and harmonious one that is free from moral decadence'. Wong Poo Yang, speaking for 'my wife and I' argued in a letter to *The Straits Times* (4 July 1991) that

To allow films that supposedly show the harsh realities of life, but the contents of which are absurd, border on voyeurism or subtly promote perversion in its many forms, is to cast away the discipline which has made Singapore what it is today. As an educator, I know how powerful a communication tool a film can be. The mind that feeds on 'trash' would be hard pressed to produce excellence in character and human relationships. Hence we appeal to the relevant authorities to reconsider the policy and set the standard for filmmakers and distributors to use movies to bring mankind to high heights of excellence rather than 'to plunge them into degradation and moral collapse'.

The idea of moral collapse is a powerful argument in a context which sees the people and its values as the major economic resource, and not long after the 1991 elections, the system was reviewed. It had been widely held amongst opposition parties, the Singapore Malay National Organisation (PKMS), for example, itself opposed very strongly to R rated movies, that the relaxation of censorship was a move 'to win the support of first-time voters in the next general election' (*The Straits Times*, 8 August 1991), and as a means of attracting more tourists to the city. Prime Minister Goh Chok Tong announced that 'We have moved too fast for Singapore, which is still an Asian Society' (*The Straits Times*, 5 September 1991). R rated movies cropped up in many cinemas in Singapore, reducing, the PAP (People's Action Party) argued, the people's choice of movies, and bringing 'soft porn' into the country.[4]

On 16 August 1991, for example, at nineteen Shaw Cinemas in Singapore, according to Hannah Pandian, 'Hong Kong actress Catrina Lau emits screams of pleasure as her character learns how to be a good prostitute in the "R" rated movie, *Gigolo and Whore*' (*The Straits Times*, 16 August 1991). With this sort of coverage the morality lobby was easily persuaded to fight. But as Lum Chan Yin rightly pointed out in a letter to *The Straits Times* (20 August 1991)

> Rape, child abuse and racism are all obscene. Their presence in our society should outrage us, challenge our attitudes and demand our action as individuals and as citizens of a maturing society. We cannot pretend that these things do not exist because they offend us. We need to be offended if that is the requirement for change. Many of the movies currently being screened are nothing more than vulgar exploitation. The fact that many people rush to see them should tell us that, at the very least, we need to re-examine our values. Pretending to be a moral society through censorship is hypocrisy; pretending to be a refined nation through enforced ignorance is farcical.

Censorship, as Lum points out, has nothing to do with morality – but this was not a point made much of in this debate. Nor was the fact that most of the R rated movies being shown did not have sex as their central focus, a point made clear by Yap Bock Seng, Secretary of the Cinematographic Film Exhibitors Association of Singapore, in response to the mounting criticism. He argued, quite reasonably, that 'the introduction of R-rated movies is an attempt to bring more serious films to mature, movie-going audiences in Singapore. It is not a shot at cheap sexploitation' (*The Straits Times*, 23 August 1991). But the fact of the matter was that R rated movies as a classification became synonymous with sexploitation, so that politicians like acting Community Development Minister Seet Ai Mee and Mr S. Dhanabalan were keen to go on record that they had never seen an R rated movie, and were able, with other politicians, to exploit the issue as a means of demonstrating to the people the effectiveness of the 'open' participatory politics of Goh's new government. 'Make your voice heard. Clamour for a change. Don't let the minority who write and speak well dictate the day' (*The Straits Times*, 25 August 1991). Mr Dhanabalan told residents at a PAP Dialogue session, 'If you feel strongly about it, make representations to the government'. 'Encourage your friends who feel the same way to speak up, or we always hear from those who agree,' said MP Dr Lee Boon Yang at another dialogue session (*The Straits Times*, 25 August 1991). 'I assure you that the government will take your views very seriously,' he continued, but asked that the system be given more time to settle down.

The Straits Times editorial of 7 September 1991 commenting on the amendment of the film classification system, recognized that the government had been strongly influenced by the strong lobby against R rated movies, but that

> we believe that censorship should ideally lie in the hands of cinema-goers, individual Singaporeans, not with a handful of civil servants and a few selected members of the public. The issue is not films *per se*. It is whether Singaporeans are ever able to learn to make decisions for themselves or forever abdicate their responsibility and ask some authority, usually the government, to decide and tell them what is best or permissible.

Discounting a widely held view that the most vehement objection to the R rated movies came from Chinese educated Singaporeans, and that, according to Leslie Fong, editor of *The Straits Times*, 'the scramble for dissent, for more freedom, more points of view, came from just one segment of society, the English-educated' (*The Straits Times*, 27 November 1991), Professor Tommy Koh, chairman of the eighteen member Censorship Review Committee, cited the results of two confidential surveys which showed, he argued, that the vocal minority against the classification system came from all ethnic, linguistic and racial groups.

The issue, then, well put by *The Straits Times*, is about social and cultural maturity, and both the government, the editorial argued, and the people of Singapore need to exercise rather more of it because 'To put on the brakes now, and risk bringing back the heavy hand of official censors, is unfair not just to them but all Singaporeans'. As Christopher Ee wrote in his letter to *The Straits Times* (9 September 1991), 'It is difficult to believe that Singaporeans cannot be trusted to decide for themselves what they want to watch . . . there is no right or wrong, only opinions.'

Erasure

Despite that, in 1993, 460 films were banned in Singapore compared to 337 in 1992 and 168 in 1991 (*The Straits Times*, 24 March 1994). *Maurice*, for example, was initially banned for screening by the Singapore Film Society because men could be seen 'hugging and kissing', despite the fact that *Pantyhose Hero* which depicted homosexual life in Hong Kong was screening concurrently in nine cinemas in Singapore (September 1990). The official response, when this was pointed out, was that *Pantyhose Hero* was acceptable because the main theme was murder, not homosexuality. *Maurice* was eventually screened (in private), again despite the fact that an issue of *LA Law* went to air at the time which showed a homosexual relationship between two men in a very positive light. The inconsistencies result, for the most part, from a slavish and mechanistic application of bureaucratic rulings on how to censor films.

One of the films which generated considerable discussion when it was screened in Singapore, for example, prior to the film classification changes was *The Accused*, where the main character (played by Jodie Foster) is gang raped on a pinball machine in a bar. In Singapore the entire scene was cut, and the Board of Film Censors announced that under the new rules for R movies the sequence would still suffer major cuts. When the movie was released in Singapore, what the audience saw was Jodie Foster being grabbed and then immediately running from the bar, thus rendering the rest of the film rather pointless. As Lim Eng Teck (a marketing executive) made clear at a Feedback Unit dialogue session held in May 1991 on the classification issue, without the crucial rape scene in *The Accused*, 'Audiences went away thinking the woman deserved to be raped' (*The Straits Times*, 19 April 1991), in reply to which the chair of the Board of Film Censors, Mr Razna Meyyappan, replied with the case of a Hong Kong movie *Erotic Ghost Story*, which was released without a lesbian scene. 'Do you want that to be allowed in the film?' he asked, as if decisions could be made so easily out of context. *Erotic Ghost Story II* was banned completely because, according to Rama Meyyappan, 'it had no storyline at all, just pornography' (*The Straits Times*, 6 November 1991). As Gopal Baratham (a leading Singapore fiction writer) made clear in an article headed 'The right to decide' (*The Straits Times*, 17 April 1991), 'the videos that I view with consenting adults and the books I take to bed with me, can, and in any society that aspires to freedom, must, be entirely my own business'. The two principal justifications for censorship in Singapore, majority wishes and the protection of Asian values, are misconceptions, he argued. They are, I would suggest, cultural smokescreens for the real political agenda of control through participation and feedback by keeping 'the silent majority' on the edge of their seats.

The process of creativity, Baratham argues, is a 'sensitive one and easily disrupted by attempts to control it'. This control, as Foucault makes clear, is 'a modality of power for which individual difference is relevant' in so much as it 'marks the moment when the reversal of the political axis of individualisation . . .

197

takes place' (Foucault 1979: 192). The cutting of the rape scene from *The Accused* was not for fear of copy cat rapes, or even of the act of rape itself, but an uncritical – deindividualized (bureaucratized) – application of controlling rules about showing sexual penetration. As Jaime Ee (Editor of *Executive Lifestyle*) argued strongly in his article 'Give adults the right of choice' (*Business Times*, 30 March 1991),

> it's hard to tell if there is anyone in the board who has a working knowledge of movies in order to decide just what is relevant to a movie's theme and what is not. The bottom line is, the board should decide if it really wants a proper film classification system. If it wants to institute conditions, then the system is not viable.

Effacement

As Singapore's Ambassador at Large, Professor Tommy Koh's brief as chair of the CRC was to 'engage the participation of many Singaporeans – some in the committee, some through public representation – so that as many of us as possible are involved in the process of deciding what our own moral standards should be' (*The Straits Times*, 22 March 1991). Just over one year later the Ministry of Information and Arts set up an Advisory Panel for Films (and a separate one for publications) (1 July 1992) comprising 'A cross-section of Singaporeans, including educationists, writers, lawyers and housewives' (*The Straits Times*, 2 July 1992). The panel reports to the BFC with the final say given, in cases of doubt, to the Films Appeal Committee, which 'is empowered to approve, classify or recommend cuts to any objectionable parts of a film' (*The Straits Times*, 2 July 1992). In a survey commissioned by the Censorship Review Committee and which became popularly known as the 'Survey on Moral Values' leading into the 'Great Debate on Moral Values' and run by Price Waterhouse Management Consultants, it was reported that 48 per cent wanted the censorship of 'obscene' language to be stricter, 17 per cent wanted less, 27 per cent were neutral and 8 per cent were don't knows; 38 per cent wanted stricter control of sex scenes, 21 per cent wanted less control, 32 per cent were neutral on the issue and 9 per cent were don't knows. A very similar breakdown occurred in the survey for violent scenes. This was interpreted in the press as 'Wanted: tougher censorship of sexual and violent scenes in films' (*The Straits Times*, 5 August 1992) with a headline of 'Singaporeans want stricter censorship of movies: survey'.

The 110 page survey entitled *Survey on Changing Moral Values and Public Perception of Certain Printed Audio and Visual Materials* interviewed 1,102 Singaporeans and was used by the Censorship Review Committee prior to its recommendations to government. In an editorial on 6 August 1992 *The Straits Times*, using the results of the survey, argued under a headline of 'Skin-deep liberalism' that Singapore was still basically a conservative society (56 per cent, for example, had agreed that films and publications which explore religious doubt should be disallowed, and 73 per cent that films and publications which offend religious groups should be banned, and over 90 per cent disapproved of sex outside marriage) and that worries about the so-called 'new values' being shaped, largely at variance with 'Eastern moderation' as a potential to erode Singapore's foundations, were largely 'ill-founded'. 'The true pulse of the nation', the editorial continued, 'beats out there in the vastness of HDB-land where the moral tone of living life the right, old way, is set.' The survey, it argued, had 'distilled two principles: religion remains the moral anchor for a good many Singaporeans, and the family as the building block of the nation is intact'. Nevertheless,

> For policy makers in government, the job of accommodating differing shades of opinion on what is wholesome and 'good' for all is harder. A way has to be found to manage the inexorable liberalising trend symbolised by space-age icons (satellite pictures, the PC and the fax machine) and their impact on values and behaviour. The state can fine-tune or micro-manage, but it is in the home that the shape of society to come is determined. Parents, take note.

Fears about the moral influence of 'inappropriate' films and publications is not the concern here – these can be controlled by censorship and the survey is used as moral and social support for that – what is of concern are the media that cannot be controlled so easily – PCs, satellite signals and faxes. Singapore may be interpreted as a generally conservative society, but the desired set of values which identify Singapore as 'Asian', for example, can still be threatened by 'liberalizing', 'non-Singaporean' influences.

However, of greater concern to many of the educated middle class in Singapore was the way in which the survey was used to confirm a government-driven conservatism for Singapore based on assumptions that what Singaporeans expressed as answers to questions about what they thought of something (the direction of most of the questions), was real rather than what they actually did in practice. Tan Sai Song, a leading English language journalist in Singapore, made the point well when she argued that what the survey told her was more about what Singaporeans 'aspire to be morally', than about who or what they are (*The Straits Times*, 8 August 1992). And this is the point, as Eddie Song Tiang Ann made clear in his letter to *The Straits Times* (6 August 1992), that notions of truth, expectations and 'appropriate' answers to questions about moral values are far more likely to reflect a socially inculcated mainstream conservatism about attitudes rather than an individual honesty about actual practices and behaviour. This was recognized by government to a certain extent. Brigadier General George Yeo, Minister of Information and the Arts, said 'We must make a distinction between moral norms that people want, and what they themselves do in private' (*The Straits Times*, 8 August 1992), and that, despite the fact that other surveys had indicated that, for example, teenage sex was increasing in Singapore, attitudes rather than behaviour was being assessed in this particular survey. 'What was valuable about the survey', he said, 'was that it was a clear articulation that Singaporeans wanted a society which was clean, wholesome and safe to bring up their children in' and that the effects of the survey upon policy would mean that 'Censorship must be applied intelligently and thoughtfully to strike a balance between preserving moral values and remaining an open, cosmopolitan society.' But, as sociologist Vivienne Wee pointed out, the survey was not even an accurate assessment of attitudes of what people think, but of what they say. 'If Singaporeans are so conservative', she suggested, 'then you don't even need to have censorship. They can take care of themselves' (*Business Times*, 8–9 August 1992).

IDENTITY CRISIS

What, in fact, the survey achieved, and presumably always was going to achieve, was a confirmation for government of so-called conservative Asian values, which would, in turn, be used as a further means of maintaining control in Singapore by incorporating the issue of what constitutes a Singaporean identity into an 'Asian' (rather than 'Western') framework. If non-Asian societies can be demonstrated to be morally bankrupt because their value systems are themselves considered to be bankrupt (families breaking down, lawlessness, street people, violence, guns in school, vandalism and so on) then the 'superiority', if you like, of 'Asian' society must, *mutatis mutandis*, rest on its maintenance of morally successful values. Denial of those values equals denial of being 'Asian' – a clever strategy for finding a new means of maintaining power in the midst of an increasingly educated and articulate middle class ready to defect from ruling party policy lines. As Jean Baudrillard observes, speaking from a completely different context, 'The only weapon of power, its only strategy against this defection, is to reinject realness and referentiality everywhere, in order to convince us of the reality of the social, of the gravity of the economy and the finalities of production' (Baudrillard 1983: 42). As Noam Chomsky (1989: 19) recognizes, when talking about the political culture of America, 'the fact that the voice of the people is heard in democratic societies is considered a problem to be overcome by ensuring that the public voice speaks the right words'. Despite the apparent positioning of Singapore as an 'open' society in recent years, Singapore is still governed by a party which, for the most part, expects a single voice to be both heard and 'right'. Foucault talked about this as the 'power of normalisation' (1977: 308), and what is essential for the maintenance of power within a discourse of normalization is not the creative *production* of new meanings, but the *reproduction* of the existing order as the 'legitimate culture' (Bourdieu and Passeron 1977: 41) imposing 'an orthodoxy of interpretation upon cultural products or attitudes' (Schlesinger 1990: 78). Singaporeans can no longer be treated as uneducated children requiring paternal guidance and control, a system which had operated for years under Lee Kuan Yew – a newer strategy of control was required, and for the most part, this has rested upon 'Asianising' Singapore so that its citizens can self-reflexively assert themselves as Asians in a rapidly modernizing/liberalizing world, but in fact be subtly controlled by the very nature of that 'Asianness'.

As George Yeo, Minister for Information and the Arts, has made clear, Singaporeans:

> must find ways to preserve our values and transmit them to subsequent generations. With each passing day, censorship becomes more difficult because of advances in technology. . . . By insisting on certain standards in the establishment media, we signal to the young the way they should behave
>
> (Yeo 1994: 105)

And further,

> Without the right social values, we could not have made economic progress in the first place. If we lose these social values, we will surely go into decline. I am not saying that our own values should be static and not evolve but we should not blindly follow the way many western societies are going. . . . Eastern societies have moved towards the centre while many Western societies are veering off to the other extreme.
>
> (Yeo 1994: 105)

He continues, 'I am confident that we can succeed beacause the tide of civilisation is again flowing in our direction' (Yeo 1994: 105).

MODERNITY AND ASIAN VALUES

Central to this argument is a recognition that civilization and modernity are changing, and that the economic power now developing in Asia can drive those changing definitions and the social, economic and cultural power that goes with them. Power it seems to me is still the key here, and despite the theoretical debates in the West about shifting centre periphery relations and the changing nature of power in a postmodern world, power is still seen by the politicians and cultural managers of the world, and in particular Asia at the moment, as a grab for the control of the centre. All of the rhetoric, all of the moves, and all of the Asian-izing of Asia time and time again demonstrates the reality of the centre for people with power.

To understand what is happening in the control of information flows and policy directions in Asia at the moment requires an understanding of the changing definitions of modernization in the region, and those definitions, and their political, social, cultural and economic realizations in the everyday life of the people of the region and their relations with other powers, are still very much about what constitutes centred power bases – centred *spaces*. Because it is, I would argue with Castells, 'The flows of power that generate the power of flows, whose material reality imposes itself as a national phenomenon that cannot be controlled or predicted, only accepted or managed' (Castells 1989: 349). It is the management of the flows, therefore, and moves to control those flows that requires analysis of agency and motivations. As Castells makes clear 'power rules through flows'

(Castells 1989: 349), but what sort of power are we talking about? For the most part, a power, I would argue, which is still totally ruled and determined by a need to generate and control economic capital in order for political, social and cultural spaces to be controlled.

Contrary to Paul Virilio, I do not believe, nor do I suspect that those making the play for power in Asia believe, that 'Ubiquity, instantaneity and the populating of time supplant the populating of space' nor that 'the durable management of continents has given way to the generalised incontinence of transfers and transmissions' (Virilio 1991: 119). The geopolitics of nation-states in Southeast Asia and beyond still assume, contrary to Virilio, 'the hierarchical privilege of centres over peripheries, of summit over basis' (Virilio 1991: 120), indeed, make it a major point of their Asianizing processes of their own nation-states. To assume with Virilio that the 'nodal' effectively replaces the 'central' as an efficient means of understanding the contemporary world is to universally map a narrow understanding of a modernized West on to a modernizing Asia, and to assume that modernization means the same thing for both. This raises important questions about the current preoccupation in some Western theoretical quarters for the increasingly unproblematized belief that what defines globalization is an emergence of, in Manuel Castells' words, a 'space of flows superseding the meaning of the space of places' (Castells 1989: 348).

This is clearly happening in some quarters but this may not be the most appropriate way of understanding the way that new technologies of information are being treated in Asia, and other places. For the most part many countries in the region are developing massive machineries of resistance to an idea which suggests that 'the emergence of the space of flows actually expresses the disarticulation of place-based societies and cultures from the organizations of power and production that continue to dominate society without submitting to its control' (Castells 1989: 349). The West may think it no longer needs to agonize about what constitutes modernity, and so therefore can argue theoretically at least that time is replacing filled up spaces, but certainly countries like Singapore, Malaysia, Indonesia, Thailand, South Korea and Taiwan do. What the West may well need to agonize about, and in some respects has been doing, is the fear that

> even democracies become powerless confronted with the ability of capital to circulate, globally, of information to be transferred secretly, of markets to be penetrated or neglected, of planetary strategies, of political military power to be decided without the knowledge of nations, and of cultural messages to be marketed, packaged, recorded and beamed in and out of people's minds.
>
> (Castells 1989: 349)

Is this an Orwellian nightmare? Castells thinks not, seeing it as 'a much more subtle, and to some extent potentially more destructive, form of social disintegration and re-integration' (Castells 1989: 349). This is certainly how, in many quarters, it is being seen in Asia. On the one hand there is a celebration of new technologies, and a recognition that they are necessary and inevitable for economic growth, but a fear of what they might do, not so much to the cultures of the region, but to the spaces of the region currently filled up, as it were, with local and regional power bases. New information technologies and the developing flows that go with them are not seen as a Western enemy out to take over the East in a different form of colonialism or imperialism, but, even more dangerously and threateningly I would argue, as a stranger. Georg Simmel made the point almost one hundred years ago now in his classic study *On Individuality and Social Form*, that the stranger 'who comes today and stays tomorrow' (cited in Yao, 1994: 46) creates an uncertainty potentially far more threatening than the enemy whose purpose can be clearly defined. Asianizing moves in Asia are reactions to that stranger in their midst. The same strategies used to cope with the West as colonizing enemy are no longer appropriate. The stranger who may or may not bring benefits needs handling in radically different, and often considerably more subtle ways, than simple resistance. One of those strategies may well be the creation of the stranger, or at least bits of the stranger, as an enemy. As Yao Souchou in a recent essay makes clear, 'the potential of the West as stranger to destabilise Asian societies and cultures becomes very real indeed' (Yao, 1994: 47) if modernization is linked to Westernization.

Understanding this puts into context the anxieties of Asian countries to construct Asia as 'morally authentic', and as Yao points out, one of the chief discursive strategies that is being used to do this is an essentialism which positions Asian values and cultures as unique, irreplaceable and pure. It is this essentialism which is seeking the spaces thought to have been replaced by time by Western theorists. As Shoesmith puts it (referring closely to the work of Harold Innis), 'the overwhelming spatial basis of electronic communications creates a disequilibrium that foreshadows shifting political power and new configurations in culture and society' (Shoesmith 1994: 115). What sort of regulations will work in a developing (and desirable) regionalization of the marketplace, if any at all, is a question exercising a good number of those holding the reins of power in the region at the moment. Understanding the context of that question in particular requires understanding of cultural markets, cultural industries, communication and information networks and flows and, importantly, understanding of regionalized audiences. The perceived danger in many parts of the region is not so much that transnational corporations have technoligized information into products rather than processes of information designed for easy consumption and profit (though that is a concern of some intellectuals), but that the values associated with those products will undermine the sorts of political, social, cultural and economic stabilities which were actively used to attract the investment capital of the multinational and transnational corporations in the first place.

Nevertheless, the development of information as an integral and necessary component of late capitalism, and its defining role in what constitutes modernity and modernization in developing countries, is such a powerful rhetoric that strategies are being sought, one way or another, to monitor and manage, according to specific national imperatives, the power that comes with that information from its 'source(es)', and what is done with the effects of that power at its 'destination(s)' (see Van Dijk 1993). The difficulty is that the parameters for determining cultural, national, ethnic and social boundaries – sources and destinations – are, because of technologized communication, continually shifting, and in some cases, breaking down altogether. Furthermore, what is so often called the 'information age', in ways which seem to suggest that we have reached a final stage in some form of post-industrial modernization process which no longer needs boundaries because we are in some form of a global village, is not particularly helpful, because it conceals, for the most part, the interdependency of communication and information development on different, localized, regionalized markets and essentialized contexts, and the opportunities opening up for specific economic and cultural niches. Transnational relations are inevitably changing the region, and increasingly 'nations, even the most powerful, are subjected to the imperatives, practices and flows of transnational capital and information' (Hoover *et al.* 1993: 110), but what needs to be addressed is not so much the content of those relations but the reactions to them.

CONTROL

At the core of this awareness is what Beniger calls 'a crisis of control' (see Beniger 1986), where regional reactions signal that, like earlier developments of communication infrastructure after the industrial revolution, the imperatives and practices of capital are often moving more quickly than the imperatives and practices of the social/cultural. Coming to terms with the control and regulation of (tele)communications, for example, is a relatively easy matter, and one in which governments have had considerable practice for the most part. Coming to terms with the control and regulation of communication, locally, regionally and globally, is a very different thing. Recognizing the increasing commodification of information at the hands of an increasingly smaller group of leading players within the context of a massively expanding and relatively inexpensive access to free-to-air satellite technology is raising all sorts of interesting questions that those governments are currently struggling to answer in policy terms. Singapore tends not to anguish too much over that struggle as its shifts and changes in cultural policies might indicate.

Dr Ong Chit Chung, MP for Bukit Batok, and member of the ruling PAP, asserts, for example, that 'Singapore is both Asian and relatively conservative, and should remain so' (*The Straits Times*, 21 August 1992), expressing, of course, a widely held view. But exactly what constitutes the nature of that 'Asianness' and 'conservatism' is exercising a great many minds in Singapore at the moment. As commentator T. Sasitharan made clear (*The Straits Times*, 14 August 1992), 'If the findings of the CRC survey should have any bearing on the review of censorship policies here, it is because the views reflected happen to coincide with independently justifiable moral axioms that both the CRC and the government deem worth preserving. Moral axioms that were in place in the minds of policy-makers long before the CRC survey was even conceived.'

Tan Tarn How, for example, a leading journalist in Singapore, commenting on the Asian films featured in the 1994 Singapore International Film Festival, made the point that 'East Asia may be riding an economic wave, but the desperate despatches from many film-makers tell a different story from the upbeat reports of progress and profit that make their way to the media' (*The Straits Times*, 7 May 1994). Discussing recent films from Hong Kong, Taiwan and China, Tan argues that these films 'chart the spiritual emptiness that is often the by-product of modern life' and 'would even go as far as to say that there are lessons here for the policy-makers in these countries – and in Singapore'. What those lessons are cluster around the observation that many of the films are cataloguing forms of discontent which

> may eventually grow into a more widespread malaise that is already evident in the more advanced [read materialistic] nations. They point to two central challenges of all modern or modernising societies from America to Europe to Asia; the problems of the marginalised and rootless.

Here, marginalized refers not simply to those individuals on the fringes of society but 'those who for whatever reasons do not subscribe to mainstream values, such as regular pay for regular work, marriage and family'. Disenchanted youth, the focus of the films, is considered to be 'newly Asian', and very much a product of 'the West'. Issues of 'soul', i.e. the 'old Asian certainties', are being 'upturned' and films as art ('which mirrors life') can also be 'a warning to society'.

The message is clear, from government to most journalists and establishment commentators in Singapore, that projecting Singapore as an 'open' society with a 'free' flow of information, within the context of a rapidly modernizing, globalized region, comes at a cost. Control of that cost has been relatively straightforward in the past, and while generally heavy-handed it has affected only a very small minority of liberal-minded Singaporeans. Mass education in Singapore, and the need to position Singapore more and more fully as a modernized independent nation, has required new strategies of control; new awarenesses; new social comment; new notions of national identity. Asserting itself as 'Asian', in the face of a morally bankrupt West, is one of those new strategies. As George Yeo was reported to have said in an interview looking at 'The changing face of broadcasting' in Singapore:

> He can accept that foreigners behave in a strange way. But he doesn't like the idea that a fellow Singaporean or a relative or a family member behaves in the same way. And that being the case, this can be a source of strength for us because it means that in an open environment you are still able to maintain the distinction between the self and the external world.
>
> (*The Straits Times*, 3 September 1994)

What constitutes the self, and indeed the external world, are of course constructed fictions which suit a particular ideology and self-interestedness. The media, print and broadcast, as well as the arts in general, are positioned as part of that constructed fiction, so much so that they 'must have a deep sense of being defenders of the establishment because, like it or not, they are symbolically very important to the community as a whole' (*The Straits Times*, 3 September 1994). The 'open' environment, therefore, is faced with a large number of restrictions in Singapore, not least of which has been the recent passing of the Singapore Broadcasting Authority Bill (August 1994), which gives the Authority 'discretionary powers to ban foreign broadcast services, and requires broadcasters in Singapore to apply for licences, which can be amended or withdrawn at any time' (*The Straits Times*, 3 September 1994). There are many others (see Tan and Soh 1994).

Consensus, certainly among well-educated Singaporeans, was that the survey could not be believed, and the creation of a 'moral majority' in this way seemed to augur very badly for what the government might do in its censorship review. But even if it could be believed, its own findings were interpreted in such a way as to confirm government thinking prior to the survey. As Koh Buck Song, a leading journalist in Singapore, pointed out (*The Straits Times*, 17 August 1992), 48 per cent may have wanted a complete ban on materials depicting homosexuality, but 46 per cent (an almost equal number) wanted some form of access to such material; 32 per cent may have disapproved of a proposal to introduce a new restricted film classification, but 40 per cent were in favour; 56 per cent may have expressed a desire to have a complete ban on films and books that explore religious doubt, but 44 per cent did not share this view. Overall, he argued, of the thirty questions relating to censorship, only four were signalled prominently in the media and that such a skewing of the findings, right or wrong, should not 'be used as a springboard for the rise of ultra-conservatism and other forms of extremism'. As academic and later secretary-general of the leading opposition party in Singapore (who was later to be publicly vilified and discredited from the National University of Singapore), Chee Soon Juan wrote, 'To urge policy makers to base their decisions on a set of findings whose methodology is open to question is both irresponsible and regrettable' (*The Straits Times*, 19 August 1992).

Three months later the recommendations of the Censorship Review Committee included exempting established theatre groups from submitting scripts for approval, relaxing the categories of videos that have to be censored (e.g. serious music, cartoons, training videos), removing the ban on magazines like *Cosmopolitan* which have more text than pictures, introducing an NC16 film classification system to prevent under 16s from watching films with adult themes, insisting that television censorship be as strict as cinema censorship, keeping the R(A) film classification age limit to 21 and keeping R(A) films in approved cinemas only, i.e. away from HDB housing estates, no video releases of R(A) films, and maintaining the ban on all pornography. Organizations like the Singapore Film Society and the cultural arms of all embassies in Singapore were given considerably more freedom than before, enabling them to make 'private' uncensored screenings of some films. Generally, all existing censorship policies were kept in place, with the chair of the CRC, Professor Tommy Koh, arguing that the committee had attempted to 'strike a balance between allowing more scope for creative expression and maintaining a morally wholesome society' (*The Straits Times*, 18 October 1992). Central to the recommendations was that despite the fact that, Singapore was an open city, Singapore should not 'liberalise just because other countries were'. 'Above all', the recommendations continued, 'we must do nothing to weaken the structure of the family.'

And this is the crux of the matter – the notion of family is central to the policy of Asianizing Singapore, because it is the so-called breakdown of the family which is seen to be the most devastating effect of modernization in 'the West'. As Prime Minister Goh Chok Tong said in his 1994 National Day speech,

> No developed country is free of problems. But the problems they face are different. They are not those of ignorance, poverty, disease and backward- ness. They are the problems of indulgence, or rather over-indulgence in materialism, in subsidies and welfare. Over-indulgence [he continued] has contributed to a loss of ethical and moral standards, the breakdown of the family, increasing illegitimate births, loss of discipline at home and in schools, and young people taking to drugs and crime. We must learn from the mistakes they made. We must not think that wealth and money can solve all social problems. For civilised living, people must have strong moral values, discipline and proper family upbringing. These are the basic virtues that societies, however high-tech, still need. The question is, how are Singaporeans to retain their basic virtues in an age of increasing materialism?
>
> (*The Straits Times*, 9 August 1994)

His answer is 'to find enough people with the selfless spirit of the older generation to form a leadership which can unite Singaporeans and get them to work together to make tomorrow's Singapore better than today's'. And, inevitably, when seen in these terms, one of the leading strategies of that 'older generation' is censorship.

CULTURAL POLICY/CULTURAL MANAGEMENT

Censorship as cultural policy is, therefore, seen to have a crucial role to play in the development, not just of the nation, but of Singapore as an 'Asian' nation because, as Tommy Koh made clear, 'Censorship is not simply a matter of enforcement; it is also a public declaration of what we want our society to be' (*The Straits Times*, 18 October 1992), and, as far as the ruling PAP are concerned, and in the words of Dr Toh Keng Kiat MP, 'The final say should rest with the censors, as I think the government should still be the moral guardian of society' (*The Straits Times*, 21 October 1992). That does not mean that in Singapore nothing goes to press or air without a government censor pencilling changes and deletions – this sort of political censorship does not happen at that level – but, as a leading media commentator, Cherian George, makes clear, political censorship still exercises power over the social and cultural, because there are still 'policies and practices of the state that restrict the communication process, and prevent people from sending or receiving information that they want' (*The Straits Times*, 25 October 1992), either by direct censorship or by self-censorship. As George clearly states,

> The CRC (Censorship Review Committee) sought a balance between maintaining a morally wholesome society and finding more scope for creativity. Singaporeans must ask themselves if a better balance can also be struck between political stability and healthy dissent. If Singapore is to mature as a polity, it is an issue that should not be consigned under the carpet indefinitely.

Despite the fact that the final decision as to whether a film will be screened in Singapore or not is made not by government but by nine (non-governmental) members of the Committee of Appeal, which can overturn decisions made by the Board of Film Censors (a government statuary board itself advised by a fifty-six member Films Advisory Panel), the climate of censorship, linked as it is to moral definitions of national identity and political, social and economic stability, is still essentially government driven. Government policy on nation building, regional-ization and its formulation on 'East/West' divides, as part of an overall economic policy insisting upon political and social stability at any cost, determines the imperatives of cultural policy, and that in turn determines the climate within which strategies of supervision, erasure and effacement, with respect to film, but also to most other forms of domestic and imported information and expression, operate. The politicians are the cultural managers of global information within a regional context.

As Roland Roberston has made clear, increased globalization implies (and usually involves) increased regionalism (Robertson 1992), and that, as a form of nationalist reaction, can be seen in many parts of the Asia Pacific today with a reformulation sometimes of those cultural practices and traditions which contri-buted significantly to the earlier establishment of national and regional identities. In that respect it is a form of post-colonial abrogation denying the global yet at the same time engaging with it. But it is not without significance. Globalization is not inevitable, despite the seemingly irreversible march of technological determinism that seems to demand it. The developing importance of ASEAN and APEC as political and economic groupings helping to position nation-states, without losing cultural sovereignties, as a powerful regional force in the face of mounting global pressure/ imperialism is a significant case in point. It is one thing for a developing nation to want an informed citizenry if it has the means to regulate and monitor the nature of the informing as part of, say, a nation building programme, quite another to lose total control to an externalized 'global citizenry', which has little or no interest, in or sensitivity towards its specific needs (see

Gurevitch *et al.* 1991). As Marjorie Ferguson says, 'a pervasive (primarily Western) electronic media popular culture does not "McDonaldize" the world. It does not and cannot impose a 'totalistic' global culture that erases local, regional or national cultures, or their expression or mediation' (Ferguson 1992 cited in Menon 1994: 42). What we need to understand is that new realities, new definitions, and new structures are being determined by powerful forces within the Asian region, driven by powerful economic capital and, aligned to that, the developing cultural capital of what constitutes Asianness. As George Yeo, Minister for Information and Arts in Singapore has said

> When we were poor we had no say. Now that we are less poor, we should begin to assert our own point of view. In the process, a better balance will be struck. One day the pendulum in the West will also swing back. . . . The tides of history are changing.
>
> (Yeo 1994: 106)

NOTES

* This paper basically covers the years 1991 to early 1995.
1 In 1980 there were eighty cinemas operating in Singapore with a total seating capacity of 77,000 and with annual attendances of 40,531,000. By 1987 the number of cinemas had dropped to forty-one, with a total seating capacity of 48,000 and with an annual attendance of 19,762,000. In 1991 the number of cinemas had grown to fifty-five with annual attendances of 20,655,000. This has expanded to 115 cinemas (with seating for 64,000) with an annual attendance of 29,000,000 in 1994 (*The Straits Times*, 22 November 1991) with the four main operators building a total of forty-six new screens in 1992 alone. The Marina Square area (a developing entertainment area built on reclaimed land) is set to have eleven new cinemas alone by 1995.
   Nevertheless, as Meileen Choo, Chief Executive Officer for the huge Cathay Organisation in Singapore, made clear in 1993, 'We may be avid movie goers, but the market is not increasing. What we have is more cinema operators sharing the same pie' (*The Straits Times*, 27 November 1993). That pie means that while Singapore is now acknowledged to have the world's highest yearly per capita cinema admissions – 7.9 films per person compared to 3.8 in the USA, 1.9 in Thailand, 1.6 in Malaysia and 1 in Indonesia – cinema operators are expanding their operations, introducing better equipment, moving towards multiplex cinemas and joining forces to open up the market. Despite the massive ownership of VCRs and the increasing use of laser discs as sources of movie watching, cinema audiences, despite some industry pessimism, continue to grow.
2 Using data from Entertainment Data Inc., *The Straits Times* published a comparison of cinema attendances around the world and suggested that Singaporeans were 'the world's most ardent movie-goers' (22 November 1991). The countries compared were US/Canada (admissions per capita, 3.8), Germany (2.1), France (2.2), Italy (1.9), UK (1.7), Spain (2.1), Sweden (2.0) and Singapore, with an admissions per capita rating of 7.9. Percentage occupancy, for example, for the week 6–12 June 1991 for the American movie *Home Alone* in Cathay 1 (a major city cinema) topped 90.8 per cent and averaged 83.7 per cent for the week. Similar figures were gained for Bedok 1, a major suburban cinema, with the highest figures topping 99.9 per cent and averaging at 85 per cent. Weekly attendance for *Front Page*, a major Chinese movie screened in

Singapore in October 1991, had upwards of 40,000 in Broadway, 35,000 in Majestic and upwards of 30,000 in Central and Regal (all major suburban cinemas). Overall, annual attendance figures have steadily increased in the last few years, from 19,766,600 in 1987 to well in excess of 25 million in 1994. The population of Singapore is approximately 4 million.

3 A recent example is the resignation of four editors from the National University of Singapore Alumni Magazine (widely circulated amongst the educated middle class in Singapore), *Commentary*, following the fears expressed by the management committee of the NUS Society that a planned issue on culture could jeopardize the society's future.

4 The Consumers Association of Singapore (CASE) conducted a survey between 1 July and 2 August 1991 and found that three 'R' rated movies were showing in twenty-six cinemas, while twelve non-'R' rated movies were showing in the other twenty-eight cinemas (*The Straits Times*, 9 August 1991), and in particular on 8 July 1991, forty-five out of the fifty-four cinemas in Singapore were showing restricted movies. Speaking a few days earlier Goh Chok Tong made the point that 'Singapore has to remain a good, clean place to bring up children, where parents do not have to worry about their children's access to low moral standards' (*The Straits Times*, 5 August 1991). 'What we have to achieve', he said, 'are what you call artistic films with occasional nudity, but that is part of art.' What he really had to achieve, at the expense of relaxing censorship, was some sense of regaining control, which was perceived to have been lost in this scramble for cinema audience dollars watching a handful of Hong Kong movies like *The Holy Virgin versus the Evil Dead*, *Erotic Nights* and *Erotic Ghost Story*, and movies like *Wild at Heart* and *Atame (Tie Me Up, Tie Me Down)*, which were playing to packed houses in all suburbs.

REFERENCES

Baudrillard, Jean (1983) *Simulations*, trans. Paul Foss, Paul Patton and Philip Beitchman. New York: Semiotext(e) Foreign Agents Series.

Beniger, J. (1986) The Control Revolution: Technological and Economic Origins of the Information Society. Cambridge, Mass.: Harvard University Press.

Birch, David (1992) 'Talking politics: Radio Singapore', *Continuum: The Australian Journal of Media and Culture*, 6: 75–101.

Birch, David (1993a) 'Staging crises: media and citizenship', in Gary Rodan (ed.) *Singapore Changes Guard. Social Poetical and Economic Directors in the 1990s*. Melbourne: Longman, Cheshire.

Birch, David (1993b) *Singapore Media: Communication Strategies and Practices*. Melbourne: Longman Cheshire.

Birch, David (ed.) (1994) *Cultural Studies in the Asia Pacific*, a special double issue of *Southeast Asian Journal of Social Science*, 22(1–2).

Birch, David (1995a) 'Information flows: Asianising Singapore', *CQU Working Papers in Communication and Culture*, 5–18.

Birch, David (ed.) (1995b) *Framing (Postcolonial) Cultures*, special issue of *Southern Review*, November, 28(3).

Bourdieu, Pierre and Passeron, Jean-Claude (1977) *Reproduction in Education, Society and Culture*, trans. Richard Nice. London: Sage Publications.

Castells, Manuel (1989) *The Informational City. Information Technology, Economic Restructuring and the Urban-Regional Process*. Oxford: Blackwell.

Chomsky, Noam (1989) *Necessary Illusions. Thought Control in Democratic Societies*. London: Pluto Press.

Dahlgren, Peter and Sparks, Colin (eds) (1991) *Communication and Citizenship, Journalism and the Public Sphere*. London: Routledge.

Ferguson, Marjorie (ed.) (1990) *Public Communication. The New Imperatives. Future Directions for Research*. London: Sage Publications.

Ferguson, Marjorie (1992) 'Globalisation and cultural industries: myths and realities', in *Cultural Industries: National Policies and Global Markets*, CIRCUIT Conference, December.

Foucault, Michel (1977) 'Revolutionary Action "Until Now"', in his *Language, Counter-Memory, Practice: Selected Essays and Interviews*. Haca, NY: Cornell University Press.

Foucault, Michel (1979) *Discipline and Punish. The Birth of the Prison*, trans. Alan Sheridan. London: Peregrine Books.

Gurevitch, Michael, Levy, Mark R. and Roeh, Itzhak (1991) 'The global newsroom: convergences and diversities in the globalisation of television news', in Peter Dahlgren and Colin Sparks (eds) *Communication and Citizenship: Journalism and the Public Sphere*. London: Routledge.

Hoover, Stewart M., Venturelli, Shalini Singh and Wagner, Douglas (1993) 'Trends in global communication policy-making: lessons from the Asian case', *Asian Journal of Communication*, 3(1):103–2.

Menon, Vijay (1994) 'Regionalisation: cultural enrichment or erosion?', *Media Asia*, 21(1): 39–42.

Robertson, Roland (1992) *Globalisation: Social Theory and Global Culture*. London: Sage Publications.

Rodan, Garry (ed.) (1993) *Singapore Changes Guard. Social, Political and Economic Directions in the 1990s*, Melbourne: Longman Cheshire.

Schlesinger, Philip (1990) 'Rethinking the sociology of journalism: source strategies and the limits of media-centrism', in Ferguson (ed.) *Public Communication. The New Imperatives. Future Directions for Research*. London: Sage.

Shoesmith, Brian (1994) 'Asia in their shadow: satellites and Asia', in David Birch (ed.) *Cultural Studies in the Asia Pacific*, a special double issue of *Southeast Asian Journal of Social Science*, 22(1–2).

Tan, Yew Soon and Peng, Soh Yew (1994) *The Development of Singapore's Modern Media Industry*. Singapore: Times Academic Press.

Van Dijk, Jan A.G.M. (1993) 'Communication networks and modernisation', *Communication Research* 20(3): 384–407.

Virilio, Paul (1991) *The Lost Dimension*, trans Daniel Moshenburg. New York: Semiotext(e).

Yao, Souchou (1994) 'The predicament of modernity: mass media and the making of the West in southeast Asia', *Asian Journal of Communication*, 4(1): 35–51.

Yeap, Soon Beng (1994) 'The emergence of an Asia-centred perspective: Singapore's media regionalisation strategies', *Media Asia*, 21(2): 63–72.

Yeo, George (1994) 'The technological revolution poses threats or opportunities?', *Media Asia*, 21(2): 104–6.

Yeo, Philip (1990) 'Economic Development – Strategic Thrusts for the 1990s', *Singapore 1990*, Govt. of Singapore, Singapore, 1–5.

Part III

INTRANATIONAL
PERSPECTIVES

12

ART AND INDUSTRY
Regional film and video policy in the UK
Steve McIntyre

INTRODUCTION

In late March 1995, two seemingly unrelated events took place which could be seen symbolically to represent and exemplify the direction which regional film and video policy took in Britain in the 1980s. At the 1995 Oscar ceremony, Peter Capaldi's short film *Franz Kafka's It's a Wonderful Life*, a production co-funded by the Scottish Film Production Fund and BBC Scotland, shared an Oscar for best short live action film.[1] The Scottish Film Production Fund is one of a network of publicly funded, culturally driven schemes across Britain and this was the first time that any such scheme has received such major official recognition. The second event was an advertisement in the 'Creative and Media' pages of *The Guardian* newspaper inviting applications for the post of Business Development Adviser to Cultural Industries in Coventry. What was most interesting and significant about this post was that it was located within the local authority – Coventry City Council. The role of the arts and cultural industries in economic development and industrial regeneration had now unequivocally found its place in the sun.

This chapter attempts to trace some of the histories that could be seen to lead up to these two events. In particular it will focus on the policies and activities promoted via public funding. There is, of course, no straightforward linear chronology that results in these particular apotheoses; rather there is a general historical drift that has seen regional arts agencies with responsibility for film and video increasingly moving away from culturally and aesthetically autonomous arts practices and embedding themselves and their work within a general rhetoric of 'cultural industries' while simultaneously increasingly successfully brokering co-funding deals with broadcasters in order that regional film and video production secures the high production values of mainstream industry and therefore can be seen to validate those rhetorical claims.

The chapter does not really attempt to deal with national British film policy – the vicissitudes of funding incentive and subsidy schemes for a British film industry. To some extent this is because there already exists a considerable literature about this.[2] It is also worth bearing in mind that for most of the century

215

(the first and last century of cinema) Britain has never really had a film policy worthy of its name and the industry in this country has periodically stumbled from crisis to crisis, only occasionally enlivened by brief (and usually eventually calamitous) moments of industrial vigour.[3] I will, however, touch on the actual and potential impact of the recently introduced UK National Lottery on both the feature film industry and 'cultural independent' film and video production

The chapter falls into four parts. First I attempt a brief description of the current ✳ structures of regional arts funding and activity in Britain. Second, and linked to this, is a brief history and interrogation of the emergence of strategies using arguments about developing cultural industries both as a mechanism for (it is claimed) supporting regional economic regeneration as well as (more certain) unlocking new sources of financial support for arts activity. The third section briefly describes and analyses regional film funding policies and structures and introduces the possibility of film production funding being made available to this area of work from the proceeds going to the arts from the UK National Lottery. The final section attempts a series of appraisals of the foregoing, of the strengths and weaknesses of exploiting arguments about cultural industries to underpin arts activity and of (some of) the issues at stake in linking public arts funding closely to the imperatives of broadcasters.

SOME DEFINITIONS

It is probably already becoming clear that this whole area is fraught with definitional and terminological difficulties. It is not the function of this chapter to map out all these difficulties, but it does need to define, more or less by fiat, what terms will mean for current purposes. The word 'culture', as Raymond Williams points out, slips between referring to 'a whole way of life' to referring to specifically legitimated, and esteemed, artistic products and practices. It is even more complex with the introduction of the notion of 'cultural industries' – industries the output of which is always ultimately concerned with the production, distribution and exchange of clusters of symbols, of signs and meanings. But the output of those cultural industries while always 'symbolic' is only sometimes 'culture' (*haute culture* as a traditionalist would understand it). It does not really help that much to introduce the notion of 'art' (although I was obliged to in the introduction) given that, at least in the Western world, the term 'artists' film and video' relates mainly to specific practices primarily (although not exclusively) concerned with questions of form, structure, texture and temporality. At one point above, the concept of 'cultural independent' practice is introduced (quite a useful term, the point of which is to re-appropriate the notion of independence from, for instance, 'independent' television operators such as Berlusconi or Murdoch).

In the main, this chapter will endeavour to adhere reasonably strictly to a fairly narrow and narrowly defined cluster of terms. 'Arts' will primarily be used here in the sense of traditional 'high art' (primarily because the term attaches to institutions such as the Arts Council of England and regional arts boards (RABs),

216

for which this is their broad understanding). 'Cultural industries' are those industrial formations concerned with the generation, circulation and exchange of symbols and attendant flows of finance (see also below). I do, however, want to attach to the notion of 'culture' (and its use in a term like 'cultural independence') a value judgement relating to issues such as quality of experience, innovation, illumination, aesthetic challenge, etc. while resisting any suggestion that these issues might be the sole property of artists' film and video practice. At heart, the subject of this article is cultural independent practice in the UK over the last couple of decades and, crudely, the story that is being told is a gradual shift from concern for cultural independence to concern for cultural industries – with inevitable attendant gains and losses.

ARTS FUNDING IN THE UK

No one really writes about arts funding and support structures – they are perhaps too contaminated with a overpowering sense of bureaucracy and officialdom to warrant the attention of cultural commentators.[4] Curiously (actually, perhaps not that curious at all) the media and television industries are written about in the British press, including, it should be said, the financial pages of quality 'broadsheets', at a length that bears very little relationship to their financial importance. Despite this dearth of serious coverage of the arts, it is worth noting that there is much at stake. There is serious money – the combined budgets of the four arts councils in the UK, the British Film Institute (and other film councils), regional arts boards, and various arts and media development agencies amounts to substantially more than £300m per annum. More than this, in a whole series of ways these funding systems act as cultural commissars determining current definitions and validations of culture – continuing to value traditional art forms (opera, classical music, theatre) while continuing to marginalize other practices (ethnic arts, new technological forms, etc.).

In 1995, these moneys have recently been massively augmented in the UK by funding from the National Lottery. Set up in 1994, the National Lottery is expected to contribute more than £250m per year to arts funding in the UK (and similar amounts to sports, charities, the national heritage and 'Millennium'-related activities). In order to distinguish this new finance from traditional arts money, National Lottery funds can only contribute to capital projects (buildings, equipment, etc.) not to revenue or ordinary arts production expense (a new play, opera or so forth). Because of UK Treasury rules, however, expenditure on film production is treated as capital expenditure because the eventual work is considered to be a capital asset (like industrial plant and machinery – it can be bought and sold). Curiously, this definition of film as a capital asset has been extended to all types of film production – not just mainstream features (for which the argument has some, albeit arguable, force), but non-mainstream work and even short films and videos. The impact on regional and national cultural film and video production is potentially massive (more on this below).

I want now briefly to describe the topography of British arts funding and then focus more on how this delivers regional film and video activities. There is something delightfully loopy and idiosyncratic about the systems and structures of funding and support for the arts in the United Kingdom – what one commentator describes as 'decidedly messy'.[5] To some extent this does little more than reflect the rather messy nature of regional government in the UK with separate (rather powerless) government departments for Scotland, Wales and Northern Ireland but very limited devolution of authority to those 'national regions'. To the political regions of England, there are to all intents and purposes no devolved policy making structures (be they political or cultural), although certain of the larger local authorities (such as Birmingham and Glasgow), because of the very scale of their economies (equivalent to a smallish nation-state), have been able to 'forge' a certain degree of local political autonomy and control. Certain of these authorities (for instance the two cited) have taken a keen interest in the role of the local arts in, primarily, image manipulation to enhance local and regional prestige. It is important to note that London has no directly-elected city government. The last one, the Greater London Council, was abolished by the radical right-wing Conservative government in 1987.

The arts system is also surprisingly resilient – reflecting possibly the status of the arts in broader political thinking. In 1989, a report by a recently retired civil servant (*The Wilding Report*), after promising a fairly radical overhaul of arts funding, eventually led to no more than twelve regional arts associations mutating into ten almost indistinguishable regional arts boards, full autonomy to the Scottish and Wales Arts Councils (instead of being sub-committees of the Arts Council of Great Britain) and very limited devolution of power and authority from the centre to the regions.

By and large, two or three years of anguish and debate surrounding Wilding's deliberations led to little more than the publication of a so-called National Arts and Media Strategy – a document which was immediately shelved and thereafter totally ignored (Challans and Webber 1993). While it is the case that literally millions of pounds was wasted on modest and somewhat inconsequential re-organization of arts bureaucracy, there was almost no public contestation of this. Perhaps this simply indicates the success of those arts bureaucracies in burying their operation and structures in a miasma of usually unspoken and almost always informal systems and operations.

At the 'centre' of things sits the Arts Council of England and the British Film Institute. ACE receives about £200 per year from central government which is used to support the so-called national companies (major drama and opera in the main) and passed on to regional arts boards (about £45m per year to support regional arts activity). The regional arts boards in turn distribute funding to regional 'clients' (supposedly) according to semi-autonomous, regionally determined cultural criteria. The vagueness of that last expression is deliberate. Throughout the system there exists profound ambiguity as to relationships of accountability (upwards to funders) versus autonomy and independence. Between central government (the so-called Department of National Heritage – the British have always worried about the use of the term 'culture') and the Arts Council of England there exists 'the arts length principle' – supposedly to protect the arts in Britain from overt and sustained political meddling and make the Arts Council an authentically artistically motivated structure. In turn, 'delegation' of funding responsibility to regional arts boards supposedly makes them responsible to regional cultural priorities. Finally the clients of a regional arts board are likewise purportedly independent companies with their own cultural autonomy. Of course it does not work out as simply as this, with these ambiguous relations of contractual financial accountability always rubbing up against a drive towards independence. Inevitably this makes the system somewhat inward looking and puzzling to outsiders. It tends to make it look as if most if not all funding is stitched up by an insider collection of charmed arts organizations. The fact that it is not always possible to identify how decisions get made, who made them and the criteria on which they were made breeds a certain cynicism and anger. The British arts funding system is not well respected.

Significantly, in the short time that it has been operating, the National Lottery has become contaminated by a similar kind of disrespect – there is emerging a cynicism about the Lottery and a feeling that public money is being distributed in non-accountable, non-transparent ways by a self-selecting 'palocracy'.

The complications of the system are multiplied by the parallel existence of arts councils for Scotland, Wales and Northern Ireland (the national regions of the United Kingdom), funded by Scottish Office, Welsh Office, etc. rather than the Department of National Heritage (whose brief outside of England exists but is ill defined). The national–regional arts councils do not have regional structures. Moreover, local authorities add to the brew. Some (usually the smaller ones) join forces with English regional arts boards against the might of the centre (usually seen as effete, bureaucratic, metrocentric). Others (the larger ones whose budget often dwarfs that of the local regional arts board) feel that they should be playing with the heavy hitters at the centre rather than with the (inconsequential) small fry out in the regions.

There are ten regional arts boards in England. RAB boundaries are based on Second World War civil defence organizations. So, even with the modest reorganization attendant on *The Wilding Report*, the overall structure of regional support for the arts harks back to the civil defence regions mapped out during the Second World War to organize against air raids. The 'morale boosting' work during the war by ENSA (Entertainments National Services Association) gave rise after the war to CEMA (Council for the Encouragement of Music and the Arts) and ultimately the Arts Council of Great Britain. When the Arts Council began to develop and support regional offices during the 1970s (which eventually lead to the establishment of regional arts associations) it fell back on this particular history. One of the most striking characteristics of the regional arts map is the way it resolutely fails to conform to the catchment areas of the independent regional broadcasters, local government or formal and informal historical communities and communities of interest!

In parallel to the delegation of regional funding by the Arts Council, the British Film Institute in turn also funds the regional arts boards – albeit at a much lower level.

There are, it must be said, not inconsiderable sums of money at stake. Not only is more than £1.8 million given as grant aid by the BFI to the RABs, but also other funding is made available directly and indirectly for regional work (see Table 12.1).

Table 12.1 Direct grants from BFI to RABs (£s)

Regional arts board	1995	1996
Eastern Arts	86,790	86,790
East Midland Arts	108,606	108,606
London Film and Video Development Agency	459,090	459,090
Northern Arts	432,028	432,028
North West Arts	214,470	214,470
Southern Arts	95,814	95,814
South East Arts	48,540	48,540
South West Arts	71,510	71,510
West Midland Arts	130,970	130,970
Yorkshire Arts	111,980	111,980
Wales Film Council	68,742	80,512
Total	1,828,540	1,840,310

In addition to these moneys (spent ultimately by the regional arts boards for their own purposes), approximately another £1 million goes to regional activity directly from the BFI by way of direct revenue grants and one-off project development grants.

The separate, distinct nomenclature of Arts Council and British Film Institute should not lead one to assume any radically clear separation of interests, for the Arts Council too operates in the moving image field, concentrating on 'artists' films and broadcasting about the arts.

RABs, therefore, answer to two 'superior' funding agencies and therefore dance to two agendas. But whereas BFI money and the activities that flow from it can be fully costed and accounted for, ACE funding to RABs is by way of a general subvention to overall programmes of work. This has led to a situation in which even though the Arts Council of England will be the hugely more significant funding partner of an RAB, the lien that the Film, Video and Broadcasting Department of ACE has on RAB film and video activity is very limited compared with that derived from the direct link to the BFI. This issue, among others, has plagued ACE/BFI/RAB relationships for years.

The BFI in turn has had its own dissatisfactions with existing structural relations between it and RABs – in particular the ways in which its concerns have traditionally been marginalized inside bodies whose principle focus has tended to be traditional performing and visual arts and whose take on an arts/industry dialectic has always been shaky. The BFI's policy for regional cultural development during the 1980s increasingly moved from a concern to develop and expand a politically radical oppositional film culture to a more pragmatic, opportunistic approach, less antagonistic to a mainstream industry and increasingly concerned to build *ad hoc* partnerships with it. Whatever the merits of this strategy (and it is considered in more detail below) it inevitably would rub up against the operating ideologies of the RABs.

For this reason, the BFI has recently undertaken an exercise to determine the desirability and viability of redirecting funding away from the RABs into a to-be-established network of media development agencies. Such agencies would be charged with executing the BFI's cultural remit in the regions of England and also, significantly, with broader responsibility for expanding the economic base of the media industries outside London. Intriguingly, the AIDA model was tried out on a kind of informal pilot basis in London, with the London Film and Video Development Agency being established in 1992!

Before examining in more detail the cultural industries development case, it is important to be aware of what a distance it represents from the radical cultural arguments being advanced not much more than a decade ago. The *locus classicus* of the political/aesthetic radical tendency is probably the BFI's own *The New Social Function of Cinema*. Published in 1981, this book attempted, as its title suggests, to delineate the parameters of nothing less than a counter-cinema. Hilary Thomson's introduction puts it absolutely frankly:

> What are the origins of this new pedagogy, this new cinema? The need for an alternative, counter, pedagogical, propagandist cinema practice in the face of a monolithic notion of audience was first indicated in this country in the Thirties. . . . From the late sixties, the British independent film movement has similarly developed, taking its impetus from the events of France in May 1968 and the upheaval of that period that fundamentally altered the relationship between State and Public. As this movement developed it concerned itself both with the 'politics of representation' and the politics of institutions. This movement, now organised in the *Independent Film-Makers Association* by people who work in many areas of our audio visual culture, challenges the basis of dominant media operation – simple production for passive consumption.
>
> (Stoneman and Thomson 1991)

Such rhetoric is unquestionably of a piece with much of the cultural and theoretical optimism (bravado) of the late 1970s and early 1980s – what Colin McCabe has called (in a transformational recantation from the author of the *Classic Realist Text*) the 'intellectual bankruptcy' of the 1970s. Much has changed. The Independent Film-Makers Association no longer exists. While central to the thinking behind the establishment of a radical, innovative Channel 4, the IFA's earnest radicalism had increasingly no place in a commercially driven independent market. Mutations of its core functions and the emergence of other representative bodies (Association of Independent Producers, Independent Programme Producers Association, etc.), coupled with the growth of small commercial independent producers, eventually led to the creation of a single *trade* association to represent independent producers in industrial and commercial negotiations with broadcaster, government, etc.

It should not be assumed that the heady, theoretically inspired optimism exemplified by *The New Social Function of Cinema* was confined to the rarefied atmosphere of London and the BFI. Indeed the regional input from Bristol, Nottingham and Newcastle based groups was crucial. And it is here, as much as in the BFI, that change has been most marked.

John Caughie and Simon Frith have trenchantly described recent history at the BFI as 'retooling the culture industry' (Caughie and Frith 1990). In the past five years or so, rather than seeing itself as oppositional in any sense, it has explicitly and deliberately attempted to align itself with an industry, campaigning vigorously on behalf of, for example, fiscal incentives and tax breaks for commercial film production. In addition, Caughie and Frith argue, market driven concerns for its 'customers', the drive for the mainstream, and shift to populism all signal a real break with the resolutely radical intellectual, educational and cultural agenda of a decade earlier. Similar if not quite so dramatically marked shifts have also appeared in regional activity.

ONE MORE DEFINITION

'[C]ultural industries' [refers] to those institutions in our society which employ the characteristic modes of production and organisation of industrial corporations to produce and disseminate symbols in the form of cultural goods and services, generally, although not exclusively, as commodities. . . .
In all these cultural processes, we characteristically find at some point the use of capital intensive technological means of production and distribution, highly developed divisions of labour and hierarchical modes of managerial organisation.
[P]ower in the cultural sector clusters around distribution, the channel of access to audiences. It is here that we typically find the highest level of capital intensity, ownership concentration and multinationalism.

(Garnham 1984: 156, 157)

A central theme of this chapter is the history of the notion of 'cultural industries' – or more particularly a specific history of the use of that term, from about the mid-1980s onwards, within *regional* metropolitan areas of the UK. This also touches on the ways in which that term mutated over these ten years or so. Almost inevitably, this kind of discussion suffers yet another terminological slippage between talking about broad 'cultural industries' and more narrowly defined 'media industries'. One reason for this slippage is that by and large specific cultural industries initiatives during the 1980s and early 1990s based themselves on broad definitions (such as that offered by Nicholas Garnham above), but tended to use film, video and television as one of the central elements – a paradigmatic case. Moreover, even when using broad definitions of cultural industries, there rarely was a consistent set of areas to be included (design, fashion, advertising, print, etc. tended to be included or not included often on what appears to be little more than whims).

I will also want to touch on some of the contradictions at the heart of the *regional* cultural industries strategies promulgated during the last decade and how certain of the 'successes' won by those strategies also led to substantial problems – for instance the break-up of the broadcasting monopolies and the growth of independent production has inevitably been accompanied by casualization and massive job losses.

THE ORIGIN OF THE POLICY

Obviously, there have always been cultural industries – from stonemason's yards to the patronage systems that traditionally supported painters and the apprenticeship systems that facilitated their work. But there is a modern usage which has a very specific provenance – the Labour controlled Greater London Council 1981–1986. In particular, it is difficult to underestimate the crucial influence of Nicholas Garnham in insinuating notions of cultural industries into the London Industrial Strategy and the thinking of the Greater London Enterprise Board (Bianchini 1987)

The Greater London Council represented an extraordinary (and in retrospect almost inconceivable) exposition of a radical left politics in London within a general political landscape characterized by the most intransigent and uncompromising radical right government since the war. The GLC introduced a series of populist, grassroots initiatives ranging from a cheap public transport policy to employment programmes addressing the needs of specific (and specifically disadvantaged) communities in the capital. It was persuaded that its industrial, economic and employment strategies should take London's cultural industries seriously.

Unlike later examples, where the focus was on job creation and economic development, the thinking behind the GLC's intervention was primarily a drive towards social engineering – in other words a strategy of grant funding in order to give a cultural voice to certain communities and constituencies traditionally marginalized within already existing traditional 'cultural industries' (black, gay, young people, the working class, etc.). In order to endow these groups with a voice, a system of business support schemes was established (start-up loans, business advice, managed workspace, etc.) focusing on those industries deemed to be particularly germane to these communities (music, film and video, design, etc.). What was crucial about these initiatives was that they endeavoured to intervene in already successful industries in order to shift and transform their social, cultural and political profiles and agendas. As Garnham put it 'the real basis of the cultural industries lies rather in the practice of everyday life, and in the many small independent producers' (Garnham 1984). The GLC's policies were not primarily, even tangentially, concerned with *overall* job creation and economic development. To put it in rather grand political terms (which are probably not inappropriate to the GLC), it was a political/hegemonic task rather than an industrial task which was being undertaken.

To situate this historically, this relates to the period 1983/84 when the Greater London Enterprise Board was set up. A key moment in all of this was a major conference, run by the GLC in 1983 at the Riverside Studio called *Cultural Industries and Cultural Policy in London*.

One of the key points about the GLC's cultural industries policies is that they failed. Possibly not because they were fundamentally flawed but because they were not really given an opportunity to work. From about 1984, the council was increasingly obsessed with its own survival. When it failed to secure this, the resulting funding and policy chaos more or less destroyed whatever had been created.

THE RISE AND FALL OF CULTURAL INDUSTRIES

The notion of public investment in cultural industries, however, rose phoenix-like from the ashes of the GLC and two to three years later, no self-respecting city in England (and England rather than Britain or the UK is used here precisely) was without a team of consultants devising a strategy for that area. What happened, however, was that the terms began to shift and the emphasis increasingly began to be placed on cultural industries as industries like any others – areas in which local authorities could intervene and thereby generate jobs, urban regeneration, economic development and so on. Increasingly the sponsoring department would be economic development rather than arts and cultural services. By the early 1990s, the shift was almost complete.

So, by the end of the 1980s there were a substantial number of media related initiatives developing across England. Around 1987, Birmingham set up a Media Development Agency, Nottingham developed the strategy of 'Nottingham as a Media Centre', a range of linked projects emerged in the north east which are examined below. Liverpool, Manchester, Bristol, Leeds, Sheffield and even humble Leicester undertook media/cultural industries mapping exercises. The Coventry example opening this chapter is emblematic of these developments. The contrast with the kinds of political activism central to *The New Social Function of Cinema* could not be more striking. Scotland and Northern Ireland came to the table slightly later, but they too are now trawling in these waters. There are fairly obvious good reasons for cities and regions grasping these apparent opportunities: the decline in traditional manufacturing industries; the need to refurbish cities' images by association with modern, clear, global arts and media activities and so on. The arguments are well known.

Also driving the process was a growing number of influential and well placed advocates of the notion of cities taking cultural industries seriously (as London had done albeit in a radically different way). Their role was vital. There emerged, in the early to mid-1980s a kind of 'invisible college' made up of academics, consultants, arts bureaucrats and independent film and video makers (possibly no more than twenty or thirty people overall). This informal group (it was never a formal 'collective' in, any way, although they mostly knew each other) were broadly responsible for 'snowballing' these ideas across the country.

Originally radicalized to some extent by cultural theory and activities of the 1970s and given an enormous shot in the arm by the investment strategies and policies of Channel 4, the main concerns of this loose group was development of structures and modes of production outside of traditional broadcasting. There was an emphasis on independent film, video and television production; there was a desire to create shared facilities and production bases; there was a heavy emphasis on training (as a mechanism of empowerment); there was often a notion of community involvement and collective practice (film and video workshops). As we will see, the trajectory of the thinking promulgated by this 'invisible college' in most significant aspects parallels that of the shift from the politically radical interventionist approach of the GLC to the pragmatic, economic regeneration strategies of later regional cities – increasingly the emphasis was on autonomous regional industries.

For two reasons, it is difficult to overstate the role of Channel 4. First it was a 'publisher/broadcaster' – it by and large did not make programmes itself but bought everything in from outside and therefore called into being a whole new cadre of independent producers. Second, through the funding strategies of its independent film and video department, it seeded a large number of film and video workshops across the UK which became the nuclei of cultural industries advocacy in their respective cities. Moreover, the success of the Channel 4 model was one of the factors leading to the eventual break up of British broadcasting, and the opening up of the airways more generally to independents.

By the early to mid-1980s, therefore, most of the elements were in place for a fairly radical shift in the terms of the debate about developing regional cultural/media industries. In effect, a meeting ground was effected between on the one hand local authorities which were looking for mechanisms and strategies for reinvigorating local economies, and on the other cultural activists attempting to develop workshop based practice but also, increasingly, to secure new private and public funding for cultural development underpinned by industrial rhetoric.

As an example of these kinds of initiatives, one of the first, and for a while most successful of public funding-led cultural industries strategies, was in the north east of England, where a group of film and video workshops (Amber Films, Trade Films, Swingbridge Video, Tyneside Cinema and A19 Film and Video) established an ambitious development programme. It established two co-ordinating agencies – the North East Media Development Council (NEMDC – a policy forum) and the North East Media Development Agency (NEMDA – the operational arm). It also set up the North East Media Training Centre (NEMTC – for technical training of new entrants) and PRIMO (to distribute the work generated). It is worth quoting from NEMTC at length as it represents, possibly in the most fully realized form, all of the issues and priorities that jostled for space within the problematic of cultural industries.

> NEMTC is helping to build a new industry, here in the North East. An industry that's growing and growing fast: the independent film, video and television industry.
>
> Much of the increasing demand for more film and TV programmes is being met by small, independent companies. Programme makers, facility houses, distributors and technical specialists of all kinds are sharing in this expansion. With the decline of the film industry's studio system, the advent of Channel Four, the arrival of cable and satellite TV and the growing use of video by institutions and businesses, the independent sector of the industry is booming.
>
> The broad aim of NEMDA is to foster the growth of a regional media industry, and to promote a model of practice based on public accountability and regional development. . . . A further role for NEMDA is as an agent for research in and development of regional cultural policy from the standpoint of the independent film and video industry.
>
> The role of PRIMO is to act as a marketing arm for regional film and video makers, functioning as the independent sector's film and video distributor. The task is to stimulate demand for film and video, especially for regionally produced titles, and to contribute to the development of new and existing sales and hire outlets across the North East and beyond. The aim is a pattern of strong and healthy outlets for product upon which regional producers can depend as a basis for growth.
>
> (North East Media Development Council Leaflet 1985)

Perhaps the most striking thing about this statement in retrospect is the emphasis on small production companies as the driving force of both industrial development and cultural empowerment, coupled with a rather unquestioned celebration of the vertical disintegration of British television. One central problem with all of this is that it tended to underestimate or downplay the importance of the broadcast establishment – in particular regional broadcasters. The focus on independent production ultimately was a focus on quite a narrow slice of the actual audiovisual pie. Looking at the bigger picture, it is clear that the vertical fragmentation of broadcasting in the UK and the growth of independent production has undermined, rather than expanded, the overall level of regional audiovisual activity. Rather than helping to wrest opportunities away from London, fragmentation has led to the consolidation over the last five years or so of metrocentric domination (Cornford and Robins 1991). At heart, the issue is one of distribution, as the opening quotation from Nicholas Garnham emphasizes. And distribution power

226

lies with broadcasters. It is instructive that the least successful and first-to-close strand of NEMDC's masterplan was PRIMO.

Another way of thinking about this is to understand the ways that broadcasters act as magnets around which all their service providers cluster. Both producers and commissioners tend to gravitate to the 'thickest market' – to the place where most work is made and most work is available (see Porter 1990). Indeed, speaking at the 'Broadcasting in the Regions' conference in Salford in 1993, Channel 4 supremo Michael Grade observed that it would be a 'commercial disaster' were Channel 4 to be based anywhere other than London. As well as most work, it is also important to recognize that television production is embedded in a whole network of other industries (design, financial services, legal, facilities) – the biggest and therefore best choice of which will always be in the capital. Accurate figures are hard to come by, but best estimates would suggest that London's domination of the television market has risen from perhaps 75 per cent to 80 per cent over the past five years.

Despite these manifest and deep-seated problems with the model, cultural industries strategies for local economies persist. The Edinburgh and Lothian Screen Industries Office is one of a number of cultural industries developments in Scotland which have emerged since the beginning of the 1990s. This is not the place to examine the late arrival on the Scottish scene of arguments which had been very common in England for more than five years (largely to do with the absence of developed film and video workshops that could act as a focus for debate about development and an absence (at least in the middle of the 1980s) of any real participants in the 'invisible college' referred to above). What is really instructive about the Scottish case is precisely that, by coming on to the scene late, it demonstrates in a clear and unambiguous form the evolution of the cultural industries arguments to a stage wherein industrial arguments are unequivocally dominant:

> Over several years, the economic development authorities within the City of Edinburgh District Council, Lothian Regional Council and Lothian and Edinburgh Enterprise Ltd have been developing a strategy for company growth and job creation which has begun to recognise the importance of the cultural industries sector within Edinburgh and Lothian. . . . The Central impulse behind the strategy is to build on current strengths through a number of targeted interventions thereby enabling the screen industries to maximise exploitation of existing and potential opportunities within Scotland and beyond. In other words, the point of the strategy is to ensure that film and television producers in Lothian secure an appropriate piece of an expanding economy.
>
> (Edinburgh and Lothian Screen Industries Office Report 1995)

Even more recently, Coventry City Council appointment of a Business Development Adviser in this area demonstrated that despite many problems with both actual performance as measured against rhetoric and intellectual credibility, arguments about the industrial and economic benefits attendant on these areas retain a serious potency. Why should this be so?

In part, the answer relates to the ways in which the regional cultural independent production sector that emerged through the 1980s for reasons outlined above has become more and more concerned with training and retraining. At least in part this derives from an ambition to open up opportunities in these areas of work to individuals and groups from constituencies which in the main have historically been denied access. It is also true to say that to a large extent this shift in emphasis was funding-led with workshops and other groups alighting on the fact that serious public money could be obtained under the central and local government training initiatives that followed the recession of the late 1980s (and which often could cynically be seen as little more than rather crude attempts to massage unemployment figures).

The link to the broader cultural industrial development argument was maintained by indicating the ways in which the workshops and independent production centres that emerged through the 1980s have increasingly turned themselves over to being training centres in an effort to maintain regional skills bases threatened by the collapse of genuine training within an increasingly casualized and fragmented broadcast industry and/or drifting towards London. The long march from *The New Social Function of Cinema* to becoming a service operation to the mainstream broadcast industries has, in many cases, been completed.

REGIONAL FILM AND VIDEO PRODUCTION

In another part of the forest, the sorts of production undertaken by and supported by the British Film Institute and regional arts boards have likewise undertaken a long march of their own. Again it is instructive to return to *The New Social Function of Cinema* and its analysis of the work of the BFI Production Board.

> The generation of film makers applying to the Board for production funds in this recent period have been frequently concerned with nothing less than a reinvention of the communication process itself: with the idea that the so-called 'language of cinema' is not limited to the familiar lexicon and syntax of naturalistic and realist forms; that it must be freed from such forms if it is to express ideas about the world other than those expressed through the industrialised modes of production – both cinema and television – and that alternative methods of distribution and exhibition need to be developed towards a most productive relationship between film maker and audience. . . .
> The films produced have therefore been starkly different to anything designed to have an unproblematic and lucrative route to a large audience and in some cases have been unfathomable by even those familiar with traditional minority cinema . . . the Board has the tradition, quite consistently maintained, that it will not finance projects that closely, resemble television programme formats – whether in drama or documentary.
>
> (Peter Sainsbury in Stoneman and Thomson 1991)

228

Even if Peter Sainsbury's meditation on the board's work begins to suggest doubts as to the overall strategic value in work distancing itself too markedly from audiences' comprehension, nonetheless this statement still encapsulates many of the threads that dominated cultural independent film production at both BFI and RAB level at the beginning of the 1980s. It is also true to say that, as an increasingly unspoken policy, it remained in place well into the second half of the decade – long after the sorts of arguments and strategies for cultural industries development had taken firm root (often among BFI and RAB clients).

Such uneven development could not be sustained and, by the end of the decade, the resolutely anti-industry approach suggested above was replaced by more and more co-production deals between RABs and national–regional film councils and regional broadcasters: First Take (Eastern Arts Board in conjunction with Anglia Television); First Cut (East and West Midlands Arts Boards in conjunction with Central Television); New Visions (Northern Arts Board in conjunction with Tyne Tees Television); Eleven O'Clock High (London Film and Video Development Agency in conjunction with London Arts Board and Carlton Television); Tartan Shorts (Scottish Film Production Fund in conjunction with BBC Scotland).

Again, the BFI's published position can be taken paradigmatically. As Ben Gibson, the current head of BFI production puts it:

> Looking back at policy statements about BFI films, particularly some of those offered in previous catalogues, one might be forgiven for concluding that this was a deeply ideological institution, locked in a long term battle over key terms of an ideal national film culture. But reading between the lines, I detect that most of this writing has really been offered in elaborate defence of a deep seated pragmatism, and not at all to install or strengthen ideologies. . . . Perhaps there really was a time when there were film makers in Britain who wished to work completely out of any relationship to the idea of an audience. I think that is mostly a myth. But as long as film making is a form of communication the abstract debate creates heat and no light . . . the contrasting of the 'good' with the 'popular' seems dangerously ideological and out of date.
>
> (Gibson 1995)

Ben Gibson's revisionist history endeavours to construct a high degree of continuity across decades in order to secure maximum cultural and historical underpinning for the Production Board's current pragmatic policy. Curiously, this strategy itself really creates heat and no light for it obscures the essential and long overdue debate about cultural value – about both the strengths and weakness of an aesthetic that by and large did fail to engage with audiences and the strengths and weaknesses of aesthetics (the plural is important) wherein cultural specificities of publicly funded work are often not clearly articulated outside of vague promises of innovation, new talent and creativity (all terms, actually, equally at home in Hollywood).

Production funding *per se* and broader cultural industry arguments have come together in the last couple of years through the success of a number of agencies in winning economic development funding for film production schemes. In Glasgow in 1992, the Glasgow Film Fund was established with financial support from the European Regional Development Fund – a European Community industry development support programme to boost economic performance of specific designated areas whose average per capita income is significantly below the European average. The European moneys were matched by funding from economic development funds available locally. Since the establishment of this fund, and since the commercial success of its first investment, *Shallow Grave* (Danny Boyle, 1994), this model has been replicated and refined in Liverpool with the Merseyside Film Production Fund – *Butterfly Kiss* (Michael Winterbottom, 1995) – and, most recently, Sheffield.

The Oscar success for the Scottish Film Production Fund's *Franz Kafka's It's a Wonderful Life*, *Shallow Grave* and (to a lesser extent) *Butterfly Kiss*, and the attendant kudos that now attaches to industrially and commercially oriented production schemes, makes the momentum in this direction almost unstoppable.

A further shot in the arm has come with the advent of the National Lottery and agreement that film production is eligible to apply for financial support (up to maximums of £1,000,000 or 50 per cent of total cost) because under UK Treasury rules, expenditure on film production is deemed to be capital expenditure (and only this can be supported by the Lottery).

Following the publishing of the guidelines, the then National Heritage Minister, Stephen Dorrell, indicated that more than £70m could be spent on film production in the five years to 2000, although the origin of this figure has never been clear and strictly speaking the Lottery legislation does not allow for particular areas of activity to have 'ring fenced' funding attached. Many industry commentators expect (or at least hope) that this figure might be a huge underestimate – some have suggested that this figure might be available *each* year.

Inevitably, this ups the stakes in considering the cultural role and responsibility of agencies such as the BFI and regional arts boards (and ultimately media development agencies). On the one hand, it will increase the magnetic pull of larger budgets, higher production values, industry 'quality' productions. On the other, it might open up some opportunity for the balance of power in co-financing and co-production deals to shift back in the direction of cultural concerns.

SOME PROVISIONAL OBSERVATIONS AND CONCLUSIONS

In considering the merits or demerits of recent historical developments, it is worth analysing where the balance of advantage lies – with the broadcaster or with the cultural agency? In many of the schemes currently operating between television and publicly funded film and video agencies, the balance of advantage certainly seems to be with the broadcaster, with the schemes acting in large part as talent spotting operations for the television industry.

The arguments, *mutartis mutandis* are much the same in the arena of production as they were earlier in the area of broader cultural industries developments. At the end of the day what is the cultural agenda which drives the rapprochement between cultural agency and industry? In the case of production, how far does an absolutely valid insistence of engagement with audiences and the pragmatics of deal making become the guiding principle? In the case of cultural industries, how valid can it be for cultural agencies to align themselves with industrial development and industry support strategies – particularly when those strategies themselves leave room for serious doubt about efficacy?

The thrust of this chapter has been the success of industry-oriented rhetoric within the cultural sector and the mechanisms through which cultural agencies have aligned themselves with film, video and television industries on the one hand and broader economic developmental concerns on the other. The polemic underpinning this analysis reflects an anxiety not just about the appropriateness of the centrality of this alignment but, certainly in terms of authentic economic development and job creation, actual delivery. In a way, this piece stems from little more than wonder that the cultural industries bets have not been called in well before now.

The present conjuncture in the middle of the decade, almost ten years after the abolition of the GLC, might, however, contain the seeds of a re-invigorated debate and more sustained analysis. Partly this is due to the very success of liaisons achieved with broadcasters. Partly it is to do with the promise of riches to film and video activities held out by the National Lottery – little concentrates the mind like the possibility of large sums of money. The 'presence' that schemes such *First Take*, *First Cut*, etc. have achieved demands, and is now beginning to receive, serious attention as to their real cultural value. While supporting new talent is a laudable objective, how far should arts money be used to subsidise a television industry in doing something that it should be doing anyway? What is the added cultural value? Even while apparently persisting with a somewhat unproblematized notion of cultural industries, the British Film Institute's interrogation of the relative merits of regional arts boards versus development agencies perforce implies an address to questions of art and industry, of balance of cultural advantage.

More than anything, however, the National Lottery changes the rules of the game. The possibility of a ten-fold expansion of funding for the sorts of work undertaken by cultural bodies will require more than a simple gearing up and taking on of (many) more staff. It will require nothing less than a radical reappraisal of the role and responsibility of these bodies. The terms of the debate are stark. On the one hand, why should public money (and Lottery money is generally considered in this way) be used to subsidise, say, television and films and videos that an industry should support itself? Why should the cash from the pockets of millions of ordinary people be used to swell the profits of already wealthy industries? On the other hand, Lottery moneys are not significantly drawn from sales to avant garde film aficionados. Why should Lottery money support non-popular forms and practices? In the course of this debate, a new cultural function of cinema might just be born.

Curiously, this might, indirectly, begin to re-invigorate and reformulate arguments around cultural industries. The micro-economic interventions promulgated to date fail (or at best underperform) because they fail to engage with the power issues of control over distribution (broadcast). At the end of the day, these are political issues – the legislative framework within which the audiovisual industries operate. For instance, a genuine and substantial Scottish audiovisual industry is unlikely to emerge from one short film Oscar and the interventionist tinkering of initiatives such as the Edinburgh and Lothian Screen Industries Office. Rather, it requires an act of political will to force genuine devolution of broadcasting to Scotland. So too with the regions of England. The profile, the presence of regional work that will be created by the injection of Lottery finance, will make arguments about real regional industries and the legislation necessary to secure them more and more urgent. In the promise of real money there might appear might emerge the possibility of regional cultural industries that deliver real culture and real industry.

NOTES

1 *Franz Kafka's It's a Wonderful Life*, Dir. Peter Capaldi, Prod. Ruth Kenley-Letts for BBC Scotland/Scottish Film Production Fund 'Tartan Shorts Scheme', 1994.
2 See, for instance, the British Film Institute's UK film initiatives series: Headland, J. and Relph, S. (eds) (1991) *The View from Downing Street*, London: British Film Institute.
Prescott, M. (ed.) *The Need for Tax Incentives*, London: British Film Institute.
Lewis, R. and Marris, P. (eds) (1991) *Promoting the Industry*, London, British Film Institute.
Smedley, N. and Woodward, J. *Productive Relationships*? London: British Film Institute.
Perilli, P. (ed.) (1991) *A Level Playing Field*?, London: British Film Institute.
Mulgan, G. and Paterson, R. (eds) (1993) *Hollywood of Europe*, London: British Film Institute.
3 The recent classic examples of this have of course been the Goldcrest and Palace Pictures fiascos. See, for instance, Eberts, J. and Ilott, T. (1992) *My Indecision is Final*, London: Faber & Faber, and Finney, A. (1996) *The Egos Have Landed*, London: Heinemann. For a gloss on the economic issues at stake in this, see McIntyre, S. (1994) 'Vanishing point: feature film production in a small country', in Hill, J., Mcloone, M. and Hainsworth, P. (eds) *Border Crossing: Film in Ireland, Britain and Europe*, Belfast: Institute of Irish Studies, and London: British Film Institute.
4 A rare exception is R. Hewison (1995) *Culture and Consensus: England, Arts and Politics Since 1940*, London: Methuen.
5 Pick, J. (1980) *Arts Administration*, p.5. See also Pick, J. and Anderton, M. (1996) *Arts Admistration (Second Edition)*. London: E. and F.N. Spon.

REFERENCES

Bianchini, F. (1987) 'GLC R.I.P. Cultural Policies in London 1981–1986', *New Formations*, 1: 103–17.

Caughie, J. and Frith, S. (1990) 'The BFI: retooling the culture industry', *Screen*, 31(2), Summer: 214–22.

Challans, T. and Webber, H. (1993) *A Creative Future – The Way Forward for the Arts Crafts and Media in England*. London: HMSO.

Cornford, J. and Robins, K. (1991) *Broadcasting and the Audio-visual Industries: A Sectoral Study for Newcastle City Council*, Newcastle: Centre for Urban and Regional Development Studies, University of Newcastle.

Edinburgh and Lothian Screen Industries Office Report (1995) Edinburgh: ELSIO.

Eberts, J. and Ilott, T. (1992) *My Indecision is Final*. London: Faber & Faber.

Finney, A. (1996) *The Egos Have Landed*, London: Heinemann.

Garnham, N. (1984) *Public Policy and the Cultural Industries*. London: Greater London Council.

Garnham, N. (1990) *Capitalism and Communications – Global Culture and the Economies of Information*. London: Sage.

Gibson, B. (1995) 'BFI production policy towards 2000' in *BFI Production Catalogue 1995*. London: BFI.

Hewison, R. (1995) *Culture and Consensus: England Arts and Politics Since 1940*. London: Methuen.

McIntyre, S. (1994) 'Vanishing point: feature film production in a small country', in Hill, J., McLoone, M. and Hainsworth, P. (eds) *Border Crossing: Film in Ireland, Britain and Europe*. Belfast: Institute of Irish Studies and London: British Film Institute.

North East Media Development Council Information Leaflet (1985) Newcastle: NEMDC.

Pick, J. (1980) *Arts Administration*. London: E. and F.N. Spon.

Pick, J. and Anderton, M. (1996) *Arts Administration (Second Edition*. London: E. and F.N. Spon.

Porter, M. (1990) *The Competitive Advantage of Nations*. London: Macmillan.

Stoneman, R. and Thomson, H. (1981) *The New Social Function of Cinema*. Catalogue British Film Institute Productions 79/80. London: British Film Institute.

13

PERIPHERAL VISIONS
Regionalism, Nationalism, Internationalism
Carole Sklan

PREAMBLE

This chapter is an attempt to look at a whole complex cluster of issues that revolve around the notion of regionalism in the film and television industry. It also tries to consider regionalism both in the national and international contexts. I would particularly like to acknowledge the contribution to this chapter that has been made by many individuals and organizations from across the country, and thank them for their time, their thoughts and their interest.

This chapter is written from the paradoxical perspective of the 'inside/outside' and should not be received as an official Australian Film Commission (AFC) paper. It is simply speaking from the perspective of someone interested in these questions in both a theoretical and a practical way. I have been working as a project co-ordinator in the Melbourne office of the AFC for the past four years, during which time I have taken leave to work on film projects based in Sydney. Prior to this, I worked as a researcher, writer, director in the industry, both in Sydney and in Melbourne, in mainstream television and the independent film sector.

STATE OF THE WORLD

There seem to be two powerful competing impulses at work today. As the globe becomes more centralized and homogenized through the workings of the giant transnational corporations who know no boundaries and no loyalties and through the formation of nations into competing trading blocs, the world is also being fragmented by the forces of regionalism.

The great monolithic empires and nation-states are breaking up into ever smaller independent nation-states. The Chechnyans in Russia, the Serbs, Croats and Muslims in the former Yugoslavia, the Basque separatists in Spain, the Eritreans in Ethiopia have all fought battles of fierce intensity over a notion of identity based on a complex of ethnic, geographic, political, linguistic and cultural affiliations.

These two competing impulses – for the greater centralization of power and the greater dispersal of power – are also at play in the film and television industry in

Australia, a national industry centralized in Sydney, catering to a small scattered population spread over a vast continent in six different states and two territories.

THE STATE OF DOMINANCE

Audiovisual production in Australia remains, as it has always been, concentrated primarily in Sydney and, to a lesser but still significant extent, in Melbourne. The traditional pattern of dominance of NSW in the share of national production has been offset slightly with the emergence of Queensland as a major site for off-shore production and large budget national production.

The breakdown for production expenditure for feature film and TV drama in 1992–3 was: New South Wales (NSW) 38 per cent; Victoria 32 per cent; Queensland 18 per cent; Western Australia (WA) 5 per cent; and South Australia (SA) 6 per cent. The average expenditure over the past five years has been: NSW 49 per cent; Victoria 30 per cent; Queensland 11 per cent; WA 5 per cent; and SA 4 per cent.

The development of NSW, the most populous state, as the centre for the national industry, has been enhanced and facilitated by the location of the major structures and institutions of training, funding, investment, broadcasting and production in Sydney. The head offices of almost all the federally funded film and television organizations are located in Sydney – the Australian Film Finance Corporation (AFFC), the AFC, Film Australia, the Australian Film, Television and Radio School (AFTRS), the Australian Broadcasting Corporation (ABC) and Special Broadcasting Service (SBS). The Children's Television Foundation and the AFI are located in Melbourne. The National Film and Sound Archive is located in Canberra.

The five national television networks are all based in Sydney, where the substantial amount of production takes place. Geographical localism in broadcasting in Australia has been severely eroded by national networking. Regional television has been stripped back to the most basic local programming and this trend has not been challenged by new broadcasting legislation, which places greater emphasis on quality and diversity than geographic localism (Cunningham 1994).

The major television drama production companies are based in Sydney – Roadshow, Coote and Carroll, Southern Star, Grundys, J & P, Kennedy Miller. Certainly all the inhouse drama production of all the television networks are centralized or controlled in Sydney.

Comedy shows traditionally tend to be based in Melbourne – *Fast Forward, Full Frontal, The Big Gig, The Comedy Company, The D Generation, D*A*A*S Kapital, Frontline*. Artists Services in Melbourne is currently developing drama for Channel 7, Simpson le Mesurier and Crawfords are producing telemovies for the Nine Network. ABC Drama in Melbourne have produced the trailblazing police dramas – *Phoenix* and *Janus*. In the other states, there tends to be local news, current affairs and perhaps some children's shows produced by the networks.

In the same way, as the argument for a distinctive Australian cinema is posed against the imminent threat of being swallowed up by the cinema of the United States of America, that terminator of local industries around the world, the argument for regional difference, regional cultural diversity, regional social specificity is mounted against the threat of being swallowed up by the dominance of NSW as the centre for film and television production in Australia.

Melbourne filmmakers argue that there are actually two major production centres in Australia, Sydney and Melbourne, and resent the regional status accorded by NSW and the lack of autonomy allowed over decisions and allocation of resources. In turn, the people working in the BAPH states, Brisbane, Adelaide, Perth and Hobart, who are also anxious to contribute to the national culture and share in the economic and cultural benefits, feel they are unfairly marginalized and ignored by the federal organizations, many of whom at least have a smaller base in Melbourne, but no representation in other states.

The successful Perth producer, Paul Barron, describes years of regular flights to Sydney every few weeks, and a large number of face to face meetings as critical to his success. He stresses that no deal can be negotiated in one meeting, that it may take years of personal liaison, getting to know the relevant people, discussion and consultation. He cites the biggest single handicap of living in Perth as being the three hour time zone. 'When I walk into the office at 8.45am, people in Sydney are going to lunch. That means there is only half a day to deal with Sydney' (phone interview with author, 1991). In Perth, the power brokers are referred to as the easterners, in Brisbane, they are the southerners. But as Paul Barron comments, 'we all know who we're talking about'.

SCREEN CULTURE

However, it's limited to talk about screen culture only in terms of the production and exhibition of commercial film and television. A country's film culture encompasses the whole environment in which films are made, distributed, seen and discussed, and in which they create meanings. There is a more extensive, rich and diverse screen culture that is circulated through a variety of ways, such as film festivals, film societies, film reviews, screen education, discussions and screenings which take place everywhere from rural halls and suburban cinemas to coffee shops and bus stops. There are also tremendously diverse possibilities in terms of production, including sponsored films, films in super 8, 16mm and video 8, which may reproduce, revitalize or directly challenge commercial codes and conventions. Interesting film work does not emerge from a cultural vacuum or as the inspired genius of 'talented' individuals loaded up with a great deal of money. There is a creative interaction between the films and the vitality of the culture from which they emerge.

It is of vital importance that local screen cultures are maintained and nurtured but local screen cultures mean much more than each state producing a mini series or a feature film which encapsulates the somehow 'magical and unique' West Australian/Queensland/Tasmanian, etc. experience.

CENTRES AND MARGINS

To understand the dynamic of the relationship between the centre and the regions, it may be helpful to look at it in terms of the relational concept of the core and the periphery. Steve McIntyre deploys this model in his analysis of the uneven development which occurs inside as well as between nation-states in his article 'National film cultures: politics and peripheries'.

> This, broadly speaking, derives from dominant groups within an emerging state systematically, politically and economically disenfranchising other groups. In other words, instead of the nation state internally diffusing homogeneity, it produces a series of 'internal colonies'.
>
> (McIntyre 1985: 68)

Another model that could be applied to the dynamics of the film and television industry is Foucault's idea of the 'Panopticon' (Shumway 1989: 133), where a particular structure of power is seen in the design of the prison or the mental hospital. In these institutions, a central administration establishes itself to see (and over-see) everything within its administration, whereas the patients, prisoners or clients are positioned so as to have very limited perspectives. I stress we are talking metaphorically, not literally here, in order to gain certain insights and understandings into structural processes. When you apply the metaphor to the film industry, a three level process can be seen at work.

1 The centre defines what is 'excellent', 'innovative', 'competent', 'relevant', 'commercially appealing', etc.
2 Its power requires the internalization of these beliefs by those in the peripheries, who seek to ape these values and preferences.
3 The centre then underdevelops the peripheries by syphoning off the 'productive' possibilities that emerge there, claiming them as their own, as evidence of their correctness. They can then point to what has been denied, excluded, devalued and suppressed in the periphery and say 'They are just not good enough, they haven't got what it takes.'

Whereas, of course, this is a projection. In fact, the centre has now got what it has taken and it has rendered meaningless what it has refused. This is the classic model of underdevelopment from the political economy of Andre Gunder Frank (Frank 1971).

Perhaps the work from the peripheries does not have the level of market attachments required. Perhaps it does not conform to notions of 'accessible drama', 'entertaining drama' or 'adventurous drama', depending on the particular corporate value systems or rhetorics deployed by the federal organization. Perhaps the work is not even 'drama'. Whatever, if the periphery claims a work which is outside the concerns and focus of the centre, then that work will be de-valued and marginalized as 'parochial'. Those on the periphery tend to internalize the sense of failure and inadequacy imposed by the centre, based on the centre's definitions and interests. The centre argues that coherent aesthetic judgements, professional competence, appropriate skills, efficient management and creative control *can* only occur in the centre and therefore *must* occur only in the centre.

One of the arguments which supports work produced from the peripheries is that work produced from the 'outside' has more of an edge, and tends to have greater artistic integrity than work produced from the more comfortable and safe position of the 'inside'. For example, the system of patronage in the centre perhaps precludes the development of a more adventurous, innovative and diverse drama, particularly with regard to television.

What tends to occur in a place like Perth, according to a commentator from Western Australia (WA), is a cultural devaluing of productions and practices other than the very expensive fantasy of feature film production and international theatrical release. The perception is that unless Perth does what the east does, then somehow the particular filmmaking practices and achievements of the west mean nothing. The cultural importance of community based film and video work, short and experimental work is little understood and the circulation of such work often happens at a sort of underground level. It is ironic that 'the cry of "regionalism" can be a demand for THEM to help US be like THEM' (Benjamin 1991: 1).

THE PRICE OF FREE ENTERPRISE

The national/regional relationship needs to be considered in the light of current debates and manoeuvres in the international context. There are significant threats posed by GATS, the General Agreement on Trade in Services, to government assistance and regulation of the Australian film and television industry. The US would like the removal of all barriers to free trade in the film and television market, where they happen to be the largest, most dominant player. However they are less disposed to apply these ostensibly ideologically driven, economic rationalist arguments to a weaker, less competitive industry, such as agriculture. Given Australia's disastrous balance of payments position, some Australian government officials do see Australia's overall economic interests being best served by a more liberal trading environment. Crudely put, this could involve the possibility of trading off the film industry in order to gain concessions from other countries over agriculture. This would help alleviate Australia's escalating deficit more significantly than the export returns from film and television. The cultural capital that comes with the manufacture and distribution of meanings is effectively erased by such positions.

At this time, Australia has not given any undertakings to liberalize our audiovisual trade relationship by reforms to local content rules or filmmaker subsidies, but certainly the Department of Foreign Affairs and Trade will come under pressure from overseas trading partners who regard these limitations to market access as highly contentious. The overall aim of the World Trade

Organisation to have full liberalization of trade by the year 2010 has serious implications for the audiovisual production industry.

In his article, 'Drama and the foreign devil', Toby Miller, writing from WA, argues that the only way to combat the threat of the application of free market economics is to champion the cause of cultural nationalism and cultural sover-eignty. He supports the hold of Sydney and Melbourne on national cultural policy because it is precisely these centres 'that can help stave off Geneva' (Miller 1991: 7). He dismisses the call for regionally based drama production in the current economic and political climate as 'whingeing from the margins' (Miller 1991: 8). Within this nationalist context, he feels there can be significant pluralism in our screen culture. Regional differences can be articulated and understood as a set of subcultural differences expressed as 'a series of careful nuances' (Miller 1991: 8).

Stuart Cunningham, in his article 'Regionalism in audiovisual production: the case for Queensland', points out that 'industry structure and economies of scale militate powerfully against local or regional content' and that 'Regionalism is far easier to achieve in cultural pursuits which do not require the levels of creative, technical and production critical mass which is necessary for audiovisual activity' (Cunningham 1994: 52). Regionalism is seen as a position frequently mobilized by reactionary forces. 'Geographic localism in Australia has often found its expression as a nostalgic states-rights chauvinism that, at the limit, has been fanned by populist demagogues actively demoting the idea of the nation' (Cunningham 1994: 52). However, these are not the only proponents of regional production.

There are compelling arguments for a strong central industry, but more problematic is the confidence that a pluralist screen culture will somehow be naturally maintained. The trouble with cultural nationalism, as perceived by Liz Jacka and Susan Dermody, is that 'it blurs and effaces so many finer, more local and more critical issues' (Dermody and Jacka 1987: 47). They go on to say:

> The more subtle, historically-precise, politically challenging set of dif-ferences that intricately complicate the construction of Australian identity – class, region, locale, sub-culture, ethnic and racial separations, and sex and age – are too easily blurred into the mirage of national identity, for the sake of broad gestures of community and collectivity. Those gestures may be useful in the short term, to oppose the threats to cultural self-determination; but they are not substantial or fine enough to sustain an indigenous cinema for long.
>
> (Dermody and Jacka 1987: 47))

A recent report from the National Indigenous Media Association of Australia argues there is a need for greater regional production for precisely these reasons:

> There needs to be an increase of representation of Australian life at a local level. . . . The tendency is to take a universal or national approach to the portrayal of Australian life. . . . It is like a head without a body. The body, particularly in the growth of Aboriginal screen culture, is where we are in

our communities and on our land; and so that we are not further divided in our conception and portrayal of ourselves we need to vitalise, and focus on, regional production development.

(Peacock 1994: 4)

Under the banner of national culture, there is no guarantee that the voices from the margins will be heard or that a significant pluralism will flourish. We need to ask whose culture is to be reflected on the national screen.

STATES OF MIND

What do we mean by regional differences? Can we talk about regional differences in any meaningful way in a country like Australia? Everywhere today is characterized by cultural hybridization, everywhere today is nowhere in particular. When we talk about Queensland as a regional production centre, are we referring to Brisbane, or do we mean the Village Roadshow Warners studio complex on the Gold Coast, or are we referring to TAIMA, the Townsville Aboriginal and Islander Media Association? Are geographic communities more significant than communities of interest based around gender, ethnicity and class? Is it more important to involve a Vietnamese woman from the outer western suburbs of Sydney in the Australian film industry or an anglo-saxon male entrepreneur from Adelaide? When we celebrate the portrayal of contemporary inner urban multi-cultural life in *Death in Brunswick*, do we also have to produce, in the name of regional equity, a *Death in Fremantle* and a *Death in Launceston*?

The film by Melbourne filmmaker Ray Argall, *Return Home*, is a nostalgic portrayal of small town life in Adelaide and the dreams and struggles of people working at a local suburban garage. It was nationally acclaimed for its portrayal of 'authentic' Australian qualities in its underlying concerns, and its depiction of character and locale. Some popular television soaps cater for this same longing for a sense of local community and attachment to place without actually identifying any specific location – they tend to be fictional, generalized notions of the suburbs in *Neighbours*, the inner city in *GP*, the country town in *A Country Practice*. These fictional locations with their fictional community identities, loyalties and sense of belonging provide an imaginary reality quite different from the isolation and commodification that characterizes contemporary life. This is nowhere more evident than in the relations and practice of television (Graffin 1991). Bracketed between incitements to buy and injunctions to watch, the world of soap provides a cosy buffer zone of friendly, concerned neighbours, colleagues and family members.

STATE BY STATE

It is tempting in a discussion of regionalism to reinforce popular mythology and make reductive generalizations in order to characterize regional differences. This popular rhetoric is generally mobilized to point to diversity and promote the need for its expression. In reality, each state is a complex layering of different, competing impulses, voices and aesthetics, which perhaps inflect and inform a range of screen cultures.

Sydney has been described as Tinseltown, the Hollywood of Australia. NSW productions are frequently driven by entertainment values, spectacle and exuberant stylization – *Sirens, Strictly Ballroom, Priscilla, Queen of the Desert.*

Queensland is often represented in films produced elsewhere as an imaginary site, a corrupt paradise, a mythic destination, populated by bizarre eccentrics. Local film, *Coolongatta Gold*, is about masculinity, sporting prowess and winning, and celebrates the narcissism and hedonism of beach culture. Another local film, *Waiting*, is about femininity, motherhood and personal relationships, and affectionately satirizes the narcissism and hedonism of the alternative culture. How can one generalize about a regional cultural identity as revealed in its films?

Victoria has a substantial low budget feature film industry whose main characters tend to be drab, idiosyncratic losers and the predominant colour scheme tends to be monochrome grey. The recent spectacular success, *Muriel's Wedding*, produced by a Victorian creative team, shot on location in Queensland and NSW, infuses this genre with the Sydney celebration of kitsch parody and brash humour. There is also a powerful tradition of heightened social realism which has informed such confronting films as *Only the Brave* and *Every Night Every Night*.

Tasmania is seen as an icy wilderness where mysterious and elemental forces permeate the landscape.

West Australia is dominated by the remarkable work of producer, Paul Barron. Films such as *Shame, Fran* and *Day of the Dog* explore difficult social subjects with considerable dramatic power and complexity. *Shame* and *Fran* are distinctive for their strong and complex female leads, *Day of the Dog* for its strong and complex Aboriginal leads. Can one characterize a region on the work of a single producer?

With regard to the *Northern Territory* our attention is drawn to unique interventions of Aboriginal communities, who are both the agents of the delivery of mainstream satellite services (through Imparja), and the champions of localized practices of production and reception at places like Yuendumu and Ernabella.

In *South Australia*, the bold, disturbing low budget feature, *Bad Boy Bubby*, is a powerful example of brilliant, idiosyncratic filmmaking that can emerge from the periphery.

THE STATE OF COMEDY

The centralization of film, TV and arts funding in Sydney has meant an underdog culture has developed everywhere else. John Clarke has developed a theory that the comedy boom in Melbourne is directly connected to the location of all the funding bodies in Sydney. Young people wanting some form of self-expression, needing an audience, with no access to grants or finance, took to cabaret as an outlet. The comedy boom took place at the low rent end of theatre and theatre restaurants, and generated a form of live theatre that was cheap, raw and local. Perhaps one could argue that this radical irreverence and a certain dark comic vision is particular to a place located, as it were, 'left of the centre'. The vicious and delicious suburban satire of Barry Humphries, of course, originates in Moonee Ponds, a suburb of Melbourne.

Since then, television has finally recognized the enormous talent and appeal of many of these local Melbourne performers and has showcased them in a series of successful programmes, *The Max Gillies Show, Australia You're Standing In It, The Comedy Company, The Big Gig, Fast Forward Rubbery Figures, D*A*A*S Kapital* and *Acropolis Now.* Television has appropriated and possibly diluted the anarchic brilliance of some of this work.

Victorian feature films reflect a comic sensibility that identifies with people on the margins of society, characters who are ineffectual, alienated and daggy – *Malcolm, Death in Brunswick, Spotswood, Stan and George* and to some extent, *Proof,* are all informed by this. *Proof* has some deftly handled comic scenes and certainly an intense engagement with a lonely, disconnected character, excluded by his physical blindness and his psychological distrust of others.

STATE OF CANADA

It is interesting to look at another model for the policies and strategies to develop a national film and television industry which also caters to regional diversity. In Canada, at least in public rhetoric, regionalism constitutes an important aspect of the political as well as the cultural agenda.

Canada is a country comparable to Australia in terms of size and population, as well as in many aspects of its historic and social conditions. The establishment of the dual centres of Ontario and Quebec has the added dimension of the explicit linguistic and cultural differences between the French and the English, which are fiercely maintained. In Canada, debates over film policy have been similar to Australia – the dominance of Hollywood product, the subordinate relation to the USA and the campaign for a state-aided industry. Again and again, in a paper written on 'The Development of regional film and television production in Canada' (Spivak 1989), government policy reiterates the need for federally funded organizations to acknowledge, reflect and cater to regional diversity. In the 1988 broadcasting policy statement, 'Canadian voices, Canadian choices', also, there is a strong affirmation of the non-economic significance of broadcasting:

> It is of fundamental importance to our political and cultural sovereignty that our broadcasting system be an accurate reflection of who we are, of how we behave, of how we view the world. It plays a major role in defining our national, regional, local and even individual identities. It is therefore, much more than just another industry.
>
> (Spivak 1989: 134)

Another example from 1988, in a paper on the national broadcaster, CBC, the government emphasized the national and regional thrusts in the CBC's mandate.

> The CBC board and management is responsible for ensuring that the corporation reflects and interprets. . . . Canada's cultural, social, political, economic, linguistic and regional reality and diversity, as well as contributing to the flow and exchange of information and entertainment between regions and Canada's two official language groups.
>
> (Spivak 1989: 7)

The Standing Committee on Communications and Culture stated in 1988, 'If the CBC ignores the regional nature of the country, its relevance, importance and effectiveness as a national public broadcasting service will be reduced' (Spivak 1989: 9).

The Canadian Film Development Corporation, now known as Telefilm Canada, has both a substantial Broadcast Fund with an annual budget of $60 million and a Feature Film Fund with an annual budget of $30 million, as well as a Project Development Fund. Acknowledging that film and television production are national undertakings, Telefilm Canada is committed to

> Take into account Canada's unique diversity of expression and the various provincial development initiatives, and has adopted a series of measures to encourage and support projects originating from across Canada, particularly those from outside the production centres of Montreal and Toronto.
>
> (Telefilm Canada Feature Film Fund Policies 1991–2: 4)

Telefilm Canada has a political brief to:

> Take appropriate measures to identify provincial and regional interests in the development of Canada's program production industry, and seek an appropriate balance in its investments so as to foster program production in all regions of Canada.
>
> (Spivak 1989: 40)

There is an Auxiliary Fund of $11.4 million set up specifically to cater to regional feature films, French language feature films, and for films of significant original content reflecting Canadian cultural diversity. There is also an Auxiliary Fund of $16.5 million set up to fund Canadian television drama productions that make a significant contribution towards celebrating Canadian cultural diversity, particularly those made originally in French or films from regional production centres, and those with highly significant Canadian creative content.

The National Film Board of Canada, unlike Telefilm, is a producer of programmes rather than a support agency. The NFB maintains regional production centres in Moncton, Vancouver, Edmonton, Winnipeg and Halifax and plays a major role in the expansion of regional production.

It can be useful to compare and contrast the Canadian model with the Australian experience. To date, the measures that Telefilm Canada has employed to encourage regional productions have not extended to quotas, with the exception of specific allocations for French and English language productions. However, recognizing the greater difficulty regional producers have in attracting private investment, Telefilm may increase its participation in regional productions beyond the limits established for all other productions. Also, minimum licence fee requirements may be relaxed for regional broadcasters, in recognition of the difficulty smaller regional broadcasters have in competing with larger national services.

STATE OF THE ART

There have been a number of tensions and paradoxes that have been endemic to the entire conception and revival of our own national industry in the past two decades – the notion of a national film culture designed to sell on the international market, an international product that should at the same time represent Australia to itself, the double-headed objectives of cultural responsibility and commercial viability, the desire for an exotic Australian product that conforms to the conventions of American cinema. Two distinct schools of thought struggle for ascendancy within almost every state in Australia as to how to most effectively address this. One school, characterized by big budgets and one or two foreign imported stars, tries to emulate American genre films – action adventure, romance, thriller. They are generally uncomfortably second rate versions of what Hollywood does consummately well – there is nothing value added coming from Australia. This school is primarily interested in the film industry as an industry of economic benefit, with little concern for its cultural interest or relevance to Australia. It advocates the use of the local industry as a cheap offshore production base for overseas companies. Australia supplies the raw resources – exotic locales, competitively priced production facilities and services, crew and cast – which can be utilized by production companies from America and Japan.

All states have established film development agencies in order to develop local creative infrastructures and to lever national and international production into their region. The mixture of cultural and economic motives are given different emphases in different times and places, according to the shifting priorities of cultural politics. Certainly a number of regional industries have seen wooing offshore production as a key strategy to establish a vigorous, viable local production sector. The current boom in Queensland is underpinned by the establishment of the major Village Roadshow Warners studio complex and the strategy to woo big budget offshore production to Queensland through the Pacific Film and Television Corp. This policy absolutely prioritizes economic development and tourism spinoffs over any local cultural development.

West Australia and South Australia have also advocated this economic underpinning as a means of bolstering a small, fragile production sector and sustaining a local grassroots industry. The elusive promise of golden bounty from a Hollywood in the South Seas might well turn out to be a Mission Impossible.

What tends to happen of course, like any enterprise set up by the First World in the Third World, is the systematic underdevelopment of key creative, technical and entrepeneurial personnel. Producers, directors and primary cast are flown in from overseas with little opportunity for locals to gain crucial skills and experience in these areas. The development and implementation of ideas is less the focus than the development of a critical mass of capital, personnel and facilities, required to sustain a local production sector.

South Australia recently merged its two separate state bodies which embodied two different objectives. The priority of the South Australian Film Corporation (SAFC) was having films made in SA, even if the projects emanated from elsewhere and the crews were imported. On the other hand, the priority of Filmsouth was to develop a local film industry emanating from SA with local creative and technical participation. The cross-fertilization provided by this merger into the SAFC can only be productive as long as the risky, creative development work does not become subsumed by the larger mainstream production.

The SAFC in recent years has suffered severe losses, compounded by its involvement with *Ultraman*, a popular Japanese television series, which incurred a budget blow out of $1.8 million. *Ultraman* is a children's television series, considered too violent for Australian palates, which features Ultraman, a super-hero who regularly saves the world, but unfortunately, omitted to save SA. The SA government bailed out the SAFC with a loan of $2.4 million. The losses on *Ultraman* were absorbed by cutbacks to local documentary filmmaking.

Another strategy in the pursuit of foreign investment and overseas distribution is the creation of the strange beast known as the co-production, an amalgam of Australian elements with overseas elements, such as Canadian, French, Italian or German. Maybe this is the real genre of the 1990s, the 'hybrid cinema', like one of those foldout children's books of characters with a lion's head, a zebra's middle and an emu's feet.

The second school of thought argues that the way for Australian films to compete on the overseas market is not to attempt to duplicate Hollywood but to explore international themes, based on our own stories and inventive ways of telling, which have a resonance in other cultures. These films would be informed by a vision that is particular and idiosyncratic, the outcome of a dynamic set up between an individual and a social imagination from a culturally specific time and place. This does not mean a desperate search for national authenticity and unity. Nor does it necessitate yards of celluloid tinted gumtree green, with tales of the bush, girls in white frocks and men on horseback chasing sheep in order to create a sense of 'difference', of 'Australianness'.

Two examples come to mind, both of which offer a critique of the dominant notion of national identity. A film from 1971, *Wake in Fright*, based on the novel by Kenneth Cook, depicted with terrifying accuracy a menace, a social violence beneath the surface of Australian mateship and jocular masculinity. It captured unnervingly certain qualities of Australian life and was directed by someone from the 'outside', a Canadian, Ted Kotcheff.

A film produced in 1988, *Celia*, by writer/director, Anne Turner, set in suburban Melbourne during the Cold War of the 1950s, tapped into the psychological hysteria and brutality generated by social repression. It explored the imaginative experience of a young girl who is shaped and informed by these forces. *Celia* was acclaimed overseas, especially in the UK, but received appallingly limited exposure in Australia.

The AFI nominees for best feature film for 1994 signal the strength and vibrancy of a regionally diverse industry: *Bad Boy Bubby* (SA), *Muriel's Wedding* (made by Victorians, filmed in Queensland and NSW), *The Sum of Us* (NSW), and *Priscilla, Queen of the Desert* (NSW, partly filmed in the Northern Territory).

The challenge is the production of new political and cultural identities rather than the fairly safe, predictable regurgitation of popular mythologies. The pursuit of the chimera of success in the international arena may involve the abandonment of both national and international formulae. The artistic power and originality of *The Piano* is an outstanding example of this. The film is claimed as an Australian film, was produced in New Zealand, financed through France, and is written and directed by a New Zealand resident of Australia, Jane Campion, trained at the Australian Film and Television School.

THE STATE OF THE NATION

The federal government allocates approximately $110 million per year to its film and television programme. This includes the AFTRS, the AFC, the AFFC, Film Australia, The National Film and Sound Archive and the Australian Children's Television foundation. This does not include the appropriations of $473 million for the national broadcaster, ABC TV, and $58 million for SBS TV, plus the recent injection of an additional $13 million for SBS Independent. Even though these are national bodies funded by taxpayers from all over Australia, with clearly defined national responsibilities, many of these organizations are not committed to a regional policy and find it fairly convenient to collapse together the national interest with the Sydney interest. We need a plurality of film cultures rather than a single, unified national cultural identity. We need peripheral visions to develop confidently and forcefully in order to generate a more critical, diverse approach rather than a centralized mainstream identity. Notions of 'the national interest', a 'national cinema', 'national artistic excellence', 'national competitiveness', can be mobilized to justify a programme defined and controlled by the centre, which obscures and transcends other competing interests. The mythology of a single nation with a unified purpose and shared interest can be recruited to conceal the fissures in the society. Steve McIntyre puts it like this:

> Both for core and peripheries it is urgent to shift definitions of nationalism away from a monolithic 'one nation' towards an awareness of a plurality of overlapping and competing discourses within which individuals and groups identify themselves and others in different ways at different times.
>
> (McIntyre 1985: 70)

246

STATE OF PLAY

Regional production is a complex and complicated question which cannot be reduced to simplistic demands for per capita equity and quotas at the expense of generating dynamic and surprising work. How do we ensure the interplay of a range of differences in Australian film and television? Will this necessarily be achieved through productions from different geographic locations? What sort of initiatives or interventions are required in order to achieve a significant pluralism in our screen culture? We need to avoid as much as possible the establishment of an AFC genre, an FFC product, and an ABC house style. Unless regionalism is seen as a policy issue at board level of the AFTRS, AFC, the AFFC, Film Australia, ABC TV and SBS, then the position of the regions will continue to be at the behest of the good will of individuals working from the centre. The federally funded organizations can continually fob off regional concerns, putting forward different agendas and priorities, unless there are management structures and processes in place to address these concerns. These will only be set up if there is an active commitment throughout the organization to acknowledge barriers of distance and access which might disadvantage outstanding and significant projects being developed, recognized, financed and produced in the regions.

Unless television stations have a commitment at a senior management level to localism and regionalism, then the situation will continue that whenever a drama production outside Sydney takes place, there is such pressure for it to perform well in the ratings that anxious executives will import a producer from Sydney, who will in turn bring with them directors from Sydney, with whom they are familiar and has worked before. There is no conscious malice or active exclusion being practised towards local producers and directors. They are simply perceived as lacking in the experience and competence that comes with continuous employment on major productions over a number of years. This of course is self perpetuating.

Regional film organizations need to initiate debate on policy and strategy between and within federal organizations. Federal bodies based in Sydney need to be flexible and responsive to the particular needs, interests and creative possibilities of other states. If there are genuine barriers to producers and filmmakers in other states conforming to requirements laid down by the national bodies, then the reasons for the difficulty needs to be addressed or even the very basis of the requirements challenged.

On the other hand, the states need a more broadly conceived notion of film culture rather than purely focusing on the need for a commercially successful TV series or a commercial feature film as the saviour of the local industry. An exclusively production-based philosophy will not generate an interesting, informed screen culture. The attempt to duplicate the production centres of Melbourne and Sydney may simply not be economically affordable, politically achievable nor may it even be culturally desirable.

We need to understand a national screen culture as being made up of national screen cultures in WA, SA, NT, etc., which do not have to replicate each other in size or in emphasis, but which are informed by and contribute to a range of contexts, international, national, local and personal.

(Benjamin 1991)

REFERENCES

Benjamin, M. (1991) Unpublished article, Perth.

Cunningham, S. (1994) 'Regionalism in audio-visual production: the case for Queensland', *Queensland Review*, August: 47–54.

Dermody, S. and Jacka, L. (1987) *The Screening of Australia: Anatomy of a Film Industry*, vol. 1. Sydney: Currency Press.

Frank, A. G. (1971) *Capitalism and Underdevelopment*. Harmondsworth: Penguin.

Graffin, G. (1991) 'Landscape and the representation of space in Australian popular culture: a study in cultural geography', Australian Cultural Studies Proceedings, Faculty of Humanities and Social Sciences, University of Western Sydney.

McIntyre, S. 'National film cultures: politics and peripheries', *Screen*, 26(1): 66–76.

Miller, T. (1991) 'Drama and the foreign devil', *In the Picture*, Spring: 7–8.

Peacock, C. (1994) *N.I.M.A.A. Report* for Australian Film Commission.

Shumway, D. R. (1989) *Michel Foucault*. Boston: Twayne.

Spivak, M. (1989) 'The development of regional film and television production in Canada', A Study commissioned by the Honourable Mira Spivak of the Senate of Canada. Montreal: Telefilm Canada.

Telefilm Canada Feature Film Fund Policies (1991–92). Montreal: Telefilm.

14

THE NATIONAL QUESTION IN QUEBEC AND ITS IMPACT ON CANADIAN CULTURAL POLICY

Ron Burnett

Since this article was written, a referendum on Quebec independence was held on 30 October 1995. The vote was preceded by a sometimes bitter campaign that saw the federal side lose ground in the polls until separists and federalists were evenly split. The result was a dead heat with the 'no', or federal, side winning by a thin margin of 50,000 votes. Canada came as close to splitting up as any modern democracy in recent times. The vote has forced both Quebec and Canada into a profound re-evaluation of nationhood, culture and the shape of governing structures within federal systems. It has placed arguments about fiscal and cultural policy into the foreground and reignited debates about the role that modern media play in shaping public opinion. In fact, questions about the public sphere and the various ways in which issues of central concern to the future of social, economic and cultural policy can be articulated are now at centre-stage in Canada.

The debate on the future of confederation has highlighted the difficulties of developing and sustaining innovative strategies that will protect the uniqueness of culture and nation within transnational and global contexts. Quebec's new Premier, Lucien Bouchard, simultaneously favours free trade and restrictive language laws. He encourages international investment while disallowing the children of foreign workers to go to English schools. He is the leader of a party (Parti Québecois) that is trying to preserve French language and culture through restrictive laws on other cultures. These contradictions are highlighted on the federal side by policy-making bodies like the Canadian Radio and Television Commission, which continues to pursue a protectionist approach to culture while simultaneously supporting monopolies in cable and telephony that actually hinder debate between federal and provincial regulatory agencies. In Canada, these sharp divisions are recast into debates about the constitution and about the viability of the country as a whole. As a result, they are discussed within a context of urgency, where every policy decision is studied for its possible impact on Quebec. The central question always is whether Quebec's cultural specificity will be protected. But there are few representative forums in which these issues can be debated, with the result that the country is more split than ever. Bouchard has promised to hold another referendum in the next few years. Recent polls suggest that the separists are now in a majority. Some have referred to this process as the 'neverendum', and the same can be said for the endless conundrums of cultural policy in a country that seems to have lost sight of its own national agenda.

In what follows I will try and present an overview of the situation in Quebec as seen through the eyes of an anglophone living through a time of intense crisis, a member of a minority which is going through one of the most difficult periods in its history. We are now at the cusp of what may well be a precipitous historical moment. Canada as we presently know it may break apart. In some respects then this is not a chapter on policy as much as it is an essay about the social, cultural and economic forces which propel governments towards policy decisions. With respect to cultural policy, Quebec has always been at the forefront in using the 'law' as a vehicle for the protection of its identity. There is a great deal which must be questioned in this regard and one of the most important questions from my point of view is why any kind of legal force is ever deemed to be appropriate in relation to cultural activity. Suffice to say that cultural laws operate at an ideal level when they are passed by parliaments – as texts – and propose a kind of juridical process which rests on an absolutism which cultural activity tends to contradict. It can be argued that even the notion of culture as constitutive, and thus necessarily in need of protection, elides the complexity of the social and economic conditions which make cultural laws seem necessary in the first place.

Certain cultural phenomena are deemed to be absolutely essential to the national survival. The idea that Quebec films better reflect Quebec than American ones means that a juridical system is introduced which stands outside of those activities, a teleology which on its own creates categories which the culture is then meant to reflect. Put another way, juridical traditions become symbolic standard bearers and then in a metaphysical twist the state is unable to account for the very activities which are being protected. The law itself becomes a window into the culture. The law freezes itself into a set of historical categories, as jurisprudence, while the culture continues with its task of defining and redefining the nature of its own processes.

Quebec is a special case in North America. Its culture has the unique characteristics which one would expect given its history of colonization by the British (in the middle of the eighteenth century) and the resistance to that by succeeding generations. Most of its cultural policy has been driven by a sense of its own uniqueness and the felt need to protect itself from the influences of American popular culture. There are many distinctions which come into play here and I do not have the time to discuss them in great detail. Suffice to say that the constitutional debate going on in Canada at the moment rests on one very central but quite ironic question. Quebec has always insisted on being recognized as a *distinct society*. By distinct it means different, other, separate as to language, culture and law. The distinct society clause which was originally proposed in the failed constitutional round of five years ago was taken up by the rest of Canada with a ferocity and anger that is surprising given the term's ambiguity. For Canadians the notion that Quebec is distinct has become a rallying point around which, as its advocates and detractors keep saying, the country will fail or succeed. The differences proposed by Quebec have been accepted at the symbolic level but the resistance to including that in the constitution, that is giving the term 'distinct' a sovereign quality, has been very intense.

Yet the notion of distinctiveness is at the centre of many of the laws which Quebec has passed in recent years in relation to culture and has become a means through which it has created the sense, though not the reality, that Quebec is being protected from the external influences which it feels do it so much harm. The idea of 'distinct' then is also a notion of weakness, of a culture which has to put up barriers to survive, of a culture which feels that it is in danger of disappearing. This paradox of identity – this inherent ambiguity as to the matrixes within which a nation defines its own orientation – is the foundation upon which the resistance to external influence has been built through the legal apparatus. But the law, as such, cannot include within it the complexity of the daily lives it addresses and attempts to control. In fact, the law is premised on notions of uniformity and regularity and can only sustain its credibility if it is perceived to be sovereign. The most difficult task for lawmakers is codifying cultural activity when that activity, by definition, transcends the boundaries which lawmakers want to put in place. The almost instant resurgence of religious belief in post-communist societies is perhaps one of the most poignant examples of this.

In addition, the notion of distinctiveness is vague enough to permit any number of laws to be created since it is premised on a contrast between cultural configurations. But ironically, much of Canadian cultural policy has also been driven by a similar concern – it can be argued that Quebec has set the tone for Canadian nationalism by revealing the potential heterogeneity at work within Canada's boundaries, but it has also given credibility to an argument which has little to stand on. As Canadian and Quebec society changes into a multi-cultural, multi-ethnic one, the constitutive elements of distinctiveness have shifted and what has been revealed by that is the fiction of the distinct, its rather mystical premise, its effort to generate a naturalized working concept of difference.

Let me turn for a moment here to a discussion of the issues which surround the national debate in Quebec before I refer more fully to the laws which have been passed to reflect the terms of that debate. I would like to work this through rather subjectively. In some senses it would be impossible for me to do otherwise.

It was an overcast day in 1977 when the great writer and Quebec nationalist, Hubert Aquin, committed suicide. I felt the pain of Aquin's death very deeply having followed his career and his writing for many years. While there was a profoundly personal side to Aquin's death, it was also a metaphoric and symbolic gesture. As he once said: 'I am the broken symbol of revolution in Quebec, a reflection of its chaos and its suicidal tendencies' (Sheppard and Yanacopoulo 1985: 25).

On 19 October 1975, a few weeks before the separatist Parti Québecois' election victory, Andrée Yanacopoulo, Aquin's wife, wrote him a letter in which she implored him to change his mind about suicide.

In Quebec we don't live a normal life like people do elsewhere. In more 'stable', countries like France, England, or the United States each individual can, in an untroubled way, feel at home but not here, not in Quebec.

For many Québecois you represent the ideals of independence, the invincibility of a nationalist spirit. This only increases the meaning of your work as a writer. Your writing is, at one and the same time, authentically Québecois and universal.

It is an act of escapism to commit suicide. It is an admission of failure. You have a responsibility to the Quebec community. If you commit suicide you will be killing a little bit of Quebec. You will be cutting of its future.

(Sheppard and Yanacopoulo 1985: 41)

She went on to say that his suicide would reinforce defeatist attitudes in Quebec which he himself had openly critiqued. She did not want to bring up their son in a country which wasn't capable of instilling national pride in its citizens. She equated his projected suicide (about which they had argued for many years) with the destruction of a collective identity still in formation.

There is an attractive romanticism to Yanacopoulo's equation of Aquin and Quebec. It is also a potentially dangerous juxtaposition, for while it might be desirable to conceive of revolution through the eyes of one individual, it is a rather different thing to transform a community of six million people. At the level of myth, however, transformations can be imagined, even thought of as real without having a direct impact on daily life. It will be my argument that many policy decisions have been taken in this 'mythic' sphere, satisfying the desire for symbolic change without the parallel development of the intellectual tools to examine and evaluate the real impact of the decisions which have been taken.

Aquin wanted a total 'national revolution'. He wanted to rebuild Quebec society from the bottom up. He wanted to start anew and this led him to analyse both the strengths and weaknesses of his own culture. He saw himself as a representative of the collective will of his people with all of the contradictions which that entails. This is an attractive formulation, a somewhat religious one in fact. It may explain the dark paradox of Aquin's suicide. He offered himself to the Quebec people as myth and this is inevitably the site of a *death*. No one individual can ever *be* the nation just as the nation can never be understood or experienced through one person. In death all of these ambiguities are *frozen*. In life they would undergo neverending change which would alter the myth, perhaps fundamentally.

Aquin experienced this gap in a very personal way. He grew frustrated with the slowness of change, with the time it takes for any community to alter its norms and values. His death was premature and a profound loss but its ambiguity may be at the heart of the dilemma which many people face in Quebec right now. The simple terms within which national identity is presently being laid out means that any considerations about the future have to be deferred. It will suffice, the modern nationalist argument goes, to regain what has been lost, to live in our own country.

In a time when the very concept of the nation is undergoing complete change, when the ideals of the market economy have triumphed over all other ideologies,

THE NATIONAL QUESTION IN QUEBEC

when Quebeckers voted for a transnational system of free trade, no border is secure, no identity untouched. Nationalism in Quebec will prosper if its discourse remains frozen and resistent to the shifts of history, if it engages with the myths of its own ideology as if they have become real. In contrast, as Eduardo Galeano has so brilliantly argued:

> What it all comes down to is that we are the sum of our efforts to change who we are. Identity is no museum piece sitting stock-still in a display case, but rather the endlessly astonishing synthesis of the contradictions of everyday life.
>
> (Galeano 1991: 125)

My voice is white, male, middle class, immigrant. I have spent most of my life in Quebec. I have married there and my children go to school in that province. However, beyond the stridency and simplicity of labels like anglophone or francophone the question of my identity cannot be reduced to the *superficial boundaries* of the nationalist debate and this applies as much to Quebec as to Canada. To say that I am either Québecois or Canadian is a caricature of the complexity of my daily life, a rather inept and derivative approach to the quandaries of self and other. But I also recognize that the terms of the debate have been set, though the agenda remains uncertain. It is just not enough to respond to the national question in Quebec with an air of complacency, to retreat and then deal with all of the contradictions as if they have come from an *elsewhere* beyond intellectual reasoning or control.

To me the history of Quebec is full of extraordinary ambiguity, ranging from a long tradition of social justice to crass anti-Semitism, from democratic practices to extreme forms of authoritarianism, from an exemplary openness to other cultures to narrowness and intolerance. This is not the place to examine all of these shifts, suffice to say that nationalists are rewriting this past in order to imagine a radically different future. Yet there is something troubling about the strategy of post-referendum (1980) nationalists, something which Aquin anticipated in the 1970s. There is a desire to downplay the *heterogeneity of identity*, to eliminate the contradictions of historical change, to freeze perceptions of Quebec's situation as if it has not evolved or undergone some fundamental shifts over the past thirty years.

It has been one of the errors of the nationalist movement in Quebec to presume that all of this complexity can be magically excised through the political process, through decisions which are thought of as administrative. On the other hand, I would also say that the national imaginary cannot be rejected as irrational. The desire to find some coherence in the maelstrom of activities, thoughts and hopes which any community experiences at an individual and collective level must not be dismissed. To do so would be to deny the role of the community in building an image for itself – to deny the way identity and identities are put in place.

'When we look at ideas about national identity, we need to ask, not whether they are true or false, but what their function is, whose creation they are, and whose interests they serve' (White 1981: viii). White's point is central and it is at the heart of many of the criticisms which have been made of nationalists in Quebec, but it leaves out the crucial need which the community of men and women in this province feel for some kind of place which they can truly call their own. This is perhaps the biggest illusion of them all, but it is also the most powerful. Ownership of place is bound up with an imagined sense of community beyond the more direct relationship of self to the immediate environment in which one lives.

People living in the neighbourhood of Outremont in Montreal do not call themselves Outremonters. We don't identify ourselves, in the sense of nationhood, with the street which we live on, or the highrise we occupy, or even the suburb we inhabit. It would be absurd to do so and yet these are a few of the most direct instances of attachment to community.

Concretely, we co-exist with small groups of people in relatively small social and economic configurations. Yet there is a longing to extend that into something greater, a sovereign realm beyond our immediate control. The only way in which that can be done is through an imagining, through a fantasy of place and then through a conferral of identity from self to an-other. Concretely this means giving over one's identity to politicians who are meant to incarnate what we ourselves lack, or cultural figures who are supposedly more in tune with what we share, than what differentiates us. But this conferral also produces a sense of loss, an almost inescapable feeling that *place* is not enough. The national imaginary is rarely satisfied with the geographic and psychological boundaries it finally creates, which may explain its link to expansionism and violence.

The 'eternal' search for Quebec, for a sovereign nation somehow above and beyond the contradictions of class interest or gender or ethnic background, reflects a desire to create a homogeneity which the social, economic and cultural practices of Quebec have long ago left behind. But a crisis of identity, of self and community is characterized precisely by this kind of contradiction. Ambiguity is the motor force, is what impells the nationalist tide to be caught in the past and to long for a utopian future, is what allows projections into the past and future to effectively deny the present.

> Finally it [the nation] is imagined as community, because, regardless of the actual inequality and exploitation that may prevail in each, the nation is always conceived as a deep, horizontal comradeship. Ultimately it is this fraternity that makes it possible, over the past two centuries, for so many millions of people, not so much to kill, as willingly to die for such limited imaginings. These deaths bring us abruptly face to face with the central problem posed by nationalism: what makes the shrunken imaginings of recent history (scarcely more than two centuries) generate such colossal sacrifices?
>
> (Anderson 1983: 16)

Hubert Aquin asked himself the same question in his very important essay entitled, 'The cultural fatigue of French Canada' (Aquin 1988: 19–48), in which he responded to Pierre Elliot Trudeau's critiques of Quebec nationalism in the early 1960s.

> I agree with him that nationalism has often been a detestable, even unspeakable thing: the crimes committed in its name are perhaps even worse than the atrocities perpetuated in the name of liberty. In the nineteenth century, the resurgence of nationalistic feeling was marked by wars which gravely tarnished every possible form of nationalism and any system of thought stemming from it.
>
> (Aquin 1988: 21)

At the same time, Aquin asserts that there is no necessary causal relationship between war and nationalism and that the concept of a national culture cannot be reduced, in a functional sense, to an anticipated future based on a sordid past. If nationalism is unpredictable, it is precisely because it unleashes forces of history which are already in place and which cannot be eradicated by an act of will or by legislation.

This is a crucial argument because it suggests that the errors of looking to the political arena for a solution to the national question are being replicated in the federal sphere as well. It makes little sense to argue against the nationalist use of the state as a vehicle for independence when the federal state is asserting its right to proceed in the same manner, albeit with a different concept of the national heritage.

Aquin is also very clear about the heterogeneity of Quebec culture and how immigration has changed the national character. The specificity of Quebec culture long ago dissolved into pastiche, into a hybrid of tendencies derived from many parts of the world. It took well into the 1960s before all of the historically embedded institutional practices of the state, the educational system, and the church recognized the characteristics of the shifts which had taken place. Quebec reinvented itself during the post-war period and, as it became more cosmopolitan, less xenophobic, more distinctively modern than any part of Canada, nationalists who were partially responsible for the changes grew fearful of the consequences.

Continuity and discontinuity can co-exist. It is possible to be a nationalist and still long for the heterogeneity of many cultures. Simultaneously it is possible to deny the results of the mix, to deny difference, to be frightened by the new images of self, negate the reinventions and transform the perception of change into a harbinger of danger. Continuity and discontinuity. Part of what is so attractive about nationalism is the way in which it preserves the past, the way it transforms complex questions of identity into simple answers about community and self. Although, as Anderson has so cogently argued, adherence to a community larger than one's immediate circle is only possible at a mythic level, this doesn't prevent or inhibit large numbers of people from believing that the interests of the community at large are also their own.

Self and identity – these are fluid, ambiguous, often contradictory concepts yet they are bandied about by present-day nationalists as a currency of exchange, a political lexicon utilized to gain votes and power. But identity can no longer be talked about in the singular, for what is driving this nation-state-province forward at the moment are the many conflicting identities which are at its very heart. The desire to purify these conflicts, to rid the present of the differences which constitute it, to protect a culture which no longer carries the same messages it did even fifteen years ago, is rooted in a nostalgia for a past seen as simpler and more manageable.

Nationalists in many countries turn to language as the unifying force upon which a new and more culturally homogeneous nation can be built. This assertion has been a consistent feature of the nationalist argument in Quebec. I am by no means suggesting that language is not the focal point for a community's perceptions of itself and of others. But it is not the simple bulwark which nationalists have made it out to be. In fact language is a contradictory site of identity because there is no simple transparent link between the rhetoric of the day and its interpretation by the community at large. More often than not language acts as a support for the community but at an abstract level. The lived relations which make up everyday life have a specificity of which language is a part, but not the whole and certainly not in the mechanical and determinist way suggested by national movements. Language does not exist in a sovereign realm and this is confirmed by the endless debates in the courts about the interpretation of laws or the circular arguments around the meaning, in the case of Quebec, of 'distinct'. The power of language resides with its practitioners. Language is an expression of identity and laws can be enacted to protect a language, but the law cannot reach into all the spheres which a community uses to define itself.

The mosaic of laws which have been enacted in Quebec to protect the primacy of the French language include a recent law which bans the exterior use of any signs which are not written in French. The consequences of this law, which actually went against the Charter of Rights in Canada, have been dramatic because, as we know, cities in particular have become the site of a plethora of advertising and sign systems. The visibility of French has increased, but the heterogeneity of the cosmopolitan context has been suppressed. This law, known as Bill 178, could not have been promulgated without the history which I have been describing to you. That is, although the government which chose to write Bill 178 is not an overtly nationalist one, it has had to respond to nationalist rhetoric in order to survive.

There clearly is a link between the legislative use of power to protect a culture which perceives itself to be under threat and the social practices which flow from that legislation. In the case of Quebec certain aspects of the nationalist discourse have become naturalized to the point where, for example, debates on a recent bill to limit the amount of time which a film in English can be shown in the theatres was centred on the regulative aspects of control, without any profound reflection on the impact or wisdom of any limitation defined in the prior sense according to language. We can begin to talk here about a legitimation of the discourse of nationalism such that, irrespective of the moral implications, a truth value is asserted which seems to transcend the possibility of debate. This is a point of contact between the legal and cultural which is closely related to a set of perceptions regarding the impact of the state on the daily lives of its citizenry. In Quebec the state plays a very powerful role in every aspect of cultural policy but has failed miserably in creating a context for precisely the kind of cultural developments which it desires. The result is that the cable television system carries a majority of English channels, a mixture of American and Canadian shows and news broadcasts, which override the policies which are developed at the macro-level. It matters little that English language films can now only play for between eight and twelve weeks before a French dubbed version must appear in the theatres because the alternative venues for viewing these films become available very quickly, either through cable or the local video store.

In other words, technological changes have made it virtually impossible to limit the perceived demands of the consumer of television. This has led to even more restrictive propositions by nationalists who see communications as the key to the control of cultural specificity. Ironically, there is a long history of laws in Canada which work on the same supposition – every time a new technology arrives on the scene, policies quickly follow and usually it is to provide protection against the presumed impact of American shows or cultural artefacts or messages in a Canadian cultural context which may suffer as a result. The language of many of these policies always talks about the big neighbour to the south and the dangers of losing cultural specificity as would happen with radio IF American broadcasters were allowed free reign in Canada. Film has always been a bone of serious contention. The following, broadly speaking, are the main arguments at the heart of these policy developments:

1 The broadcasting systems should be effectively owned and controlled by Canadians;
2 The right to freedom of expression;
3 The requirement of balance and quality in programming of 'high quality' which would rely on predominantly Canadian and other resources;
4 The guarantee of broadcasting services in English and French;
5 The placement of special obligations on any national broadcasting service;
6 The reaffirmation that the broadcasting undertaking (including cable) constituted a single system;
7 The conclusion that all broadcasting should be regulated by a single, independent public authority (CRTC).

(Finlay 1991: 65–6)

The effort to assure national unity through the use of broadcasting policy and to see that process as a point of resistance to American influence has, of course, been duplicated in Quebec, but premised on a different sense of the national and on a radically separate explanation of identity.

The problem here is between regulation in the national interest and techno-logical innovation which outstrips and overwhelms the former. The difficulty is that with regard to culture, and especially in relation to film, policy is attuned to *product* and industrial notions of consumption and marketing, while cultural processes are never reducible to the simplicity of that formulation. A film, for example, circulates in a sphere which can be described as transnational with none of the specificity so desired by nationalists. It does so because its mode of communication doesn't rely exclusively on the local or the national for success. Genre categories may have a specific relationship to the context in which they have been shot, but the film which results quickly moves beyond the initial parameters which have been set up for production. In fact, the nationalist claim has another deeply embedded one within it and that is that there must be some way of accounting for authorship. Ironically, the culture industry makes use of the symbolic importance of the author as a way of transcending national boundaries. Thus, for example, one of the most famous pop stars in Quebec, Celine Dion, learned English in order to produce for the American market while at the same time, in Quebec, claiming a central role in the nationalist debate. Her music and her lyrics changed to suit the exigencies of a transnational marketplace with a parallel concern for the local. She kept her roots in place while extending far beyond the boundaries of Quebec and her albums have sold very well. She was, in her own terms if not culturally, finally confirmed in America when she appeared on the Johnny Carson Show and then on the Emmys.

The intersection of the national and commercial is full of contradictions which make their appearance to the fullest in the debate over film policy. One of the central arguments in the Applebaum–Hebert Report, which was also called the Federal Cultural Policy Review Committee, was that a direct policy intervention was needed in film because without it there wouldn't be an industry. As the argument goes a feature film industry didn't exist in Canada before the 1970s and this was due to the tiny marketplace and population. This tended to make the profit margins for Canadian films small, if not inexistent. I will not go into the federal organisms which were created in response to this, suffice to say that many of the laws which were put in place were duplicated in Australia, for example. I am interested in the underlying contradiction between concerns for the marketplace, survival, and the central notion of cultural difference – the presumption of homologous interests between the presumed need for profit and the national interest. (The central metaphor for this and one that sticks in my mind is the way in which research and development is subsidized in Canada. American companies came in and set up shop in order to get the subsidy. They export the results of the research to the US without paying any taxes. They then re-import the products at a premium price but because the R&D was done in Canada they pay no taxes on the profit. They then export the profits back to the US and begin the cycle all over again. There are virtually no benefits to be derived from this arrangement except for a small increase in employment, which is a high price to pay for the loss of investment.)

In a similar vein, film policy has in large measure been determined by a concern for 'made in Quebec' or 'made in Canada' products with a parallel argument against American control of cultural production. The problem is that the root of this concern is a strong dislike for 'those numbingly anonymous films with American flags and Home Box Office formulas to the exclusion of the more economically marginal French language, regional, or even Canadian productions' (Gathercole 1984: 44–5). As Gathercole goes on to say,

> Public subsidy schemes which require matching private funds actually exacerbate this branch plant syndrome by making producers dependent on investment which is increasingly available only from American sources. Consequently companies such as HBO are able to lever a disproportionate degree of control over publicly subsidized Canadian films. Any traces of Canadian origin left in by a Canadian producer may be removed by fiat from New York.
>
> (Gathercole 1984: 45)

The link between cultural uniqueness and policy making, between notions of community, state, nation and instruments of communication, proposes a vertical model of national difference which the policy process is somehow meant to represent and regulate. What must be kept in mind here is that more is at stake than the cultural product. The problem is that the model of filmmaking, which at a stylistic level is dominated by the conventions which have been constructed by Hollywood, transcend national boundaries and put in place a form of cultural production which is very costly, but in contrast is not cost effective in a Canadian context. This has less to do with the availability of viewers (the argument that we are a small nation) than it has to do with a concern for a professional product where the guidelines for production create risk. The imperative to budget a film at $8 million, for example, and the presumption that this is the only way to produce an idea or a script is very much at the root of the problem. Policymakers have accepted the implications of this because the cultural community has bought into it as well.

In Quebec this has become a very serious problem because the pool of production funds is so small. Rather than confronting the contradictions head on, the imperative has been to go for co-production as a way of increasing the financial base. Ironically then, just as the nationalist wave has hit its peak the cultural movement, in collusion with government policy makers, has been moving towards the international arena and Quebec filmmakers and television producers have been quick to grasp on to the federal monies which have become available to them as a result of international agreements.

In the midst of this rush, questions of cultural specificity become reduced to points on a scale of presumed values with regard to what will benefit the industry and what won't. Points are awarded for jobs which may not have to exist and for a style of production which may not have to be followed or reproduced.

Policy becomes a vehicle for national claims on identity while in actual fact serving the needs of a naturalized notion of market economies and a very specific notion of cultural production and also reinforcing the political power of the agents involved. Quebec's desire to control the flow of cultural production within its own borders looks more and more like an attempt to maintain the discourse of an elite, now identified as the nation. But this argument is not new except that it has taken on an autonomy which threatens the possibility of countervailing discourses. This may explain why the conundrum of the national debate in Canada and Quebec seems to go on and on as if it has become the necessary condition for *any* discourse in the country.

It can be argued that the very notion of culture as a reflection of 'who we are' has been a powerful invention. What has been created are simulated national identities and inevitably when these flounder, as simulations are wont to do, policy makers rush in with defined and easily codified rules to keep the system from falling apart. The contradictions seem so self-evident that it takes a legal infrastructure to give any credibility to the rules which are created. But what are we to make of as famous a Quebec filmmaker as Denys Arcand, the creator of *Jesus de Montrèal*, which arguably can be described as culturally specific, who has been identified with the nationalist wing of Quebec culture for two decades, saying in a recent interview that he wanted to be an international filmmaker? Celine Dion and Arcand have understood that specificity as such can best be identified from the outside and that the distinctions which we so arbitrarily use to maintain our sense of identity rarely survive without being affirmed by observers from other cultures. The necessity of the other in this case, and without putting an absolute dichotomy in place, makes policy necessary for culture but only if policy itself is seen as a cultural product and thus as open to change and re-evaluation as any cultural production might be. Any transformation of policy into law in this regard closes off the very channels of discourse and exchange which have made the creation of culture possible in the first place.

A final example. Although the cable industry is fundamentally a monopoly in Canada, it has managed to convince the regulatory agencies to prevent the introduction of satellite technologies into Canada. This is because the largest firms are American and they clearly intend to make more of the American product available to Canadian viewers. The result of this decision is that the cable operators (who do precisely the same thing) will maintain their monopoly in the major cites in Canada. Cable operators have done virtually nothing with regard to Canadian production. Their desire to avoid competition is couched in the language of nationhood, although it is a transparent defence of their economic strength. This contradiction highlights the collusion between vague concepts of nation and policy making. Ironically, Canada and Quebec are no different in this respect and share a terrain which links them together, even as their politics may lead to an ill-timed and poorly thought out break-up of the very 'nations' they seek to protect.

REFERENCES

Anderson, B. (1983, 1993) *Imagined Communities: Reflections on the Origin and Spread of Nationalism*. London: Verso.

Aquin, H. (1988) *Writing Quebec: Selected Essays by Hubert Aquin*, ed. by Anthony Purdy. Edmonton: University of Alberta Press.

Canada Broadcasting Act, R.S.C. 1970 c. B–11, quoted in Marike Finlay (1991) 'The social discourses of law and policy on communication', *Social Discourse*, Montreal: 65–6.

Galeano, E. (1991) 'Celebration of contradictions' in *The Book of Embraces*. New York: Norton.

Gathercole, S. (1984) 'The best film policy this country never had', in Seth Feldman (ed.) *Take Two*. Toronto: Irwin.

Sheppard, G. and Yanacopoulo (eds) (1985) *Signé Hubert Aquin: Enquête sur le suicide d'un écrivain*. Montréal: Boréal Express.

White, R. (1981) *Inventing Australia: Images and Identity 1788–1980*. Sydney: George Allen & Unwin.

15

SPEAKING OUT

Indigenous film policy debates in Australia, New Zealand and Canada

Michael Meadows

INTRODUCTION

Indigenous people in Australia, New Zealand and Canada were amongst the first subjects recorded on film by the early colonists. British anthropologist Alfred Cort Haddon's movies shot on Murray Island, in the Torres Strait region in far northern Australia in 1898, are often claimed as the world's first ethnographic films. Murray Island or *Mer*, as it is known by Torres Strait Islanders, was to become the focus of a landmark High Court decision in 1992, effectively casting aside the legal fiction of *terra nullius* – the notion that Australia was an empty continent at the time of British invasion. The full ramifications of this legal decision, which acknowledged the continuation of Native Title in some areas, have yet to be realized. Treaty rights have been used by indigenous people in both New Zealand and Canada to argue for greater access to cultural resources – like media. At the time of writing, this aspect of the Australian legislation has yet to be tested in areas like indigenous education and media access (Harris 1994).

Since those first few unsteady images were captured on film in Australia's far north, a struggle over, in Gail Valaskakis's words (1993: 285), 'who can represent whom, who can tell the stories of others – and how they should be told', has ensued. Valaskakis argues that the debate today often veers uneasily between claims of political correctness and censorship, thus ignoring the real world struggles of the subjects. What is often forgotten is a consideration of the relations which maintain inequalities – relations which link representation, appropriation and access, and social and political questions. In such an environment, identity is continually contested and re-constructed with representation a central site of cultural struggle (Valaskakis 1993: 285–95).

We should not need to resort to the draft Universal Declaration on the Rights of Indigenous Peoples to remind us that First Nation Peoples have the 'right to the use of and access to all forms of mass media in their own languages' (Knudtson and Suzuki 1992: 205). New Zealand's national organization of Maori communicators, Te Manu Aute, claims such rights in its constitution, stating that 'every culture has a right and a responsibility to present its own culture to its own people' (Barclay 1990: 7). Indigenous cultural rights are acknowledged in broadcasting regulation governing environments in New Zealand and Canada. The 1992 Australian Broadcasting Services Act includes no such provision although the link between land rights, knowledge rights and cultural rights is inseparable (Meadows 1993).

A range of discourses compete for legitimacy through cultural institutions, like film, which act to secure consent for particular ideas and assumptions about the world. More often than not, alternative views are systematically marginalized or ignored. But alternatives do exist – alternative ways of thinking, alternative ideologies which might re-frame interpretation of events, and alternative ways of constructing and maintaining notions of culture. From the time of the first European contact with indigenous cultures in Australia, New Zealand and Canada, indigenous people have been represented in terms of non-indigenous ideologies – as the exotic Other, the noble savage, the ignoble savage, the dying race, the welfare dependant, the drunk, the activist, the threat to existing order, the invisible. None of these images is the product of indigenous people themselves. A pattern of indifference emerged from the earliest explorers' journals and writings – a discursive construction, a 'structure of attitude and reference' (Said 1993), which has proved difficult to challenge. Consistently absent from this ideological framework is an acknowledgement of the existence of diversity *within and between* indigenous communities (Meadows 1993). As Valaskakis (1993: 284) reminds us, First Nation people's expressions of anger, frustration and distrust are grounded in the politics of difference and its oppositional strategies of cultural and political struggle – and identity. Part of this identity is pan-cultural, linking indigenous people in Australia, New Zealand, Canada and other countries in a global struggle for social justice. But the process also enables a diverse range of cultural identities to emerge. Thus the Inuit, the Cree, the Maori, the Warlpiri and the descendants of the Jagera people are able to employ diverse ways of using media, like film, as a 'strategic management of cultural goods' to advance this continuing process of cultural definition and re-definition (Meadows 1994). And as Martín-Barbero suggests, this entails a complex interweaving of resistance and submission, opposition and complicity (1988: 462).

Derek Tini Fox (1993) attributes the 'spectacular development' of Maori tribal radio in Aotearoa (New Zealand), for example, to disaffection with mainstream media representation. There are moves to set up a national Maori television station there for the same reason. Similar moves are underway to set up community television stations in Catalonia, a film and video workshop movement in Scotland, Wales, Northern Ireland and the north east of England, indigenous control of media in Papua New Guinea, and community television on the Caribbean island of St Lucia. All seek media access as a form of cultural control (Dowmunt 1993). Bruce Girard (1992) has similarly charted the alternative uses of community radio, driven by similar needs. Many suggest that international links between indigenous media producers are crucial in highlighting the widespread nature of struggle, with the creation of diversity a key factor in community video development (Thede and Ambrosi 1991).

Concessions in the policy process have been won by indigenous people only following protracted battles. As Jock Given (1994) suggests, governments intervene in audiovisual policymaking as film and programme makers, broadcasters, providers of subsidy, regulators, educators and archivists. Policy emerges from the combined results of these and other multifarious activities. But what is often missing from this formula is the notion of social justice, reflecting a general shift in approach to broadcasting regulation in Australia, New Zealand and Canada (Cunningham 1994). Social justice is a topic which seems to have been banished from public rhetoric (Langton 1993: 81). It is evidence of powerful ideological forces at work, effectively setting the limits of the debate – particularly from an indigenous perspective.

In this chapter, I plan to examine indigenous film policymaking in terms of cultural resource management. Film production – indigenous film production, in particular – might be thought of as the strategic management of cultural goods. This theoretical approach is derived from Gramsci's cultural theory. Gramsci (1988), in his cultural writings, focuses on genre, concerned not with its meaning but with its 'tactical orientation and usages'. This points to the *ways* in which cultural forms like media production might be used and negotiated according to 'implicit' cultural instructions (Mercer 1989). So *how* indigenous communities, for example, might use a cultural resource like film, or television or radio becomes crucial. The strategic use of film and film policy by indigenous communities might be theorized in this way because cultural forms, like media, continue to make a significant contribution to the way in which we 'imagine' ourselves and our place in the world (Geertz 1973; Anderson 1984; Robinson 1994).

AUSTRALIA

Since the Lumiere brothers' first crude cinematograph made its debut in Australia in 1896, around 6,000 Australian films have been made about indigenous people here – the bulk made by scholars and missionaries. This amounts to around 8,000 hours of film stock. Australian historian Michael Leigh (1988: 79) laments that, despite this vast resource, the white community is still generally ignorant of Aboriginal culture. The problem, he explains, is in the types of representation – or, rather, misrepresentation – adopted by filmmakers for almost a century. It was not until the late 1970s and 1980s in Australia that some creative control was transferred to indigenous people in some independent films. At this time, too, indigenous writers, producers and directors began to emerge, along with broadcasting organizations like the Central Australian Aboriginal Media Association (CAAMA) and its offshoot, Imparja Television, in Alice Springs. More recently, successful co-productions involving indigenous communities and non-indigenous filmmakers represent a progressive shift in filmmaking ideologies. Ethnographic film making techniques, too, have begun to reflect the need for collaboration and community control (Larkin 1984a, 1984b; Dunlop 1979, 1986; MacDougall 1969, 1978). The crucial issue is control over the means of production.

Indigenous media producers (Wharton 1994) have suggested the need for the regulation of indigenous content on Australian television – in the same way as Australian content is defined under the Broadcasting Services Act. Plans to set up a national indigenous television station are part of a separate agenda to gain 'air rights'. Indigenous production units have operated with varied success within both the national broadcaster, the Australian Broadcasting Corporation (ABC), and the multicultural broadcaster, the Special Broadcasting Service (SBS). According to Aboriginal broadcaster Rachel Perkins (1994), working in the mainstream is essential: 'It's good for us to produce our own media because we know who we are. We can transmit our identity in a true form in the ways that we want to.' The ABC set up its Aboriginal Programs Unit in 1987 and broadcaster Frances Peters (1994) explains that one of the first questions to be addressed by it was, 'What is indigenous filmmaking?' As a result, the regular programme produced by the unit, *Blackout*, features no presenters or narrators. Production methods demand community accountability and recognition of cultural protocols. This, according to Peters, ensures its indigenousness.

The Australian Film Commission (AFC) set up in 1993 an Indigenous Branch in an attempt to deal with some of these continuing questions at an industry level. The AFC came into being in 1975, replacing the Australian Film Development Corporation. The commission's practice in assisting indigenous filmmakers has been erratic over the years. Robinson (1994: 159) argues that a framework for such assistance has never been established. In the mid-1980s, an Aboriginal Advisory Committee existed within the AFC but was ineffective because of tensions over the interpretation of its role. But in 1993, attempts to set up a workable framework began anew. The Indigenous Branch's objectives are to develop filmmaking and related skills amongst indigenous people. It also has a mandate to facilitate effective participation of indigenous people and to promote the quality and diversity of indigenous films. In late 1993, the AFC released draft guidelines for funding on projects with significant indigenous content which gives preference to those which have indigenous people in positions of creative control.

Head of the Indigenous Branch, Wal Saunders (1993b), argues that many of the images of indigenous Australians have been created by those in power and it is these people who oppose change, perpetuating the invisibility of indigenous culture – 'the same invisibility which has seen white Australians knowing more about Native American tribes, their massacres and their battles of resistance than about indigenous Australia' (1993b: 6). Two alternatives emerge: either stop non-indigenous filmmakers from using government money to make films about indigenous people; or allow only collaborative projects which ensure that indigenous people have the right to creative and artistic control (1993b: 7). The debate on this thorny issue continues, with the Indigenous Branch gaining some access, at least, to the AFC's decision-making processes.

In the Torres Strait, moves are underway to set up a film/video production studio in an attempt to give Torres Strait Islanders some control over the construction of their identities. Torres Strait Islander media workers believe strongly that there is only one real solution – Islander control (Noah 1988). Their experience with other media supports this (Meadows 1995). The funding for such projects comes largely through the Aboriginal and Torres Strait Islander Commission, ATSIC. Set up in March 1990 following an amalgamation of the former Department of Aboriginal Affairs and the Aboriginal Development Commission, ATSIC has funded Aboriginal filmmakers and organizations involved in indigenous film production like Film Australia, the ABC, community TV in Melbourne, SBS and independent film companies (Christopher 1994). It continues to provide support for community radio and television production in about ninety remote indigenous communities around Australia. This programme, called the Broadcasting for Remote Aboriginal Communities Scheme (BRACS) attracted funds of around $10 million in 1994–5 (Meadows 1992; Molnar 1993). Like indigenous control, the issue of identity remains central.

Marcia Langton (1993) and others (Beckett 1988; Attwood 1989) suggest that the dynamic notion of identity – Aboriginality – is created from an historical interaction between black and white. Langton identifies three categories of construction: Aboriginal people interacting *within* Aboriginal culture; *stereotyping* by non-Aboriginal people who have had little first-hand contact with Aboriginal people; and Aboriginal and non-Aboriginal people engaging in *dialogue* (1993: 34–5). By considering Aboriginality as a 'mobilised political identity', it becomes 'counter-hegemonic', as an expression of status and claim, critical of much non-Aboriginal discourse (Pettman 1992: 112–13).

From this, it would seem that there is a need to re-examine ways in which indigenous identities are constructed through the management of cultural resources like film. The suggestion of greater collaboration between filmmakers and their subjects is one solution. But merely being indigenous may not necessarily enable an understanding of how to represent indigenousness. Albeit discussing black filmmaking in Britain, Stuart Hall suggests that cultural producers like filmmakers must not only control production but also must examine their position within (and their relationship to) their own media. He continues (1989: 68): 'Films are not necessarily good because black people make them. They are not necessarily "right on" by virtue of the fact that they deal with the black experience.' Maori filmmaker Barry Barclay acknowledges the problematic nature of the definition, 'a Maori film', suggesting that 'we shall know what a Maori film is when we get a chance to make more films' (Barclay 1990: 20). Policies which enable this process would seem to be essential, with access to the means of production the key.

NEW ZEALAND

Just as North American Native stories were appropriated for Western consumption, Maori myths, too, were romanticized and adapted to satisfy European tastes, with white actors commonly 'blacked up' for the indigenous roles (Watson 1994: 121–4). With the production of six documentaries about Maori life, 1974 was a crucial year for indigenous filmmaking. The director was Barry Barclay and the series was called *Tangata Whenua*. This helped to sensitize New Zealanders – indigenous and non-indigenous – to seeing themselves on screen.

The Treaty of Waitangi signed in 1840 between the British colonial government and the Maori set in place a framework for policy making which pervades the New Zealand communication policy environment. Poata (1994) argues that it is impossible to separate film policy from land claims made under the Treaty of Waitangi and all future policy must be framed with this document in mind. Since 1950, $3 billion has been allocated to broadcasting in New Zealand but, until recently, Maori cultural producers have received nothing. But perhaps the drought has broken (Poata 1994: 155–6). Maori have successfully used the Treaty of Waitangi as a framework to gain access to radio and television in New Zealand with varied outcomes – although Maori control remains a central issue (Wilson 1993).

The key policymaking body, the New Zealand Film Commission (NZFC) was established within the Department of Internal Affairs in 1978 at a time when the film industry was on a high. The commission has clear objectives: to ensure availability of New Zealand films and to show that such films and the industry are reflective of New Zealand's cultural richness – including the aspirations of Maori filmmakers (Jeffrey 1994: 45–7). The commission is in the process of shifting its *modus operandi* from that of a funding body to that of a development corporation. The challenge is to make the commission's processes accessible to Maori. Access for Maori filmmakers is available through the Creative Film and Video Fund of the Arts Council of NZ. In addition, the NZFC supports Maori drama production for television (Lyndon 1994).

Maori in the industry at large are represented by their own group, Te Manu Aute. The New Zealand Film Commission meets regularly with Te Manu Aute in public forums to discuss relevant issues. Despite all this, the NZFC does not have a Maori film policy *per se* but tries to cater for Maori needs through existing assistance programmes. The commission has appointed six Kaumatua/Kuia (council of elders representatives) to enable regional input and cultural advice. The commission has a bi-lingual Maori Industry Support Officer, appointed in early 1993, and there is Maori representation on the board of the film commission, the Short Film Fund Committee and amongst general staff (Lyndon 1993).

Like their counterparts in Australia and Canada, many Maori filmmakers have turned to video as an emancipatory technology because of the possibility of using it in culturally-appropriate ways. Barclay (1990) recounts how, on some occasions, the use of video enables the images (and knowledge) captured to be returned to the tribe immediately. This not only recognizes sanctions or *tapus* placed on certain knowledge, but also returns control of that information to its owners – Barclay describes this as 'keeping the trust' (1990: 93). The gesture of returning control of the images to their owners, he explains, is culturally important as are notions that Maori film and video makers should not *take* pictures, they should be *given* them by the community (Barclay 1990: 84). This is an important concept which has some parallels within indigenous communities in Australia and Canada. The perception of the audience-producer barrier is important here.

The New Zealand Broadcasting Act has at least tried to recognize the significant cultural space Maori occupy in New Zealand society. New Zealand's broadcasting authority, NZ on AIR, has a mandate under the 1989 Broadcasting Act to reflect and develop New Zealand culture and identity by promoting programmes about the country and in promoting Maori language and culture (NZ on AIR 1993). Broadcast funding by NZ on AIR was split in July 1993 with a new Maori broadcasting funding agency, Te Mangai Paho, being formed. From 1995, it began allocating funds to Maori radio and television (Ministry of Commerce 1993).

Recognition of the need for Maori access to the means of cultural production has been won through the Treaty of Waitangi. In Australia, the 1992 High Court decision on Native Title remains a possible framework for negotiating media access. But cooperative moves in both Australia and New Zealand are an indication that ideologies are changing – even though the process is being accelerated by legal means. The inclusion of indigenous culture in film offerings from both countries is perhaps what will, in the future, distinguish these cultural productions from those driven by the commercial imprimatur of Hollywood. But, as Black observes, the tensions remain.

> There is every indication in Aotearoa [New Zealand] now that Maori people are asserting their own distinctiveness. More and more we want to hang onto the roots of our language and culture. As technology thrives in the area of film the more the striving should be to develop resources in a way that is amenable to a tribal perspective.
>
> (Black 1993: 17)

CANADA

Native North Americans, too, have been the subject of thousands of films both by Hollywood and independent documentary producers (Weatherford and Seubert 1988: 7). An indigenous perspective essentially was absent from such film images until the 1970s when the rise of independent film and video enabled alternative perspectives to emerge. This coincided with a growth in Native American political activism – the stand-offs at Wounded Knee and Alcatraz Island are examples.

In both Canada and the United States at this time, indigenous people were able to participate in radio and television training programmes along with independent film projects. The National Film Board in Canada, set up by John Grierson just prior to the Second World War, trained producers and funded the production of documentaries as part of a 'Challenge for Change' programme. It was in the 1970s that the Native American Public Broadcasting Consortium was formed to try to increase the number of programmes about indigenous issues on United States' television. However, it was largely unsuccessful (Weatherford and Seubert 1988: 7). Canada's National Film Board set up its Cape Dorset film workshop on Baffin

Island in Canada's north in 1972 (Valaskakis 1992: 71). Its aim was to enable the production of films more reflective of Native culture than earlier, more infamous offerings. Canadian filmmaker Robert Flaherty's *Nanook of the North*, for example, was more a re-creation of past practices than it purported to be – a documentary of Native life in the Arctic – when it was made in 1921. Present day Inuit audiences 'roar with laughter' at the film's staged hunting scenes (*Inuktitut* 1984: 11).

The Canadian film industry – sometimes dubbed 'Hollywood north' – has been shaped to a large degree by policy influenced by the critical reception of Canadian films in Canada (Morris 1994: 79). The Canadian Film Development Corporation was founded in 1967 and became Telefilm Canada in 1981. But attempts by seven federal ministers to strengthen Canadian content on Canadian screens through political means have failed (Lewis 1994: 16). Until recently, there was even less success with indigenous content. Native people's participation in radio and television have dominated indigenous media production in Canada. In 1992, this took a major step forward with the advent of Television Northern Canada (TVNC), a dedicated Native satellite television network which broadcasts to an audience of around 100,000 across Canada's remote north. TVNC has enabled the broadcasting of around seventeen hours each week of programming in both Native languages and English made by a range of Native communities north of the 60th parallel (Television Northern Canada 1994). While this focus is on television production, it has nonetheless enabled the creation of a pool of experienced programme makers, many of whom have turned their attention to film.

A major focus of indigenous filmmaking in Canada is a National Film Board of Canada initiative in Edmonton, Alberta. Called Studio One (for First People), it was set up in 1991 aiming to 'explore the condition of indigenous peoples'. It does this by providing a training ground and a home for Aboriginal talent from which the rest of the NFB as well as the private sector can draw. Studio One's mandate recognizes the right of First Nation peoples to tell their own stories, not just to each other, but to all Canadians (Studio One 1994): 'At a critical point in the history of North America our storytellers face the serious task of communicating the National Destiny and National Character of the Indian and Inuit people through an emerging Nativist film-making industry.'

Studio One is also involved in developing archival and community-based education projects on First Languages and Culture to be delivered through fibre optics and CD ROM in the future. The studio offers a hands-on approach where people work for between two to three years to develop their own projects with production guidance – documenting 'a living history of North America's First Peoples' (Studio One 1994). The NFB claims to be Canada's only national media educational programming source not governed by commercial interest – the 'conscience of Canadians'. This sets it apart from Telefilm Canada and the CBC. It has plans to pioneer the delivery of a television network for Canada's southern Native people. Of an estimated one million people of Native ancestry in Canada, 75 per cent live in the south and are not served by TVNC or southern networks.

TVNC, too, has plans to extend its coverage south and this could provide a valuable source of programme material.

Across North America, a Native American Producers Alliance exists to enable indigenous filmmakers to organize at grassroots level to develop a Native cinema. Cheyenne/Arapaho filmmaker Chris Eyre suggests that such organizations will enable eventual access to mainstream audiences:

> There's going to be a breakthrough in the next five years, maybe sooner. Someone will make a feature film that'll get distributed theatrically and reach the populace, the American populace. Once the gate opens – it enables Native actors to show what they can really do.
>
> (Bowannie 1994: 10)

CONCLUSION

> We are beginning to discover that its [moving imagery's] most profound effects may be upon the people it has portrayed, offering them an historical and cultural resource more vivid and accessible than any they can find in books. At the same time, Aboriginal people, both individually and collectively, are turning to film, video and television as the media most likely to carry their messages to one another and into the consciousness of white Australia.
>
> (MacDougall 1987: 58)

While no firm indigenous film policy exists in any of the countries dealt with in this discussion, moves towards a new spirit of cooperation between indigenous and non-indigenous filmmakers perhaps heralds a new era in representation. However, ample evidence exists of continuing media assumptions of the *absence* of indigenous people – their interests largely ignored and their voices seldom, if ever, heard. The pattern of development of indigenous cultural production worldwide has been influenced by the recognition of the possibility of using various media as tools for cultural and political intervention – allowing the dispossessed to 'speak as well as hear' (Girard 1992; Dowmunt 1993). Weatherford and Seubert (1988) suggest that this response is driven by several impulses – combating stereotypes, addressing information gaps in non-Native society, and reinforcing community cultures.

These media responses have grown out of a commitment to the multifarious communities they serve. While in one sense this process exists at the periphery of mainstream society, the implications are far more profound. Behind much of the impetus for the development of indigenous broadcasting is the fear of further cultural and language shifts because of the influence of mainstream values. Indigenous media production could well be one of the most dynamic sites in the age of information technology. And what this represents is essentially management of cultural resources in Gramscian terms (Meadows 1994). Policy, of course, plays a critical role in determining the outcome of central questions like access.

Indigenous cultural production is a hybrid process – 'a multifaceted and heterogeneous mix of policy issues, practices, and tactics' (O'Regan and Batty 1993: 230; Ginsburg 1991, 1993). So the nature of the products which emerge – largely *as a response* to insensitive and ideologically bound mainstream media representation – is diverse although the mission is clear. It is about reclaiming identity and the right to participate in identity construction. It is about appropriating technologies and managing them as cultural resources whether they be computers, telephones, cameras or satellites. The operation of culture as an authorizing agency is evident in these many locations (Bhabha 1991). Involvement in policy making is just one facet of this complex process but it is a crucial one. The *ad hoc* approaches of the past must be recognized for their exclusionary framework. New ways of 'imagining' ourselves surely lie in recognizing new ways of working co-operatively with indigenous knowledges and practices. It is this which may well determine how each of the nations considered here will be perceived in the late twentieth century.

As Renate Holub suggests, the impulse for change does not emerge from privilege but from those who continue to be politically, economically and socially marginalized. As modern intellectuals, she argues, we move in a 'structure of feeling' which not only enables us to speak about other cultures but which also enunciates our complicity in the exploitation of these cultures. She concludes:

> In spite of various struggles we undertake against domination, our bodies move, none the less, in immense privilege, inordinately saturated with material and cultural goods, technology and consumer products, on a scale incommensurable with that which governs the practices of everyday life for millions of people. While we do not choose the place where we were born, we can choose the places and ideas deserving of our energies.
>
> (Holub 1992: 189)

REFERENCES

Anderson, Benedict (1984) *Imagined Communities: Reflections on the Origin and Spread of Nationalism*. London: Verso.

Attwood, Bain (1989) *The Making of the Aborigines*. Sydney: Allen & Unwin.

Barclay, Barry (1990) *Our Own Image*. Auckland: Longman Paul.

Beckett, Jeremy (1988) *Past and Present: the Construction of Aboriginality*. Canberra: Aboriginal Studies Press.

Bhabha, Homi (1991) 'The postcolonial critic: Homi Bhabha interviewed by David Bennett and Terry Collits', *Arena*, 96: 47–63.

Black, Taiarahia (1993) 'Anei Ahau', paper presented at the Australian History and Film Conference, 30 November–4 December, La Trobe University, Melbourne.

Bowannie, Mary K. (1994) 'Tenacious focus', *Aboriginal Voices*, 1(4): 10–11.

Christopher, Rod (1994) 'Film policy and ATSIC', in A. Moran (ed.) *Film Policy: An Australian Reader*. Brisbane: Institute for Cultural Policy Studies, Griffith University.

Cunningham, Stuart (1994) 'A policy primer for our times', in A. Moran (ed.) *Film Policy: An Australian Reader*. Brisbane: Institute for Cultural Policy Studies, Griffith University.

Dowmunt, Tony (1993) *Channels of Resistance: Global Television and Local Empowerment*. London: BFI Publishing and Channel 4 Television.

Doxtator, Michael (1994) Personal communication, letter, 26 September.
Dunlop, Ian (1979) 'Ethnographic film-making in Australia: the first seventy years (1898–1968)', *Aboriginal History* 1(2): 111–19.
Dunlop, Ian (1986) 'Strangers abroad – fieldwork: but whose film?' *Anthropology Today* 2(6): 15–16.
Fox, Derek Tini (1993) 'Honouring the treaty', in Tony Dowmunt (ed.) *Channels of Resistance: Global Television and Local Empowerment*. London: BFI Publishing and Channel 4 Television.
Geertz, Clifford (1973) *The Interpretation of Cultures: Selected Essays*. New York: Basic Books.
Ginsburg, Faye (1991) 'Indigenous media: Faustian contract or global village?', *Cultural Anthropology*, 6(1): 92–112.
Ginsburg, Faye (1993) 'Aboriginal media and the Australian imaginary', *Public Culture*, 5: 557–78.
Girard, Bruce (1992) *A Passion for Radio: Radio Waves and Community*. Montreal: Black Rose Books.
Given, Jock (1994) 'Guerillas in the mist – film policy and process', in A. Moran (ed.) *Film Policy: An Australian Reader*. Brisbane: Institute for Cultural Policy Studies, Griffith University.
Gramsci, Antonio (1988) *A Gramsci Reader: Selected Writings 1916–1935*, trans. David Forgacs. London: Lawrence & Wishart.
Hall, Stuart (1989) 'Cultural identity and cinematic representation', *Framework*, 36: 68–81.
Harris, Stephen (1994) 'Pay the rent: Mabo and the big picture of Aboriginal education', *Social Alternatives*, 13(3–4): 20–2.
Holub, Renate (1992) *Antonio Gramsci*. London: Routledge.
Inuktitut (1984) 'Search for Nanook', Winter: 11–19.
Jeffrey, Ruth (1994) 'Film policy in New Zealand', in A. Moran (ed.) *Film Policy: An Australian Reader*. Brisbane: Institute for Cultural Policy Studies, Griffith University.
Knudtson, Peter and Suzuki, David (1992) *Wisdom of the Elders*. Sydney: Allen & Unwin.
Langton, Marcia (1993) '*Well, I heard it on the radio and I saw it on the television': An essay for the Australian Film Commission on the Politics and Aesthetics of Film Making By and About Aboriginal People and Things*. Sydney: Australian Film Commission.
Larkin, C. (1984a) 'Ethnographic film', *Filmviews*, 120: 27–35.
Larkin, C. (1984b) 'Problems of ethnographic film practices', *Filmviews*, 121: 46–50.
Leigh, Michael (1988) 'Curiouser and curiouser', in S. Murray (ed.) *Back of Beyond*. Sydney: Australian Film Commission.
Lewis, Brian (1994) 'A thoroughly colonised industry: Canada's quiet subversion', in A. Moran (ed.) *Film Policy: An Australian Reader*. Brisbane: Institute for Cultural Policy Studies, Griffith University.
Lyndon, Pierre (1993) Letter, 27 August.
Lyndon, Pierre (1994) Letter, 19 September.
MacDougall, David (1969) 'Prospects of the ethnographic film', *Film Quarterly*, 23(2): 16–20.
MacDougall, David (1978) 'Ethnographic film: failure and promise', *Annual Review of Anthropology*, 7: 405–25.
MacDougall, David (1987) 'Media friend of media foe?', *Visual Anthropology*, 1(1): 54–8.
Martin-Barbero, Jesus (1988) 'Communication from culture: the crisis of the national and the emergence of the popular', *Media, Culture and Society*, 10: 447–65.
Meadows, Michael (1992) *A Watering Can in the Desert: Issues in Indigenous Broadcasting Policy in Australia*. Brisbane: Institute for Cultural Policy Studies, Griffith University.
Meadows, Michael (1993) *The Way People Want to Talk: Media Representation and*

Indigenous Media Responses in Australia and Canada, unpublished PhD thesis, Griffith University, Brisbane.

Meadows, Michael (1994) 'The way people want to talk: indigenous media production in Australia and Canada', *Media Information Australia* 73: 64–73.

Meadows, Michael (1995) 'Voice blo mipla all ilan man', in Jennifer Craik, Julie James-Bailey and Albert Moran (eds) *Public Voices: Private Interests: Australia's Media*. Sydney: Allen & Unwin.

Mercer, Colin (1989) 'Antonio Gramsci: E-Laborare, or the work and government of culture', paper delivered at TASA '89, La Trobe University, Melbourne, December.

Michaels, Eric (1986) *Aboriginal Invention of Television Central Australia 1982–1985*. Canberra: Australian Institute of Aboriginal Studies.

Michaels, Eric (1987) *For a Cultural Future: Francis Jupurrurla makes TV at Yuendumu*. Melbourne: Manic Exposeur.

Ministry of Commerce (Te Manatu Tauhokohoko) (1993) *Maori Broadcasting Policy Newsletter*, 25 March.

Molnar, Helen (1993) 'Indigenous use of small media: community radio, BRACS, and the Tanami Network', paper delivered to Enhancing Cultural Value: Narrowcasting, Community Media and Cultural Development, CIRCIT, 4 December.

Moran, Albert (1994) *Film Policy: An Australian Reader*. Brisbane: Institute for Cultural Policy, Griffith University.

Morris, Peter (1994) 'Public policy, public opinion', in A. Moran (ed.) *Film Policy: An Australian Reader*. Brisbane: Institute for Cultural Policy Studies, Griffith University.

Noah, Aven (1988) Regional Program Manager, Torres Strait Islander Media Association, Personal interview, 5 September.

NZ on AIR (1993) 'New television developments', *Background Notes*, April.

O'Regan, Tom with Batty, Philip (1993) 'An Aboriginal television culture: issues, strategies, politics', in Tom O'Regan (ed.) *Australian Television Culture*. Sydney: Allen & Unwin.

Perkins, Rachel (1994) 'Aboriginal television', in A. Moran (ed.) *Film Policy: An Australian Reader*. Brisbane: Institute for Cultural Policy Studies, Griffith University.

Peters, Frances (1994) 'The Black Film Unit at the ABC and Aboriginal filmmaking', in A. Moran (ed.) *Film Policy: An Australian Reader*. Brisbane: Institute for Cultural Policy, Griffith University.

Pettman, Jan (1992) *Living in the Margins: Racism, Sexism and Feminism in Australia*. Sydney: Allen & Unwin.

Poata, Tama (1994) 'Maori filmmaking and policy questions, New Zealand', in A. Moran (ed.) *Film Policy: An Australian Reader*. Brisbane: Institute for Cultural Policy, Griffith University.

Robinson, Cathy (1994) 'Films, policies, audiences and Australia', in A. Moran (ed.) *Film Policy: An Australian Reader*. Brisbane: Institute for Cultural Policy Studies, Griffith University.

Said, Edward (1993) *Culture and Imperialism*. New York: Vintage.

Saunders, Walter (1993a) 'The Australian Film Institute', in *My Life as I Live it* (film catalogue). South Melbourne: Australian Film Institute.

Saunders, Walter (1993b) 'The owning of images and the right to represent', *Filmnews*, May: 6–7.

Search, Patricia (1993) 'The rhythm and structure of multicultural communication', *Media Information Australia*, 69: 62–9.

Studio One (1994) *Background Notes*. Edmonton: National Film Board of Canada.

Television Northern Canada (1994) *Background Notes*.

Thede, Nancy and Ambrosi, Alain (1991) *Video the Changing World*. Montreal: Black Rose Books.

Valaskakis, Gail (1992) 'Communication, culture, and technology: satellites and Northern

Native broadcasting in Canada', in S. Riggins (ed.) *Ethnic Minority Media: An International Perspective*. Newbury Park: Sage.

Valaskakis, Gail (1993) 'Parallel voices: Indians and Others – narratives of cultural struggle', *Canadian Journal of Communication*, 18: 283–96.

Watson, Chris (1994) 'The effect of funding policies on New Zealand's film culture', in A. Moran (ed.) *Film Policy: An Australian Reader*, Brisbane: Institute for Cultural Policy Studies, Griffith University.

Weatherford, Elizabeth and Seubert, Emelia (1988) 'Currents: film and video in native America', in Elizabeth Weatherford and Emelia Seubert (eds) *Native Americans on Film and Video: Volume II*. New York: Museum of the American Indian.

Wharton, Wayne (1994) 'Film and video making in North Queensland', in A. Moran (ed.) *Film Policy: An Australian Reader*. Brisbane: Institute for Cultural Policy Studies, Griffith University.

Wilson, Helen (1993) *'Te Wa Whakapaoho i te Reo Irirangi:* some directions in Maori radio', paper presented at the Post Colonial Formations Conference, Griffith University, Nathan, 7 July.

INDEX

Paramount Communications 28, 34
Parker, R. A. 76
Parkfield Group 109
partnerships: domestic 30–3;
    independents 31–3; international
    33–4
Passeron, J.-C. 200
Pauwels, C. 80
pay-TV 23, 24, 25, 43
Paz, O. 134
Pendakur, M. 152
Perkins, R. 265
Peters, F. 265
Peters, J. 35
Pettman, J. 266
Piano, The (Campion) 246
PKA 43, 47, 56 (n2)
du Plantier, D. T. 74
Poata, T. 267
Polanski, R. 88, 90
politics: and cinema 157–62; cultural
    xii, 79–82
Pollack, A. 29
pornochanchada 137, 142
Porter, M. 227
Porter, V. 93
Positif 90
Potter, S. 90
Prague (Sellar) 90
Primestar 41–2
Proctor, E. 90
production: *see* film production
propaganda films 4
Prosser, T. 111
protectionism 7; France 75–6, 81, 93;
    Indonesia 176; Latin America 135–7
Ptak, J. 77
public service broadcasting 40, 63–4
public service cinema 122
Puenso, L. 90

quality, and entertainment 78
Quebec: cinema 121–4; funding
    259–60; heterogeneity 255;
    language 256–7; nationalism
    250–60; separatism 251–2
Quester, G. H. 78
quota system 26, 102, 135–6

Rajesh, Y. P. 165
Ramachandran, T. M. 156, 162
Rambo films 24
Ray, S. 149, 151

Redstone, S. 34
regional arts boards 219–21, 229
regionalism 234–6, 240–6
Relph, S. 109
Renn Productions 90
research, films 11–12
Resnais, A. 87
Resnick, 118
Roberge, G. 122
Robertson, R. 172, 208
Robins, J. M. 33
Robins, K. 2, 6, 108, 226
Robinson, C. 264, 265
Robison, R. 176, 178
Rockett, K. 7
Routt, W. D. 10
Roy-Chowdhury, S. 162

Said, E. 263
Sainsbury, P. 228
Saint-Laurent, M. 124
Sánchez, A. R. 141
Sasitharan, T. 204
Sastry, K. N. T. 160
satellite broadcasts 27–8, 41–2, 48–9,
    70
Satellite Business News 42
Satyu, M. S. 157
Saunders, W. 265
Scannell, P. 10
Schatz, T. 76
Schatzberg, J. 89
Schild, S. 143
Schiller, H. 11
Schindler's List (Spielberg) 81, 194
Schlesinger, P. 11, 12, 172, 200
Schnitman, J. 133, 137
Schroder, K. 10
Schwarzenegger, Arnold 24
Scott, R. 89, 92
Scottish Arts Council 218
Scottish Film Production Fund 215,
    230, 229, 230
screen culture 236
Screen International 111
screen quotas 135–6
Screen 166
Sellar, I. 90
Sen, K. 174, 180, 182
Sen, M. 151
services 72, 73–4, 79, 238
Setzer, F. 40, 44, 51
Seubert, E. 268

282

INDEX

World Trade Organisation 72, 74, 81, 238–9
Worth, D. 188

Yanacopoulo, A. 251–2
Yao, S. 172, 203

Yeo, G. 185, 193, 199, 201, 205
Yeo, P. 185–6
Zaharom, N. 172
Zecchinelli, C. 81
Zier, J. 53
Zinnemann, F. 88